Class, Race, Gender, and Crime

Class, Race, Gender, and Crime

The Social Realities of Justice in America

Fourth Edition

Gregg Barak
Paul Leighton
and
Allison Cotton

ROWMAN & LITTLEFIELD
Lanham • Boulder • New York • London

Published by Rowman & Littlefield
A wholly owned subsidary of The Rowman & Littlefield Publishing Group, Inc.
4501 Forbes Boulevard, Suite 200, Lanham, Maryland 20706
www.rowman.com

16 Carlisle Street, London W1D 3BT, United Kingdom

British Library Cataloguing in Publication Information Available

Library of Congress Cataloging-in-Publication Data

Barak, Gregg.
  Class, race, gender, and crime : the social realities of justice in America / Gregg Barak, Paul
Leighton, and Allison Cotton.
    pages   cm
  Includes bibliographical references and index.
  ISBN 978-1-4422-2072-0 (cloth : alk. paper) — ISBN 978-1-4422-2073-7 (pbk. : alk.
paper) — ISBN 978-1-4422-2074-4 (electronic)
  1. Criminal justice, Administration of—United States. 2. United States—Social conditions.
I. Leighton, Paul, 1964– II. Cotton, Allison M., 1969– III. Title.
  HV9950.B34 2014
  364.973—dc23

                                                                                    201400885

Printed in the United States of America

Contents

Figures, Tables, and Boxes

FIGURES

TABLES

BOXES

Preface

"Those who won our independence by revolution were not cowards," wrote Supreme Court associate justice Louis Brandeis. "They did not exalt order at the cost of liberty" (*Whitney v. California*, 274 U.S. 357 [1927]). The radicals who founded this country were not afraid to state their belief in the importance of freedom and argue it through to its logical conclusion: a government dependent on the people, who were free to change it. They wrote in the Declaration of Independence: "We hold these truths to be self-evident, that all men are created equal, that they are endowed by their Creator with certain unalienable Rights, that among these are Life, Liberty and the pursuit of Happiness."

It is ironic that many of those talking about liberty and equality were slave owners, leading some to wonder exactly how "self-evident" these truths really were. Indeed, the declaration contains a list of grievances against England to justify violent rebellion, and the original declaration attacked the king for waging "cruel war against human nature itself, violating its most sacred rights of life & liberty in the persons of a distant people who never offended him, captivating & carrying them into slavery in another hemisphere, or to incur miserable death in their transportation thither" (Christianson 1998, 66). The capture and transportation of African people into slavery was similar to the British policy of transportation, whereby convicts—as well as poor people kidnapped for cheap labor—were put on boats bound for indentured servitude in Australia or the American colonies. At the request of southern men, this passage was deleted and replaced with the more general "long train of abuses and usurpations."

The Founding Fathers not only had slaves but also prohibited all women and many poor men from voting for a government supposedly "of . . . by . . . and for the people." Supreme Court associate justice William O. Douglas reminds us that "the enduring appeal lay in two of its conceptions: First, that revolution can be a righteous cause, that the throwing off of chains by an oppressed people is a noble project; and second, that all men have a common humanity, that there is a oneness in the world which binds all men together" (1954, 3). A modern expression of that sentiment would more explicitly include women, but the basic sentiment is correct and shapes the contours of this book. Specifically, we believe in social justice, a concept that will be developed throughout the book, and we strongly value the ideals of freedom and equality. Yet, at the same time, we are all too aware of the numerous current inequalities and ways in which the United States is not living up to its ideals as well as the intense struggles it took to get the country from the limited notions of equality at its founding to the more expansive—but still incomplete—understanding of it today.

Because freedom and inequality are such broad topics, this book focuses on the areas of crime and criminal justice. The criminal justice system has a monopoly on the coercive use of force through the powers of the police to detain, arrest, and use deadly force against people suspected of committing crimes; the court system's power to find guilt and pass sentence against people convicted of crimes; and the prison system's ability to deprive people of their freedom and to execute condemned citizens. The law defines what actions are harmful and thus gives direction to the formidable powers of the criminal justice system. Thus, "law and order" can be an oppressive mechanism employed to protect privilege in an unequal society, or it can be the call of conscience reminding the country about its promises of equality and liberty for all.

While this book focuses on law and criminal justice, our method is to connect those topics to social structures of inequality that systematically deny liberty to many people. A key to linking these is through the integration of class, race, and gender, categories that represent some of the most fundamental divisions in the United States. Indeed, Marx argued that all of human history was a class war that involved the struggle between the haves and have-nots—and that law was a tool in this struggle. Feminists point out that Marx's analysis of the workers and owners of the means of production left out women, some of whom were at home doing unpaid housework and reproductive labor and others of whom have always worked alongside men in the fields, factories, and businesses of American civilization; the battle of the sexes is thus also crucial, including issues of sexual access and reproductive control. Finally, race has also been a key issue throughout history in terms of conquest and empire, and any honest telling of US history should start with whites taking land from Native Americans and then building the wealth of the country through the use of African slaves, who provided hundreds of years of unpaid labor. Laws in the United States along with the criminal justice system allowed other immigrant groups to be exploited for cheap labor that also built America's capitalist economy.

Of course, it is important to understand not only how class, race, and gender work separately but also how they work in combination. For example, historians frequently report that the Fifteenth Amendment gave the former slaves the right to vote. A more accurate statement is that it gave the former male slaves the right to vote if they could somehow overcome the many physical and mental barriers to political participation that white society erected for them, such as physical barricades, paying poll taxes, and proving extraordinary competence on literacy tests; black women had to wait for the passage of the Nineteenth Amendment in 1920 before they, and white women, could vote. This book emphasizes the integration of class, race, and gender to create a more sophisticated or nuanced analysis that comes from looking at multiple aspects of identity. It can also reveal some stark discrepancies, as in chapter 9's analysis of incarceration rates: while 3.4 percent of whites born in 2001 will spend time in prison, 18.6 percent of blacks will; while 1.5 percent of women will spend time in prison, 11.3 percent of men will; while 0.9 percent of white women will spend time in prison, 32.2 percent of black men will.

Some may believe that black men are overinvolved in crime and drugs and thus should be overrepresented in prison. But the statistics indicate that disparities in street crime do not explain that much of the excess prison population, and whites and blacks use illegal drugs in rough proportion to their size in the population. Further, using street crime as an assessment for how "criminal" a group is leaves out the problem that much harm done by corporations is not criminalized, even though such actions hurt workers, consumers, communities, and the environment. As but one example, a manager's willful violation of safety regulations that results in a worker's death is punishable by a maximum of six months in prison, while a few grams of crack cocaine results in mandatory sentences of much longer for many poor minorities.

One of the underlying assumptions that drives this study of criminal justice has to do with the fundamental distinction anthropologists, sociologists, and others make between insider and outsider groups. Whether we are talking about matters within nations or between nations, the ages-old interactions and conflicts among social groups have always possessed an element of we/they or us/them. Accordingly, "insiders," or members of one social group, tend to see themselves as possessing virtues not possessed by "outsiders," or members of the other social groups. For example, members of one's own group of origin are typically seen as less violent, aggressive, or criminal and more trustworthy, peace loving, and law abiding than members of the "other" group.

But the fact of the matter is that no one race, class, or gender group holds a monopoly on common decency. Within each and every race, class, or gender group there are "decent" people and there are "deviant" people. Within each and every family there are some members who conform to society's expectations and there are those who reject the same. Some race, class, and gender groups, however, receive extra scrutiny and reprimand for deviance than others. This book seeks to raise issue with some of the beliefs, policies, and procedures that undermine social justice in this way.

Still, for many millennia and throughout the world, these ethnocentric beliefs have shaped social relations across lines of what we now think of as class, race/ethnicity, gender, nationality, sexuality, religion, and more. In our own contemporary period, when it is politically incorrect to hold bigoted views about some "others" (i.e., racial and ethnic minorities, women, gays, Jews), it is still politically accept-able to hold such views about "criminals." So when public discourse has dwelled on "welfare cheats" or "violent offenders," what typically comes to mind are racially/ethnically charged subtexts with derogatory images of the "other." In the 1980s, this phenomenon of stereotyping was classically demonstrated when the media and ethnographers alike talked about drug-addicted mothers while simultaneously and relentlessly using racial images of African American women trading sex for crack rather than middle-class white women snorting the more expensive powder cocaine. While pregnant poor and black women became targets of the criminal justice sys-tem, middle- and upper-class women escaped the scrutiny of criminal justice agents into the confines of private detoxification facilities (Flavin 2009; Humphries 1999). While it is not politically correct to hold overtly sexist views, many still focus on why women stay in an abusive relationship or what a woman was wearing when she was raped rather than asking about why some men abuse their intimate partners or why some men rape.

In other words, this book treats crime as more than the violation of a legalized social norm and justice as more than the equal application of laws. Similarly, we see the study of crime and crime control as more than analyzing the behavior of criminals and the institutional agents of the criminal justice system. As Livy Visano has emphasized:

> The study of crime is an analysis of being, becoming and experiencing "otherness." Crime is a challenge to a particular socially constructed and historically rooted social order. The study of crime, therefore, is an inquiry into expressions of power, cultural controls and contexts of contests. Accordingly, the designated criminal is set apart and relegated to the margins according to a disciplining discourse about differences. (1998, 1)

This book is an attempt to locate the study of crime and crime control in the context of being and becoming persons of "class, race, and gender." And while those terms are typically reserved for the poor, minorities, and women, everyone fits into a class, whites have race, and men have gender. In communicating and experiencing "otherness" in the social realities of crime and justice, we are interested not only in how class, race, and gender biases become reflected in the administration of everyday criminal justice but also in the roles played by criminology, law, and the mass media in helping to (re-)create the "other." In short, our effort here is to show that "crime" and "criminals" as well as the "criminal justice apparatus" as a whole are socially constructed phenomena, reproduced daily through various discussions in the streets, the media, the home, the governing bodies, the courts, and other cultural bodies; they are a product of moral agents, social movements, political interests, media dis-semination, and policymakers (Best 1990; Jenkins 1994; Potter and Kappeler 1998). In the process, crime control becomes the regulation of a relatively small number of acts that have been designated as threatening the social order, and the administration of criminal justice becomes the institutionalized or patterned responses for process-ing those threats. This way of criminal justice functioning becomes accepted and normalized; ideologies, legal and otherwise, convince people that the patterns are inevitable and just, when in fact they are mutable and discrepant.

For reasons like this, concepts of "equal protection" and "due process" are important but limited. Although the police might not coerce a suspect into confessing and the defendant might have a lawyer for representation in court, the late judge David L. Bazelon once noted, "It is simply unjust to place people in dehumanizing social conditions, do nothing about those conditions, and then command those who suffer, 'Behave—or else!'" (quoted in Leighton and Reiman 2001, 39). Justice Brandeis, in the case noted at the opening of this preface, would have agreed, because he noted that the Founding Fathers "knew that order cannot be secured merely through fear of punishment for its infraction; that it is hazardous to discourage thought, hope and imagination; that fear breeds repression; that repression breeds hate; [and] that hate menaces stable government" (*Whitney v. California*, 274 U.S. 357 [1927], 375).

The narrow rational-legalistic conceptions of crime and justice are valid and pragmatic, but they are not sufficient by themselves for a full understanding of justice. Instead, the analysis of criminal justice is strengthened when the broader social, cultural, and historical conceptions of crime and justice are added to the mix and then investigated and evaluated together. This kind of comparative inquiry sheds more light on important (but frequently neglected) questions of "equal justice for all." In the spirit of critical pedagogy, we believe that this type of integrative analysis and its implications can help move the administration of justice closer to the ideals of peace, equality, and human liberation. Finally, we concur with Jock Young (2011, 225), who writes in *The Criminological Imagination*, "We are privileged to work in an area which has its focus on the fundamental dislocations of justice that occur throughout our social order, a place of irony and contest, of vituperation and transgression."

ABOUT THE FOURTH EDITION

After substantially changing the organization in each of the earlier editions, this fourth edition keeps the structure of the third edition and makes a small change to the order of chapters in part 1, "Crime Control and Criminology." What was chapter 1 in the third edition ("Criminology and the Study of Class, Race, Gender, and Crime") is now chapter 2, and chapter 1, which had been chapter 2 ("Criminal Justice Work and the Crime Control Enterprise"), is now "The Crime Control Enterprise and Its Workers." This organization provides an overview of the criminal justice system, its actors, and its actions before focusing on theories of crime and criminals. We have, of course, updated statistics, events related to the themes of this book, and theoretical and empirical developments in the areas of policy inquiry and justice practice, and we have furthered our evolving analysis of the intersections of class, race, gender, and crime.

The major change facilitating this updated edition is a new coauthor, Allison Cotton. While Jeanne Flavin has continued to work in areas relevant to this book, other professional interests and personal events have taken her further from this particular project. Gregg and Paul worked to update areas that were Jeanne's strength, but they recognized that the strength of this book lies in having multiple authors with different (but overlapping) strengths. Rather than have the coverage of issues become unbalanced, they sought a new coauthor whose strengths would ensure full and thoughtful coverage of class, race, gender, and their intersections. Gregg had worked as the series editor for Allison's book, *Effigy: Images of Capital Defendants* (2008), and recommended her. Paul agreed, and Allison accepted. We are all pleased with how this edition came out and look forward to the prospect of a fifth edition. Allison would like to thank her department chair, Dr. LiYing Li, and the administration of Metropolitan State University of Denver for approving her sabbatical proposal to participate in this project.

Through the changes and updates, we have kept what we believe to be the strengths of the book: it is the only authored rather than edited book in the field to thoroughly and systematically address class, race, and gender in relationship to crime and justice. We have kept the chapters that provide substantive introductions to class (chapter 3), race (chapter 4), gender (chapter 5), and their intersections (chapter 6) in part 2, "Inequality and Privilege." The chapters in part 3, "Law and Criminal Justice," on victimization (chapter 7), criminal law (chapter 8), policing and prosecution (chapter 9), and punishment (chapter 10) all share a common structure, with headings for class, race, gender, and intersections. As with the previous edition, each chapter starts with an opening narrative of interest that sets the tone for the chapter.

The authors would like to thank Natalie Morin of Eastern Michigan University, who worked as a research assistant for this edition. Natalie collected and delivered many of the updated figures, tables, and other data—and during this process, she provided valuable feedback about the new data that have been incorporated into the discussions in this edition. In addition, Natalie prepared the *Instructor's Manual* and *Test Bank* materials. The authors would also like to thank Jennie Brooks of EMU for her work on the index. Finally, the authors would like to thank some of the previous students whose work lives on in this edition, especially Maya Pagni Barak and Dana Horton.

GB, PL, AC

Introduction

Crime, Inequality, and Justice

The standard view of criminal justice is that criminal law is built on a consensus about harmful acts that reflect social norms; that police investigate crime and arrest wrongdoers; that prosecutors weigh the strength of the evidence and then decide when to press charges; that juries decide on guilt or innocence; that judges sentence according to guidelines that eliminate disparities; and that people objectively study crime and criminals to ultimately reduce the amount of victimization. That view is not wholly incorrect, but the standard view is problematic because in the bigger picture, changing social, political, and economic conditions shape the formation and application of the criminal laws of the United States. Crime and criminal justice are shaped by the political economy, which is a structural analysis of how politics, law, and economics influence one another. As such, official crime rates do not explain the dynamics of the criminal justice system as much as they explain social stratification, the surplus population—those who are unemployed or unemployable and are thus considered the "dangerous class"—technology, and prevailing ideologies. This means that the realities of crime and justice have always reflected, and usually re-created, class, race/ethnic, and gender relations.

For example, slavery rather than prison had been the dominant form of social control for African Americans before the Civil War. When the Thirteenth Amendment (ratified in 1865) freed the slaves, it removed that system of control and created serious anxiety among the white population. Slaves went from property to economic competition; black men were freed at a time when many Southern white women were widowed or single because of the large number of young white men killed during the war. Southern whites wanted another system for social control, but building prisons at that time was impossible. The war had been fought primarily in the South, and that was where most of the destruction had occurred. The repairs required labor, which was in short supply, again because of the large number of young men killed in

the war. Additionally, labor-intensive crops grown on plantations still required attention. Thus, Southern states passed black codes that penalized a number of behaviors
by blacks that whites found rude, disrespectful, or threatening. After the blacks were
convicted, they would be leased for labor to serve their sentence. Plantation owners
could now lease inmates rather than own slaves. Prisons also changed form during
the Industrial Revolution, and more recently, boot camps came about because the
government was closing military bases but had an increasing criminal—and juvenile—justice population.

Because crime and justice are shaped by the political economy, crime and crime
control are also inseparable from the changing relations of inequality, hierarchy, and
power. Crime and crime control are thus important locations where inequality is re-
created or challenged. Domestic violence, rape, and fraud by financial institutions
that enriches executives while devastating millions—each crime, while committed
by different types of offenders for very different reasons, reflects and re-creates an
aspect of inequality. Likewise, inequality and hierarchy are re-created or challenged
by both the explanations given for these different crimes and the decision of whether
the perpetrators are pursued or not by the criminal justice system.

This book sees crime and criminal justice as socially created and as having both
subjective and objective realities. That is, harms done to people are real, but the law
chooses to criminalize only certain ones. Manslaughter is a death because of negligence, but it applies only to individuals; there is no corporate manslaughter law in
the United States. Great Britain, Canada, and Australia all have various corporate
manslaughter provisions that apply to workplace deaths caused by negligent conduct
of supervisors and/or executives. The social reality of crime and crime control are
further shaped by the decisions of police about who is arrested, by prosecutors about
whether to pursue a case and which charges are most appropriate, by judicial processes that find certain offenders guilty, and by judicial decisions about who goes to
prison (Reiman and Leighton 2013). Statistics appear to be objective measurements
about crime but are the result of decisions and processes that are influenced by class,
race, and gender. Media decisions about what to report and which "frame"—or
"spin"—to put on a story add to the ways that the reality of crime and justice is
socially created.

These structural-legal relations are dynamic, subject to the changing needs of the
dominant relations in the prevailing political economy. Over the past millennium,
for example, different types of laws have evolved in response to the complexity of
political, economic, and social relations. For example, the division between "public" law (acts or omissions that offend or injure the state) and "private" law (acts
that offend or injure only persons) has evolved over time in response to changing
conditions and political powers. (Public laws include administrative and regulatory
law, constitutional law, and criminal law. Private laws, also referred to as civil laws,
include the laws of property, contracts, and torts.)

Historically, during the ancient regime or before the rise of mercantilism in the
fourteenth and fifteenth centuries, there were no criminal laws as we know them.
There were only civil offenses or torts. A tort was (and still is) a private or civil wrong

and/or injury that breaches a legal duty or obligation allegedly independent of the interests of the nation-state. For example, one person sues another for personal injury rather than having the state file assault charges. When a tort occurs, the offense or harm (injury) is subject to a fine, restitution, or some other form of compensation to make the victim whole again. Civil offenses, in other words, are not punishable by loss of liberty or life subject to the intervention of the "nation-state." By contrast, criminal prosecutions and punishments first appear with the simultaneous decline of feudalism and the rise of capitalism, which ushered in the early developments of the modern state, capital, labor, private property, and mercantilism. Many of these laws, some six hundred years old, are still operating today. Many other criminal laws have come and gone during this same period.

For example, the "crime of bankruptcy" was punishable by death in the English courts in the late 1700s because it was defined as an "act of debtor fraud, de facto theft by absconding with property and avoiding judicial process and the paying of just debts" (Pomykala 2000). While it was never treated as a capital offense in the United States, the framers of the Constitution did add bankruptcy to the list of federal powers used to prevent fraud. Until the mid-nineteenth century, plaintiff creditors could accuse defendants of bankruptcy or "debtor-perpetrated crime" in a court of law. Eventually, "bankruptcy was transformed from a branch of law for the relief of creditors against debtor fraud intended to foster the payment of debts into a pseudo-social welfare program for debtor relief. Modern bankruptcy law legalized what antecedent jurisprudence first sought to prevent, the nonpayment of debt" (Pomykala 2000). Now corporations routinely engage in strategic bankruptcy, which is legal and encourages "firms to use bankruptcy to avoid lawsuits; to decrease or eliminate damage awards for marketing injurious products, polluting or other corporate misconduct; [and] to abandon toxic waste sites" (Delaney 1999, 190). Even in bankruptcy that involves reorganization rather than liquidation, "financial risk can be shifted away from more powerful institutional creditors and the corporation itself and onto the backs of more vulnerable" and less organized groups, meaning workers and consumers (Delaney 1999, 190).

By contrast, many criminal laws that first emerged to control poverty, street crime, and the disorder of the dangerous classes in mercantile England are still with us today in one form or another. Some laws can be traced back to the British vagrancy statutes of 1349 or the Elizabethan Poor Law of 1601. In 2014, these and other related crimes of the marginal and powerless classes overwhelmingly consume and preoccupy the activities of the US criminal justice system as a whole. In fact, most histories of crime control acknowledge that the criminal justice policies of the postindustrial United States are the preferred methods for managing rising inequality and the surplus populations of the United States (Michalowski and Carlson 1999; Parenti 1999; Shelden 2000). *Surplus populations* refer primarily to economically marginal persons and those who are unemployed or unemployable; they are people with little attachment to the conventional labor market and little "stake in conformity" (C. Anderson 1974). Because of this status, surplus populations are also called "marginal classes" or "dangerous classes." Of course, the war on crime is not publicly discussed as an explicit war on the "down-and-out" or conceptualized as involving the enforcement of inequality and privilege. But the result of the current war on crime has been to fill an ever-expanding prison system with the poor and a disproportionate number of young minorities.

These dynamics are not new, and a historical overview of social control reveals that on the frontier as well as in the industrial United States, the administration of justice was about regulating and controlling the "dangerous classes." Freed black slaves were subject to harsh Jim Crow laws, and the Chinese were highly criminalized after they finished work on the transcontinental railroad. Still, over time, the criminalizing of behavior has been subject to periods of legal and constitutional reform that have gradually expanded the meanings of "due process" and "equal protection" for a wider and more diverse group of people.

Despite the vaunted democratization of criminal justice during the late nineteenth and twentieth centuries, the effects of crime control have always been to the disadvantage of the nation's most disentitled and marginalized members (Auerbach 1976; Barak 1980; Harring 1983; Walker 1980). When it was a young nation, the political and legal apparatuses of the United States were dominated by the organized power of wealthy, white, and male interests to the detriment of slaves, freedmen, workers, nonworkers, women, people of color, and (ex-) convicts. Since our nation's beginnings, then, the various struggles for justice, inside and outside the administration of criminal law, have included the goal of empowering people and granting all access to the same political and legal bodies of rule making and rule enforcing. As the notion of struggle suggests, history is not a linear progression of ever-greater equality. Achievements can result in backlashes, and those who are "more equal" always resist gains of the "less equal." Moreover, new forms of inequality often arise to take the place of old forms, and being granted a right in law does not make it a reality.

The next sections provide brief overviews of how class, race, and gender have been intertwined with the history of crime and justice. This is not meant to be definitive but to start a process of thinking separately about class and race and gender before trying to understand what happens at their intersections. To that end, the section that follows emphasizes the importance of understanding intersections and highlights some assumptions that guide our analysis. Because criminal justice is so often referred to as a "system," a subsequent section discusses some additional frames of reference for understanding crime control so that readers can have a fuller sense of the complexities of criminal justice.

CLASS, RACE, GENDER, AND JUSTICE: A HISTORICAL OVERVIEW

Class Justice

Throughout most of the nineteenth and well into the twentieth century, a blatant kind of class justice prevailed in the selective enforcement and differential application of the criminal and civil laws to the "haves" and the "have-nots" (Auerbach 1976; Barak 1980). The law was heavily influenced by a reverence for private property and laissez-faire social relations ("let them do as they will," meaning few regulations beyond the protection of private property). In terms of commercial transactions, the philosophy of the day was caveat emptor, "buyer beware"; businesses sometimes used their freedom to produce dangerous goods or to misrepresent their product. In the area of business, farmers and merchants alike were subject to few regulatory laws of any kind. In other words, both groups were allowed the freedom to expand their particular domains and to compete and acquire both property and capital with little legal interference. By contrast, labor was highly regulated. Unions were an illegal interference with "freedom of contract" and an unlawful conspiracy that limited an employer's property rights.

Railroads were crucial to the expansion of the economy at the beginning of the twentieth century, and companies amassed large fortunes from this industry. However, they fought attempts at minimum wages for employees and often required employees to live in a company town, rent dwellings from the company, and shop at company stores. The prices charged by the company were usually more than the wage, so the debt bound families to the company as indentured servants. For industry as a whole, the average workweek was sixty hours. Fatigue, combined with the employers' indifference to workplace safety, created "an appalling record of industrial accidents. An incomplete survey showed that at least half a million workers were killed, crippled, or seriously injured on the job in 1907" (Gilbert 1998, 57).

In other areas, exposés of the meatpacking industry shocked the public and motivated legislators to enact the first food and drug acts. Certain journalists, called muckrakers, believed that "big business was 'bad business' insofar as it was more concerned with profit than human life" (Lynch and Frank 1992, 13). Lawyers such as Louis Brandeis, who would soon become a US Supreme Court associate justice, shared their concerns. Brandeis wrote about the "curse of business" and the problems of companies becoming large in the interests of being a monopoly—one that violated public trust rather than worked in its interest. "No country," he wrote, "can afford to have its prosperity originated by a small controlling class" (in W. Douglas 1954, 187). Justice Douglas (1954) explained, "Brandeis did not want America to become a nation of clerks, all working for some overlord."

The administration of criminal (and civil) justice was chaotic, often corrupt, and subject to the buying of law enforcement and juries (Barak 1980). An independent and decentralized criminal justice system designed for a more homogenized, pioneer, and primarily agricultural society was ill adapted for the needs of an increasingly complex, urban, and industrialized society. A social and cultural environment experienced increasing numbers of immigrants from southern and eastern Europe, a changing means of rapid communication and transportation, and an expanding presence of wage-earning working classes—and it all called for a coordinated system of criminal justice.

By the turn of the twentieth century, the buying of justice that had prevailed earlier (available to those who could afford representation in the legislatures, in the courts, and in the streets) was threatening the very legitimacy of criminal justice in the United States (Cantor 1932). The initial laissez-faire emphasis on the right to acquire private property had blossomed into a full-fledged national preoccupation with wealth and power. Political corruption became widespread, and political machines dominated urban areas: "The machines controlled city governments, including the police and the courts. Payrolls were padded and payoffs were collected from contractors" (Edelstein and Wicks 1977, 7). Graft and other forms of bribery contributed not only to the buying of justice by those who could afford it but also to a changing national morality. "Rackets," "pull," and "protection" were common antidotes for stubborn legal nuisances. Prevailing values of wealth and success predominated as guiding principles of right and wrong. "The ability to 'make good' and 'get away with it' offsets the questionable means employed in the business as well as professional world. Disrespect for the law and order is the accompanying product of this scheme of success" (Cantor 1932, 145).

Those who were marginalized, especially the poor, unemployed, women, and people of color, were rarely, if ever, in a position to buy justice. As the marginalized groups of immigrants and others grew in urban cities across the United States and the miscarriages of justice flourished, the need to reform the institutions of criminal justice grew because the country was beginning to experience bitter class wars. The working classes aggressively resisted exploitation through on-the-job actions and wide social movements. To combat challenges to the emerging monopoly or corporate order of industrial capitalism, the wealthy and ruling classes initially employed illegal violence, such as the hiring of thugs and private armies. Later, they retained the services of private security companies, such as the Pinkertons, to infiltrate and break up worker organizations. However, as the number of violent incidents increased, as the contradictions of American democracy became more apparent, other methods for regulating and controlling the masses were needed—methods reflective of a modern, rational system of crime control and a criminal justice system based on a more equal-appearing application of the rule of law (Barak 1980).

During the Progressive Era of the early twentieth century, the plight of the poor gained the attention of some industrialists and political leaders. The discontent of those who were not benefiting from the expanding economy threatened the growing prosperity of those who were. As a response to the growing resentment of the lower and working classes and to the middle-class Progressives who believed in the "perfectible society," the ruling strata sought to stabilize the social order in general and to reform the administration of criminal justice in particular. There emerged a number of reforms, some "hard" and some "soft" (Center for Research on Criminal Justice 1975).

Examples of the harder, or technical, reforms included the formation of systems of state policing, the initiation of truancy laws, and the forced sterilization of some "mentally defective" persons, poor people, and sex offenders. Examples of the softer, or humane, reforms included the development of the juvenile justice system, the public defender system, and a bit later, systems of treatment and rehabilitation. Each of these soft reforms aimed at a fairer, more objective, scientific, and humane administration of criminal justice. In combination, these reforms helped secure and legitimate the needs of an emerging corporate capitalism as they contributed to more rational, bureaucratic, and efficient systems of criminal justice. At the same time, these legalistic reforms not only improved the practices and the images of due process and equal protection under the law, they also legitimated greater state intervention into the lives of those marginally defined and segregated on the basis of their class, race, and gender. The practice of forced sterilization, for example, continued until as recently as the 1970s and provided the foundation for chemical castration as well as policies aimed at getting women who receive welfare to agree to be implanted with the contraceptive Norplant.

Generally, with the crimes of the powerless, the governmental legal agents wage "wars" like the ones on illicit drugs or undocumented families and have "zero tolerance" for a range of petty crimes. Such acts receive a disproportionate priority with investigations, surveillance, arrest, and prosecutions and during what is likely to be a negotiated settlement (plea bargain). When convicted, perpetrators are typically sentenced to prison or placed on probation. Either way, the poor and powerless are disproportionately represented as "common criminals" or the "dangerous class," and they are treated accordingly.

By contrast, many crimes of the very powerful are "beyond incrimination" or not subject to the criminal law in the first place because of lobbying and donations to politicians. Thus, the possibility of criminal liability and prison does not even exist. Police do not investigate, and it is a regulatory matter to be dealt with by a fine and a consent decree. Even when there is an actual crime, offenders can receive a "deferred prosecutorial agreement," which means charges will be dropped if there is no additional wrongdoing. Through these various means, the powerful Wall Street securities fraudsters responsible for the recession of 2009 to 2012, for example, were not investigated, prosecuted, or held accountable for their actions (Barak 2012). The sentiment is concisely, if crudely, expressed by a quote appearing in "Why Isn't Wall Street in Jail?" by *Rolling Stone* columnist Matt Taibbi (2011): "Everything's f**ked up, and nobody goes to jail." The white men who overextended their speculative risks, engaged in multiple misrepresentations, and caused a financial implosion felt around the world are still in charge today because the financial institutions that they run were—and are—"too big to fail" or jail (Barak 2012).

Racial Justice

The consistencies in the practice of racial injustice in the Americas date as far back as Christopher Columbus's ill treatment of the indigenous peoples, followed by the early colonists' treatment of American Indians and the enslavement of Africans. This intense and sustained history of mistreatment has raised questions about genocide in the United States with respect to both American Indians (Weyler 1992) and African Americans (Johnson and Leighton 1999; Patterson 1970, 1971). Katheryn Russell has shown that one constant remained as the slave codes became the black codes and the black codes became the Jim Crow segregation statutes:

> Blackness itself was a crime. The codes permitted Blacks to be punished for a wide range of social actions. They could be punished for walking down the street if they did not move out of the way quickly enough to accommodate White passersby, for talking to friends on a street corner, for speaking to someone White, or for making eye contact with someone White. (1998, 22)

Each of these "systems of racial justice" operated in racially oppressive and discriminatory ways. Some were blatantly racist, and some were subtly so, as in the "separate but equal" ruling in *Plessy v. Ferguson* in 1896 (see chapter 4). In either situation, these forms of racial (in)justice, until midway into the twentieth century, were ruled to be both "moral" and "rational-legal" by the highest court in the land.

Slave codes, from 1619 to 1865, constituted the criminal law and procedure applied against enslaved Africans (Gorman 1997; Oshinsky 1996). The codes regulated slave life from cradle to grave and were virtually uniform across the states in upholding the institutions of chattel slavery. "Under the codes, the hardest criminal penalties were reserved for those acts that threatened the institution of slavery (e.g., the murder of someone White or a slave insurrection). The slave codes also penalized Whites who actively opposed slavery" (Russell 1998, 15). But their primary purposes were to enumerate applicable laws and to prescribe the social boundaries for slaves: where they could go, what types of activity they could engage in, and what type of contracts they could enter into. Slaves were subject not only to the administration of separate, special tribunals but also to procedural practices that did not accord them the same rights as those of free white men, such as the rights to a jury trial, to be convicted by a unanimous verdict, to be presumed innocent, and to appeal a conviction. Nor were slaves permitted to serve as jurors or to act as witnesses against whites. In short, "the codes create a caste system under which Whites, Blacks, and mulattoes were accorded separate legal statuses and sanctions. This meant that in addition to the blatant double standards of the slave codes, Blacks were further marginalized by laws that assessed punishment by 'degree of Blackness'" (Russell 1998, 15).

Under such a caste system, the slave codes of most states allowed whites to beat, slap, and whip slaves with impunity. Punishment for crimes involving interracial relations also involved racial double standards: "A Black man who had sex with a White woman faced the most severe penalty, while a White man who had sex with a Black slave woman faced the least severe penalty" (Russell 1998, 16). In fact, more black men were executed for raping white women than for killing white persons. Similarly, under Virginia law, the only law carrying the punishment of castration was the rape of a white woman by a black man. According to most slave codes, however, the rape of a black woman by a white man or by a black slave was not a crime. Under the slave codes, the prevailing modes of enforcing slavery were not only through separate and unequal laws and tribunals but also by the notorious slave patrols or the precursors to the first American forms of policing. Slave patrollers, working in conjunction with the militia, were allowed to stop, search, and beat slaves who did not have proper permission to be away from their plantations. Slave laws also sanctioned extrajudicial forms of justice, such as "plantation justice," which permitted slave owners to impose sanctions, including lashes, castration, and hanging, and to hire bounty hunters to catch runaway slaves (Russell 1998).

After the Civil War and emancipation, newly freed black men and women were given the right to enter into contracts and to marry. At the same time, the first black codes adopted in 1865 created a new system of involuntary servitude, expressly prohibited by the recently adopted Thirteenth Amendment. For example, the adoption of vagrancy laws allowed blacks to be arrested for the "crime" of being unemployed, and licensing requirements were imposed to bar blacks from all but the most menial of jobs in the South. Finally, the newly granted rights for blacks served to mobilize white vigilantes, including the likes of the Ku Klux Klan. The harsh nature of racial justice also can be seen by the institutionalization of the "lynching ritual," an extreme form of vigilante racial justice that between 1892 and 1964 claimed the lives of three thousand to ten thousand black Americans (Tolnay and Beck 1995).

Jim Crow laws began to take hold in the early 1900s following the *Plessy v. Ferguson* decision. These laws mandated separate public facilities for blacks and whites and applied to cemeteries, hospital wards, water fountains, public restrooms, churches, swimming pools, hotels, movie theaters, trains, phone booths, lunch counters, prisons, courthouses, buses, orphanages, school textbooks, parks, and prostitution (Myrdal 1944). The segregation statutes and covenants in the South (as well as in the North) dictated where "Whites, Coloreds, and Negroes" could rent or buy property, which spoke to how extensively these laws sought to regulate both the private and public lives of blacks. Both before and after *Brown v. Topeka, Kansas, Board of Education* in 1954, which outlawed "separate but equal," the world of social etiquette made no pretense regarding social equality. Russell offers this explanation:

> Rules of racial etiquette were an integral part of Jim Crow. These unwritten rules required that Black men refer to White men as "Mister" or "Sir." At the same time, however, Whites would commonly refer to a Black man as "boy." The rules governing racial manners also required Blacks to step aside and bow their heads in the presence of Whites. This system of verbal and physical deference reflected the White belief that no matter how much racial equality the Constitution promised, Whites would never view Blacks as their social equals. (1998, 22)

African Americans are not the only nonwhite groups who have experienced racial injustice, imposed separation, and cultural imperialism. The thefts of land from American Indians and the government's subsequent breaking of treaties have left many of them on small, isolated reservations (Lazarus 1991). Similarly, there were the thefts of personal property and land as well as the internment of Japanese Americans in "relocation camps" during World War II. Many Latinos today live in rural and inner-city barrios, not unlike the proliferation of Chinatowns and black and brown ghettos that grew up all across the United States in the past century.

Patterns of residential segregation have remained the rule, even though "separate but equal" was struck down (Massey and Denton 1993). The social isolation experienced by these racial others has created "many deleterious effects, both structural (e.g., systematic differences in opportunities to acquire disposable income and to generate wealth) and psychological (e.g., being unable to understand what life is like for members of other groups)" (Mann and Zatz 1998, 5).

Gendered Justice

The differential treatment of men and women—and later of boys and girls— reflected a gendered double standard that dated back to the chauvinistic sexual customs and conceptions of private property first articulated in ancient Greek and Roman laws (Posner 1992). Until recently, these customs explicitly prevailed in US law. Women were considered chattel or possessions of their fathers and husbands, forbidden from holding property in their own names or from entering into business deals or contracts. Women were treated as different or as "second-class" citizens, and they were subject to the patriarchal rules of family, usually under the guise of protecting them and controlling them "for their own good." Whether in the public or private sphere, gendered justice denied women equal protection under the law. In fact, it was not until the 1980s that husbands could be charged with the crime of raping their wives. Moreover, the burdens of legal proof involved in extramarital rape cases before then were always hard to meet, making rape the single most difficult crime to successfully prosecute on behalf of women victims seeking justice from the criminal law.

Early European feminists worked to raise awareness of women's oppression, a tradition that continued in spite of social revolutions in Europe and passionate discourses about equality and brotherhood. Indeed, in the late 1700s, Mary Wollstonecraft, in the name of "sisterhood," observed "the inconsistency of radical males who fought for the freedom of individuals to determine their own happiness and yet continued to subjugate women, leaving them to 'procreate and rot'" (Kandal 1988, 12). In the United States, few advocates of abolishing slavery saw any connection with women's suffrage. For example, the Grimké sisters used their status as part of a prominent southern family to argue that female slaves "are our sisters" and have a "right to look for sympathy with their sorrows and effort and prayer for their rescue." But the New England abolition society chastised them for forgetting "the great and dreadful wrongs of the slave in a selfish crusade against some paltry grievance . . . some trifling oppression" of their own (Kandal 1988, 214).

With the arrival of the Progressive Era, social reformers sought to address the widespread prostitution and venereal diseases that resulted from the temporary shortage of women that accompanied the great waves of immigration in the late nineteenth and early twentieth centuries. Laws were passed that tried to suppress abortion, pornography, contraception, and prostitution. Federal laws such as the

Mann Act of 1910 outlawed the importation of contraceptives, the mailing of obscene books and other materials, and the interstate traffic in prostitutes. The selective enforcement of those laws disproportionately against the female sellers rather than the male purchasers of sex remains a component of the social relations of gendered justice and social control.

To be sure, persons handled formally by the criminal justice system and who ended up in prisons through the nineteenth and twentieth centuries were 95 percent male and 5 percent female (Rafter 1990). However, at least since the nineteenth century, the social control of girls and women has also included the patriarchal institutions of marriage and family, the associated treatment of females for their recalcitrance and waywardness, and the medicalization and the hospitalization of their problems (Foucault 1980; Platt 1969).

Women also experienced gendered justice in other ways besides the chivalry that has been shown primarily to white women but denied to other women. For instance, when the first wave of organized imprisonment of women occurred between 1870 and 1900, many reformatories were opened as alternatives for white women. These women were regarded as in need of moral reform and protection. Women's case files in the American West in the late 1880s "rarely expressed an official opinion that an incarcerated female offender represented a threat to society. Instead, parole boards denied a woman freedom because she 'had not been sufficiently punished,' or she 'traveled with bad companions in the past,' or she 'broke the hearts of her respected parents'" (Butler 1997, 226).

While the reformatory movement "resulted in the incarceration of large numbers of white working-class girls and women for largely noncriminal or deportment offenses," such offenses did not extend to women of color (Chesney-Lind 1996, 132). Rather, African American women, for example, continued to be warehoused in prisons, where they were treated much like male inmates (Butler 1997). In the South, black women often ended up on chain gangs and were expected to keep up with the men in order to avoid beatings (Rafter 1990).

Gendered justice has also socially constructed the "normal" criminal as male and the "abnormal" criminal as female. In other words, men were seen as rational creatures of culture and women as governed by their nature. Thus, criminology constructed crimes by men as being bad choices that reflected a normal weighing of gain and loss, but crimes by women were seen as "unnatural" because they went against the allegedly docile and submissive "nature" of women (Hart 1994; Rafter 1990). Links have also been made between the "unnaturalness" of female criminality and lesbianism (Faith 1993; Hart 1994).

THE SOCIAL RELATIONS OF
CLASS, RACE, GENDER, AND CRIME

Examining class, race, and gender in relationship to law, order, and crime control provides an appreciation for the unique histories of the individual social groupings and interrelated axes of privilege and inequality. At any given moment, class, race, or gender may "feel more salient or meaningful in a given person's life, but they are overlapping and cumulative in their effect on people's experience" (Andersen and Collins 1998, 3). Class and race and gender are all required in order to begin to describe an individual's experience in the world, and they are likewise all required in order to understand crime and criminal justice. For example, rape generally leads to few arrests and convictions, but that statement also needs to acknowledge the hyperenforcement of rape laws against black men when white women were thought to be involved.

Dorothy Roberts's (1993) work also draws attention to these intersections by examining black women, who are often rendered invisible because "black" tends to mean "men" and "women" tends to mean "white." Roberts links crime, race, and reproduction to show how racism and patriarchy function as mutually reinforcing systems of domination that help determine "who the criminals are, what constitutes a crime, and which crimes society treats most seriously" (Roberts 1993, 1945). More specifically, in terms of abortion, birth control, and social control, Roberts discusses how this domination is meted out through the control of black women's bodies that discourages procreation, subordinates groups, and regulates fertility. As part of our integrative analysis of class, race, and gender, we also attempt to explore how each of these hierarchies helps sustain the others and how they reinforce the types of crime and justice in our society.

Our study of class, race, gender, and crime reveals that while class, race, or gender may feel more important at a specific point, one is not obviously more important than the others over time or situations. Only by studying their combinations and integrating them can one come to fully appreciate how bias undergirds the construction of what will and will not become criminal, as well as the effects of implementation and administration of those biased rules. This bias also shapes the construction of individual experience and identity, including experience of crime and the criminal justice system. More specifically, we bring several assumptions to the study of the social relations of class, race, gender, and crime control:

- First, these categories of social difference all share similarities in that they convey privilege on some groups and marginalize others, so they relate to power resources in society. Ideology works to naturalize privilege, so those who have privilege do not see themselves as having it and are much more likely to believe there is a "level playing field."
- Second, systems of privilege and inequality derived from the social statuses of class, race, and gender are overlapping and have interacting effects that can be more than the sum of their parts. Here, 1 + 1 is more than 2, or gendered racism is much more powerful than simply adding gender and race.
- Third, while class, race, and gender privilege all tend to be similarly invisible because of ideology, the experience of marginalization will vary considerably, depending on the specific nature of the prejudice and stereotypes. Understand-

ing marginalization also requires appreciating the diversity within categories—American Indians represent hundreds of different tribes; Hispanics and Asians represent dozens of different countries and cultures.

• Fourth, there are connections between these systems of class, race, and gender. Few people are pure oppressors or victims, so it is a complex matrix in which all people are more aware of their victimization than of their privilege.

Subsequent chapters use an array of material to unravel the complexities of class, race, and gender as they interact with the cultural and social production of crime, justice, and inequality. Our analysis of crime and justice further assumes that the inequalities in crime control and the administration of criminal justice are an essential element of popular culture, market society, and the social constructions of class, race, and gender differences as these are experienced in relation to one's place, order, conflict, and perception.

Perceptions, public and private, of what constitutes unacceptable social injuries and acceptable social controls are shaped by the underlying elements of social organization, including the production and distribution of economic, political, and human services (Michalowski 1985). We are not talking about conspiracies of elites and decision makers here, but rather about crime and crime control institutions that both reflect and re-create the changing nature of capitalist social relations. So "serious crime," defined from above or below, from the suite or the street, and from official reports of the Federal Bureau of Investigation or by the unofficial cultural media, becomes a statistically mediated and socially constructed artifact.

In popularly organized numbers, narratives, and images alike, a distorted view and limited perception of harmful behavior emerges. Crime and criminals are restricted primarily to the tabulations and representations of the conventional criminal code violations: murder, rape, burglary, robbery, assault, and face-to-face larceny-theft. Almost all crimes in the suites, if not ignored, are typically downplayed rather than focusing on human decisions and harms done to society. There are no databases or publications for corporate crime like the FBI has for street crime, so many white-collar corporate frauds and offenses against the environment, workplace, and consumer are not captured in FBI press releases about "Crime in America." Reporters and authors, including academics, analyze data that are more readily available, and those findings get reported in textbooks on criminal justice that focus on street crime.

Culturally produced images of crime and criminals reinforce one-dimensional notions that criminality and harmful behavior are predominantly the responsibility of the poor and marginal members of society. As mass consumers, we all share mediated facsimiles of lawbreakers and crime fighters. Common stories of crime and criminal justice appear and reappear over and over in the news, in films, on television, and in literature, helping to reproduce or reconstruct in the imagination of the American psyche similar renderings of crime, criminals, law enforcement, adjudication, and punishment. It is no wonder that when most people try to picture the typical American crime, the common image that emerges is one of young male victimizers. There are also the numerous police-action reenactments that can be viewed regularly on such television programs as *Top Cops* or *America's Most Wanted* that similarly recycle images of these young men as dangerous drug dealers whose dwellings must be invaded during the early hours of dawn by "storm troopers" and other law enforcement personnel in order to pursue, secure, and repress the dangerous faces in the "war on crime." (USA Network does have a program, *White Collar*, which focuses on art theft, counterfeiting, and smuggling—not corporate crime or ways in which elites victimize employees, consumers, and the environment [Leighton 2010].)

Moreover, the images of crime control that are constructed of the criminal justice system as one moves from law enforcement to adjudication and from sentencing to incarceration again serve to reinforce fairly limited and often distorted realities of criminal justice in action. For example, images of a criminal courtroom come to mind from relatively long and involved trials exposed in feature-length films, or from Court TV's gavel-to-gavel coverage of celebrated trials, or from other cable network television outlets on the trials and acquittals of celebrities and unusual cases. The public is also led to believe, based on artist sketches or succinct and curt shots of highly charged courtroom scenes from various television series such as *The Practice* and *Law and Order: Special Victims Unit*, that attorneys for each side, engaged in vigorous battle, always do their legal best to secure justice for all. However, in these dramatizations, whether fictional or "reality-based television" (with editing), the images that do not come to mind are the overwhelming majority of criminal cases (90 percent) that are plea-bargained every day in courthouses throughout the United States. These negotiated deals in lieu of trials usually take less than a few minutes for judges and courts to process and uphold. The coercion to "go along" is hidden, and the deals virtually eliminate the possibility of appeal (Kipnis 2001).

With punishment, popular images of dangerously violent offenders who need to be locked up indefinitely are prevalent in the media. For more than thirty-five years, politicians have appeared before the media talking about a "get tough" platform that criticizes the "leniency" of previous election cycles. More recent presidential elections (2004, 2008, 2012) have been dominated by other issues such as wars on terror and a slumping economy rather than declining crime rates. Nevertheless, the United States is left with a legacy of harsh penal policies that continue to make it unimaginable even to consider the possibility of reuniting the offender, the victim, and the community in some of kind of restorative form of justice. As part of the inherited politics of a war on crime, the political economy of incarceration, and the privatization of penal services ("bodies destined for profitable punishment"), the languages and images of dangerousness and retribution continue to contribute to the United States' criminal justice–industrial complex (J. Dyer 2000; Leighton and Selman 2012).

Representations of dangerous offenders convey the images of feuding convicts divided into racial and religious cliques doing "scared time," not of inmates engaged in school or the learning of a vocation or of former offenders reintegrating or fitting back into society. The recently discontinued and award-winning HBO dramatic series of life in a maximum-security prison, *Oz*, portrayed a based-on-facts fictional account of the complexity of one of those "hell-on-earth" archipelagos. On the one hand, its representation ignored the social realities of some 1,500 other state and federal prisons of lesser pain. On the other hand, *Oz* did not actually do justice to the continuing apartheid-like conditions of crime and punishment that disproportionately affect marginal black and brown Americans.

CRIMINAL JUSTICE THEORIZING

Among other important assumptions that undergird this work is that the administration of criminal justice may be viewed as both a "system" and a "nonsystem" (Bohm and Haley 2004); it may also be viewed as an "apparatus" involving both public and private or state and nonstate sectors (Duffee 1980; Kraska 2004). Hence, when scholars of crime and justice speculate about "criminal justice" in this or any other country, they do so as a means of orienting themselves to various symbolic and cognitive frameworks for understanding the causation of crime and crime control as well as the underpinning of norms, values, and beliefs surrounding the administration of criminal law.

Compared to theories of crime/criminality, theories of crime control/criminal justice are underdeveloped. In *Theorizing Criminal Justice* (2004), Peter Kraska has identified eight essential orientations or theoretical metaphors that attempt to explain the workings and expansion of the areas of "criminal justice" dating back to the 1950s. He also notes that four of these orientations are primarily concerned with the formal criminal justice system and that four are concerned with criminal justice as a broader apparatus. The first group views criminal justice as *formal models of the administration of criminal justice as a system*. These include rational/legalism, system, crime control versus due process, and politics. The second group views criminal justice as *informal models of a criminal justice apparatus as a nonsystem*. These include socially constructed reality, growth complex, oppression, and late modernity.

The *rational/legal* theoretical orientation "does not constitute a well-defined area of scholarship. It exists, instead, as a way of thinking dispersed throughout various literatures in criminology/criminal justice" (Kraska 2004, 19). The intellectual roots of this model may be traced back to the legal formalism of the classical and neoclassical schools of economic thought with their emphases on the social contract, utilitarianism, and the rule of law. These models argue that criminal justice operations are the product of rational, impartial decision making based on the rule of law, at least in the ideal if not the practice. The systems *theoretical* orientation has been considered the dominant paradigm in criminal justice studies for more than fifty years. The intellectual roots of the *system* models come from three other traditions: the biological sciences, sociological functionalism, and the field of organizational studies. As a biological metaphor, criminal justice is viewed as larger than the sum of its parts or subsystems—police, courts, and corrections. As a way of thinking, it was also a social movement in organizational behavior, with various stakeholders within the criminal justice system stepping forward to research and study criminal justice primarily as a means to make it operate more efficiently and effectively (Barak 1980; Walker 1992).

Both the rational/legal and systems models view the recent expansion and growth in size and power of the criminal justice system as a "forced reaction" to a worsening, real or imaginary, crime problem rather than a policy choice. The next two orientations, crime control versus due process and politics, require different explanations. These move from a condition of the criminal justice system being forced to act to one where it chooses to act in a particular fashion, based on its own (or the government's) value preferences.

By contrast, the *crime control vs. due process* and the *politics* models view these developments as a matter of human will subject to different ideological values, political preferences, and material conditions. These models contend that crime and crime control are not some kind of inevitability or natural phenomenon. In elaborating on the *crime control versus due process* orientations, Herbert Packer (1964) discusses how the criminal justice pendulum swings back and forth, conservatively and liberally, favoring crime control at certain times and favoring due process ("rule of law") at other times. He also makes it clear that crime was a sociopolitical artifact, not a natural phenomenon, dependent on what we choose to count as criminal and the ways in which we process (i.e., order versus liberty, efficiency versus equity) those whom we define as criminal. The *politics* orientation to criminal justice is inclusive of Packer's two political models, but it expands the political metaphor by assuming that politics "is at play at all levels of the criminal justice apparatus—from the everyday actions of the corrections or police practitioner, to the political influence of local communities, to agencies involved in criminal justice policy formation and implementation, and to lawmaking at the national and state levels" (Kraska 2004, 206). In short, these two orientations view all criminal justice activity and thinking as interest based, involving inherent conflicts, power struggles, influence building, and hardened ideological positions. They both argue that the strategies of criminal justice are products of a complex mix of political and social interests.

The next four models, with their focus on the criminal justice apparatus, broaden the object of criminal justice study to include the activities of numerous state and nonstate responses to the crime problem, including "1) crime control practices carried out by state and non-state entities; 2) the formal creation and administration of criminal law carried out by legislators, the police, courts, corrections, and juvenile subcomponents; and 3) others involved in the criminal justice enterprise, such as the media, academic researchers, and political interest groups" (Kraska 2004, 7–8). The apparatus-oriented models view crime control as involving more than the activities of state agencies and the political negotiation over the appropriate means of carrying out the administration of criminal justice according to the rule of law. These four model types regard criminal justice administration not only as a nonsystem of state bureaucratization but also as part of the larger culture and other nonstate and privatized activities and networks that coalesce to sustain the hierarchy and legitimacy of the prevailing political, economic, and social arrangements.

In the context of the larger culture and society, these apparatus-oriented models view the police, courts, and corrections agencies as engaging in ritualistic ceremonies and in promoting various myths of crime and crime control for the purposes of establishing and maintaining their legitimacy in relationship to the prevailing hierarchical order. For example, the *socially constructed reality* orientations, such as "symbolic interactionism," "dramaturgical analysis," or "moral panic," adopt interpretative approaches to criminal justice that do not assume that reality is pre-determined or given (much as the previous four orientations do). In other words, reality, criminal justice or otherwise, is not taken for granted, but rather, it's a human accomplishment. Social realities of criminal justice do not simply exist; they are the result of an intricate process of learning and constructing meanings and definitions of situations through language, symbols, and interactions with other people, crime fighters and non–crime fighters alike. The scholarly roots of the socially constructed models come from interpretive philosophy, symbolic interactionism, and cultural studies. They argue that the products of criminal justice administration are derived from the most believable stories about crime and justice.

Similarly, the *growth complex* orientations to criminal justice are about believable stories of "crime fighting" and the legitimacy of the criminal justice bureaucracy's survival and growth as a social industry. The arguments for the ideals of equal justice for all or of administering justice and controlling crime become subordinate to the divergent and competing interests of the various subsystems of criminal justice, on the one hand, and to the common and mutual interests of the criminal justice system as a whole, on the other hand. The intellectual roots of the growth complex models stem from a hybridization of systems theory, bureaucratic rationalism, critical theory, and the Frankfurt school of thought.

The *oppression* orientations to criminal justice have varied from those that take a more instrumental approach to those that take a more structural approach, the former arguing that the criminal justice apparatus is simply a tool of the economically powerful to control the behavior of the poor, the disadvantaged, and the threatening classes, and the latter arguing that in addition to the instability issues of "class," there are also the instability issues of "race" and "gender." The social roots of these latter oppressive models emerged with the struggles for social justice and the critical theories of class, race, and gender inequality. These models argue one dimensionally or in some kind of combination that the selective enforcements and differential applications of the law experienced by some (and not other) groups of people is a reification of the dominant economic, ethnic, and patriarchal interests interacting.

Finally, the *late modernity* orientations to criminal justice explain changes in crime and punishment as adaptations to late modern social conditions or risks, such as the rise in economic globalization, telecommunications, privatization, and the decline of state sovereignty. The philosophical roots of these models may be traced back to the traditions of existentialism, postmodernism, and critical materialism. Applied to recent criminal justice trends, these models locate crime and crime control within the macroshifts of a rapidly changing world, and they attempt to explain how the various responses to crime and injustice over time occurred. According to Kraska, these are potentially the most theoretical of the eight essential orientations because they offer a perspective capable of fusing or integrating the other orientations. However, from an integrated approach, none of the eight theoretical metaphors are capable of standing alone or of being more than partial explanations for the developing changes in criminal justice behavior. When holistically brought together, the explanatory powers of these models are enhanced.

I

CRIME CONTROL
AND CRIMINOLOGY

1

The Crime Control Enterprise and Its Workers

In his farewell address as president, Eisenhower warned of a military-industrial complex. The World War II general was concerned that defense policy was being driven by the businesses that politicians and the military contracted, insulated from public view and thus from accountability. He noted (1961) that until World War II, "the United States had no armaments industry"—other businesses converted to manufacture them as necessary—but having a permanent armaments industry of "vast proportions" (millions of employees and substantial military spending) was new and troubling. The economic, political, even spiritual" influence of these interests was

felt in every city, every Statehouse, every office of the Federal government. We recognize the imperative need for this development. Yet we must not fail to comprehend its grave implications. Our toil, resources, and livelihood are all involved. So is the very structure of our society. In the councils of government, we must guard against the acquisition of unwarranted influence, whether sought or unsought, by the military-industrial complex. The potential for the disastrous rise of misplaced power exists and will persist. We must never let the weight of this combination endanger our liberties or democratic processes. We should take nothing for granted. Only an alert and knowledgeable citizenry can compel the proper meshing of the huge industrial and military machinery of defense with our peaceful methods and goals, so that security and liberty may prosper together.

Similar to the military-industrial complex is a criminal justice–industrial complex born from the drastically increased size of the criminal justice system from the 1970s until the financial crisis of 2008. That is, while prisons and the criminal justice system have had contracts with businesses for supplies and consultants for much of their history, the nature of these relationships and the amount of money involved reached a critical mass because of the war on crime and drugs, which began in the 1970s. It expanded to include private prison companies traded on the stock exchange and regular Las Vegas–style

21

conventions for businesses selling goods and services to criminal justice officials (Selman and Leighton 2010). The increases in spending from the wars on crime and drugs have created a new type of permanent crime control industry with "grave implications" for criminal justice policy:

> *Three decades after the war on crime began, the United States has developed a prison-industrial complex—a set of bureaucratic, political, and economic interests that encourage increased spending on imprisonment, regardless of the actual need. The prison-industrial complex is not a conspiracy, guiding the nation's criminal-justice policy behind closed doors. It is a confluence of special interests that has given prison construction in the United States a seemingly unstoppable momentum. It is composed of politicians, both liberal and conservative, who have used the fear of crime to gain votes; impoverished rural areas where prisons have become a cornerstone of economic development; private companies that regard the roughly $35 billion [$80 billion in 2010] spent each year on corrections not as a burden on American taxpayers but as a lucrative market; and government officials whose fiefdoms have expanded along with the inmate population. (Schlosser 1998)*

The criminal justice and military-industrial complexes share more than a common idea. By the mid-1980s, the Cold War against Russia—called the "evil empire" by then-president Reagan—and "peace through strength" was winding down, and defense firms were looking for new markets to bolster revenue. The Department of Defense had already signed a memorandum of understanding with the Department of Justice for technology development and commercialization, and companies in the defense industry increasingly became suppliers to local law enforcement and criminal justice agencies. The drug war served to fuel the growth of military-style Special Weapons and Tactics (SWAT) teams across small and large urban areas.

After the tragedies of 9/11, the criminal justice complex developed stronger ties with intelligence agencies, the Department of Homeland Security, and Immigration and Customs Enforcement (ICE). Many citizens do not fully appreciate the sweeping changes to law enforcement, court processes, and government surveillance initiated by the Uniting and Strengthening America by Providing Appropriate Tools Required to Intercept and Obstruct Terrorism Act (USA Patriot Act), passed to improve homeland security on October 25, 2001, nor by the passage of the Homeland Security Act of 2002, which has added significantly to the reconfiguration of federal and local law enforcement since its passage.

What has emerged is a security-industrial complex (SIC) with a cumulative private- and public-sector spending spree estimated to have exceeded $1 trillion over the past decade. Echoing its kissing cousins, the military- and criminal justice–industrial complexes, the SIC has annual meetings with eight hundred companies exhibiting products and technology to combat terrorism. Today, the monies flowing into the military and homeland infrastructure are at the cutting edge of the digital revolution. Some argue that "a pleasant side effect of all the spending on anti-terror technology will be a reduction in crime" (M. Mills 2004). Others contend that "homeland security" will be a short-term economic stimulus. Like military spending, the emerging security-industrial complex will *ultimately add to inequality, become a drag on the nation's domestic production, and even become counterproductive in its war on terror (N. Klein 2007).*

As the American crime control enterprise has attempted to integrate many new criminal justice, intelligence, and security roles, social control has become more systemic compared to the more decentralized patterns of law enforcement and the administration of justice during the previous two centuries. But threats to "our liberties or democratic processes" persist. Consider:

- *Guantanamo Bay, Cuba, houses a number of foreign enemy combatants. Although on a military base and thus on American soil, they are in a "legal black hole": subject to indefinite detention without a trial, discovery of evidence, the ability to cross-examine accusers, or any other provisions of the Sixth Amendment.*

- *Presidents Bush and Obama have asserted their rights to kill those labeled as enemy combatants, a process that happens without notice to the person being labeled. Even when that person is an American citizen, there is no right to notice or to challenge the information that culminates in what may be a death sentence. This power has been used abroad, and the administration has neither claimed nor denied the right to kill an American citizen labeled as an enemy combatant who is in the United States.*

- *The attacks on those designated as enemy combatants occur in the context of "drone attacks," in which unmanned small airplanes help target missiles. Such attacks also kill innocents in foreign nations and increase anti-American sentiment, but the American government has claimed that there was no role for US courts in reviewing lawsuits filed by the family of a sixteen-year-old American citizen killed in a raid aimed at killing an older relative who was designated as an enemy combatant.*

- *US police departments are increasingly using unarmed drones for surveillance, which can be useful in armed standoffs but becomes a concern when "all the pieces appear to be lining up for the eventual introduction of routine aerial surveillance in American life, a development that would profoundly change the character of public life in the United States" (Rosenwald 2013).*

- *Documents leaked by former National Security Administration (NSA) technologist Edward Snowden have revealed widespread and routine surveillance of all Americans through their cell phones and Internet usage. The chief judge of the court supposedly overseeing the NSA, the Foreign Intelligence Surveillance Court (or FISA Court), "has admitted that the court can't verify what the agency says and thus can't provide full oversight over it" (BloombergView, 2013).*

- *A secret branch of the Drug Enforcement Administration (DEA) has been using information from the NSA and other intelligence agencies for fighting ordinary drug crimes. Local law enforcement agencies have either been misled about the origins of the information or "coached to conceal the existence of the program and the source of the information by creating what's called a 'parallel construction,' a fake or misleading trail of evidence" (O'Hehir 2013). This limits defendants' rights to challenge information against them and results in false testimony in court, but it is not clear whether there will be a judicial response or what it will be. "Should we be confident that NSA intercepts and foreign-intelligence wiretaps and 'parallel construction' will never be used to build criminal cases against hackers, leakers, Occupy activists, investigative journalists, unfriendly pundits and any other dissidents on the left or the right whom the government decides to persecute?" (O'Hehir 2013).*

The conventional view is that the criminal justice system is composed of police, courts, and corrections. While that is not inaccurate, it is still only a partial understanding of the work, mission, problems, issues, and career opportunities related to criminal justice. In addition to providing opportunities for expanded thinking about employment, study, and reading, we hope this chapter serves as a reminder of the challenges to democracy posed by the criminal justice–security complex. These problems are likely to continue into the foreseeable future because the war on terrorism appears to be open-ended and because a renewal of the 2001 Congressional Authorization for Use of Military Force law that was passed within days of the September 11 attacks could provide a license to wage a "war on terror" indefinitely.

Of course, funding obstacles and legal uncertainties make it unclear as to what exactly the mission or mandate will become for the twenty-first-century "criminal justice worker." However, the first sections below highlight four areas that will have an enduring impact on criminal justice work and workers: globalization and immigration, militarization, privatization, and cybercrime and security. Another section provides an overview of criminal justice workers that is focused on law enforcement, courts, and corrections.

GLOBALIZATION AND IMMIGRATION

Globalization refers to the growing interdependency among events, people, and governments around the world that are increasingly connected through trade, expanding communications, transportation, and computer networks. With a globalizing political economy, goods, labor, and money move more freely around the world, a situation that leads to some benefits but also leads to intensified inequality of wealth and income. The chief economist of Wall Street investment bank Morgan Stanley noted: "Billed as the great equalizer between the rich and the poor, globalization has been anything but." Indeed, "only the elite at the upper end of the occupational hierarchy have been spared the pressures of an increasingly brutal wage compression. The rich are, indeed, getting richer but the rest of the workforce is not" (Roach 2006). Today, globalization emphasizes "free trade" and deregulation as corporations look for locations with the cheapest labor, the least number of laborers, and the fewest environmental and other regulations. Even after the 2009 economic crisis and pressure at the Global Economic Summit from the European Union, China, and India to establish international regulatory agencies, President Obama and many Wall Street banking institutions rejected the idea.

Globalization policies can lead not just to inequality between countries but also to inequality within a country because of job losses, stagnating wages, and/or greater benefits to those at the top (through greater profits because of low wages and fewer restrictions) (Faux 2006; N. Klein 2007; Perkins 2007). In some countries, globalization has led to an expansion in pain and social injustice as measured by higher rates of disease, poverty, and hunger. Studies carried out by the United Nations reveal that the top 20 percent of those living in high-income countries account for 86 percent of the world's entire private consumer spending. At the same time, tens of millions of people succumb annually to famine and preventable diseases. For hundreds of millions of others, life has become a daily preoccupation with obtaining safe water, rudimentary health care, basic education, and sufficient nutrition (Barak 2007). Nations around the world are shrinking their welfare states while governments have been busy deregulating, downsizing, privatizing, contracting out, reducing taxes, and cutting social spending.

Ultimately, globalization and inequality create expanding opportunities for "legitimate" capitalists as well as criminals because the need for both licit and illicit goods or services grows in tandem (Nordstrom 2007). "Free trade" does not explicitly include the sexual trafficking of women and children, but encouragement of the "free flow" of goods also makes it easier to traffic persons, drugs, intellectual property, weapons, and exotic wildlife. It also encourages the fraudulent and unfair trade practices in commerce, the laundering of unauthorized drug and arms trade profits, the smuggling of illegal immigrants into and out of nations, the dumping of toxic waste and other forms of ecological destruction, the acts of terrorism committed by and against various states, and the behavior of multinationals to move capital and technology to exploit cheap labor (Barak 2001, 66).

Meanwhile, the contours of some criminality are currently undergoing fundamental change as they become part of the growing transnational character of organized, financial, sex, immigration, and computer crime (Edwards and Gill 2003; Sheptycki and Wardak 2005; Travis 1999). As crime becomes transnational, crime control must do the same, requiring workers who are fluent in different languages and who have an understanding of other regions of the world where the United States must collaborate with other nations' crime control agencies. The technological control of cybercrimes that threaten to victimize not only individuals but also the homeland security and financial health of the nation are blurring the boundaries of law enforcement and military engagement.

An important aspect of globalization is immigration, which is also considered a security issue. A *New York Times* editorial noted that the Bush administration conducted "mass raids to net immigrant workers while leaving their bosses alone," using heavy weapons, dogs, and helicopters "to spread the illusion that something was getting fixed" (2009a). In eight years these policies netted six thousand undocumented immigrants out of about twelve million employees and 135 employers out of who knows how many. In the process, they managed to destroy families, tearing parents and grandparents from children, many of whom are citizens of the United States. Raids, no matter how sensible or tactfully designed, will not fix the problems of immigration in a global economy. On the contrary, such policies have proved themselves to be counterproductive as the "fear they caused went viral in immigrant communities, driving workers further into the arms of abusive employers" (*New York Times* 2009a).

During the spring of 2009, the Obama administration issued new guidelines for Immigration and Customs Enforcement that emphasized prosecuting employers who knowingly hire illegal immigrants. Homeland Security secretary Janet Napolitano asserted during a CNN appearance that illegal immigration or "crossing the border is not a crime per se." She argued accordingly, "What we have to do is target the real evil-doers in this business, the employers who consistently hire illegal labor" as well as "the human traffickers who are exploiting human misery" (quoted in Meyers 2009). Hence, the proposed shift on immigration policy has not had a positive impact on altering the lives of illegal immigrants or the working conditions of US citizens. Nevertheless, the Obama administration deported 410,000 undocumented immigrants in 2012 and 369,000 in 2013 (Dinan 2013). What these policies do not fix are the long backlogs in legal immigration—the single biggest issue related to immigration today.

The delays in processing paperwork and cases often extend years or decades, "forcing people who want to follow the rules to make an agonizing choice between intolerable separation from their families or lawbreaking" (*New York Times* 2009a). Nor do these policies protect captured illegal immigrants from the arbitrary cruelties of the detention and deportation system in which due process is limited at best and unacceptable risks of sickness, injury, and death at worst prevail as a condition of imprisonment. As the editorial of the *New York Times* (2009a) succinctly articulated the situation:

> The new enforcement regime, like the old, might lead employers to purge their payrolls of people they merely suspect are here illegally, to avoid the hassle and expense of a raid. . . . Without a path to earned legalization, undocumented workers who lose their jobs will have nowhere to go—except to endure ever-lower wages and worse abuse from bottom-feeding employers.

While modifying raiding policies seems sensibly motivated and slightly more humane, the new guidelines as a whole are a smarter version of a bad idea that does not address the underlying problems of immigration. Far better, critics argue, would be for government to redouble its efforts to enforce the minimum wage, to grant the right of immigrants to organize, and to provide health and safety protections. Such polices would have the effect of reducing the incentive to hire the undocumented while raising conditions for all workers.

MILITARIZATION

Although law enforcement has always been a quasi-military organization, the civil unrest of the 1960s led to the modern escalation in the militarization of the American police (Strauss 2007). Militarism is "a set of beliefs, values, and assumptions that stress the use of force and threat of violence as the most appropriate means to solve problems. It glorifies the use of military power, hardware, operations, and technology as its primary problem-solving tools" (Kraska 2007, 164–65). Accordingly, the militarization of law enforcement includes the processes of arming, organizing, planning, training for, and sometimes pursuing violent conflict.

Peter Kraska argues that assessing the degree to which crime control in general and police behavior in particular have become militarized hinges on the clarity of its concepts. He has also argued that the "similarities between a police paramilitary drug raid [at home in the United States] and the latest Iraq war" represents "the cultural, organizational, operational, and material blurring of the line between war and law enforcement, on the one hand, and between U.S. military and civilian criminal justice, on the other hand" (Kraska 2007, 166). Certainly police departments across the United States have experienced dramatic growth and use of specialized units such as Special Weapons and Tactics (SWAT) teams and Special Response Teams (SRTs) that are based on similar units within the military. In 1983, only 13 percent of towns with populations between twenty-five thousand and fifty thousand had a SWAT team, but 80 percent of these small towns had one by 2005 (Balko 2013). Between 1980 and 2004, these units in towns of all sizes, mostly as part of the war on drugs, increased from 2,884 deployments to 45,000 per year (Kraska 1999, 2007).

Further, these units were once thought of primarily as *reactive* units for handling hostage standoffs and other unique situations, but in an age of zero-tolerance policing, these units have become *proactive* forces, specifically trained to execute police raids in poor, urban communities as a result of the war on drugs. But SWAT teams are also used to break up poker games and wagering on college football games ("illegal gambling"), underage drinking in bars, and "Tibetan monks who had overstayed their visas while visiting America on a peace mission" (Balko 2013). In fact, by 2004, 85 percent of raids were no-knock and quick-knock contraband raids inside private residences. Twenty-five years ago, these police paramilitary raids and "forced investigatory searches using the military special operations model, employed during hostage rescues, was almost unheard of and would have been considered an extreme and unacceptable police tactic. Today, it defines the bulk of activity most police paramilitary teams are engaged in, and this is true of both very small and large police departments" (Kraska 2007, 163).

Military personnel train and assist these specialized units, and they also arm local police with the latest in military technology, surveillance equipment, body armor, less-than-lethal use of force devices, "various gases, and explosives to breach doors" (Strauss 2007, 456). The economic boon to suppliers of these paramilitary law enforcement teams (in weaponry, body armor, training, jails, and vehicles, for example) has been fortified by the increased arrest rates and subsequent incarceration rates of poor minorities who are convicted of nonviolent drug crimes. In 2011, the Pentagon gave away $500 million to assist local law enforcement agencies in acquiring military equipment (Balko 2013). Most visible is the adoption of military weapons, including the 9mm Heckler pistol, Koch MP5 submachine gun, and the M4 carbine. The M4 carbine is a smaller, modified version of the US military's M16 assault rifle.

The militarization of policing has been accompanied by an escalation in violence, lethal and otherwise. No-knock or quick-knock paramilitary raids—used to collect evidence, such as drugs, guns, or money—naturally surprise citizens and put both citizens and police in potentially volatile situations. Dealing with these potentially dangerous situations justifies further extraordinary measures:

> These include conducting searches during the predawn hours, usually in black military battle-dress uniforms, full body armor, ninja-style hoods, and an array of enhanced listening and seeing devices—sort of a twenty-first century cyborg style. It also includes a rapid entry into the residence using specialized battering rams or sometimes entry explosives, the use of flash-bang grenades designed to temporarily disorient the occupants, a frantic room-by-room search of the entire residence where all occupants are expected to immediately comply with officers' screamed demands to get into the prone position. If a citizen does not comply immediately because he or she is confused, dazed, obstinate, or doesn't know that the people raiding the house are police, more extreme measures are taken. Finally, the police ransack the entire residence for contraband. (Kraska 2007, 167)

The adverse effects from these military-style raids on American citizens include situations such as the deaths of Branch Davidians in Waco, Texas, in 1993; the killing of children; unintentional (but still lethal) gun discharges; raids on the wrong house; and college students shot for violations of marijuana laws because of quick entry. The commonality of these types of tragedies is not known because data on SWAT teams gone wrong are not officially recorded. The National Center for Women in Policing also notes that "many women are discouraged from applying to law enforcement agencies because of policing's aggressive and authoritarian image, an image based on the outdated paramilitary model of law enforcement" (2002, 3). This, in turn, is detrimental to public safety because "women police officers utilize a style of policing that relies less on physical force and more on communications skills." Thus, when it comes to policing in general, "women are substantially less likely to be named in a citizen complaint, sustained allegation, or civil lawsuit" that results in a payout (2002, 3).

PRIVATIZATION

Privatization refers to the process of government outsourcing certain tasks to for-profit businesses. While prisons have frequently contracted out food service and health care ("nominal privatization"), privatization escalated in the 1980s with the creation of businesses that built, owned, and managed prisons ("operational privatization"). A number of private prison companies later had initial public offerings in which they raised money by selling shares to the public and became traded on the stock exchange (Selman and Leighton 2010). Indeed, in the opening of his book

The Perpetual Prisoner Machine, Joel Dyer comments on the sign hanging outside the Northeast Ohio Correctional Center that reads, "Yesterday's closing stock price." The stock price is for the prison's owner, the Corrections Corporation of America (CCA), the leader in the private prison business. To Dyer, what the sign means "is that anyone—anyone with money, that is—can now profit from crime" (2000, 10). As the industry has grown, so too have concerns about the number of (poor, black) "bodies destined for profitable punishment" (Leighton and Selman 2012).

The movement to private prisons started as a way to offset the high correctional expenses resulting from the incarceration binge in the United States. With the expansion of prisons, jails, parole, and probation, the number of companies involved in delivering services has expanded, and they have diversified into providing more services (see chapter 10). For example, the privatization of punishment is not solely the construction and management of prisons but also includes: housing illegal immigrants (including families), juvenile offenders, and the mentally ill; contracting to provide health care and food services for incarcerated persons; contracting to provide community-based forms of surveillance, including electronic monitoring; and, most recently, contracting for reentry services for the formerly incarcerated (Selman and Leighton 2010). Indeed, some local governments are considering using taxpayer money for private police as well—a notable departure from the historical situation where the clients of private security companies were private businesses.

The reality of contemporary corrections is that it includes several multinational prison businesses with billions of dollars' worth of stock and billions more in debt to Wall Street banks. The money from investors and banks allowed private businesses to build many facilities and thus continue the unprecedented expansion of the prison population—an example of understanding the political economy of punishment, or how politics and economics exert influence on punishment more significantly than on arguments about retribution, deterrence, and sentencing guidelines (Rusche and Kirchheimer [1939] 1968). Killingbeck (2005, 169) summarizes how at each stage of history, the reliance on imprisonment in its different forms was tied up in a political economy of punishment:

> When society was manual-labor based and dependent on the production of goods and cheap labor, imprisonment included prison labor. It was not until the use of prison labor was no longer economically viable and politically advantageous that reforms were instituted. . . . With the advent of new technologies that reduced the demand for manual labor, imprisonment served to warehouse the surplus labor supply. As capitalism became more service oriented, imprisonment became a *service* to be provided. As capitalism becomes a combination of technology, service and information, so too does punishment, in the forms of electronic monitoring and GPS tracking. (emphasis in the original)

With outsourcing and globalization, wages of most workers go down while those at the top do much better, leading to an overall situation of greater inequality. In private prisons, guards tend to be paid less and have fewer benefits than government workers, and the antiunion stance of private prisons makes it difficult for workers to substantially improve work conditions. Median earnings in 2010 for all correctional officers and jailers were $39,040, but private prisons paid $30,460 (Bureau of Labor Statistics 2012–2013). Meanwhile, the chief executive officer (CEO) of a private prison company makes more than the average head of a department of corrections who manages a substantially higher number of inmates. For example, the CEO of CCA had total compensation of $2.8 million for 2012, down from $3.7 million in 2011 (CCA 2013); the CEO of GEO made almost $6 million in 2012, up slightly from $5.7 million the previous year (GEO 2013). The managers of state departments of corrections of a similar size make less than $200,000 (Selman and Leighton 2010).

The free-market ideology suggests that business will be more efficient and cheaper than government. But the research does not support the contention of cost savings. Private prison companies have substantial overhead because of executive pay, payment for the compensation committee to set executive pay, and executive compensation consultants; they also pay money to Wall Street banks and corporate attorneys for activities such as Securities and Exchange Commission filings, mergers, acquisitions, shareholder lawsuits, advertising, lobbying, campaign donations, accounting complexities from operating in multiple states and nations, and so on. In order to be competitive and turn a profit given all their overhead costs, they use cheaper, non-union labor. The end result is staff turnover, apathy, and poor judgment—which can combine to precipitate riots, unconstitutional conditions of confinement, or inmate abuse (Carceral 2005; Greene 2002; Selman and Leighton 2010). The other result is increasing inequality as states pay private prison companies, which pay their top leadership far more than the head of a department of correction would make and pay their employees in the prison less than the salary a state would pay.

As more companies generate revenue from corrections, there is more potential for misplaced power in the multibillion-dollar prison-industrial complex to distort sentencing and criminal justice (and mental health and immigration) policy: the interests of corporate shareholders become increasingly important, causing increased corporate lobbying and campaign donations, while public safety and public accountability become less relevant. Basic free-market principles dictate that companies with shares traded on a stock exchange have a duty to make money for their shareholders. Thus, businesses involved in incarceration have no duty to balance their desire for ever-increasing profits with the larger public good that would come from, say, crime-prevention funding or money for schools. Indeed, sentencing reform and declining crime rates are "risk factors."

CYBERCRIME/SECURITY

President Obama brought some of the functions and responsibilities for the nation's digital security to the White House when he announced in late May 2009 that he would appoint "the nation's first cyber security czar to help protect the nation's telecom infrastructure and information systems that have grown so crucial to industry, the military and individual citizens" (*Denver Business Journal* 2009). On the heels of President Obama's declaration of a new security czar, the Pentagon announced "the formation of a Cyber-Command to both defend against cyber attacks and wage cyber warfare against our enemies" (ChattahBox 2009). It is now common knowledge that the United States and Israel committed cybercrime vis-à-vis their jointly developed "Stuxnet" computer viruses used to repeatedly sabotage nuclear reprocessing plants in Iran as far back as 2005, during the George W. Bush presidency (Arthur 2013).

Cybercrime involves an expanding assortment of "virtual dark markets"—underground sites that auction or sell hard drugs, child pornography, fraudulent passports, counterfeit dollars, military weapons, and stolen identities. Technological developments help both law enforcement and cybercriminals. Recently, for example, commerce in these illicit goods and services has been made possible by the Deep Web, a place where the NSA cannot surveil a part of the web that can be considered off the grid:

> Technically the Deep Web refers to the collection of all the websites and databases that search engines like Google don't or can't index, which in terms of the sheer volume of information is many times larger than the Web as we know it. But more loosely, the Deep Web is a specific branch of the Internet that's distinguished by that increasingly rare commodity: complete anonymity. Nothing you do on the Deep Web can be associated with your real-world identity, unless you choose it to be. Most people never see it, though the software you need to access it is free and takes less than three minutes to download and install. (Grossman and Newton-Small 2013, 28)

The Deep Web has thus become a tool for criminals, political dissidents, hackers, intelligence agents, law enforcement, and any who need or want to conduct their online affairs in private. Thus, some prosecutors and government agencies regard the Deep Web as a potential nightmare, an electronic haven for thieves, human traffickers, and peddlers of state secrets. Moreover, the FBI, the DEA, the ATF (Bureau of Alcohol, Tobacco, Firearms and Explosives), and the NSA are now spending tens of millions trying, ironically, to crack into a system that the US military built in the first place. For example, in 2012 these agencies, joined by the US Marshals Service, established the National Domestic Communications Assistance Center (NDCAC) in Quantico, Virginia. A tech start-up, the NDCAC received "at least $54 million in funding for the 2013 fiscal year that's focused on helping law enforcement penetrate areas of the Web that are currently unsearchable" (Grossman and Newton-Small 2013, 32).

The Deep Web also has its own digital payment system and a currency called Bitcoin that may be used for both legitimate and illegitimate dealings. Bitcoin has no physical form, and its worth is "determined by supply and demand and is valuable only insofar as individuals and companies have agreed to trade it" (Grossman and Newton-Small 2013, 29). A government does not back this currency; it is completely decentralized, and users can transfer bitcoins from one digital wallet to another without banks brokering the transactions or imposing fees. In short, bitcoins are basically cash (anonymous transactions) for the Internet. Because of the workings of encryption and cryptography, they are virtually anonymous and extremely difficult to counterfeit.

CRIMINAL JUSTICE WORKERS

Although this chapter opened by introducing the larger criminal justice–security complex, there are too many occupations and work possibilities to meaningfully discuss in part of a chapter. Thus, this section focuses on law enforcement, judicial workers, and corrections. For each of those areas, we provide an overview of the occupation and those who do the job. Table 1.1 provides a more expansive list of careers within the more traditional understandings of what the criminal justice system is.

Table 1.2 provides a breakdown of criminal justice system expenditures, including the payroll for employees and the number of workers. The US Department of Justice (as of May 23, 2013) had a budget of about $28 billion and employed about 112,000 people. Federal law enforcement functions made up about $13 billion of that total, prisons and detention were more than $8 billion, litigation expenditures were about $3 billion, another $3 billion was spent for grants and assistance, and another $1 billion went to administration and technology. The criminal justice budget proposal from state governors totaled about $13 billion for 2013–2014, down from a high of about $15 billion in 2007–2008 (Taylor 2013).

The totals in the previous paragraph do not include expenditures or workers in private security, private detection, or other related security occupations not funded by government. Jobs within the criminal justice enterprise are diverse, and different occupations have unique dynamics with respect to class, race, and gender. What follows are the roles and functions of the principal occupations in the three primary areas of criminal justice practice—law enforcement, courts, and corrections—as well as other characteristics, such as the number of workers, working conditions, educational requirements, and professional salaries as available.

Law Enforcement Workers

In 2008, the United States had almost eighteen thousand public law enforcement agencies and about 1.1 million full-time personnel, including about 765,000 sworn personnel (with the power to arrest) at the local and state levels of government (Bureau of Justice Statistics 2011). Another one hundred thousand employees were part-time, including forty-four thousand sworn personnel. Another 1,700 agencies served a special geographic region—public schools, universities, parks, forests, airports, mass transit, and so on—and employed another ninety thousand people full-time, including fifty-seven thousand sworn officers.

Table 1.1.   Careers in Criminal Justice

Law Enforcement/ Security	Courts/Legal	Corrections/Rehabilitation
BATF agent	Arbitrator	Activity therapist
Border patrol agent	Attorney general	Business manager
Campus police officer	Bailiff	Case manager
Computer security advisor	Clerk of court	Chaplain
Computer crime investigator	Court reporter	Chemical dependency worker
Crime prevention specialist	Jury coordinator	Child care worker
Crime scene processor (evidence collection)	Juvenile magistrate	Classification officer
Criminal investigator	Law clerk	Clinical social worker
Criminal profiler	Law librarian	Community liaison officer
Customs officer	Legal researcher	Correctional officer
Deputy sheriff	Mediator	Dietary officer
Deputy US investigator	Paralegal	Fugitive apprehension officer
Drug enforcement officer	Public defender	Home detention supervisor
Environmental protection agent	Public information officer	Job placement officer
FBI special agent	Specialty court (drug, veteran, domestic violence, etc.) worker	Juvenile detention officer
Fingerprint technician	Trial court administrator	Juvenile probation officer
Forensic scientist	Victim advocate	Medical doctor
Highway patrol officer		Mental health clinician
INS officer		Nurse
Inspector general's office investigator		Parole/probation officer
Insurance fraud investigator		Postal inspector
Laboratory technician		Presentence inspector
Loss prevention officer		Prison industries supervisor
Military police officer		Programmer/analyst
Park ranger		Psychologist
Police administrator		Rehabilitation counselor
Police dispatcher		Residence supervisor
Police officer		Secret service agent
Polygraphy examiner		Sex offender therapist
Private investigator		Social worker teacher
Private security officer		Vocational instructor
Researcher		Warden/superintendent
State trooper		Youth service worker
		Youth supervisor

Table 1.2.   Criminal Justice Expenditures, Payroll, and Employees, 2010

	Total Expenditures (in billions of US$)	Employee Payroll (in billions of US$)	Total Employees
CJ system total	$260.5	$11.8	2,468,795
Police	$124.2	$6.0	1,163,354
Judicial and legal	$56.1	$2.5	519,791
Corrections	$80.2	$3.2	785,650

Source: BJS 2013. "Justice Expenditure and Employment in the United States, 2010—Preliminary." NCJ 242544, tables 1 and 2.

Note: Detail may not add to total because of rounding. Payroll as of March 2010.

A breakdown of occupational police types and the employment data for 2006 and projected for 2016 are presented in table 1.3. While this section does try to paint a general picture, Bohm and Haley (2005, 160) point out that virtually no two police agencies in the United States are structured alike or function in the same way. Police officers themselves are young and old; well trained and ill prepared; rural, urban, and suburban; generalists and specialists; paid and volunteer; and public and private. These differences lead to at least three generalizations about law enforcement in the United States:

1. The quality of police services varies greatly across the nation.
2. There is no consensus on professional standards for police personnel, equipment, and practices.
3. Expenditures for police services vary greatly among communities.

Starting salaries and median annual earnings for police and patrol officers in 2012 across local, state, and federal law enforcement agencies ranged from $52,600 to $62,800, although pay for police at colleges and schools was less (Bureau of Labor Statistics 2012–2013). However, supervisory salaries for federal law enforcement workers topped out at around $85,000 to $106,000, compared with a range of $50,000 to $85,000 for local and state supervisory law enforcement workers.

Educationally, only 1 percent of municipal police departments required new recruits to have a four-year college degree, and only 9 percent required at least a two-year degree in 2003. A high school diploma or higher educational achievement was required by 81 percent of local police agencies across the nation (Bureau of Justice Statistics 2006b, 9).

At the federal level in 2008, there were about sixty-five law enforcement agencies employing about 120,000 full-time personnel authorized to make arrests and carry firearms (Bureau of Justice Statistics 2012). The Department of Homeland Security (Customs and Border Protection, Immigration and Customs Enforcement) and the Department of Justice (Federal Bureau of Prisons, FBI) employ about 80 percent of

Table 1.3.   Police Types and Employment, 2006 (with Projections for 2016)

Occupation Title	Employment, 2006	Employment, 2016	Change, 2006–2016	
			Number	Percent
Police and detectives	861,000	959,000	97,000	11
First-line supervisors/ managers of police and detectives	93,000	102,000	8,500	9
Detectives and criminal investigators	106,000	125,000	18,000	17
Fish and game wardens	8,000	8,000	0	0
Police officers	654,000	724,000	70,000	11
Police and sheriff's patrol officers	648,000	719,000	70,000	11
Transit and railroad police	5,600	5,900	400	6

Source: US Bureau of Labor Statistics 2009. *Occupational Outlook Handbook.* Washington, DC: US Bureau of Labor Statistics. http://www.bls.gov/oco/ocos160.htm#earnings.

Note: Data in this table are rounded.

all officers. In these and other federal law enforcement agencies, women and minorities are underrepresented, but they fare better than at the local levels of law enforcement. For example, in 2008, women accounted for 16 percent of federal officers; almost 20 percent were Hispanic, 10 percent were African American, 3 percent were Asian American, and 1 percent was Native American (Bureau of Justice Statistics 2012). Total minority representation at the federal level was thus about 33 percent, compared with almost 24 percent at the state and local levels. The Bureau of Justice Statistics does not publish data broken down by race and gender, which would reveal the number of minority women employed as federal officers.

Local law enforcement activities constitute the bulk of police work and are carried out primarily by municipal (i.e., city, township) police departments that typically (94 percent) employ fewer than fifty sworn officers. The larger the police agency, the more likely it is to employ women and minority officers. While white males are still highly overrepresented, the overrepresentation has been declining. From the early 1900s until 1972, when the Equal Employment Opportunity Commission (EEOC) began to assist women police officers in obtaining equal employment status with male officers, policewomen were responsible for protection and crime prevention work with women and juveniles, particularly girls. Today, women engage in virtually all of the duties that men do, but according to the National Center for Women in Policing (2002, 6), the number of women within large police agencies declined from 14.3 percent in 1999 to 12.7 percent in 2001. The center also notes that women hold only 7.3 percent of top command positions (chiefs, deputy chiefs, and captains) and 9.6 percent of supervisory positions (lieutenants and sergeants); women of color hold 1.6 percent of top command positions and 3.1 percent of supervisory positions (2002, 4, 7).

Like most municipal police departments, most sheriffs' departments are small. In addition to enforcing the criminal and traffic laws of the state, sworn and not sworn personnel of sheriffs' departments perform functions that range from investigating crimes to supervision of jailed inmates. Unlike municipal police departments, sheriffs are directly elected, so they operate in the context of partisan politics and have the authority to appoint special deputies and to award jobs based on political support. Generally, they have a freer hand in running their agencies than police chiefs, who usually serve as mayoral appointees, but sheriffs are also subject more to local politics than they are to measures of effectiveness and professionalism.

In making sense of the statistics and the overall environment, a number of points are important. First, all women and racial minorities interested in working in most areas of criminal justice share the challenge of entering overwhelmingly white male work environments, with women of color being doubly disadvantaged. For example, Susan Martin (1992) concluded that white patrolmen tended to be protective of white women but not black women. Moreover, black men could not be counted on to support and assist black women, and some (as with some white men) were opposed to women on patrol. Further, white female officers tended to view gaining acceptance by male officers as more important and valuable than being accepted by other women, leading one black female supervisor to conclude that "getting unity is like pulling teeth."

Second, sexual and racial discrimination acts to preserve some criminal justice professions, especially law enforcement, as disproportionately white male domains. These forms of harassment can be separate and unrelated or combined, for example, in the form of "racialized sexual harassment" that serves to keep some women of color from entering, advancing, or remaining in a predominantly white male occupation. In general, women of any color and minority males are forced to consider the world through the eyes of the white male cop. Both of these groups, by definition, lack access to the "old boy" networks in law enforcement, a situation that can be conducive to a catch-22 state of affairs, especially for women. On the one hand, if men of color or women in general do not socialize (either by choice or exclusion), they risk not learning information related to their job or promotion opportunities and may be labeled as aloof or "cold." On the other hand, if women in particular socialize with male colleagues, they may be perceived to be sexually available, which reflects negatively on women's professionalism (Belknap 2007; Fletcher 1995; Martin and Jurik 1996). Gay and lesbian officers, white or of color, have another set of issues to be addressed by law enforcement.

Third, the National Center for Women in Policing (2002, 3) notes that "once on the job, women often face discrimination, harassment, intimidation, and are maliciously thwarted, especially as they move up the ranks." When such behavior is on the basis of gender discrimination alone, women may encounter sexual harassment in a variety of forms. Such harassment may contribute to a hostile working environment in which submission to unwelcome sexual advances and comments becomes a condition of employment. In fact, oftentimes colleagues ostracize women who complain (see chapters 5 and 9).

Fourth, women of color have additional barriers even though some people believe that they receive a double benefit because of their underrepresentation as both women and people of color. In reality, cases like *United States v. City of Chicago* are more typical (Martin 1992). There, the judge imposed quotas for promotion to encourage the hiring of more racial and ethnic minority officers and women. Initially, black women were called from the promotion list as blacks. When the white women officers realized the black women officers were being promoted ahead of them, the white women filed a claim asserting that all women should be treated as one single minority group—women. The judge ruled that black women could not be given double benefits and that they had to be judged against other women and not men, with the approval of the lawyer from the African American Police Officers League (which was representing all black officers), who failed to consult the black women involved in the case. This decision advantaged the black males and disadvantaged the black females, because in many ways, white women are culturally and educationally closer to white males (who set the standard in law enforcement) than black males are. Of course, the ruling could have placed black women in the minority category of black rather than that of female, wherein the result would have been that black women would have been promoted over black men. Interestingly, when the black female officers filed a lawsuit protesting the decision, the judge agreed that they had a valid complaint but deemed their concerns "not timely." So what can be said about this decision is that it, rather predictively, redistributed advantages to the benefit of white males and females in law enforcement and to the detriment of black males and females in law enforcement in much the same way that social and political forces outside of law enforcement operate to maintain "white privilege" (see chapter 4 for a more complete discussion of this topic).

Fifth, racial and/or ethnic minorities, blacks and Hispanics in particular, not only have to deal with being forced to fit in and with being told they are not as good as their white male counterpart majorities, but they often, especially in impoverished ethnic communities, find that their community identities or loyalties are subject to questioning. In cases of police brutality or when excessive force is used by black police officers against those in the black community, some see it as evidence that the incident was about brutality and excessive force, not race. But people should not jump to that conclusion without considering that black officers are capable of holding prejudices about black offenders. Ronald Hampton of the National Black Police Association observed, "Success [in a department] is defined in white male terms. So these guys internalize the racist, oppressive culture of the police department in order to succeed" (Ripley 2000). But instead of viewing black and Latino police officers who engage in police brutality against black and Latino criminal suspects as a symptom of a larger problem, which is overreliance on policing poor and minority communities, police brutality against the most powerless people in society is sometimes viewed as a normative behavior because both black and Latino officers also participate in it.

Finally, undercover work requires the involvement of detectives whose brown skin permits them to blend into certain neighborhoods, but they sometimes fear that a white officer will accidentally shoot them (Winerip 2000). Accidental shootings of minorities by white cops are not uncommon and are attended by numerous studies that suggest that brown faces are more threatening than white faces: "There is over-whelming evidence that young, black men are stereotyped as violent, criminal and dangerous. Indeed research suggests that black men are associated with threat both implicitly as well as explicitly" (Trawalter et al. 2008, 1322).

For all the problems, there are some who say that sexism and racism in the work-place is declining. However, affirmative action myths still abound, such as the myth that police or corrections departments must meet quotas in hiring women and mi-nority men, regardless of whether or not they are qualified. For example, scrutiny of the text of the original Affirmative Action Executive Order 11246, signed by Presi-dent Lyndon Johnson in 1965, specifically prohibits hiring of unqualified people to fill positions in occupations and requires in section 202(2) that: "The contractor will, in all solicitations or advertisements for employees placed by or on behalf of the contractor, state that all qualified applicants will receive consideration for employ-ment without regard to race, creed, color or national origin."

So in reality, affirmative action programs were designed to determine the percent-age of qualified women and minorities available to an organization (such as a police department) and to set flexible goals to be reached in good faith. The courts, in short, imposed quotas only in the case of blatant discrimination against clearly quali-fied minorities, and this system disappeared after the Supreme Court decided quotas were unconstitutional when used in college admission in *University of California v. Bakke* (438 U.S. 265 [1978]).

In conclusion, there are significant limitations on essentializing gender relations or police-race relations in an occupational setting. Statements such as "all white officers engage in racial profiling" or generalizations about the behavior of female officers are too simplistic. The social reality is that people are influenced not only by their per-sonal attitudes and experiences but also by the context in which they live and work. Whites are capable of recognizing the problems of racial profiling and brutality, and racial and ethnic minority officers are charged with the responsibility of not falling victim to them. But the contributions of women and minorities and women who are minorities should be both valued and incorporated into the ways that law enforce-ment agencies operate today so as to eliminate racism, minimize discrimination, and maximize fairness in the administration of justice. Certainly, it is useless to continue to expect minorities and women to adapt to the white majority without reciprocal efforts being made on the part of the white majority to include them, especially since globalization has ramped up. To suggest otherwise is to diminish everyone by treat-ing people as if their actions are solely dictated by their racial categorization rather than by a variety of individual, occupational, organizational, situational, and other contexts. However, this should not mask some underlying dynamics of privilege, because when it comes to harassment based on gender, sexual orientation, or race/ethnicity in law enforcement, women, gays and lesbians, and people of color each still experience the status of "outsider." They are all subjects of police subordination in an occupation that punishes them for entering male-only or white-male-only domains (Martin and Jurik 1996).

Judicial Workers

Both the expenditures (see figure 1.1) and the number of judicial workers involved in criminal tribunals, from the charging to the sentencing stages, is considerably smaller than the number of dollars spent on or workers involved in law enforcement. Comparatively, law enforcement workers are essentially made up of professional

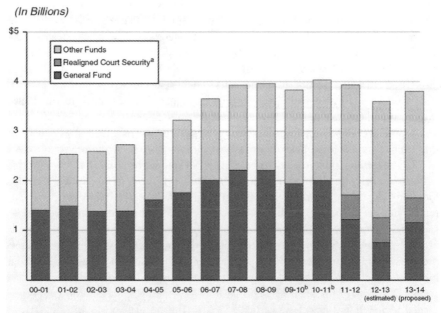

(In Billions)

[a] 2011 realignment shifted responsibility for funding most court security costs from the state General Fund to counties. Figure displays estimated county spending on court security for comparison purposes.

[b] General Fund amounts include use of redevelopment funds for trial courts on a one-time basis—$1.3 billion in 2009-10 and $350 million in 2010-11.

Figure 1.1. Total Judicial Branch Funding in Billions, 2000–2001 to 2013–2014

Source: Mac Taylor, "The 2013–14 Budget: Governor's Criminal Justice Proposals," report, Legislative Analyst's Office, http://www.lao.ca.gov/analysis/2013/crim_justice/criminal-justice-proposals/criminal-justice-proposals-021513.pdf.

persons with and without college degrees. Similarly, judicial workers can be divided up into two distinctively educated workers whose professional class also varies from working to middle class.

First, there are the members of the legal bar—attorneys and judges—who have overwhelmingly graduated from a four-year college or university as well as a three-year law school, passed a state bar examination, and been certified to practice law. The *Sourcebook of Criminal Justice Statistics* indicates that in 2005, the median salary of prosecutors was $85,000, although this figure includes part-time offices. Full-time prosecutors had a median salary of $95,000 to $149,000, depending on the size of the jurisdiction (*Sourcebook* online, table 1.87.2005). For states, the median salary for judges in 2012 ranged from about $132,500 for a general trial court up to a median of almost $147,000 for the highest court (*Sourcebook* online, table 1.90.2012). However, salaries varied widely by state, so general-level judges in Mississippi made about $104,200 while their counterparts in Illinois made $180,800. The *Sourcebook* does not provide any data on public defender salaries.

It should also be pointed out that the share of the nation's lawyers who are minorities and women, which had been growing slowly but steadily for years, fell in 2010 for the first time since the National Association for Law Placement began keeping statistics in 1993. Not only did the deep economic recession lead businesses to make diversity programs less of a priority, but a growing number of states—including Arizona, Michigan, Nebraska, New Hampshire, and Oklahoma—also moved to ban race-based affirmative action in recent years. These states joined California, Florida, and Washington, which had already banned affirmative action back in the 1990s (Schwartz and Cooper 2013). Figure 1.2 reports on the diversity of judges appointed to US district courts and to the US courts of appeals by the past three presidents. An important criterion for appointment to a federal judgeship is having served as a clerk to a US Supreme Court justice, and this issue is explored in box 1.1.

Second, there are the nonlawyers, primarily bailiffs and stenographers but also including the much less frequently occurring occupations of victim-witness or domestic violence advocates. With the exception of bailiffs, the other nonlawyers (especially stenographers) are primarily women and white. The educational backgrounds of these nonlawyers vary greatly, from those with a high school diploma or GED to those with undergraduate and postgraduate degrees. These judicial workers' annual incomes place them in the working and middle classes. For example, the average annual 2012 salary for paralegals and legal assistants was $50,200; court reporters earned $53,100; and law clerks earned $52,610 (Bureau of Labor Statistics 2012).

The rest of this discussion on judicial workers focuses on the three key actors in the criminal court process: the prosecutor, the defense attorney, and the judge. These positions influence some of the direct actions taken by police and correctional personnel in the name of crime control, and they also indirectly influence some behavior of general citizens as they conform to the "rule of law." Despite the relative power of these legal actors, they are still captives of a legal order and rigid judicial processes that are, for the most part, well beyond their control.

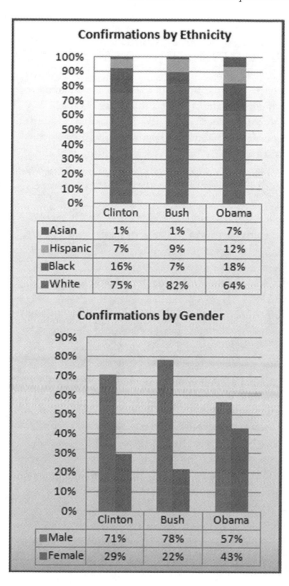

Figure 1.2. Total Federal Judicial Confirmations by the Past Three Presidents as of May 20, 2013

Source: "Composition of the Federal Courts of Appeal," Judicial Nominations.org, http://judicialnominations.org/statistics.

BOX 1.1.   THE LACK OF DIVERSITY
AMONG SUPREME COURT CLERKS

Federal laws barring workplace discrimination do not cover the US Supreme Court. The lack of diversity among law clerks reflects this omission in the law as it raises the question of "supreme hypocrisy." For example, between his appointment to the Supreme Court in 1972 and the beginning of 1999, former chief justice William Rehnquist had eighty-two law clerks. During that time, he had only one Hispanic clerk and only eleven women clerks. Not once did he hire a black clerk. Overall, only 1.2 percent of his clerks had been members of minority groups.

The track record of his colleagues had not been much better. Of the 428 law clerks hired during the respective terms of the current justices, only seven were black, five were Hispanic, eighteen were Asian American, and not a single one was Native American. Despite the fact that over 40 percent of law school graduates in the 1990s were women, they made up only one-quarter of all clerks hired by current justices.

These figures prompted Rep. Gregory Meeks (D-NY) to conclude: "If the court were a Fortune 500 company, the statistics alone would demonstrate illegal discrimination." In an article, "Does the Supreme Court Need Affirmative Action for Its Own Staff?" Meeks (1999, 24) criticized the Supreme Court's hiring practices. He reasoned that becoming a clerk is a stepping-stone to other legal positions, including that of a Supreme Court justice. Thus, the hiring practices of the highest court in the land create a structural barrier to obtaining those positions. Moreover, Supreme Court law clerks wield considerable power, playing an extremely influential role in the court's functioning.

As Meeks writes: "Clerks have the ear of the justices they serve. They have input on which cases the justices choose to consider. They write the initial drafts of most decisions. The Supreme Court's decisions are the law of the land and thus affect lives, determine how government resources are allocated, [and] force legislatures to reformulate public policy choices." In other words, the influence clerks have on both the cases heard and the opinions the court renders should not be underestimated.

For example, recent Supreme Court decisions have narrowed opportunities for people of color as a result of limiting or ruling unconstitutional critical affirmative action programs or by diluting the application of the Voting Rights Act. The fact that clerks preview and review these cases means that they have had an impact on rulings involving civil rights, access to education, workplace discrimination, religious freedom, voting, welfare reform, immigrant rights, school desegregation, sexual harassment, police brutality, and death penalty appeals. Many of these cases have a disproportionate impact on minorities or women, so it is conspicuous that minorities and women did not have any influence over the preview or review of these cases. Diversity in the background (as well as the foreground) would not only provide a more well-rounded approach to dispensing justice in an increasingly diverse nation, but it would also go a long way toward displaying the image of color-blind justice in an era that lays claim to such.

Court observers note that virtually all the Supreme Court clerks are chosen from clerks for the United States courts of appeals. Thus, the lack of diversity of judges in the courts of appeals influences the pool of clerks for the Supreme Court. While the data do not allow for the analysis of intersections, the clear implication is that judgeships are very much male and white. To the extent that judges seek clerks they are comfortable with because the clerks are "like themselves," judges re-create the pattern set by the white, male presidents who appointed them. In short, without a more balanced or diversified group of clerks, there is an obvious loss of valuable counterweight to the established court's largely majoritarian tendencies (Benson 2007).

With the election of Barack Obama, the first biracial president, some of these patterns will start to change. His first appointment to the Supreme Court was Sonia Sotomayor, the court's third woman and first Hispanic woman. But more generally, "Whites still comprise a full 84 percent of the federal judiciary. Women constitute only one in five federal judges. African Americans make up only 8 percent of the bench," and less than 1 percent are Asian Americans (Tobias 2009). As of year-end 2013, there were 874 federal judgeships, of which 94 were vacant. Through 2012, President Obama has appointed 173 people—not all of whom are minority and/or female (Uscourts .gov 2012).

Having diverse clerks is thus important because clerks help to provide justices with a broader, more rounded, and varied perspective on critical issues. Only by setting a proactive example of inclusion can the Supreme Court fulfill the ideal of justice that it purports to protect. Indeed, the same argument, more or less, can be applied to all careers associated with the administration of justice in the United States.

Prosecutors

Violations of federal law are prosecuted by the US Justice Department, headed by the US attorney general and staffed by ninety-three US attorneys (one assigned to each of the federal district court jurisdictions), all nominated by the president and confirmed by the Senate. Within states, district attorneys are generally employed by a county to prosecute violations of state laws. Most chief prosecutors for each county are elected, and they select their assistant or deputy prosecutors who carry out the day-to-day work of the prosecutor's office in all but the small and rural offices. Since most crimes violate state law, these offices receive most of the attention in this section.

In 2005, the last year there was a survey of prosecutors, there were 2,344 prosecutors' offices in the United States, employing more than 78,000 attorneys, investigators, victim advocates, and support staff (Bureau of Justice Statistics 2006d, table 1). The combined annual budgets in 2005 for state ($4.9 billion) and federal ($3.2 billion) prosecutors came to $8.1 billion (Bureau of Justice Statistics 2006d, 1, 4). State prosecutors' offices closed more than 2.4 million felony cases and nearly 7.5 million misdemeanor cases in 2005. This amounted to about ninety felony cases per assistant prosecutor. The median number of felony jury trial verdicts per office was only six, and these represented approximately 3 percent of the total number of felony cases. The Bureau of Justice Statistics notes that "felony trial verdicts were relatively rare" (2006d, 6), underscoring the preference of judicial players for the plea-bargaining system (DeFrances 2002). The real role of prosecutors and defense attorneys, then, has become that of a private negotiator rather than an advocate in a trial. Disposing of more cases via plea bargains, however, may be unwise since the Bill of Rights authorizes jury trials as a necessary part of due process. In short, the right of citizens to be judged by a jury of their peers is one of the essential components of due process; but overreliance on plea bargaining may have usurped that right as a matter of convenience and economy.

Depending on the state, the prosecutor may be called the district attorney, the county attorney, the state's attorney, or several other variations. Whatever the name, the prosecutor is the most powerful actor in the administration of justice. Not only do prosecutors conduct the final screening of each person arrested for a criminal offense, and therefore decide whether to pursue criminal charges, but in most jurisdictions they also have unreviewable discretion in deciding whether to charge a person with a crime and whether to prosecute the case. In other words, regardless of the amount (or lack) of incriminating evidence, and without having to provide any reason to anyone, prosecutors have the authority to charge or not to charge a person with a crime and to prosecute or not prosecute the case (Bohm and Haley 2005, 278). Importantly, a study of "known wrongful convictions involving African American men that occurred since 1970," which had a sample of 343 individuals, reported that prosecutorial misconduct was a factor in 36.2 percent of the wrongful murder convictions in the study and 15 percent of the rape and sexual assault cases (Free and Ruesink 2012). Overall, they concluded, "the lack of diversity among actors in the criminal justice system makes it easier for nonwhites to be processed through the system without the necessary safeguards to minimize the probability of a wrongful conviction" (2012, 196).

Like all attorneys, prosecutors are officers of the court. In addition, although police typically recommend that a suspect be charged with a crime, the final decision rests with the prosecutor. To charge or not to charge and what to charge are all decisions within prosecutorial discretion, which is what gives prosecutors their formidable power. The only check on the power of the prosecutor's arsenal of legal weapons are the "rules of discovery" mandating that a prosecutor provide defense counsel with any exculpatory (favorable) evidence on behalf of his or her client.

Once the decision to prosecute has been made, prosecutors are then involved in virtually all stages of criminal adjudication, including whether to plea bargain a case (and the negotiated punishment to be doled out) or take it to trial, the trial itself, and the sentencing phase as well. Other duties, depending on jurisdiction, that add to the power of prosecutors are recommending whether a person should receive bail and/or the amount; acting as legal advisers to other local governmental agencies; and managing a legal and political bureaucracy.

With few exceptions, partisan politics plays a controlling role in the recruitment of prosecutors, both county and federal. For attorneys with any political aspirations or ambitions, choosing to work, as a district attorney is a wise decision. As a political office engaged in the "war on crime," the only office to rank higher for those with political desires is the mayor's. In short, it's not the money but the power, status, and political potential that attracts persons to prosecutors' offices, often cementing their allegiances to the political status quo and state-legal apparatuses in the process (Jacob [1973] 1980).

Breakdowns of prosecuting attorneys by gender and/or race/ethnicity were not available; however, the number of chief and assistant prosecutors belonging to the National Black Prosecutors Association in 2005 was eight hundred. Historically, women, blacks, Hispanics, and other minorities have been highly underrepresented. Although there are certainly more women prosecutors today compared to three decades ago (when there were virtually none), the presence of persons of color is still statistically marginal. In other words, the cultural gap between the majority of white, middle-class prosecutors and the overwhelmingly indigent majority of defendants, nonwhite or white, remains wide. Also, those who become assistant and chief prosecutors are not traditionally of the same class backgrounds as those members of the bar who take cases against American big businesses and corporations. As Herbert Jacob, the political legal scholar, pointed out ([1973] 1980) in one of his classic works:

> There are substantial indications that in many cities, most of the assistant prosecutors come from local law schools. In Chicago, for instance, more assistants come from De-Paul and Chicago Kent than from the University of Chicago or Northwestern University law schools. They are likely to come from more modest backgrounds than students in elite law schools; they are often graduates of local high schools and colleges and come from families that have lived a long time in the city. The backgrounds of prosecutors suggest that they are particularly sensitive to political implications of their work; they are usually part of the political clique that dominates their locale and, therefore, may be more protective of their fellow officeholders than others would be.

Little has changed about these fundamental political, social, and economic realities of prosecuting criminal defendants in the contemporary United States.

Defense Attorneys

Backgrounds of defense attorneys are similar to those of prosecutors, working class and middle class. Both groups of attorneys are usually homegrown and typically attended nonelite law schools within their native states. Unlike prosecutors, however, defense attorneys are generally not connected to the local political scene. It is also safe to assume that if prosecutors closed 2.4 million felony cases in 2005, then defense attorneys of some kind were present in each of these cases, although some of the seven million misdemeanors might have been closed without the benefit of a defense counsel.

Privately retained lawyers, court-appointed lawyers, public defenders, and contract lawyers do criminal defense work. Regardless of the type of lawyer that one has, the Sixth Amendment to the US Constitution as well as several twentieth-century Supreme Court decisions guarantee the right to "effective assistance" of counsel to people charged with a crime (Barak 1980; Loftus and Ketcham 1991). Besides the right to representation at trial, the right extends to several other critical stages in the criminal justice process where the "substantial rights of the accused" or convicted may be affected. These stages may include police lineups, custodial interrogations, preliminary hearings, plea-bargaining sessions, first appeal of a negotiated or post-conviction sentence, sentencing hearings, and probation and parole revocation hearings. The Supreme Court has also extended the right to counsel to minors in juvenile court proceedings.

Defense attorneys often receive a "bad rap" from the public for defending obviously guilty clients or for getting them off through legal loopholes or technicalities. However, the defense attorney is playing a part as an officer of the court by making sure the prosecutor can prove guilt beyond a reasonable doubt while playing by the accepted rules of procedure. The constitutional right to effective assistance of counsel and the adversarial nature of the adjudicative process would become meaningless if lawyers refused to defend their clients on the grounds that they knew (or believed, or the community generally believed) that a defendant was guilty. Hence, their jobs are to provide the best possible legal counsel and advocacy within the ethical standards of the profession and the limits of the law in order to compel the state to legally prove its case beyond a reasonable doubt.

On the whole, defense attorneys differ markedly from both prosecutors and judges. First, defense attorneys come on the stage after prosecutorial discretion has engaged in its gatekeeping functions, deciding which cases to drop, to pursue, to negotiate, or to take to trial. In effect, prosecutors initiate cases, and defenders respond. Some may argue that such discretion, in and of itself, gives the prosecutor a head start in preparing a case. Similarly, although defenders may influence the decisions to plea-bargain or to try a case, they exert no systematic impact over the courtroom flow of criminal cases unless they are members of a large public defender's office (Barak 1980). Moreover, unlike prosecutors and judges, criminal defenders are not elected public officials (whose employment is based on approval ratings). They are all private citizens whether they are self-employed or salaried employees of local government.

Second, as a group, criminal defense attorneys are alienated and isolated from local politics; their chief alliances are with the vagaries of the legal marketplace and/or the civil service system to which they belong. In other words, not only are defense attorneys not part of a political patronage system, they are also generally not centrally located in one downtown office building, as prosecutors and judges are. Nor do they wield influence comparable to that of prosecutors with either bar associations or legislators.

Third, unlike prosecutors, not all lawyers who represent criminal defendants are adequately trained or prepared to specialize in the practice of criminal law. Most lawyers while in law school have typically taken one or two courses in criminal law and criminal procedure. Like most of the other law courses and like most practicing attorneys, the areas of law they specialize in relate to such lucrative fields as corporate, tax, or tort law or to the less remunerative, yet still financially secure, areas of the law such as probate, divorce, custody, or real estate. Comparatively speaking, the practice of criminal law provides its practitioners, with some notable exceptions such as Alan Dershowitz, Gerry Spence, or the late Johnnie Cochran Jr., less income, prestige, and status in the community.

This discussion provides some of the reasons why both academics and the US Department of Justice estimate that about 34,250 persons are wrongfully convicted each year in American courts (Bohm and Haley 2005, 286). The wrongful convictions generally involve defendants who had public defenders or assigned counsel, not the few who can afford nationally prominent, highly paid lawyers. Such high-end attorneys, however, are generally retained for one or more of three reasons: (1) the crime is sensational or highly publicized, (2) there are large legal fees involved, or (3) the chance to make new law, usually in the area of criminal procedure, is a distinct possibility.

If defendants are upper-middle-class, they may still have access to privately retained competent counsel. In most large cities, there is another small group of criminal lawyers who make a very comfortable living by defending professional criminals, such as gamblers, pornographers, drug dealers, and members of organized crime. Other defendants of the middle classes or working classes, who may or may not be able to afford private counsel, have access to the vast majority of criminal lawyers who practice predominantly in the large cities across this country. By and large, these solo criminal practitioners or small partnerships of two or three attorneys struggle to earn a decent living, often practicing other kinds of law to make ends meet.

The majority of criminal defendants who are too poor to retain their own counsel must rely on one of three types of criminal attorneys: a court-appointed lawyer, a public defender, or a contract lawyer. Nearly 70 percent of state prison inmates had attorneys appointed by the courts; blacks (77 percent) and Hispanics (73 percent) had slightly higher rates (Bohm and Haley 2005, 287–88).

In sum, most practitioners of criminal defense work can be described as either "those who have failed to establish a successful practice and therefore accept criminal cases as a way of enlarging a legal practice, or those who relish the excitement in criminal work and feel that their practice secures some justice for the accused" (Quinney 1975, 213). However, in terms of the relatively few who fall into the latter category, most practice for many years as career civil servants in the public defender's offices, justifying their roles "as mediators between the poor and the courts, resigned to seeking occasional loopholes in the system, softening its more explicitly repressive features, and attempting to rescue the victims of blatant injustices" (Platt and Pollock 1974, 27). As for most young defense attorneys who are busy learning and developing their litigation skills, they sooner or later become bored, cynical, and burned out fighting for "justice for all," whereupon, if they have become competent in their trade, they leave the field of criminal law altogether for middle-class clients and the greener pastures of civil law.

Judges

The vast majority of judges at the state level oversee trial courts of general jurisdiction, with substantially fewer sitting on intermediate appellate courts or courts of last resort (state supreme courts). Judges who oversee most felony cases sit on the benches of what are variously called "district," "superior," or "circuit" courts (depending on jurisdiction). These trial courts, of which there are more than three thousand across the nation, have the authority to try both civil and criminal matters and to hear appeals from the "lower courts" or trial courts of limited jurisdiction (i.e., city courts, municipal courts, county courts, justice-of-the-peace courts, magistrate courts) that primarily handle misdemeanors, traffic violations, and ordinance offenses.

In several states, judges of the lower courts are not required to be lawyers or have any formal legal training. In other jurisdictions, before being elected or appointed to office, the judges will have been practicing lawyers, but many of them will have no background in criminal law before joining the judiciary. In jurisdictions where judges are elected to office, these may be partisan or nonpartisan elections. Where city councils, mayors, legislatures, or governors appoint judges, they are subject to the politics of local and state bar associations. Like prosecutors, then, whether elected or appointed, judges are also sensitive to the political process that generally serves the interests of the people who elected or appointed them rather than the goals of social change.

Like prosecutors and criminal defenders, most judges in the United States are overwhelmingly white and male. Judges tend to come from upper-middle-class families, average more than fifty years of age, attend college and law school in their home states, and are typically born in the communities in which they preside (Satter 1990). Better educated than the average citizen, a majority of these judges were previously in private legal practice, making more money than they usually do as judges. In 2012, the median lawyer made $113,530 annually—which includes both criminal and civil attorneys—while the median salary for judges and magistrates was $115,760 (Bureau of Labor Statistics 2012). In 2010, there were 728,200 lawyers and 62,700 judges in the United States.

Compared to prosecutors and defenders, trial judges command more respect, status, and deference from citizens at large. According to imagery, judges are presumed to have enormous power over the adjudication or criminalization process. Actually, though, judicial discretion is far more limited than prosecutorial discretion because judges are subject to appeal and legal review by higher courts. Legislators establish sentencing guidelines, and even when they are technically "advisory," they exert a great deal of control over the outcome. In effect, while trial judges do in fact possess a great deal of power, discretionary and otherwise, they are still less powerful in the administration of criminal justice than prosecutors.

Since more than 95 percent of criminal cases are resolved by plea bargains, a judge's principal role becomes that of a "bureaucratic stamp" for negotiated deals worked out between prosecutors and defenders rather than one of an interpreter of complex legal matters. What Herbert Jacob wrote about judges and criminal adjudication more than thirty years ago is just as accurate today as it was back then:

> The massive flow of cases through their courts precludes anything but a cursory examination of the issues brought to their attention. Judges, like many factory workers, sit on an assembly line. They repeatedly perform routine tasks, with each task consuming only a fraction more than a minute. For such judges, the role is exactly the opposite of the intellectual challenge a judgeship is presumed to pose; it is a mind demeaning, stupefying post. (Jacob [1973] 1980, 67)

Corrections Workers

When it comes to prisons and imprisonment, correctional officers represent the vast majority of workers. They are generally responsible for the security of the institution and have the most frequent and closest contact with inmates. As Richard Hawkins and Geoffrey Alpert (1989) have observed, correctional officers experience a number of conflicts in their work, often become bored (tower workers) or overstimulated (cell block workers), depending on the nature of their jobs, and are subject to role ambiguity or role strain resulting primarily from the contradictions between custody and treatment objectives. Overall, these "officers generally have considerable discretion in discharging their duties within the constraints of rules, regulations, and policies. Yet, because they lack clear and specific guidelines on how to exercise their discretion, they feel vulnerable to second-guessing by their superiors and the courts" (Bohm and Haley 2005, 405).

Gresham Sykes's classic study, *The Society of Captives* (1958), pointed to some ambiguities in correctional officers' power and discretion because they are outnumbered by prisoners and depend on their compliance to keep the daily routine of prison functional, a situation Sykes referred to as one of the "defects of total power." Hawkins and Alpert (1989) have identified three responses of officers to their working conditions. First, officers may become alienated and cynical and withdraw into some relatively safe niche within the prison. Second, some officers in their efforts to control inmates become overly authoritarian, confrontational, or intimidating. Finally, there are those officers who adopt a human-services orientation, seeking to make prisons a constructive place for themselves and for inmates. This latter orientation is not about waiting on the inmates and "serving" them in that sense but rather about a community-policing type of orientation within the cell block rather than out on the streets (R. Johnson 2002).

While correctional officers are most directly engaged with inmates, there is a larger prison bureaucracy that accounts for many jobs. By 2006, correctional agencies employed about five hundred thousand people. About three of every five jobs were in state correctional facilities, about eighteen thousand in federal institutions, and about sixteen thousand in privately owned and managed prisons. Median earnings in 2010 for correctional officers and jailers were $39,040, with the federal government paying more, local government paying less, and private prisons paying much less ($30,460) (Bureau of Labor Statistics 2012). Salaries at both levels of government were subject to increases after completion of preservice training and/or a probationary period (Camp and Camp 2002, 168–69).

Although corrections workers for the Federal Bureau of Prisons are required to have a bachelor's degree and some related work experience, paid or volunteer, applicants for state correctional systems need only be eighteen or twenty-one years of age and possess a high school diploma or GED. Slightly more than one-third (35 percent) had at least some college, and about 10 percent of all correctional workers have a bachelor's degree or higher (Sumter 2008). At the same time, there are efforts to upgrade prison work from that of a mere job to that of a professional career. However, low pay, the nature of the work, the lack of prestige associated with it coupled with the remote or rural location of many prisons makes recruitment of better-educated officers difficult if the economy presents other opportunities. Conover (2000) sums up the situation from a discussion he had with a fellow guard:

> "Officer after officer will tell you: there's no way in hell you'd want your kid to be a [correctional officer]." He said that probably ninety percent of the officers he knew would tell a stranger they met on vacation that they worked at something else—carpentry, he liked to say for himself—because the job carried such a stigma. Sure it had its advantages, like the salary, the benefits, the job security, and with seniority, the schedule: starting work at dawn, he had afternoons free to work on his land . . . but mainly, he said, prison work was about waiting. The inmates waited for their sentences to run out and the officers waited for retirement. It was "a life sentence in eight-hour shifts."

In terms of gender and race, "77 percent of uniformed staff, including correctional officers, were male (though 35.5 percent of correctional officers hired in 2000 were female), and about 66 percent were white" (Bohm and Haley 2005, 404). When looking more broadly at all employees in state and federal prisons, about 33 percent are female (*Sourcebook* 2003, table 1.104, 96). And while it is commonplace for women correctional officers to work in federal and state high-security institutions today, the first woman to do so was hired in 1978. Interestingly, women make up a greater percentage of employees in state facilities than they do in federal facilities, and there is a higher percentage of female employees in the South than in other regions.

This discussion of corrections workers has focused mainly on workers in prison. However, there are also probation and parole officers working in the field of "community corrections." Indeed, as inmate populations have soared over the past several decades, so have the numbers of persons on probation and parole. For example, between 1980 and January 2011, the number of offenders subject to probation rose from 1.1 million to 4 million, and parole increased from 250,000 to almost 853,900 (Bohm and Haley 2005; Bureau of Justice Statistics 2012). Statistics on employment, including race and gender breakdowns, are not available.

IMPLICATIONS

This chapter has highlighted such factors as globalization, militarism, privatization, and the Department of Homeland Security that are affecting the criminal justice enterprise of both today and tomorrow. It has also provided an overview of some of the main categories of workers within the criminal justice system. In examining these workers, the overall conclusion is that criminal justice work is becoming more diverse. Proportional representation of women and people of color working in the administration of justice still seems important for at least two reasons. The first issue is of fairness and confidence in the system: the more closely the criminal justice labor force represents the distribution of diverse groups in society, the more the system appears to represent "we the people." The second issue is of incorporating substantively different group backgrounds into the criminal justice process: women and people of color are more likely to bring experiences and insight into the field that repetitive generations of white males may not (W. Williams [1982] 1991).

For example, the National Center for Women in Policing (2002) suggests that women have a positive impact on policing by helping to reduce police brutality, increasing the efficacy in police response to domestic violence, and more generally by promoting an emphasis on the use of conflict resolution over the use of force. Similar arguments are made about women correctional officers, emphasizing interpersonal communication and reducing the conflict and violence behind bars. The presence of women prosecutors and judges can challenge the patriarchal and paternalistic attitudes of the judiciary and, in the process, impact the treatment of women lawyers, victims, and defendants (Spohn 1990). Likewise, although the presence of women or people of color may result initially in "affirmative action" tensions and even backlash caused by misguided application of the rules of affirmative action, over time the cognitive dissonance between the "in" and "out" groups dissipates, and mutual identification sets in.

Even while the criminal justice system is slowly changing because of the infusion of more women and minorities, forces of globalization, privatization, militarization, and homeland security are also changing it. One aspect of globalization and privatization is outsourcing to the lowest bidder and moving where costs are cheapest.

The result in both cases is the "increasingly brutal wage compression" as mentioned by Morgan Stanley's economist Stephen Roach (2006). In other words, just as the United States is likely to continue to lose jobs because of globalization, it is also likely that more services of the criminal justice system will be privatized. The result will be low-wage, contingent, and no-benefit employment for those at the bottom and greater wealth for those at the top. Additionally, the large increases in criminal justice expenditures have attracted the interest of many businesses, which want to find ways to tap into an expanding source of potential revenue brought about by the new securitization. As they do so, many of these penal-surveillance entrepreneurs also become advocates for "tough on crime" policies that lead to more expenditure and potentially more business and which do very little to solve the crime problem. Ironically, as more of criminal justice is directed by private-public enterprise for profits, concern for public safety, prevention, and rehabilitation becomes secondary.

Globalization creates issues related to immigration, terrorism, and cybersecurity (as anyone in the world with a computer can attack the United States). Robert Johnson offers a poignant reminder that "we forgot that our Global Village was a stepchild of technology, not the flowering of community" (2001). People around the world did not consciously decide they all wanted to be closer and set out to invent telecommunications technology and systems to easily move money around. Rather, "technology happened," and people are still catching up with its effects, good and bad. Likewise, the criminal justice system is playing catch-up with homeland security and cybersecurity czars. As with the military, it is not clear whether the criminal justice system is still fighting the last war or preparing for future ones. But it is clear that the war on terror and emphasis on homeland security can lead to further militarization of the criminal justice system, even though the militarization accompanying the war on drugs has not led to increased justice. Indeed, it may very well aggravate many existing concerns about racial profiling and other forms of discrimination such as disproportionate minority contact throughout the apparatus of criminal justice.

REVIEW AND DISCUSSION QUESTIONS

1. What are some of the perceived benefits to increasing the number of minorities and women in law enforcement?
2. What are the similarities and differences between prosecutors, defenders, and judges? Which one has the most power? Why?
3. In terms of adapting to the working conditions of prisons, what are the three common responses employed by correctional officers? Which one do you think is the most effective?
4. Define globalization, privatization, and militarization. What is one way that each is having an impact on the criminal justice system?
5. What are some of the drawbacks to increasing the privatization of prisons? Whom does it hurt?

2

Criminology and the Study of Class, Race, Gender, and Crime

The story of criminology is the story of three revolutions: the revolution of reason, the revolution of science, and the revolution of reflexivity. These classical, positivist, and critical revolutions, respectively, are spaced roughly one hundred years apart, at 1764, 1876, and 1976, which is not to suggest that the ideas of each of these schools of criminology did not coexist more or less throughout the past 250 years. Today, each of the three schools of criminology still has its adherents and is expanding its ideas, methods, and research, and each of these schools still has its relevance to the varied practices of, respectively, equal, restorative, and social justice.

These revolutions in criminological thinking or theory may also be thought of as moving from supernatural to naturalistic, to scientific, to deconstructive (or critical) explanations of crime and justice. For most of early Western history, the dominant theory of crime was the "demonic perspective" (Pfohl 1985) that saw crime as sinful behavior or an offense against God (or the gods). People engaged in crime because evil forces either possessed them or they had succumbed to the temptations of evil forces, such as Satan or demons. Crime was thought to be the result of supernatural forces, and brutal methods, including torture, were used to discover and to punish those who were possessed or who had surrendered to the devil.

Until the middle of the eighteenth century, the demonic perspective, which focused on the supernatural, was dominant. Then it was challenged by a group of individuals who would become known as classical criminologists. Characteristic of the Enlightenment, classical theory argued that crime was the result of natural, observable, or "worldly" forces, such as the absence of swift, certain, and effective punishments. According to the classical perspective, all people were more or less equal, rational, and free willed; they had self-control and chose to engage or not engage in crime because they were rationally pursuing their own interests, trying to maximize their pleasure and minimize their pain. The response to the pursuit of self-interested criminal behavior, therefore, became the rational employment of "swift, certain, and appropriate" punishment to deter potential offenders who calculated the pleasure of crime versus the pain of punishment. This criminology was developed in reaction to the harsh, corrupt, and often arbitrary nature of criminal justice in the 1700s and was inspired by a desire to bring about rational legal reforms. This classical perspective dominated criminology from the late 1700s until the late 1800s, when it was challenged by a more modern and scientific approach, influenced to varying degrees by the introduction of Darwin's theory of evolution.

The positivist school, with its divergent and yet related biological, psychological, and sociological orientations to the study of criminal behavior, argues that criminals are not in fact normal, rational human beings who choose to engage in crime to maximize their pleasure and minimize their pain. Instead, criminals are viewed as different from noncriminals—and it is their differences that compel them to engage in crime. Such "criminogenic properties" call for intervention, reform, treatment, and reconstruction to environmentally control crime and to socially engineer individual criminals away from deviance.

While still the dominant model or paradigm in criminology today, positivism has been successfully challenged by the emergence of the critical school of criminology in the 1970s, which was part of a larger philosophical critique of "value-free, objective, and neutral" social and behavioral science. Rooted in the sixties and in the crisis in American institutions, critical criminology (at least in the United States) reflected the reality that with racism, sexism, imperialism, and other types of inequality, social justice remained an American dream. This "newest" of criminologies stressed the fact that the traditional older criminologies, classical and positivist alike, both ignored and thus left unchallenged the powerful interests that benefit from both the attention paid to crime in the streets rather than crime in the suites and the lack of concern about inequality. In contrast, critical criminologies—feminist, peacemaking, constitutive, and so on—turn their focuses not only to the social relations of crime and punishment but also to the very structural forces that sustain them. They examine, for example, the mean streets of American inner cities, complete with drive-by shootings, as well as the cutthroat operations of a deregulated Wall Street where the infamous boys of Enron, Arthur Andersen, and AIG were busy robbing people through very sophisticated Ponzi schemes and other financial weapons of mass destruction.

Finally, the critical school of criminology focuses its attention on social, political, and economic justice rather than on retributive and therapeutic justice per se. The institutional and structural emphases of critical criminologists would move away from policies and practices of adversarialism (e.g., warmaking) and toward those of mutualism (e.g., peacemaking). In general, critical criminology focuses on the "justice" part of criminal justice by striving to bring about more equitable and peaceful societies, locally and globally.

Criminology is the study of crime and criminal justice. It includes theories of criminal behavior as well as criminal law and the operation of the criminal justice system.

There are essentially two types of parallel criminology at work in the contemporary world, one consisting of positivists and classicists or "mainstream" criminologists, the other consisting of an eclecticism of culturists, feminists, political economists, and postmodernists or "critical" criminologists. The first type of criminology is a creation of the "culture of control," a product of the movement from penal reform to one of situational crime prevention (Garland 2001). Mainstream criminology, writes Jock Young, is

> minimalist in its theory, one-dimensional in its portrayal of human action. Its genealogy stretches from Lombroso in the late nineteenth century to the work of Travis Hirschi, James Q. Wilson and Marcus Felson today. It is the world of positivism and rational choice theory, a stance which denies meaning and minimalizes social structure; it is constructed around analytical individualism which is contrary to the main thrust of sociological thinking. (Young 2011, 223)

On the other hand, the second type of criminology is the creation of the intersection of biography and history and the struggles for human liberation and social justice. This critical criminology is

> informed by sociology, which concerns itself with meaning and power, and understands that humans create cultural solutions to their life problems in social structures which are largely not of their own making. [It] traces its lineage through the Victorians, such as Mayhew, Booth and Engels, via the Chicago School of the 1930s to the revolutionary developments of the new deviancy theory in the US in the late 1950s and 1960s, and through to the new criminology and subcultural theory of Britain in the 1970s and early 1980s. (Young 2011, 222)

In different words, researchers approach topics of study with a theory implicitly or explicitly in mind. Their theories, perspectives, and assumptions thus shape decisions about what constitutes a problem worthy of study (or publication), what method is appropriate for the study, and what the results mean. Further, researchers are embedded in a world where class, race, and gender dynamics affect many aspects of life—and this includes theories of crime, approaches to studying criminal law, and understanding the operation of the criminal justice system. Thus, the first part of this chapter elaborates on the opening narrative by further exploring the classical, positive, and critical perspectives on criminology. The second part of the chapter explores the roles that class, race, and gender have played in the field of criminology.

CLASSICAL CRIMINOLOGY

Classical criminology emerged and developed during the second half of the eighteenth and first half of the nineteenth centuries in the midst of the Enlightenment in Europe, especially in France and England because of their strong emphasis on rationalism and humanitarianism. As part of a reaction to the turmoil and disorder

in many countries across Europe—the harsh and barbaric punishments administered by a highly arbitrary state and the many rebellions and fewer revolutions—the
classical school of criminology set out to study the relationship of citizens to the
state's legal structure. The emphasis was on reforming the state's antiquated, ineffective, and cruel systems of administering crime and punishment, which would
result in increased legitimacy for the state and its rule of law. Influenced by a part
of the related logic of two new doctrines, the *social contract* and *free will*, classical
criminologists adopted the view that "reason and experience, rather than faith and
superstition, must replace the excesses and corruption of feudal societies" (Beirne
and Messerschmidt 1991, 286).

Classical criminology builds on the idea of the social contract, Thomas Hobbes's
(1588–1679) notion that people create government and civil society rather than
pursue their own narrow self-interests in a perpetual, unproductive "war of all against
all." Other philosophers explored the idea of a social contract, not as a historic event
but as a theory that citizens submit to government in exchange for social order, represented by the idea of an agreement that specified the rights and duties of both people
and the government. For example, in the bargain that was struck, citizens were to
"surrender some measure of their individuality so that government [could] enact
and enforce laws in the interests of the common good; the government, in return,
[was to] agree to protect the common good but not to invade the natural, inviolable
liberties and rights of individual citizens" (Beirne and Messerschmidt 1991, 287).

As part of the Enlightenment agenda, the doctrine of free will asserted that men,
at least those who were free and who possessed property, rationally and voluntarily
chose to participate in the social contract. Further, "those who challenged the social
contract, those who decided to break its rules, and those who pursued harmful
pleasures and wickedness were liable to be punished for their misdeeds" (Beirne and
Messerschmidt 1991, 287). The two principal classical theorists were Cesare Beccaria (1738–1794) and Jeremy Bentham (1748–1832), both of whom applied the
doctrines of free will and rational, pleasure-maximizing choices to the study of crime
and punishment.

Reacting against the cruel and inhumane legal practices of the time, these two
leading classical criminologists objected to the inequities in the administration of
the criminal law. They proposed substantive and procedural reforms of penal justice
consistent with their conceptions of human life, reforms that sought to balance the
good of society with the rights of the individual. Human beings were to be viewed
as responsible for their own actions because they were rational and free to engage in
rightful or wrongful behavior. Accordingly, punishment was to fit the social harm
caused by the crime, with the formal and institutionalized reactions to crime more
important than the informal and individualized efforts to control crime. Throughout
the twentieth century and into the present, classical theory has been an integral part
of legal and economic thought, and it has influenced the nature of punishment and
sentencing in this society, moving it toward and then away from treatment as a rationale for punishment. Recent related approaches would include "crime as rational

choice" and "routine activity theory" developed in the 1980s and later (see Cullen and Agnew 1999, chapters 26 and 27).

POSITIVIST CRIMINOLOGY

In the late nineteenth century, the theoretical movement of positivism, which began to study crime as a social phenomenon, buttressed the emergence of a scientifically based criminology. Relying on the point of view of the natural sciences and borrowing from their methodology, positivists sought to analyze crime not by speculation and observation alone but also by the collection of scientific "facts" through systematic data collection and analysis. The positivist analyses of crime, following such disciplines as physics, chemistry, and biology, began a process that still continues of uncovering, explaining, and predicting the ways in which observable facts occurred in regular patterns.

Positivist criminology turned its focus away from law and crime and toward behavior as a reaction to the failures of classical criminology to stem the rising tides of criminality through moral reformation (e.g., religious teachings) and humanitarian reform (e.g., incarceration rather than corporal or capital punishment) and to differentiate between delinquent and pathological inmates (who included the likes of syphilitics, alcoholics, idiots, vagabonds, immigrants, prostitutes, and petty as well as professional thieves). Based on a variety of determining forces or causal factors, positivist criminologists also began to assert that the "treatment should fit the criminal" rather than the "punishment should fit the crime." In effect, positivist criminology maintained that criminal actions were not the product of free wills but rather arose as a result of biological, psychological, economic, and social forces that propelled individuals into engaging in them.

One of the most influential early positivists was the Belgian astronomer Adolphe Quetelet (1796–1874). Using scientific methods and social statistics, he set out to develop a "social mechanics" of crime in which he attempted to demonstrate that the same lawlike regularity existing in the world of nature also existed in society. Quetelet argued that there were many causes of crime that could be divided up into three categories: *accidental* (wars, famines, tsunamis), *variable* (personality), and *constant* (age, gender, occupation). Society, too, was a cause of crime, but Quetelet ultimately concluded that crime had biological causes.

Other influential theorists came from the fields of anthropology, medicine, and psychiatry in the early and middle nineteenth century, such as Francis Gall's work on phrenology (head shape), Gregor Mendel's work on genetics, Charles Darwin's work on the origin of species, and Benjamin Rush's work on the diseases of the mind. Biology found its criminological proponent in the father of modern criminology, Cesare Lombroso (1835–1909). Rounding out the Italian school of positivism were two of Lombroso's students, Enrico Ferri (1856–1929) and Raffaele Garofalo (1852–1934). Ferri argued for a sociopolitical criminality that emphasized the interrelatedness of social, economic, and political factors that contribute to crime; Garofalo argued for a doctrine of "natural crimes," a social Darwinist approach that viewed crimes as offenses "against the law of nature."

Throughout the rest of the nineteenth century and into the twentieth, positivist criminologists debated the relative importance for crime of *nature versus nurture*, or heredity versus social environment. The turn of the twentieth century had already seen the rise and fall of biological determinism as exemplified by the discrediting of Herbert Spencer's "bioevolutionary" model of society and Lombroso's "born criminal" who was an "atavistic throwback" to an earlier evolutionary stage. Rising to replace biology in popularity was the psychogenesis school of criminal causation, influenced by the psychiatrist Sigmund Freud (1856–1939), followed by the rise of sociology and the related influence of sociologist-criminologist Edwin Sutherland and his theory of "differential association," first presented in 1939.

During the twentieth century and into the early twenty-first century, the powers of positivism and the methods of quantitative science have dominated much of criminology. At the same time, each of the theoretical orientations or schools and disciplines of positivist criminology has continued to evolve and develop, including areas such as the following: individual traits and crime; social disorganization and crime; learning and crime; anomie/strain and crime; control and crime; and labeling and crime. The past several decades also witnessed the rise of integrated theories within (and without) positivist criminology. Among the shortcomings of positivism is its overemphasis on individual as compared with social or organizational analyses of criminality and on the belief that changes in the behavior of offenders can occur independent of changes in the social conditions, including the political and economic arrangements.

CRITICAL CRIMINOLOGY

The newest school of criminology is the critical school. About forty-five years old, this school first emerged as radical criminology and now encompasses feminist criminology, left-realist criminology, peacemaking criminology, constitutive criminology, newsmaking criminology, integrated criminology, cultural criminology, postmodern criminology, green (or environmental) criminology, and anarchist criminology. Despite the diversity of critical criminologies, they have in common an agreement on the limitations of criminological knowledge and justice policy inherent in the classical and positivist criminologies.

For example, critical criminologists are skeptical of the rational and positivist belief that an orderly universe can necessarily be organized by knowledge and the manipulation of the external world. Critical criminologists are skeptical about objectivity and point out that there are no "value-free" standpoints—everyone has certain assumptions and values. Certain assumptions and points of view may seem "natural" or objective because they are widely shared by the dominant groups. Critical criminologists therefore acknowledge their subjectivity, that they are part of a moral and political endeavor. Finally, with their rejection of mechanistic conceptions about how facts are related and gathered, critical criminologists typically do not present causal models of crime; explanations and arguments about crime and justice revolve around both social and cultural interactions as well as the structural relations of the political economy as these intersect with the everyday activities of people (Barak 2009).

The emergence of a critical criminology in part represents a departure from the traditional practices of criminology that have focused attention on changing the behavior of the lawbreakers either through punishment (classical criminology) or treatment (positivist criminology). Not that critical criminology is unconcerned with punishment and treatment or with reforming the administration of criminal justice—on the contrary, it is, but it prefers to locate these changes within the contexts of social, political, and economic justice. Critical criminology is thus concerned not so much with "law and order," but "whose law?" and "what order?" (Chambliss and Mankoff 1976)—that is, with the power relations involved in the law, the fairness of social order that law is protecting, and solutions that promote justice rather than simply repress criminals.

In sum, unlike classical and positivist criminologists, critical criminologists are also reflexive criminologists, meaning they question the privilege that goes with having one's viewpoint be seen as "objective" and how such privileged standpoints and "knowledge" contribute to inequality. They have turned the activity of explanation back on itself: in the process of reflection and introspection, critical criminology asks about "first principles," such as the basic assumptions and thought processes of criminological inquiry that generate our "knowledge" about crime. Morally and politically, critical criminology questions the status quo, official versions of reality, and prevailing ideologies about the "solutions" in crime control. Critical criminology represents alternative modes of analysis and better pathways to human liberation and crime reduction in all its forms, but it also remains committed to empirically supporting its scholarship and interventions into policy formation.

CLASS AND CRIMINOLOGY

Social and economic class are generally discussed less than race or gender. Indeed, the ideas that the United States is a classless society and that "anyone can make it if they try hard enough" drown out analysis of the distribution of income and wealth. Unfortunately, both are unequally distributed, and class mobility is more limited than most people would like to believe. These assertions are developed in chapter 3, and this section reviews some of the important ways that understanding class and economic power relates to criminology. For example, criminological theory is frequently based on an unquestioning acceptance of how the criminal law defines crime. But class is related to political power and lawmaking, so it is also deeply implicated in understanding what has been defined as crime and why almost forty years of being "tough on crime" has hardly applied to white-collar crime. Economic resources also play a role in the working of a justice system to process those defined as criminal. The first part of this section provides an overview of these issues, followed by a discussion of the link between inequality and crime and the relative neglect of white-collar, corporate, and governmental crime.

Crime theory frequently assumes that criminal law is a direct reflection of consensus, or of folkways hardening into custom and finally law rather than the contingent outcome of a political process that includes class conflict and class biases. As Jeffrey Reiman notes, "Criminology is in the unusual position of being a mode of social inquiry whose central concept is defined officially, by governments," so "politics openly, necessarily, insinuates itself into the heart of criminology. Political systems hand criminology a ready-made research agenda" (in Reiman and Leighton 2013, 243). In other words, criminologists' focus on street crime, and thus the crimes of the marginally poor, becomes seen as a "natural state of affairs" rather than as an expression of inequality and privilege, so criminology develops theories about the criminality of the poor rather than examining harms of the rich. In turn, the criminal law's controlling of the offenses of the poor rather than the offenses of the rich appears to reflect the legitimacy of an agreed-on definition of "dangerous" crime.

When crime theory unreflectively takes the criminal law as a given, the fiction of crime as neutral law sets in (Platt 1974). Working within the confines of "crime" as defined by the law cedes control of criminology to lawmakers and the political process that produces law. Thus, many social harms—from tobacco smoke to environmental pollution, from workplace injuries to defective products, and from neocolonialism to extraordinary crimes against humanity—are excluded from study, even though they present more of a threat to people's well-being and security than much of what is officially designated as crime (Barak 1991a; Reiman and Leighton 2013). If criminology makes

> no moral judgment independent of criminal statutes, it becomes sterile and inhuman— the work of moral eunuchs or legal technicians. If moral judgments above and beyond criminal law were not made, the laws of Nazi Germany would be indistinguishable from the laws of other nations. (Quoted in Simon 1999, 37)

Among the main theorists in exposing the myth of the neutral criminal law were the nineteenth-century philosophers and political economists Karl Marx and Friedrich Engels, who noted that the law, along with the order it upholds, is one based on a very unequal distribution of property and resources. Marx and Engels thus "insisted that the institutions of the state and law, and the doctrines that emerge from them, serve the interests of the dominant economic class" (Beirne and Messerschmidt 2000, 110). For them, crime was not about the defects of morality or biology, but rather about the defects of society and the product of the demoralization and alienation caused by the horrible conditions encompassing industrial capitalism.

Subsequent Marxian analyses of crime and crime control in the United States can be subdivided into "instrumental" and "structural" models of crime and criminal control. Some of the earlier work, for example, of Richard Quinney (1977), is representative of the instrumental model. He argued that within the overall conditions of the capitalist political economy, two kinds of crimes emerge: *crimes of domination* and *crimes of accommodation*. Crimes of domination include "crimes of control" (i.e., acts by the police and the FBI in violation of civil liberties), "crimes of government" (i.e., political acts such as Watergate, Iran-Contragate, or torturing suspected terrorists), "crimes of economic domination" (i.e., corporate acts involving price-fixing, pollution, or planned obsolescence), and "crimes of social injury" (i.e., acts that may not be illegal but that deny basic human rights, such as racism, sexism, and economic exploitation). The crimes of domination, according to the instrumentalist view, are necessary for the reproduction of the capitalist system itself.

In contrast, relatively powerless people of the lower and working classes commit crimes of accommodation. Quinney identified three crimes of accommodation, or adaptation to the oppressive conditions of capitalism and to the domination of the capitalist class: "predatory crimes" (i.e., burglary, robbery, drug dealing), "personal crimes" (i.e., murder, assault, rape), and "crimes of resistance" (i.e., protests, sabotage). For Quinney, the real (greater) danger to society comes from the crimes of domination rather than the crimes of accommodation. However, the former acts are not criminalized (or are minimally so) because they serve the interests of the ruling classes; the latter acts are criminalized and punished as they threaten the political and economic status quo. Hence, crime control becomes class control.

As an example, consider the following quotation taken from one of the founding fathers of the classical school, Beccaria, in his book, *Essay on Crimes and Punishments*, first published some two hundred years ago and still in print today. In trying to reason through the appropriate punishment for an offender, he takes the imagined voice of the criminal:

> What are these laws that I am supposed to respect, that place such a great distance between me and the rich man? He refuses me the penny I ask of him and, as an excuse, tells me to seat at work he knows nothing about. Who made these laws? Rich and powerful men who have never deigned to visit the squalid huts of the poor, who have never had to share a crust of moldy bread amid the innocent cries of hungry children and the tears of a wife. Let us break these bonds, fatal to the majority and only useful to a few indolent tyrants; let us attack justice at its source. I will return to my natural state of independence; I shall at least for a little time live free and happy with the fruits of my courage and industry. The day will perhaps come for my sorrow and repentance, but it will be brief, and for a single day of suffering I shall have many years of liberty and of pleasures. (Quoted in Vold and Bernard 1986, 29)

The speaker points out the social injuries that are part of the crimes of domination that help secure the unequal distribution of resources. At the same time, the speaker advocates unspecified crimes of accommodation in response to oppression. George Vold and Thomas Bernard (1986) note that the revolutionary implication behind the passage is obvious and that crimes of need could be better prevented by a more equal distribution of money than by the severity of the penal law. Instead, Beccaria argues that the death penalty is an ineffective deterrent that should be replaced by the more protracted suffering of life imprisonment.

William Chambliss (1988) articulates a structural-contradictions theory of crime and class control, in which recognition is given to the resistance and pressures from other classes besides the ruling classes. In his model, Chambliss identifies certain contradictions inherent within capitalism, such as those between profits, wages, and consumption—or between wages and the supply of labor. These contradictions ultimately culminate in crime as underclasses are formed that cannot consume the goods that they were socialized to want as necessary for being happy. One solution for these underclasses is to resort to criminal or illegitimate behavior. The state then responds to these acts in the name of crime control.

Although research on the link between social disadvantage and crime is no longer a priority as it once was for a brief period during President Lyndon Johnson's Great Society of the 1960s, criminologists have continued to explore it. An important finding is that poverty itself is not the key, because "if that was the case, then graduate students would be very dangerous people indeed" (Currie 1998, 134). The important theoretical concepts relate to inequality, relative deprivation, and blocked opportunities. As Elliott Currie (1998, 34) points out, the important contribution to crime and violence is "the experience of life year in, year out at the bottom of a harsh, depriving, and excluding social system [that] wears away at the psychological and communal conditions that sustain healthy human development."

Further, high levels of inequality mean that there are more poor and destitute than would exist under a more even or equal distribution. Thus, "there are criminals motivated by the need for a decent standard of living, where 'decent' can mean what they perceive most people in their community enjoy, what whites but not blacks enjoy, what they used to enjoy before they lost their jobs, or what they were led to expect to enjoy by advertising and dramatization of bourgeois lifestyles on television" (Braithwaite 1992, 82). Inequality also produces more structural degradation, which John Braithwaite argues is important because of the links among humiliation, rage, and violence. Ultimately, the "propensity to feel powerless and exploited among the poor and the propensity of the rich to see exploiting as legitimate . . . enable crime" (94).

Because most of criminology tends to be guided by the criminal law, the focus of crime theory is almost exclusively on the behavior of the poor. Notably, one of the first important mentions for criminology of "crime" in relation to the behaviors of the upper classes was in 1908, when E. A. Ross promoted the notion of a "criminaloid." David Friedrichs (1996, 2) notes that Ross used this term to discuss "the businessman who committed exploitative (if not necessarily illegal) acts out of an uninhibited desire to maximize profit." Ross's discussion, however, did not immediately inspire sociologists to explore the topic, partly because criminology was attempting to establish itself as a "science," which meant distancing itself from the passionate outrage that characterized many of the journalists who were busy condemning robber-baron industrialists and pointing to the excesses of the capitalist system.

But this work did get the attention of Sutherland, who was interested in the criminality of the rich because of his attempt to develop a general theory of crime. He believed that a major deficiency of criminological theory was that it could not explain crime by the rich, which made for not only class-biased criminological theory but also for a practice and policy of criminal and juvenile justice steeped in class biases as well (Platt 1969). In 1939, Sutherland introduced the term *white-collar crime* in his presidential address to what is now the American Sociological Association. The key elements included that the perpetrator be an upper-class or white-collar person, the crime be committed in the course of one's occupation, and the crime be a violation of trust.

Once again, criminology was slow to follow up on Sutherland's research, and its primary focus still remains with street crime, although crimes by the upper class exact a far heavier toll in terms of dollars and lives (Reiman and Leighton 2013; Simon 1999). The criminological literature spends little time trying to explain or understand financial fraud compared with the time spent on trying to explain or understand drug use and graffiti. An analysis of 4,878 articles in 15 criminology journals from 2001 to 2010 showed that only 6.3 percent were about white-collar crime—and only 3.4 percent in the ten journals ranked highest in prestige (McGurrin et al. 2013, 9).

Further, many categories of white-collar crime include crimes committed by both the powerful and the relatively unpowerful. For example, embezzlement and improper use of a credit card qualify as types of "white-collar" crime, but they should not be confused with those crimes committed by large corporations, financial institutions, or the federal government (Leighton and Reiman 2013). A careful examination of these acts thus requires looking at the relative power of the criminal and victim. The most frequently discussed white-collar crimes are employee pilfering and credit card fraud, in which businesses, corporations, and financial institutions are the victims. The least frequently discussed are corporate and government crime, in which the powerful are the perpetrators who are victimizing employees, consumers, taxpayers, and/or the environment. When white-collar crimes are discussed, they rarely highlight the executive who harms employees by cutting corners on workplace safety, who knowingly markets unsafe products, or who causes environmental damage in order to help boost corporate profits. Further, criminologists, politicians, and the media take insurance fraud to mean false claims against the industry and do not also include improper denials of claims by insurance companies. Likewise, workplace theft means stealing by employees but should also include improper withholding (theft) from paychecks.

Significantly, those white-collar crimes committed by the relatively powerless that are more likely to be officially defined as crime, such as employee theft or embezzling money from one's employer, have virtually nothing in common with the actual "crimes of the powerful" except that all of these abuses involve some kind of violation of trust. Accordingly, studies of white-collar crime should pay attention to crimes of the powerful whose actions and practices knowingly violate the rights of groups of people or cause harm to workers, consumers, communities, and/or the environment.

For the most part, the crimes of the powerful are relatively invisible to the average person, taxpayer, politician, or journalist because they are generally not acknowledged or discussed in the mass media. When they are covered and discussed, if they are not denied outright, then they are typically excused, justified, and/or neutralized to the point that they are viewed as "not really crime" after all. These "noncrimes" committed by the powerful may include corporate crimes, crimes of globalization, environmental crimes, financial crimes, organizational white-collar crimes, state crimes, and state-corporate crimes. While these seven categories of "crimes of the powerful" represent separate or independent areas of harm and injury, they often involve overlapping areas of criminality, employing organizational and institutional networks—locally, nationally, and multinationally—of powerful people. As already suggested, these crimes may include actions committed against workers, market-places, taxpayers, political systems, and the air we breathe as well as crimes against humanity, such as acts of torture, genocide, or state terrorism.

Individuals in a corporation who violate the law in the corporation's interests, who also benefit themselves individually through bonuses and promotions, perpetrate *corporate crimes*. These involve a range of practices that victimize employees, consumers, the environment, stockholders, and/or creditors. Acts also may include fraud against the government, which victimizes taxpayers, and anticompetitive practices that cause higher prices for consumers. *Corporate violence* refers to acts that inflict physical and emotional suffering rather than simply monetary losses, as in the case of dangerous or defective products, unsafe working conditions, and medical conditions caused by pollution or toxic exposure. These harms, injuries, or violations may be national or transnational in scope. *Environmental crimes* are typically perpetrated by corporations but may also include public policies and practices that add to environmental degradation. Similarly, *crimes of globalization* may involve the superexploitation of workers in developing countries as well as the related policies and practices of global financial institutions such as the International Monetary Fund, the World Bank, or other mega-international banks located in places such as New York, London, Singapore, Tokyo, or Zurich.

Public officials who are trying to perpetuate a specific administration, exercise general government power, or accomplish undue influence on behalf of large campaign contributors perpetrate *state crime*. The victims can be as widespread as all taxpayers who are forced to pay for corruption, fraud, and sweetheart deals. Victims can also be a specific political group—or even its leaders—who are denied basic political rights through surveillance and harassment (Barak 1991a). Finally, *state-corporate crimes* represent hybrid forms of state and corporate organized crimes working together.

With all these various forms of crime and white-collar crime, class biases operate in the social construction of "perpetrators" and "victims." Serial killers who commit street crimes are a trendy topic of study for criminologists, but criminology devotes little attention to trafficking in human beings or to mass slaughter, including genocide. Indeed, criminologist Margaret Vandiver notes that "if we had as much research and theory on genocide as we do on shoplifting, we would be far ahead of where we are now" in reducing human suffering (1999, personal communication).

RACE AND CRIMINOLOGY

Race is socially defined by a constellation of traits that include physical character-istics, national origin, language, culture, and religion. That is, while people have real differences, racial and ethnic categories are made up based on prevailing beliefs, political pressures, and a host of nonobjective reasons. Consider that the racial cat-egories used in the United States have changed over time and that no other country uses them. "Hispanic" is an ethnicity rather than a race because of lobbying by the Mexican government, which did not want Mexicans categorized as nonwhite. These issues are further explored in chapter 4, and this section reviews some of the connections between criminology and the racial hierarchies that privilege some and disadvantage others.

Historically, research on crime has consciously and unconsciously reproduced the racism of prevailing social attitudes, while it has also been a site for resistance. For example, Lombroso wrote, "The white races represented the triumph of the human species, its hitherto most perfect advancement" (quoted in J. Miller 1996, 185). This belief influenced his criminal anthropology and its implications that criminality was related to atavistic or evolutionary throwbacks. In contrast, Willem Bonger's 1943 study, *Race and Crime*, was written as a critique against the growing fascist movement in Europe and arguments about the superiority of Nordic peoples (Hawkins 1995, 23). Today, many criminology texts do not mention Lombroso's early racism or his repudiation of such ideas as those in *Criminal Man* (1870) over the course of his career. Most texts without an interest in race and/or ethnicity ignore altogether the critical work of Bonger on race and crime, though they almost always mention his work on economics and crime.

American criminology and social science have generally been characterized by a "liberal political tone and assumptions" that document, for example, black disadvan-tage and attribute it to white prejudice rather than biological notions of inferiority (Hawkins 1995). Hawkins starts his analysis with some of the work of W. E. B. Du Bois (1868–1963), a prominent black intellectual and writer who is typically omitted from criminology texts. He is an important figure because "many of the most virulently racist, social Darwinist critiques of black life were published during the period he wrote [and] Du Bois was among the first to provide a retort to their argument" (Hawkins 1995, 13). Du Bois seemed to accept the higher rates of black (street) criminality; he ascribed them to the social disruption and urban migration that occurred after the end of slavery as well as to the degradation and legacies of slavery.

Criminologists such as Sutherland and Thorsten Sellin shared some of Du Bois's analysis of crime, although they both urged much more caution in concluding, based on official statistics, that blacks had a higher rate of crime than whites. At the same time, Sellin (1928, 64) recognized that black crime rates might still be higher than whites', but he argued this was not a condemnation of blacks because "it would be extraordinary, indeed if this group were to prove more law-abiding than the white, which enjoys more fully the advantages of a civilization the Negro has helped to create." Sutherland and Sellin did recognize the salience of *culture* as relevant to criminality but argued that culture is somewhat different from nationality (based on political boundaries) and race. Important data for them included the observation that immigrants from the same culture would have different rates of criminality, depending on the age at which they arrived in the United States and the number of generations their family had been here—data that cannot be explained by reference to biology or genetics.

Clifford Shaw and Henry McKay's study of social ecology in Chicago neighborhoods also raised questions about the importance of biology and genetics because "no racial, national or nativity group exhibits a uniform, characteristic rate of delinquents in all parts of Chicago" (Shaw and McKay 1942, 153). The key factor for them in explaining delinquency was social disorganization and community attributes rather than the racial traits of those who lived in certain areas. Marvin Wolfgang and Bernard Cohen (1970) later elaborated on the persistence of high rates of criminality among blacks while other immigrant groups had moved out of socially disorganized communities and zones of transition. In particular, they noted that blacks faced more blocked opportunities because of racism than white immigrants and that the legacy of racial oppression might make blacks less ambitious than immigrants, who would be more optimistic about achieving the American dream.

Wolfgang and Cohen's *Crime and Race* (1970) also critiques biological determinism by noting that there could not be a genetic predetermination to general criminality because neither crime nor the definition of crime is stable in time and place. They note that most criminals obey most of the laws and generally break laws carefully so as to avoid drawing attention from the police. Like Bonger, they argue that criminality is not a specific trait like eye color:

> According to Mendel's rule of inheritance of specific traits, if criminality were genetically determined, we should inherit specific tendencies for embezzlement, burglary, forgery, etc. And if we inherited specific *criminal* forms of behavior, and some of us were genetically destined to be burglars or stock embezzlers, rapists or check forgers, we would also have to inherit specific *noncriminal* occupations, which would mean some of us would be genetically destined to become police officers or truck drivers or school teachers, as to have red hair. (Wolfgang and Cohen 1970, 92, emphasis in the original)

The critique in the preceding paragraphs does not mean criminology should exclude the disciplines of biology, physiology, and genetics from a comprehensive and integrated approach (Barak 1998). Indeed, the emphasis here is that there are no genetic bases for race, which makes the link between race and crime problematic. The physical and other characteristics that are often used to create racial categories are socially constructed; they do not correlate with criminality but can mean that minority groups are subjected to greater social control because they are more involved with the criminal justice system.

Hawkins concludes his thoughtful overview of literature on race and crime by noting that the liberal tradition tries to balance a recognition that racial bias inflates the officially counted criminality of minorities with an awareness that minorities frequently live in criminogenic conditions. He is skeptical of efforts to find the "real" rate of crime and of attempts to get more accurate counts of real misconduct. Instead, he argues for the development of a conflict perspective, which examines official records of minority crime as an index of social control that shows "how the criminal justice system is used by the dominant ethnic and racial groups to maintain their status" (Hawkins 1995, 34). This perspective, which is developed in chapter 7, contends that contact with the criminal justice system has as much to do with social standing as it does with criminal conduct, and perhaps more.

More recently, criminologists have explored how experiences with "injustice at the hands of criminal justice officials support existing societal inequalities" and the ways in which "ethnoracial inequalities in the United States in education, employment, and health are exacerbated by the disproportionate imprisonment of groups of color" (Krivo and Peterson 2009, 9–10). *A Theory of African American Offending* tries to recognize that centuries of subordination have created a worldview—one that is "continually being reaffirmed and shaped as African Americans confront everyday racism" (Unnever and Gabbidon 2011, xvii)—that is related to offending. Factors such as unjust treatment at the hands of criminal justice system employees can also weaken respect for the law. The theory also recognizes that blacks are disproportionately poor and have higher exposure to environmental toxins such as lead, which can increase criminality.

GENDER AND CRIMINOLOGY

Sex generally refers to the biological components that characterize males and females. Gender typically refers to femininity and masculinity or to the roles and behaviors dominant society encourages for males and females. Gender thus refers to the social expectations for how males should be masculine and how females should be feminine. While sex is a relatively fixed biological anchor, gender involves the social processes through which people learn and are socialized into acting according to the ever-changing notions of what is appropriate for men and women in our society. Women are a majority of the American population, but men are the dominant gender. These issues are further explored in chapter 5, and this section reviews some of the connections among criminology, gender roles, and male domination.

A wide variety of people (family, friends, coworkers) and institutions (schools, advertising, mass media) help create expectations about appropriate gender behavior and apply pressure for conformity. Further, "as an official agent of social control, the criminal justice system responds not only to crime but also transgressions against gender norms" (Flavin 2009, 4). One important way the criminal justice system achieves this end is by becoming involved in matters of reproductive choice. As Jeanne Flavin explains in *Our Bodies, Our Crimes* (2009, 4):

> By restricting some women's access to abortion and obstetric and gynecological care, by telling some women not to procreate and pressuring them to be sterilized, by prosecuting some women who use drugs and become pregnant, and by failing to support the efforts of incarcerated women and battered women to rear their children, the law and the criminal justice system establish what a "good woman" or "fit mother" should look like and how conception, pregnancy, birth and child care and socialization are regulated.

(Generally, the women prosecuted and subject to this type of control are poor and/ or minority women, which highlights the importance of looking at intersections.)

Until recently, gender has not been important to criminology because men have been the vast majority of criminal offenders and have dominated the criminal justice system from lawmaking to parole officer. Women have made up a small percentage of offenders and have tended to commit less serious crimes than men. Until the mid-1970s, these and other factors contributed to a lack of interest in female criminals and their experience within the criminal justice system. However, over the past forty years, interest has increased in the study of women, gender, and crime. During this sustained period of criminological interest, the areas of both gender and women's studies have evolved in their analyses and sophistication. A five-stage framework developed by Peggy McIntosh (1984) and others (Andersen 1988; Daly 1995; Goodstein 1992) provides an overview of the ongoing process by which the fields of criminology and criminal justice have considered, do consider, and could consider women (Daly 2006; Flavin 2001).

Stage One: The Intellectual Falklands

The Falklands are a series of islands whose total area is smaller than Connecticut located between South America and the Antarctic. Up to the nineteenth century, most researchers ignored women's criminality, and the study of female criminality was considered "an intellectual Falklands"; that is, "remote, unvisited, and embarrassing" (Heidensohn 1995, 124). Theorists who did consider women saw them as being particularly determined by their biology. Lombroso, for example, studied female offenders to support his theory that criminals were physically anomalous. His methodology involved extensive measurements of criminals to isolate the "born criminal." Lombroso concluded that the born female offender was closer to a normal man than a normal woman. However, he also seemed to distinguish between different types of female criminals: "Unlike the 'semi-masculine, tyrannical and selfish' born criminal who wants only to satisfy her own passions, the occasional [female] offender puts trust in her male protectors and regains confidence in men—especially her lawyer, and in some cases that Lombroso is fond of relating, her executioner" (Hart 1994, 23).

Other positivist theorists, especially those with a psychological or psychoanalytic approach, perceived women's deviance as peculiarly sexual. For example, Otto Pollak (1950) argued that women's tendency toward deceit stemmed from their physiological ability to hide their true sexual feelings and the social expectation that they will conceal menstruation and menopause.

Stage Two: "Add Women and Stir"

In the twentieth century, criminologists moved away from viewing deviant behavior as inherently abnormal and pathological and toward seeing deviance as normal. Thus, models that examined external sources of crime, such as poverty, social structure, and racial discrimination, gradually replaced those older models that examined internal sources such as biology and psychology. Once again, before the 1970s, most studies of crime continued to look exclusively at men and boys. In the mid-1970s, however, women insisted they be included in criminological research and analysis about crime and the criminal justice system. Unfortunately, the result was simply to "add women and stir" them into existing research rather than reconsider and challenge what was or is "known" about crime.

Eileen Leonard's work (1982, 1995) provides perhaps the most comprehensive attempt at using traditional positivist theories of crime such as anomie/strain, differential association, subcultural labeling, and Marxism to explain women's low involvement in crime. Because these theories excluded consideration of women's criminality, Leonard developed hypotheses that the theorists might have constructed had they been so inclined or informed. For example, Robert Merton's anomie theory holds that when people lack legitimate means (e.g., a job, a savings account) to achieve socially accepted goals (e.g., material and monetary success), they are more likely to innovate (e.g., steal, write bad checks) to achieve these cultural ends. Leonard points out that although women are overrepresented among the poor and thus arguably are subjected to more strain than men, women are less likely to deviate. Leonard also challenges whether monetary success is as salient a goal for women as it is for men. She further critiques Merton for assuming that women's goals (and men's, too) are shared across class, race, and ethnicity. Following her systematic review and analysis of traditional theories, Leonard concludes that these theories are unsuited for explaining female patterns of crime. She calls on scholars not to develop a separate "criminology of women" but to reconsider the understanding of women *and* men's criminal behavior.

Stage Three: Enter Feminism

The first of the feminist stages reflects some scholars' realization that women have been excluded from crime theories or that when women *are* discussed their behavior is distorted. This stage focuses more attention on crimes that adversely affect women more than they affect men, such as domestic violence. Also, increasing attention is paid to the ways in which women's experiences differ not just from men's but also from one another's based on characteristics such as race, ethnicity, class, age, and sexual orientation.

While this stage is a marked improvement over ignoring women altogether or "adding and stirring," it still has its shortcomings. Most notably, this stage reflects a tendency to treat men as normative and women as anomalous. Labeling one sex the "anomaly"—relegating its members to a marginalized status—is incompatible with aims to achieve more equal opportunities for men and women on the professional golf circuits as well as in a court of law. It reflects male privilege (discussed in chapter 5), and the implications of androcentric or male-centered thinking for the criminal justice apparatus are significant. For example, the historically male-centered legal system meant delays in recognizing marital rape and stalking as crimes, providing vocational programs for women prisoners, and addressing sexual harassment in the workplace.

The development of feminism has helped raise consciousness about the male biases reflected in criminology, and it has re-created its theoretical understandings and practice. While feminist theories of crime and justice do try to correct the exclusion or silences about women's beliefs, experiences, and achievements, most acknowledge that the understanding of women's lives also requires consideration of masculinity and male sex-role expectation. When neither males nor females are the hidden or invisible norm of criminological analysis, then the discipline is in a better position to understand the fact that men also have a gender, whites also have a race, the wealthy have a class, and straight people have a sexual orientation. These types of feminist insights help move criminology in the direction of describing gendered oppression in all of its forms, of identifying and explaining its causes and consequences, and of prescribing strategies for the political, economic, and social equality of the sexes (Rice 1990; Tong 1989).

Stages Four and Five: "An Emerging Whole New Pie"

The fourth and fifth stages are still at conceptual or imaginary levels because women and minority men do not currently form enough of our basis of knowledge, although that too has begun to change over the past decade or so. The current literature does reflect a growing willingness to reconsider what is "known" about women and crime and to examine racial and ethnic differences among women and men. In the fourth stage, scholars have begun not only to locate women with men at the center of research but also to study women on their own terms without reference to male norms. As an established body of feminist theory and research grows, it is becoming possible to build on feminist knowledge itself rather than merely dedicating time and attention to critiquing and evaluating traditionally male-dominated criminological theories and research.

During the fourth stage, rather than addressing how the study of crime and criminal justice contributes to our understanding of women's criminality, research has begun to emphasize how feminist insights contribute to our understanding of crime and men's high incidence of criminality. At this point, the research goes beyond a sociology or criminology of women. The work of such scholars as Jody Miller (2001, 2002, 2008) and James Messerschmidt (1993, 1995, 2004), for example, does in fact suggest that we have crossed into the fourth stage, where we are increasingly integrating our knowledge of masculinities and femininities.

In the fifth stage, our knowledge base will be fully transformed and feminist, and it will include a theoretical and analytical focus on multiple relations of class, race, and gender. Kathleen Daly (1995) has identified a number of challenges to be met in the process of reaching this stage (which will be taken up later, in part 3 of this book). Among these challenges is the fact that our inherited ways of thinking obstruct our ability to imagine alternative ways of viewing crime and punishment. In other words, the existing biases built into our knowledge bases make it difficult to imagine what a fully inclusive and transformed body of knowledge, gendered and otherwise, will be like.

INTERSECTIONALITY AND CRIMINOLOGY

Discussions of intersections and intersectionality refer to efforts to combine the analysis of class *and* race *and* gender. While each is important in its own right, by themselves they provide an incomplete description of a person's life experiences and "social location." A person may be white, but multibillionaires are different from those considered "white trash"; rich and poor white women will have some different experiences than their male counterparts. Figure 2.1 illustrates the social location of

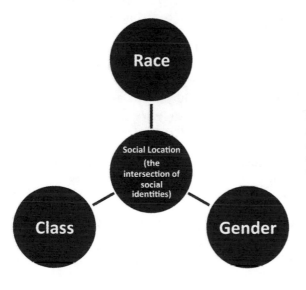

Figure 2.1. An Integrated Illustration of Class, Race, and Gender as It Shapes Crime and Experiences with the Criminal Justice System

the intersecting formation of class-race-gender identities, identification, and representation.

While it may seem obvious to use class and race and gender to get a "fix" on a person's social location, it is also easier said than done. One of those dimensions may be more important than the others in a specific situation, but that factor will not always be most important—and theorists have not created good models to understand whether class or race or gender will be most important (and why). Further, the combination of factors does not work in a simple additive way like 1 + 1. Combining devaluation because of gender with devaluation because of race creates gendered racism, which can be far more powerful because of the interacting dynamics.

Intersectionality is further explored in chapter 6, and this section provides an overview of criminology's limited efforts to explore how class and race and gender all apply at the same time. Too frequently, researchers focus on one of these three social relations to the near exclusion of others. For example, the short-lived *radical* perspective in criminology that emerged in the late 1960s and early 1970s drew heavily from Marx's ideas about capitalism and the social relations of production, so it emphasized how class conflict was at the root of most crime.

Eventually, the almost exclusive focus on class would broaden to give greater and increasing importance to race and gender because they are independent structuring forces that affect, shape, and influence areas of criminological concern: how people act, how others respond to and define those actions, how certain actions are viewed as more or less serious or as more or less "criminal" and deviant, and how the law and legal systems are organized to control behavior in highly stratified and unequal societies (Lynch 1996). By the 1990s, race and gender had surpassed class in being viewed as key concepts of society, prompting Robert Bohm (1998, 18) and others to call for a reemphasis of "class and class struggle in an understanding of crime and social control in market societies." Currently, *The Rich Get Richer and the Poor Get Prison* (Reiman and Leighton 2013) is one of the few book-length treatments of class and criminal justice.

Today, there are a variety of race, gender, and hybrid analyses of crime and justice, such as those involving feminist perspectives, critical race theory, or critical legal studies. For example, building on critical sociology, neo-Marxism, and postmodern approaches, *critical race theory* assumes that racism is an ordinary, ingrained aspect of American society that cannot be readily remedied by law. Developed in the late 1970s through the efforts of scholars who were discontent with the slow pace of achieving racial justice (Delgado 1995a), critical race theorists argue that the racism that permeates society is part of a socially constructed reality that exists to promote the interests of men and women in elite groups. Hence, not only do they expose the ways in which existing arrangements support racism, they also pursue alternatively constructed social realities.

Similarly, *critical race feminism* emerged from critical race theory to address the gap between what tended to be white feminism and critical race theories focusing on men (Wing 1997). Specifically, critical race feminists have objected both to feminist approaches that presume white middle-class women's experiences are representative of all women's experiences and to critical race scholarship that presumes minority women's experiences are all the same and can be represented by the experiences of their minority male counterparts. The effect of essentialist perspectives has been to "reduce the lives of people who experience multiple forms of oppression to addition problems: 'racism + sexism = straight black women's experience'" (A. Harris 1997, 11). In other words, racial and ethnic minority women—as victims, offenders, and workers—are not simply subjected to quantitatively "more" disadvantage than white women; their oppression is of a qualitatively different kind.

Critical legal scholarship in the form of narrative or storytelling is used as one means of analyzing, challenging, and resisting the dominant myths, presuppositions, and "truths" that make up the mainstream culture's views of race, gender, and law. Too often, the scholarly accounts of dominant groups have suppressed, devalued, and marginalized the experiences and perspectives of women and minority men. Narratives are used to break the silence and convey complex issues in a readily accessible form designed to promote understanding. For example, law professor and critical race theorist Richard Delgado (1995b) explains the debate surrounding essentialism with his fictional alter ego, Rodrigo Crenshaw. In one of his chronicles, Rodrigo has gotten "caught in the crossfire" at a Women's Law Caucus meeting:

> The "debate about essentialism has both a political and a theoretical component," Rodrigo began. . . . "In its political guise . . . members of different groups argue about the appropriate unit of analysis—about whether the Black community, for example, is one community or many, whether gays and lesbians have anything in common with straight activists, and so on. At the Law Women's Caucus, they were debating one aspect of this—namely, whether there is one, essential sisterhood, as opposed to many. The women of color were arguing that to think of the women's movement as singular and unitary disempowers them. They said that this view disenfranchises anyone—say, lesbian mothers, disabled women, or working-class women—whose experience and status differ from what they term 'the norm.'"
>
> "And the others, of course, were saying the opposite?"
>
> "Not exactly," Rodrigo replied. "They were saying that vis-à-vis men, all women stood on similar footing. All are oppressed by a common enemy, namely patriarchy, and ought to stand together to confront this evil. . . . [Black feminists' focusing] on their own unique experience contributes to a 'disunity' within the broader feminist movement. . . . [It is troubling] because it weakens the group's voice, the sum total of power it wields. Emphasizing minor differences between young and old, gay and straight, and Black and white women is divisive, verging on self-indulgence. It contributes to the false idea that the individual is the unit of social change, not the group. It results in tokenism and plays into the hands of male power." (Delgado 1995b, 243–46)

In a similar fashion, *critical white studies* (Delgado and Stefancic 1997) is the most recent body of scholarship that considers what it means to be white in the United States. Far from being a safe haven for white supremacists, critical white studies prompts whites and nonwhites alike to consider the legacy of whiteness and to ask such questions as: How do whites as members of the dominant race benefit (or not), depending on their place in the social order of stratification? What does white privilege mean to the poorest whites—sometimes called "white trash"—and to the poorest white women especially? How has our culture constructed "whiteness" and "blackness" such that they are not neutral descriptors but laden with meaning, value, and status?

Several more specific examples of analysis close out this section on intersections and criminology. As noted in the previous section, privilege may present itself in terms of the preferred masculinities or femininities. The form of femininity most valued and supported in US culture, for example, emphasizes marriage, housework, child care, fragility, and sociability. More generally, this idealized femininity is based on white, middle-class, and heterosexual norms. In this respect, Lynda Hart's work (1994) on depictions of lesbianism and female killers suggests that the category "woman" is reserved for white, upper-class, heterosexual females. This categorization serves a disciplinary function, patrolling the boundaries of "normal" femininity by creating an "othered" (not woman) category onto which women's deviance can be displaced. Thus, "the ultimate violation of the social instinct, murder, and the perversion of the sexual instinct, same-sex desire, was linked as limits that marked the boundaries of femininity" (Hart 1994, 30). Lesbians and killers (and women of color) reside together in the "not woman" category.

Three noteworthy studies of crime that have captured various nuances in the interactions of class, race, and gender are Esther Madriz's (1997) examination of women's fear of crime, Mark Totten's (2000) investigation into adolescent girlfriend abuse, and Jody Miller's (2008) detailed excavation of the multiple dimensions of violence experienced by black inner-city girls. In these ethnographies, the authors are able to encapsulate the qualitative differences in the life experiences of men and women, boys and girls, majorities and minorities, in relation to class, crime, and the administration of justice. They demonstrate that there is no standardized "class" experience, "race" experience, or "gender" experience but rather a repertoire of interacting class, race, and gender identities. Figure 2.1 illustrates the social location of the intersection of these forming identities.

In *Nothing Bad Happens to Good Girls* (1997), Madriz explores the fear of crime among young and old, African American, Latina, and white upper-, middle-, and working-class women. In the process, she is able to demonstrate how fear of crime perpetuates gender inequalities and contributes to the differential social control of women by class and race/ethnicity. For example, Madriz was able to capture the differential responses of informal social control that were in play where women of lower socioeconomic class or women of color were more inclined to restrict their movement and activities in the public sector than middle-class white women.

In *Guys, Gangs, and Girlfriend Abuse* (2000), Totten explored the relations between early childhood abuse, family and gender ideologies, and the construction of masculinity on the one hand and the marginal male socialization experiences of straight, gay, white, black, and Asian teenagers on the other hand. In his integrated analysis, Totten is not only able to make sense out of the patterned differences of girlfriend abuse with respect to the physical, sexual, and emotional violence meted out by boyfriends, but he is also able to explain how the reproduction of violence and social control in these young people's lives is related to the abuse of gays and racial minorities. Adolescent males' bashing of girlfriends and gay people is related to feelings of powerlessness, despair, and humiliation regarding their future economic prospects and living up to the masculine ideal of "breadwinner" as well as their anxieties about and fears surrounding their heterosexuality.

Finally, in *Getting Played: African American Girls, Urban Inequality, and Gendered Violence* (2008), Miller captures the ways in which gender, class, and race inequality exposes many disadvantaged African American girls to sexual harassment, sexual assault, dating violence, and even gang rape. Miller points out that "urban violence" is exclusively about African American men, and women's victimization in that context tends to be invisible. She explains how gendered victimization, racial discrimination, and the perpetuation of violence toward these adolescent females, by boys and men alike, are linked to structural inequality. Miller's analysis also significantly demonstrates how young African American women struggle to navigate this dangerous terrain, where those who do not stand up for themselves against the daily "testing" of men can become targets for assault but also where deflecting male attention in the wrong way can get them labeled as a "bitch" deserving of assault.

IMPLICATIONS

The criminal law furnishes the basis for much of criminology and criminal justice study as though the law were objective or neutral. However, while some laws serve the interests of most people, most laws reflect the special or partisan interests of elected people who have conscious and subconscious desires in maintaining the privileged orders or status quo of which they are obvious benefactors. Reiman asserts that criminology needs philosophical reflection on the nature of crime "to establish its intellectual independence of the state" and thus declare "its status as a social science rather than an agency of social control, as critical rather than servile, as illumination rather than propaganda" (in Reiman and Leighton 2013, 243). Similarly, criminology also needs reflection on and independence from class, race, and gender constructs if it is not to become simply another tool of social control and propaganda for the status quo in these areas, too.

This reflection on the nature of crime and crime control—which is related to critical criminology and explored throughout this book—is especially important because the definition of crime drives the resources of policing and the rest of the criminal justice system. It also becomes the basis for theorizing about crime as well as the collection of official data that is used for research about crime and presented in criminology books to explain crime. Without critical reflection, the criminal law appears neutral and above question because its values seem reinforced by police activity that is focused on street crime rather than white-collar crime and by criminological theory, data, and books that also have the same emphasis or focus as the criminal law.

Class, race/ethnicity, and gender are each important in understanding the production and social construction of crime and the administration of justice. Understanding that some groups are privileged because of their class, race/ethnicity, and gender is also important because privilege is the unifying concept underlying these three variables. In the United States, each of these variables has been involved in many of the laws that are selectively made (or not made) or that are differentially applied to offenders. These variables are both implicit and explicit in the theories used to explain behavior and provide direction for criminological investigation. In the processes of crime and crime control, however, separating these variables out from one another is as difficult as separating the ingredients out from a person's identity. For example, when minorities are disproportionately poor, separating class from race can be problematic.

However, it is relatively easy to identify the class, race, and gender biases at work in the study of crime and crime control. For example, for a brief period in the 1960s, the President's Commission on Crime and Law Enforcement identified the roles of inequality and discrimination as contributing to the "breakdown" in law and order. Some thirty years later, at a retrospective sponsored by the US Department of Justice, criminologist Todd Clear was one of the few speakers who mentioned the issue of inequality in crime and crime control. Clear also discussed the backlash to President Johnson's Great Society ideas that had been the backdrop for the commission's report, *The Challenge of Crime in a Free Society*. The commission advocated government taking a lead in crime prevention through social programs and opportunities for disadvantaged citizens. The subsequent rise of the law-and-order mentality and the bipartisan war-on-crime policies led to a different and more limited "get tough" pro-incarceration role for the government because crime was seen more as the result of individual failings rather than of discrimination and structural inequality and privilege.

It is also relatively easy to see how privilege is reflected differently in the two prevailing legal interpretations—the *jurisprudential model* and the *sociological model*—of class, race, and gender on "justice" outcomes. The jurisprudential model of criminal justice is an ideal, not a reality per se. It is based on "rationality, equality before the law, and treating of like cases alike" (Agozino 1997, 17). To consider such factors as class, race, and gender, then, is to violate the due process rights of the involved individuals. Because social characteristics are not *supposed* to influence the handling of a case, the jurisprudential model assumes that they do not; it regards law as constant and universal, with the same facts resulting in the same decisions. Consequently, when class, race, or sex discrimination occurs, it is considered the exception, not the rule.

In contrast to the jurisprudential model of justice, the sociological model assumes that political, economic, and social characteristics influence the administration of justice. Far from being constant from one case to another, law is assumed to be variable, changing with the social relations of the parties. Whereas the jurisprudential model is concerned with how the system *should* work, the sociological model examines how it actually *does* work. Sociological models, then, are interactive models of the administration of justice as they incorporate both the ideal and real representations of law and order, involving a variety of extralegal characteristics that include class, race, and gender.

REVIEW AND DISCUSSION QUESTIONS

1. What are the key points of the classical, positivist, and critical revolutions of criminology? How are all three still relevant to contemporary discussions of crime and justice?
2. What are the strengths and weaknesses of classical, positivist, and critical criminologies?
3. Why do the authors believe that reflection and critique of the criminal law is so important for criminology and criminal justice?
4. Briefly explain how the authors define class, race, and gender. What is one example of how each is important for criminology?
5. What is the basic idea of intersectionality? Why is intersectionality difficult to apply, and why would criminology benefit from the effort?

II

INEQUALITY AND PRIVILEGE

3

Understanding Class
and Economic Privilege

The novel Snow Crash *(Stephenson 1992) is set in an alternative United States at a time when the four things we do best are music, movies, software, and high-speed pizza delivery. Hiro lives in a 20' by 30' U-Store-It, formerly intended for people with too many material goods. The storage room has its own door and doesn't share walls with other units, so he tells himself there are worse places to live.*

Hiro is a freelance computer hacker; he also belongs to the elite order of Deliverators, those entrusted with the task of thirty-minute pizza delivery for the Mafia-owned businesses (specifically, CosaNostra Pizza franchise #3569). In contrast with his own residence, deliveries are to the "burbclaves"—suburban enclaves, gated communities. All burbclaves have the same layout because the "Development Corporation will chop down any mountain ranges and divert the course of mighty rivers that threaten to interrupt this street plan." Some of them are Apartheid Burbclaves such as White Columns: "WHITE PEOPLE ONLY: NON-CAUCASIANS MUST BE PROCESSED." As he approaches the gate, a laser scans his bar codes and he rolls through the immigration gate and past "customs agents ready to frisk all comers—cavity search them if they are the wrong kind of people."

Hiro's partner, a skateboard courier named Y.T., gets arrested in the burbclave by MetaCops Unlimited ("DIAL 1-800-THE COPS All Major Credit Cards"), who also enforce traffic regulations for one of the major companies that operate private roads. Many of the Franchise-Organized Quasi-National Entities prefer to have their own security force rather than engage a general contractor. Security is a big deal because they're "so small, so insecure, that just about anything, like not mowing your lawn, or playing your stereo too loud, becomes a national security issue." The burbclave doesn't have a jail, but "any half-decent franchise strip" has one, either the cowboy themed Hoosegow or The Clink, Inc. The MetaCops quickly see the sign: "THE HOOSEGOW: Premium incarceration and restraint services. We welcome busloads!"

While Snow Crash *is frequently considered science fiction, its author considers it an "alternative present." Indeed, the world he paints in the first pages of the novel satirizes many features of the present day, including the shift from manufacturing to a service-based economy, rising income inequality, residential segregation, the popularity of gated communities, the privatization of justice functions, the predictable, franchise-based world George Ritzer describes in* The McDonaldization of Society *(2004), and the growth in corporate power to rival the resources of states and many nations in the global village.*

While Americans like to think of themselves as a "classless" society, the United States has both a highly stratified workforce and extreme inequality in the distribution of income and wealth. This class-based society is also spatially separated, divided into urban and suburban spaces, a new "geography of inequalities" (Body-Gendrot 2000). The white flight by upper and middle classes circa the 1960s to 1990s that facilitated the development of "gated" and "walled" communities separated socially, mentally, and spatially from the poor has probably now peaked in many urban areas such as New York City, Detroit, and Washington, DC. Due to gentrification and the more recent supergentrification, or the transformation of previously gentrified upper-middle-class neighborhoods into much more exclusive and expensive enclaves, there are currently reversing "flight" trends where the poor and working classes are now being forced out of places such as Brooklyn Heights, New York City (Lees 2003). For example, in the 2000s, the Fort Greene area of Brooklyn changed rapidly and dramatically. In 2000, the black population in the area had been 93 percent; by 2010, the white population had increased by nearly 30 percent, qualifying it as one of the fastest-gentrifying neighborhoods in the United States (Moss 2014). Nevertheless, urban spaces still elicit a recurrent fear of crime and lack of trust in the public institutions responsible for law and order, and either way, whites and minorities find themselves inhabiting worlds that rarely meet either socially or spatially:

> *The residential environment of suburban whites is overwhelmingly white (82 percent), native born (92 percent) and non-poor (94 percent). In contrast, the living environment of most minorities is non-white, foreign, and disadvantaged. City-dwellers are twice as likely as suburbanites to live in female-headed families, 56 percent more likely to be unemployed, and their incomes are about 26 percent lower than those in the suburbs. (Body-Gendrot 2000, 31)*

These social realities of the urban and suburban worlds of class difference also yield very different rates of arrest. While 30 to 40 percent of boys growing up in the urban United States were being arrested, only about 6 percent of suburban youth under the age of eighteen had ever been arrested (Greenwood 1995, 92). These very real class differences in experiencing crime and the administration of juvenile/adult criminal justice have lasting consequences not only for these youth but also for the ways in which the larger society and its institutions come to view crime, criminals, and crime control. In those places where reurbanism and supergentrification are "reversing" wealthy white flight, it will be interesting to see whether or not the actual practices of law enforcement and the administration of justice and/or the mediated views of public safety change. It should also be of interest to discern the ways in which crime and its control as well as new technology and securitization adapt to the age of reurbanism.

As for life inside the overprotected, gated communities of suburbia, living has been redefined along with the meaning of community, engendering a sense of what used to be called the "me generation" and the notion that individuals must protect themselves and their families from the "Other." This preference for living in the suburbs and for the levy of separate taxes has caused drastic shortfalls in the fiscal budgets of urban American cities. In addition to the tens of millions of residents, mostly white, living in such autonomous, unincorporated communities, there are also nearly eleven million households located in gated communities as of 2009 (Mohn 2012), about 10 percent of all occupied homes (Benjamin 2012).

By the turn of the twenty-first century, Americans were spending about $65 billion for their private security, and the number of private police officers had exceeded the number of public. Much of the cost was not in the suburbs but inside such cities as Los Angeles, New York, Chicago, and elsewhere because there is no access to the "defensible" spaces that are protected by new technologies of surveillance. Consequently, these urban areas claim to have private police on duty twenty-four hours a day because of the rising property values of such spaces and the needs of the affluent who live there. In this two-class divided society of rich and poor, "the privatization of safety . . . and the freedom to carry weapons in the public space (taken advantage of by one-third of U.S. citizens) distinguish the American landscape" at the turn of the twenty-first century (Body-Gendrot 2000, 32).

The Constitution of the United States claims that everyone is entitled to equal protection under the law. The statues of Lady Justice that adorn many courts show her blindfolded so that she can impartially weigh the claims on the scales she carries. But most Americans know that being rich has its advantages, including in the areas of crime and law. Death-row inmates joke that people who have capital do not get capital punishment, and the data support their observation. Being wealthy makes it more likely that someone can literally or figuratively get away with murder.

Some observers see this pattern as so pervasive that they argue the criminal justice system is about controlling the poor and keeping them in their place (Chambliss and Seidman 1982; Quinney 1977; Shelden 2000). Further, "crime" refers to "crime in the streets" rather than "crime in the suites," or white-collar crime, which is more prevalent and more costly to society. Inequality and roadblocks in achieving the "American dream" are key concepts in strain theory and its offshoots, although few texts note that the wealthy also desire more and may turn to (white-collar) crime because they have a limited number of legitimate ways to achieve their aspirations. Thus, understanding class is important for gaining insight into many facets of criminology and criminal justice.

Fundamentally, class revolves around questions of the distribution of income, wealth, and status. (These questions clearly are related to racial and gender identity since many women and minority men tend to occupy the lower levels of income distribution, as we will explore in subsequent chapters.) Yet despite its importance, class is currently less frequently discussed than race and gender. Gerry Mooney, for example, notes that while "class remains a primary determinant of social life," most public "discourses about modern society have been largely de-classed" (2008, 68). The neglect of class occurs in a context where "the scale of this inequality is almost beyond comprehension, perhaps not surprisingly as much of it remains hidden from view" (2008, 64).

In the context of the recent economic collapse and recovery, people were briefly willing to speak about class and the transfer of wealth from all taxpayers to the very rich through bonus payments to companies bailed out by the government (Barak 2012; Ritholtz 2009a). However, very few were willing to talk about "capitalism's dirty little secret: excessive lending was the only way to maintain the living standards of the vast bulk of the population at a time when wealth was being concentrated in the hands of an elite" (Funnell 2009). Outside of times when a financial crisis happens, conversation about class is more muted because getting vital information about class is still more difficult than with race or gender as basic sources do not contain a table with key information such as how much wealth the top 1 percent of the country controls.

Consider that four members of the Walton family, whose wealth comes from Wal-Mart stores, are "wealthier than the bottom third of the U.S. population put together—about 100 [million] people" (Funnell 2009). The members of the Walton family appear on *Forbes* magazine's list of the four hundred wealthiest Americans for 2012 in ranks six through nine, with between $33 billion and $35 billion in wealth *each* (Forbes 2013a). But despite increasing inequality, the issue was never raised in the most recent presidential election. The presidential debates contained no substantive discussions of wealth inequality or proposals to help achieve a more egalitarian distribution of wealth. The national media also failed miserably to bring this critical issue to the attention of the voters and to question the candidates about it.

Discussions of class are not easy because information about the distribution of income and wealth can potentially disrupt deeply held beliefs about a United States where everyone is middle class and anyone can get ahead if they try hard enough. It is easier to talk about "working families," which includes people of all classes, than about the specific needs of the working class, the middle class, and the upper class. The clear pattern is that since the mid-1970s, the distribution of wealth has become more unequal, and the top 1 percent has disproportionately benefited from the recent weak economic recovery (Cronin 2013). But saying that "the rich are getting richer and the rest of us are getting taken" is seen as inciting "class warfare" (Hightower 1998b, 105), even though a senior editor of *Forbes* magazine said, "The mega rich are mega richer" (B. Fowler 2013) and surveys show many people are experiencing downward mobility. The financial crisis and bailouts of "too big to fail" banks should have moved discussions of class, inequality, and privilege to the forefront of discussion, but popular outrage faded quickly.

This chapter starts an investigation into class to explain important concepts and introduce facts about inequality. What follows is an overview of what class means, how income and wealth are distributed, and what studies say about the ease of mobility between classes. Although these issues often receive less attention than race and gender, a three-week special series on class in the *New York Times* began by noting, "Class is still a powerful force in American life." It concluded that over the past thirty years or so, class "has come to play a greater, not lesser, role in important ways" (Scott and Leonhardt 2005, A1).

SOCIAL CLASS AND STRATIFICATION IN SOCIETY

In a broad sense, *class* may be defined as "any division of society according to status," or social ranking (*New Webster's Dictionary of the English Language* 1984, 186). For example, Paul Horton and Chester Hunt (1976, 234) defined social class as "stratum of people of similar position in the social status continuum." Consequently, the janitor and the college president are not of the same class and are not treated the same way by students. The *New York Times* series conceptualized class as a hand of cards, with the suits representing education, income, occupation, and wealth (Scott and Leonhardt 2005). But we believe primary attention should be placed on the stark inequality in the distribution of economic power and resources.

Further, income and wealth are more important than other aspects of class for understanding the nature of crime control and the functioning of the criminal justice system. Money is ultimately the primary factor involved in motivations and opportunities to commit crime as well as in the responses of the criminal justice apparatus. For example, wealth means political influence to lobby for more favorable laws and less oversight; and, except for isolated cases related to widespread financial scandals, it is generally the case throughout history that poor defendants are the ones seen as "noncredible and/or disreputable persons regardless of their actual moral proclivities" (Emmelman 2004, 50, 63). Thus, the focus of our discussion of class is economic because it is convenient shorthand for understanding the larger issues, especially as these relate to crime, law, and justice.

Many social thinkers have tried to devise meaningful ways to divide up the spectrum of income and wealth. Karl Marx identified the *bourgeoisie*, who owned the means of production (factories, banks, and businesses); the *petty bourgeoisie*, who do not have ownership but occupy management or professional positions; and the *proletariat*, or workers, who need to sell their labor to make a wage. Marx also identified the surplus population, or *lumpenproletariat*, who have no formal ties to the system of economic relations because they are unemployed or unemployable (see Lynch, Michalowski, and Groves 2000). In developing his theory, Marx contributed a useful critique of capitalism, involving his belief that history could be described as an ongoing war of the rich against the poor for control of wealth. Although Marx himself did not write much about crime, his suggestions that law and criminal justice are tools used in this class warfare have been used by criminologists over time to provide important insights and questions that are explored throughout the text.

Many other attempts to describe the class system have been less useful because they are not tied to a theory of power relations or offer less useful insights for understanding law, crime, and justice. They tie class to sources of money (rent, wages) and the amount of it to separate people into different groupings. Other attempts to describe the distribution of wealth tend to be variations on upper, middle, and lower classes, although there is some discomfort in describing others as "low class." To avoid possible value judgments, the lower segment of the income distribution has been described by such terms as *working class* and *working poor*, while *underclass* refers to the poorest of the poor, who seem to lack class mobility and are locked into poverty.

Also, a growing literature in the field of "white-trash studies" examines the poorest whites who have none of the power and prestige of most whites. These people tend to have resources equal to or even less than minorities but have white skin, so studying them can potentially shed theoretical light on issues of race and class (Wray and Newitz 1996). Many schemes for understanding class have difficulty placing women who work in the home and are not wage earners. Indeed, radical feminists often argue that women represent a social class. More generally, feminists argue that women's relationship to class structure is mediated by "the configuration of the family, dependence on men, and domestic labour" (quoted in Gamble 1999, 206). Chapters 5 and 6 examine these issues in more detail.

One interesting attempt to describe the distribution is Paul Fussell's typology of nine classes: top out-of-sight (rich), upper, upper middle, middle, high proletarian, midproletarian, low proletarian, destitute, and bottom out-of-sight (1983). People in the first category include those such as media mogul Ted Turner. One of his seven properties is a New Mexico ranch that covers 578,000 acres, or enough room for twenty-two lakes, thirty miles of fishing streams, and more than eight thousand elk (Gilbert 1998, 90). People in the bottom category include homeless people, such as mentally ill people and veterans of recent wars who live in the subway tunnels of major cities (Barak 1991b; Toth 1995).

More recently, the term *precariat* has come into use to describe those who have a precarious financial existence because of low job security, poor pay, and/or a pay-check-to-paycheck existence (Ritholtz 2011). Relatively small unexpected expenses can cause substantial problems for this group. But because many high-salary earners also live paycheck to paycheck—or perceive themselves to be in this situation—it is not a term that directly identifies class privilege. For example, if a family has no money at the end of the month because of having an expensive mortgage for a big house, credit card bills from travel and eating out, and funding college savings and retirement accounts, they still have class privilege. Box 3.1 has some statements that help further identify class privilege.

The important point is that underlying all these ideas about how to create meaningful divisions are some basic concepts related to income, wealth, and financial assets. *Income* is the most straightforward indicator of class. It represents sources of individual revenue such as salary, interest, dividends (payouts from owning stocks),

BOX 3.1.   YOU KNOW
YOU'RE PRIVILEGED WHEN . . . (PART 1)

In 1988, Peggy McIntosh's frustration with men who would not recognize their male privilege prompted her to examine her own life and identify ordinary ways in which she experienced white privilege. "I think whites are carefully taught not to recognize white privilege, as males are taught not to recognize male privilege" ([1988] 1997, 292). Since then the idea of privilege checklists has gained widespread acceptance, and people have applied the idea to many different types of privilege.

This box covers the issue of class privilege, and each of the next three chapters will have a similar box to cover white privilege (chapter 4), male privilege (chapter 5), and intersections (chapter 6).

You know you have class privilege when

- I can buy things for my comfort and because they are fashionable.
- I do not fear being hungry or homeless.
- I have the time and money to take care of my body (if I choose).
- I do not worry about my access to medical care.
- I can advocate for my class without being seen as looking for a handout.
- Whenever I've moved out of my home it has been voluntary, and I had another home to move into.
- I hunted for sport, not because of food insecurity.
- I can employ people to help with household tasks and child care.

Source: Adapted from Pease, Bob. 2010. *Undoing Privilege*. London: Zed, 77–78.

capital gains (money made on the sale of stocks), and other items reported on income tax forms. By contrast, *wealth* includes possessions such as cars, savings accounts, houses, stocks, bonds, and mutual funds; it also subtracts debts and loans. *Financial assets* is a measure of ownership of the economic system, so it excludes houses, cars, and items people could turn into cash at a garage sale. Instead, it focuses on stocks, bonds, and trusts—"the kind of ownership that gives a person distinct advantages in a capitalist society" (Brouwer 1998, 13).

The study of class is also part of a larger question about what sociologists call *stratification*, which is concerned with the distribution of social goods such as income, wealth, and prestige. Because most of these goods have an unequal distribution, part of stratification attempts to explain how small minorities maintain control over a disproportionate share of the social resources—an explanation that involves the role of the criminal justice system and the phenomenon of how *The Rich Get Richer and the Poor Get Prison* (Reiman and Leighton 2013).

ECONOMIC DISTRIBUTIONS

Income, wealth, and financial assets are all distributed more unequally in the United States than in other developed nations we would consider to be our peers. As figure 3.1 demonstrates, the top 10 percent in the United States have a much greater percentage of the total net worth than the top 10 percent of other nations, and the bottom 50 percent have among the lowest shares of net worth. Americans have mixed reactions in their moral evaluation of this inequality. Some people believe it is unjust for some to starve and live in poverty while others have so much, for example, that in 2010 the highest-paid hedge-fund manager took home $4.9 billion in salary (Creswell 2011) while 21.6 percent of American children lived in poverty (Macartney 2011). Others see the inequality as a necessary part of the American dream, where the possibility of nearly unlimited wealth motivates everyone to work harder to achieve the "good life." In this section, we try to describe the income and wealth distributions.

The facts about economic distributions are important for furnishing a concrete picture of inequality and concepts such as relative deprivation, which focuses on people's evaluations of their place relative to what others have and/or what they believe they are entitled to. As discussed further in chapter 8, John Braithwaite argues that "inequality worsens both crimes of poverty motivated by *need* for goods for *use* and crimes of wealth motivated by *greed*" (1992, 81; emphasis in the original). Crime can be related to the powerlessness and exploitation of those at the bottom of the class system as well as by the unaccountability and manipulation by those at the top. Class mobility and crime are related to the notion of blocked opportunities

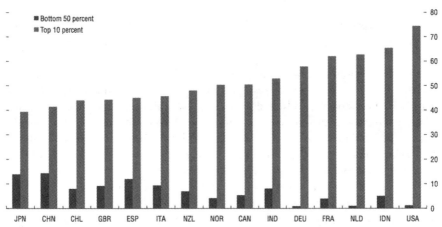

Figure 3.1. Shares of Net Wealth Held by the Bottom 50 Percent and Top 10 Percent in Selected Countries

Source: International Monetary Fund, "Taxing Times," *Fiscal Monitor*, October 13, http://www.imf.org/
external/pubs/ft/fm/2013/02/pdf/fm1302.pdf. © International Monetary Fund. Reprinted by permission of
the IMF.

and poverty in strain theory, yet crime is seldom discussed in terms of class mobility, stratification, and greed.

Income Distribution

To illustrate income distribution, Dennis Gilbert (1998) uses the example of a parade, where all the households in the United States pass by in one hour. The height of the marchers in the parade is used to represent their income, with the shortest being the poorest and the tallest being the richest. In updating Gilbert's idea with current data, the parade is built around a median family household income in 2012 of $51,017 (DeNavas-Walt, Proctor, and Smith 2013, 5) and a median height for people in the United States of approximately five feet seven. (The median is the number that half of the distribution is above and half is below. *It is also worth pointing out that the 2012 median family household income was nearly $7,500 less than the $58,407 median back in 2006.*)

First Twelve Minutes

In this part of the parade would be the lowest 20 percent of income earners, who all together received 3.2 percent of all income (DeNavas-Walt, Proctor, and Smith 2013, 10). Imagine that one hundred marchers represented all the people in the United States, and the total income they shared was $100. In these first twelve minutes, twenty marchers would pass by whose income all together amounted to $3.20.

Gilbert suggests that the parade opens on an odd note because "it seems that the first people are marching in a deep ditch" (1998, 86). These people have suffered income losses, such as self-employed people whose expenses are higher than their income. Many people in this opening part of the parade receive at least part of their income from public assistance, social security, or veteran's benefits. Women, minorities, and children are overrepresented in the first part of the parade, especially children in female-headed households. Only 7.3 percent of white, non-Hispanic families were in poverty in 2012, compared with 25.6 percent of black families and 24.6 percent of Hispanic families (DeNavas-Walt, Proctor and Smith 2013, 54 and 57).

As of July 2009, the minimum wage was $7.25 an hour, so those who work forty hours a week for fifty weeks out of the year earn $14,500. They would appear in the parade as being nineteen inches tall. (The minimum wage is not indexed to inflation, so it increases irregularly, whenever Congress decides to raise it.)

At the close of the first segment of the parade, marchers would be earning $20,599 annually and be two feet four.

From Twelve to Twenty-Four Minutes

Next comes the 20 percent of income earners who collectively received 8.3 percent of all income. The poverty level for a family of two adults and two related children in 2012 was $23,283, and families earning this amount would be represented by a marcher almost two and a half feet tall.

In this category are families that have multiple-wage earners at marginal jobs and single-income families living off a wage from production or nonsupervisory work (average salary was about $20 per hour before taxes in 2012). Wages for this group tend to appreciate at about the rate of inflation, so "the average worker's wages are stuck in neutral" (Porter 2005). That is an accurate assessment about the recent past, but a longer-term view shows this group losing ground: in 1980, this group collectively received 11.6 percent of the income, about 3 percent more than it shared in 2012.

At the end of this part of the parade, with 40 percent of the families having passed by, marchers would be earning $39,764 and be almost four and a half feet tall.

From Twenty-Four to Thirty-Six Minutes

Now comes the middle 20 percent of income earners, who collectively received 14.5 percent of all income.

The median income of $51,017 crosses the line at thirty minutes into the parade. While there is a great deal of debate about who is included in the middle class, the median should be the midpoint of it. However, many households with incomes well over $100,000 see themselves as middle class even though they are in the top 20 percent of income earners.

At the end of this part of the parade, with more than half of the population represented, marchers would earn $64,582 and would be just over seven feet tall.

From Thirty-Six to Forty-Eight Minutes

The next 20 percent of income earners collectively received 23 percent of all income.

At the end of this segment, with the parade 80 percent finished, the marchers would earn $104,096 and be almost eleven and a half feet tall.

From Forty-Eight to Sixty Minutes

The highest-earning 20 percent of income earners collectively received 51 percent of all income, so this last twelve minutes represents more than half of all the income earned in the United States. The last twelve minutes show a greater range than other segments—from under twelve feet to miles tall—illustrating the large income that a relatively few households command.

At fifty-four minutes, 90 percent of the marchers would have passed by, and their height would now be sixteen feet ($146,000). At fifty-seven minutes, the top 5 percent of wage earners—who receive 22.3 percent of the income—would walk by, and their height would be almost twenty-one feet ($191,156). These marchers are likely to be professionals such as doctors and lawyers. Fifty-nine minutes into the parade, "We would be looking at 50-foot Goliaths, seconds after that, 200-foot King Kongs, and then the towering leviathans, thousands of feet tall" (Gilbert 1998, 89–90). Marchers from the last minute are likely to be corporate executives, hedge-fund managers, and a mix of celebrity entertainers and people in sports. For example, Sean Payton, coach for the National Football League's New Orleans Saints, was the highest-paid coach at $8 million a year (C. Smith 2013), making him 875 feet tall.

For CEOs, salary tends to be a small part of the overall pay or "compensation package," which includes stock options, spending allowances, and generous pensions that are frequently protected even during bankruptcy proceedings. In 2011 the average Standard & Poor's 500 CEO made $10.5 million (DeCarlo 2012), meaning he or she would stand 1,150 feet tall in the parade. However, the highest-paid CEO, John Hammergren of McKesson, made $131 million, making him nearly three miles tall.

Historically this top group has managed impressive gains, as revealed by a comparison with the average worker: in 1980, CEOs of the largest companies were paid forty times as much as the hourly wage earners at their companies, but in 2013 the average S&P 500 CEO made 204 times the average wages of the rank-and-file workers (Smith and Kuntz 2013). If the minimum wage increased at the same rate as the earnings of the top 1 percent, it would be $28.79 an hour in 2013 instead of $7.25 (Light 2013).

CEO pay grows faster than profits and other company performance measures. It remained high even as the financial crisis hit and firms went bankrupt or received bailout money. In a report, the New York attorney general noted, "When the banks did well, their employees were paid well. When the banks did poorly, their employees were paid well. And when the banks did very poorly, they were bailed out by taxpayers and their employees were still paid well" (Cuomo 2009, 1).

In the last minute of the parade are a number of celebrities—athletes and entertainers—who add some diversity to the largely white male CEOs. Rap star Kanye West and tennis star Serena Williams had incomes of $20 million, according to the most recent *Forbes* celebrity list (Forbes 2013b), making them almost 2,200 feet tall. Actress and singer Jennifer Lopez made $45 million, making her almost a mile tall. Oprah Winfrey's pay was $77 million, making her more than 8,400 feet (1.6 miles) tall. The top earner on the celebrity list was pop star Madonna, who made $125 million, making her 2.6 miles tall.

While the celebrities are visible and diverse, the top earners in any given year are hedge-fund managers, who tend to be white, male, and out-of-sight rich. In 2010, the twenty-five highest-paid hedge-fund managers earned four times what all five hundred CEOs of Fortune 500 companies earned (Lenzner 2013). So in the closing seconds of the parade for 2012 would be the tenth-highest-paid hedge-fund manager, Daniel Loeb, who made $380 million (Creswell 2013), and he would be almost eight miles tall. Number four, James Simons, crossed the *billion*-dollar mark by taking home $1.1 billion for the year, making him almost twenty-three miles tall. The final marcher would be David Tepper, who made $2.2 billion and would be just over forty-five miles tall.

Overall, the uneven distribution of income can be seen by considering that median income at thirty minutes was the median height of five feet seven inches, but at fifty-seven minutes marchers are twenty-one feet tall, and several minutes later the last marcher is more than 240,000 feet tall. Further, income is becoming more unequally distributed over time. Since 1990, the top 5 percent has increased the proportion of income it receives, while the bottom 80 percent has seen its share shrink.

Wealth Distribution

Income is only one way of examining the finances of households, and in many ways measures of wealth are more important. Measures of income look at salary for a year, whereas wealth looks at the accumulated assets and debt over a lifetime. Wealth includes bank accounts, ownership of stocks and bonds, retirement accounts, houses, cars, and ownership of businesses; it also includes debts such as car loans, student loans, mortgages, and credit card balances. Wealth thus provides security for setbacks in life, such as job loss, employment transition, and/or medical hardship. But because wealth also includes the ownership of financial assets such as businesses and stock—especially large blocks not held through a mutual fund or retirement account—it is also important for understanding economic and political power.

To help see the difference between income and wealth, compare boxer Michael Tyson and businessman Michael Dell. During his boxing career, Tyson earned about $400 million in income but managed to spend it in ways that left him declaring bankruptcy after hitting $34 million in debt (Schlabach 2005, E1). In contrast, Dell makes a lower salary per year than Tyson received for many individual fights, but as founder of Dell computers he has substantial business and stock ownership. As with others, his wealth will rise and fall along with the value of his company's stock, but his ownership of the business will continue to provide economic and political power.

More generally, whites had about eight times the wealth of blacks in 2010, the latest available data at the time of publication. The median wealth of whites was $130,600 compared with $15,500 for blacks (Bricker et al. 2012, 17, 21). Likewise, lists of people with high salaries tend to include minorities and women who are athletes and entertainers, but the lists of those with the largest wealth are much more likely to be white male businessmen. Indeed, the only minority on both the Forbes Celebrity 100 and Forbes Richest 400 was Oprah Winfrey at $2.7 billion in wealth, which put her at number 184.

To convey a sense of the wealth distribution, the income parade can be turned into a wealth parade, with the median height of five feet seven inches corresponding to median family net worth in 2010 of $77,300 (Bricker et al. 2012). Data from an earlier study indicated that the "typical" family

> has about $3,800 in the bank. No one has a retirement account, and the neighbors who do only have about $35,000 in theirs. Mutual funds? Stocks? Bonds? Nope. The house is worth $160,000, but the family owes $95,000 on it to the bank. The breadwinners make more than $43,000 a year but can't manage to pay off a $2,200 credit card balance. (N. Irwin 2006, F01)

Since this was written, a number of families in the lead-up to the financial crisis took on increasing housing-related debt, but the houses themselves are now worth less, so the households have lower net worth. Unemployment also erodes wealth as families dip into any savings and then sell stocks, bonds, and retirement account holdings.

The information for the parade is the Survey of Consumer Finances, which is done every three years. The survey deliberately excludes people in the Forbes 400, who are the four hundred richest people in the United States. Because of the large amount of wealth held by those at the top, their exclusion means the survey results understate inequality. For example, the survey indicates that in 2010, the top 1 percent of wealth holders has 34.5 percent of the wealth (Kennickell 2012, 12), but this figure excludes about $2 trillion in wealth held by the Forbes 400 (Kroll 2013).

While the discussion of the parade provides further breakdowns and additional information about wealth distribution, table 3.1 provides a summary of wealth and the distribution of certain assets and debt for 2007. (The Federal Reserve Board, which publishes the results of the survey, has not published this information for the 2010 survey—an example of declassed public discussions at a time of increasing inequality.) As noted above, direct ownership of stock and business is an important measure of ownership of the economy that translates into economic and political power. Even the more general measures of net wealth indicate that the combined worth of the poorest 50 percent of the population (about 150 million people) is only slightly higher than that held by the richest four hundred families (Kennickell 2009; see also Sum and Forsell 2009).

First Thirty Minutes

While this is a large segment of the parade to discuss at once, this 50 percent of families in the United States collectively owned only 1.1 percent of all wealth in 2010. Other countries have lower degrees of wealth inequality and report the owner-ship of wealth for each 10 or 20 percent of the population. But in the United States, the least wealthy have so little that the ownership of wealth by half of the country

Table 3.1. Shares of Net Worth and Distribution of Components, 2007

	Wealth Percentile Groups				
	0–50	*50–90*	*90–95*	*95–99*	*99–100*
Percentage of all net worth owned	2.5	26	11.1	26.6	33.8
Percentage of all stocks owned	0.6	9	8	30.5	51.9
Percentage of all business owned	0.4	6	5.4	25.5	62.7
Percentage of all credit card debt	43.1	45.8	5.6	4.3	1.2

Source: Kennickell 2009.

Note: The Forbes 400, the four hundred wealthiest families in the United States, were not included in the Survey of Consumer Finances used to produce table 3.1. In 2007, the Forbes 400 collectively had total wealth of over $1.5 trillion; the minimum wealth to make the list was $1.3 billion, and the wealthiest family had $59 billion in wealth.

is reported in one category—and at the other end, the top 1 percent has so much wealth that its members can be reported in one category.

As with the income parade, the first marchers would look as if they were in a ditch. Their bills and debts would be higher than their assets. About 10 percent of people have negative net worth (more debt than assets), so it would be six minutes into the parade before even the smallest of marchers appeared. Those marching from six until fifteen minutes have so little that the average net worth of the first fifteen minutes of marchers (25 percent of the population) is *negative* $13,000.

For these families, credit card debt tends to be high, along with auto loans that exceed the value of the car. Student loans contribute to the negative segment of the parade, but the education provides an increase in human capital, which relates over time to better income and jobs. Thus, while young people appear early in the parade, many of the students will start to accumulate some wealth over their lifetimes, while many of the women and minorities—who are also overrepresented here—will remain in this group. The median wealth of African Americans was $15,500, representing a marcher just over one foot tall.

The marchers who appear at twenty minutes, closing out one-third of the population, would be about two feet tall and have a net worth of about $30,000.

During the first half hour, assets tend to be in the form of checking and saving accounts plus vehicles. A majority of those marching after fifteen minutes own a home, although large mortgage balances mean the house does not contribute greatly to wealth. Ownership of business is negligible, reflecting both low levels of ownership and relatively small businesses. On the other hand, this 50 percent of the population has almost 50 percent of all the credit card debt. At the end of this segment of the 2010 parade, marchers would have the median wealth of $77,300 and be the median height of five feet seven.

Thirty to Fifty-Four Minutes

This segment, representing the fiftieth to ninetieth percentile, owned 24.3 percent of the wealth in 2010. In addition to larger checking and savings accounts, families are more likely to own stocks, bonds, and mutual funds; they are more likely to have retirement accounts that are better funded. They have larger houses, less debt, and a greater likelihood of owning rental property or second homes. This group still owns only a small amount of all business equity.

In this segment, the inequality is starting to show. At thirty minutes, the marchers were five foot seven inches; at thirty-seven minutes, they are more than eleven feet tall ($157,200), and at fifty minutes they are thirty-five feet tall ($482,700).

Fifty-Four to Fifty-Nine Minutes and Twenty-Four Seconds

This part of the parade represents the ninetieth to ninety-ninth percentile, which owned 40 percent of the net worth. At fifty-seven minutes, the top 5 percent of the wealth holders starts to parade by, starting at a height of more than 134 feet ($1,864,100).

Fifty-Nine Minutes and Twenty-Four Seconds to End (Final Thirty-Five Seconds)

This brief part of the parade covers the top 1 percent of wealth holders, who owned 34.5 percent of all wealth in 2010. The bottom 90 percent owned 25.4 percent, so there is substantially more wealth in the last thirty-five seconds than in the first fifty-four minutes of the parade.

In writing about wealth, a *Forbes* author noted that $50 million in net worth was common around Silicon Valley:

> The $50 million crowd typically owns a $5 million house—that's only 4,000 square feet on one acre in Atherton or Los Altos Hills—and a $2 million vacation place near, but not on, Lake Tahoe. They might own a golf membership or two at fancy clubs, costing $300,000 each, or perhaps sail around the world in their Hunter 50 cruising yacht or fly around the world in their Pilatus PC-12 turboprop. (Karlgaard 2011)

But that's still a long way from the Forbes 400 list, which for 2012–2013 required $1.3 billion in wealth. They would be almost one hundred thousand feet (eighteen miles) tall, which is a huge increase from the 134-foot marchers representing the start of the top 5 percent.

Even within the Forbes 400, there is a substantial distance between those at the bottom and top of the list. Many people are crowded together at the bottom, where several hundred million dollars in additional wealth can catapult a person many ranks up the list. But breaking into the top one hundred wealthiest requires $4.6 billion, which would be represented by a height of about sixty-three miles, another large increase in only a second or so of parade time.

Rupert Murdoch, owner of Fox media, is number thirty at $13.4 billion, making him 183 miles tall and a powerful figure in global politics because of his media properties. Mark Zuckerberg, founder of Facebook, is number twenty, with $19 billion (260 miles tall). Breaking into the top ten requires $31 billion (424 miles) and is a place held by New York City mayor Michael Bloomberg, who also owns Bloomberg financial media. The top spot belongs to Microsoft founder Bill Gates, at $72 billion in wealth and a height of 985 miles.

SOCIAL SPHERE

The market structure and venture capital system in the United States do provide degrees of openness and opportunity for changing one's class. Because of high levels of inequality, citizens potentially have a high degree of mobility, but that should not be confused with the likelihood of social mobility. Stories of self-made millionaires and billionaires are likely to be popular because they confirm the idea of mobility and the American dream, but stories are different from a study of exactly how often it happens. Further, Americans seem willing to tolerate higher levels of inequality than other countries because of the belief that there is more mobility here—but that is, unfortunately, not the case.

According to the Organisation for Economic Co-operation and Development (OECD), rising levels of inequality "can stifle upward social mobility, making it harder for talented and hard-working people to get the rewards they deserve" (quoted in Corak 2013, 79). An economist with the Federal Reserve Bank of Chicago notes that "income mobility has declined in the last 20 years" (Francis 2005) as inequality has increased. The article "The American Dream Gains a Harder Edge" notes that most Americans do not believe mobility has declined, "but academic studies suggest that income mobility in the U.S. is no better than in France or Britain."

A number of researchers have approached this topic and looked at the earnings of parents and adult children to measure upward and downward mobility across generations. They find that inequality produces an "inequality of opportunity":

> Socioeconomic status influences a child's health and aptitudes in early years—indeed even in utero—which in turn influences early cognitive and social development, and readiness to learn. These outcomes and the family circumstances of children, as well as the quality of neighborhoods and schools, influence success in primary school, which feeds into success in high school and college. Family resources and connections affect access to good schools and jobs, and the degree of inequality in labor markets determines both the resources parents have and ultimately the return to the education the children receive. This entire process then shapes earnings in adulthood. (Corak 2013, 85)

We would add that with law enforcement and criminal justice focused on those at the bottom, criminal records are also more likely, which adds to social exclusion and limits a person's earning potential.

This explanation is not meant to be deterministic and recognizes that mobility happens; it is attempting to explain why it happens less frequently than people think (Scott and Leonhardt 2005). Specifically, in "Finland, Norway, and Denmark, the tie between parental economic status and the adult earnings of children is weakest: less than one-fifth of any economic advantage or disadvantage that a father may have had in his time are passed on to a son in adulthood. In Italy, the United kingdom and the United States, roughly 50 percent of any advantage or disadvantage is passed on" (Corak 2013, 81).

Notice that while much of this discussion is presented as being about mobility in general, the underlying research is based on studies of men's mobility. Drawing conclusions about everyone based on studies of men is a common problem in social science, medical, criminological, and other research (see chapter 6). While women have claimed a permanent role in the workforce, their struggle to enter the workforce and break glass ceilings (that limit upward mobility) is erased; most research implies that they have the same mobility patterns as men when they do not, or it implies that their mobility does not matter. Many key issues about the labor force are then not discussed, such as the male models of successful leadership that women are expected to emulate even while they are criticized for acting assertively. Male standards of success require women to work long hours away from their families, which by itself is unproblematic when gender expectations are widened to include dual caretaking responsibilities for men. But many women still face social ridicule for spending more time at work than at home when they have families and even more ridicule when women choose to remain unmarried and child-free. So while some businesswomen are still expected to work the same number of hours as men when they have children, men are still not expected to stay at home or to pull a "second shift" at home after work.

POLITICAL SPHERE

For at least some purposes, American law treats corporations as "persons." The legal fiction of corporate "persons" means their size should also be considered in order to have a full understanding of how income and wealth affect the treatment of persons under the law. The intense concentration of wealth in corporations generates considerable political power, makes accountability increasingly difficult, and increases inequality in a way that is invisible to criminological theory.

Corporations now grow to unlimited size so that their money power now dwarfs that of (most) individuals. For example, Facebook is number 482 on the 2013 list of *Fortune* magazine's five hundred largest companies (Fortune 2013), and with revenue (income) of $5.1 billion they would be 106 miles tall. Wal-Mart is the largest of the Fortune 500 companies, with revenue of $469.2 billion, which would represent a height in the income parade of more than fifty-one million feet—well over 9,700 miles tall, compared with the average height of five feet seven inches! Such an income makes it gargantuan in relation to not only individuals but also cities, states, and even the federal government that is supposed to regulate and control corporations.

Indeed, rather than comparing modern corporations with individuals, they can instead be compared with countries. Specifically, the revenue of a corporation can be compared with the gross domestic product (GDP) of a country, which is the total value of all the goods and services that it produces (Leighton 2013). The result, displayed in table 3.2, shows how corporations and countries compare in terms of the largest economies in the world.

Moreover, the large concentrations of wealth by these megacorporations translate into political power that is also exercised through corporate lobbyists and political action committees (PACs). PACs that donate thousands—or even millions—of dollars can achieve considerable clout, especially because only 0.08 percent of the adult population gave more than $200 to a political party or candidate during the 2012 election cycle (OpenSecrets.org, n.d.). Many corporate interests donate heavily to both political parties to ensure access to legislators and favorable action on their legislation, regardless of which party wins the election. Further influence and

Table 3.2. World's Largest Economies: GDP and Fortune 500 Revenue, 2010

Overall Rank	Country Rank	Company Rank	Country/Company	GDP/Revenue (in billions of US$)
1	1		United States	$15,064.8
11	11		Canada	$1,758.7
21	21		Saudi Arabia	$560.3
30		1	Wal-Mart Stores	$421.8
31	30		United Arab Emirates	$358.1
32		2	ExxonMobil	$354.6
51		3	Chevron	$196.3
52	49		Romania	$185.3
53		4	ConocoPhillips	$184.9
57	53		Kuwait	$171.1
62		6	General Electric	$151.6
63	57		Hungary	$147.9
65		8	General Motors	$135.6
66		9	Bank of America Corp.	$134.2
70	58		Vietnam	$121.6
71		13	JPMorgan Chase & Co.	$115.5
72	59		Bangladesh	$115.0
73		14	Citigroup	$111.1
86		23	Wells Fargo	$93.2
134		54	Goldman Sachs Group	$46.0
136	81		Uzbekistan	$43.7
146	84		Costa Rica	$40.0
147		63	Morgan Stanley	$39.3

Source: Fortune 500 from CNNMoney.com. http://money.cnn.com/magazines/fortune/fortune500/2011/full_list/. International Monetary Fund, World Economic Outlook Database, September 2011. http://www.imf.org/external/pubs/ft/weo/2011/02/weodata/index.aspx.

Note: Gross domestic product is expressed in current (2011) US dollars.

consideration comes from the corporate use of "the slush fund, the kickback, the stock award, the high-paying job offer from industry, the lavish parties and prostitutes, the meals, transportation, housing, and vacation accommodations, and the many other hustling enticements of money" (Simon 1999, 24).

The result of this influence can be tax breaks, less regulation and/or policing, and/or limits on the extent of punishment (harms are misdemeanors rather than felonies, are civil matters rather than criminal, or have limits on the size of damages juries are allowed to award against businesses). An excellent example is the process to establish sentencing guidelines for corporate misconduct. In 1984, Congress established the US Sentencing Commission to help create guidelines that would make federal sentencing more certain and uniform in criminal cases. The guidelines are a grid that judges use to plot both the severity of the offense and an individual's record to find an appropriate range for the sentence. The first set of guidelines in 1987 did not address corporate crime, although the 1990 ones did.

Instead of $5,000 or less—the amount levied in four-fifths of all corporate convictions from 1975 to 1976—fines were set as high as $364 million (Etzioni 1990, C3). After a "steamroller of business lobbyists" took notice, the commission released a revised set of guidelines in which the potential fines were "slashed." Mitigating factors were given more weight, and aggravating factors (such as a prior record) were removed from consideration (Etzioni 1990). Penalties for a level 25 offense were revised down from $136 million to $580,000, and the maximum fine went from $364 million to $12.6 million. Later, then attorney general Dick Thornburgh, who had called fighting crime in the suites one of his top priorities, "withdrew the Justice Department's long-standing support for tough mandatory sentences for corporate criminals following an intense lobbying campaign by defense contractors, oil companies and other Fortune 500 firms" (Isikoff 1990, A1).

After the half-*trillion*-dollar savings and loan scandals of the late 1980s, Congress did increase penalties for some financial crimes and added some financial regulations. But according to the authors of *Big Money Crime*, soon after the savings and loan crisis Congress went on a spree of "cavalier" financial deregulation, spurred on by lobbying and political donations and creating the "paradox of increasing financial deregulation coming on the heels of the most catastrophic experiment with deregulation in history" (Calavita, Pontell, and Tillman 1997). In turn, this deregulation created the conditions for the string of corporate corruption in 2001–2002 that included Enron, WorldCom, and many others (Leighton and Reiman 2002). Congress passed the Sarbanes-Oxley Act to correct some of the systemic causes of widespread fraud. But with the passage of time, businesses felt increasingly comfortable lobbying against many of the safeguards put in place to protect shareholders (Leighton and Reiman 2004).

Further, the financial services industry lobbied to deregulate many aspects of their business, which resulted in the financial crisis of 2008–2009, and now they have been lobbying quietly behind the scenes to block much-needed reform after the $700 million bailout (Barak 2012). Indeed, Barry Ritholtz—the CEO of an investment research firm and author of *Bailout Nation* (2009a)—argues that the financial crisis has been "wasted": there was "smoldering resentment" among people because of the "massive taxpayer wealth transfer to inept, corrupt, incompetent bankers." This provided the "best chance to clean up Wall Street in five generations," but "what we got instead, was the usual lobbying efforts by the finance industry. They own Congress, lock stock and barrel, and they throttled Financial Reform" (2009c). Congressman Barney Frank, cosponsor of the Dodd-Frank financial reform legislation, says the bill is "facing a death through a thousand cuts" because of lobbying (Rivlin 2011). Financial institutions aim their sights both at putting loopholes in new rules and at reducing the budgets of enforcement agencies.

Although real people convicted of felonies lose their voting rights, corporations convicted of multiple felonies lose none of their political rights—and in some cases try to lobby Congress to weaken the law under which they were convicted. Further, corporate charters themselves act as a shield from the public and give corporations permission to act in the best interests of shareholders rather than the larger public good. Thus,

> the corporation is now a superhuman creature of the law, superior to you and me, since it has civil rights but no civil responsibilities; it is legally obligated to be selfish; it cannot be thrown in jail; it can deduct from its tax bill any fines it gets for wrongdoings; and it can live forever. (Hightower 1998b, 34)

While many of the individual men and women who work in the corporation make good neighbors, the corporation itself can be a problem because "the corporation's legally defined mandate is to pursue, relentlessly and without exception, its own self-interest, regardless of the often harmful consequences it might cause to others" (Bakan 2004, 2). Indeed, Joel Bakan asked Robert Hare, a noted expert on psychopathologies, to apply his diagnostic checklist to corporations and found a close match: they are irresponsible by putting others at risk; manipulative of everything, including public opinion; lacking in empathy for others and unable to feel remorse; unwilling to accept responsibility; and superficial in relating to others (2004, 56–57). Just as psychopaths are known for their superficial charm, corporations may "act in ways to promote the public good when it is to their advantage to do so, but they will just as quickly sacrifice it—it is their legal obligation to do so—when necessary to serve their own ends" (118).

Thus, protecting people—citizens, workers, consumers, communities, and the environment—from the excesses of corporate behavior is an important function of law. But this social control is brought into question by donations and strategic lobbying on the part of corporations. When the size of corporate actors is combined with their institutional personality, the dark side of big business becomes visible. Obviously, not all businesses are bad, and the point is that there is a problematic antisocial tendency that must be kept in check, but the control mechanisms to regulate and hold corporations accountable have become less powerful relative to the corporations themselves.

IMPLICATIONS

This chapter began by noting the reluctance in our society to discuss issues of economic class. In spite of real differences in class, in popular media "people dwell in a classless homogenized American Never-Never Land" where "the pecking order of sex and looks has replaced the old hierarchy of jobs and money" (McGrath 2005). Class thus becomes less visible and less subject to honest conversation. This chapter has made class more visible by reviewing the economic facts and setting a foundation for how this impacts criminology and criminal justice. This chapter has not made a case for or against the current distributions of income and wealth, but we would like to leave readers with some thoughts about how to evaluate the justice of the current situation.

John Rawls has written some important contemporary works about justice in which he argues that justice is the result of decisions that people would make about society from behind a "veil of ignorance." That is, people would design a fair society if they had to make choices not knowing their position in that society, so they could appear as rich or poor, white or minority, male or female, and so on. So, a starting point for examining economic inequality would be to ask: If you were going to be randomly placed in a society, what would you want the distribution of income and wealth to look like?

Researchers actually put this question to a sample of five thousand people and found a high degree of consensus from people across the political spectrum for distributions of wealth that are far more equal than what currently exists in the United States (Norton and Ariely 2011). The researchers did more than simply compare this "ideal" to the actual distribution of wealth; they asked people what they believed the distribution of wealth to be. The researchers conclude that

> Americans also construct ideal distributions that are far more equal than they estimated the United States to be—estimates which themselves were far more equal than the actual level of inequality. Second, there was much more consensus than disagreement across groups from different sides of the political spectrum about this desire for a more equal distribution of wealth, suggesting that Americans may possess a commonly held "normative" standard for the distribution of wealth despite the many disagreements about policies that affect that distribution, such as taxation and welfare. (Norton and Ariely 2011, 12)

The full results are available in table 3.3, which indicates that Americans believed the top 20 percent should own 32 percent of the wealth, when in fact they own 84 percent. On the other side of the distribution, Americans believed the bottom 60 percent should own 45 percent of the wealth, when in reality they own less than 5 percent.

The other striking aspect of this research is that Americans' beliefs about the amount of inequality the country really has underestimate inequality by a substantial amount. People believe the top 20 percent own 59 percent of the wealth when they really own 84 percent; people believe the bottom 60 percent own 20 percent of the wealth when they really own less than 5 percent. These mistakes about economic facts hide the true amount of inequality and thus support the unequal status quo. When ideas—whether intentionally or not—"distort reality in a way that justifies

Table 3.3.   Actual, Perceived, and Ideal Distributions of Wealth in the United States

Wealth of Poorest 60%		Wealth of Richest 20%
5%	Actual amount of wealth	84%
20%	Perceived amount of wealth	59%
45%	Ideal amount of wealth	32%

Source. Calculated from Norton and Ariely 2011.

the prevailing distribution of power and wealth, hides society's injustices, and thus secures uncritical allegiance to the existing social order, we have what Marx called ideology" (Reiman and Leighton 2013, 195).

Criminology and criminal justice have a role in creating ideology because income and wealth are not part of the "official knowledge" about crime and crime control, even though they are important factors to understand. Indeed, a twenty-five-year retrospective on the 1967 President's Crime Commission stated: "While evidence shows that criminal justice procedures are more evenhanded than in the past, it is also painfully obvious that the growing gap between rich and poor, and white and black, continues to make criminal justice a social battleground rather than a mechanism to increase social peace" (Conley 1994, 66).

Because of the long history of racism, blacks, Hispanics, and Native Americans are disproportionately poor, so issues of class and race are tied together in ways that will be explored in other chapters. The current and evolving problem is that criminal justice is contributing to the differences between rich and poor and the separation of whites from minorities. Current domestic policies of crime control operate as if "Americans have concluded that the problems of the urban poor are intractable and therefore they [apparently agreed to have their money] spent on a vast network of prisons, rather than on solutions" (quoted in Welch 1996a, 101) and basic social and educational services for the poor. Some of these programs are cheaper than prisons and have the potential to reduce crime by preventing child abuse, enhancing the intellectual and social development of children, providing support and mentoring to vulnerable adolescents, and doing intensive work with juvenile offenders (Currie 1998, 81).

John Irwin and James Austin captured the essence of this problem almost two decades ago, and the "enormous policy dilemma" they articulated ultimately as a problem of inequality and economic class has only intensified since then:

> On the one hand, we are expending a greater portion of our public dollars on incarcerating, punishing, treating and controlling persons who are primarily from the lower economic classes in an effort to reduce crime. On the other hand, we have set in motion economic policies that serve to widen the gap between the rich and poor, producing yet another generation of impoverished youths who will probably end up under control of the correctional system. By escalating the size of the correctional system, we are also increasing the tax burden and diverting billions of dollars from those very public services (education, health, transportation, and economic development) that would reduce poverty, unemployment, crime, drug abuse and mental illness. (1997, 10–11)

While the levels of inequality and economic mobility have important implications for the American dream and for criminological theories such as strain or conflict theory, criminology does not pursue these ideas in a way that would increase consciousness of class, inequality, and stratification. Sadly, the criminal justice system reflects the class biases in society—and helps to reinforce them. The United States has enlarged its apparatuses of criminal justice and crime control against the poorest members in society while the rich, especially corporations, continue to gather more wealth and feel unaccountable for the adverse consequences of their privileged behavior on the "teeming masses."

REVIEW AND DISCUSSION QUESTIONS

1. Why don't Americans know the actual levels of inequality between classes?
2. Discuss the differences and overlaps among income, wealth, and financial assets.
3. If you were going to be randomly placed in a society, how would you distribute wealth in that society? Would it look like the United States?
4. What are some of the problems caused by class inequality? What are some of the problems caused by unaccountable corporations?
5. Why is the issue of class important for understanding criminology and criminal justice?

4

Understanding Race and White Privilege

In Plessy v. Ferguson *(163 U.S. 537 [1896]), the Supreme Court set the precedent of "separate but equal": separate facilities for blacks did not offend constitutional provisions about equal protection so long as they were equal to those provided whites. Louisiana law required separate railway cars, and when Plessy sat in a car designated for whites only, the conductor told him to leave. As the court described it, on Plessy's "refusal to comply with such order, he was, with the aid of a police officer, forcibly ejected from said coach, and hurried off to, and imprisoned in, the parish jail."*

The court found that the requirement of separate accommodations was a reasonable regulation, made "with reference to the established usages, customs, and traditions of the people, and with a view to the promotion of their comfort, and the preservation of the public peace and good order." Social prejudices cannot be overcome by legislation, and if the races "are to meet upon terms of social equality, it must be the result of natural affinities, a mutual appreciation of each other's merits, and a voluntary consent of individuals." Although Plessy argued that enforced separation "stamps the colored race with a badge of inferiority," the majority held that it is "not by reason of anything found in the act, but solely because the colored race chooses to put that construction upon it."

What is less known about the case is that Plessy "was seven-eighths Caucasian and one-eighth African blood; that the mixture of colored blood was not discernible in him." The suit involved a claim "that he was entitled to every right, privilege, and immunity secured to citizens of the United States of the white race." Plessy argued that "in a mixed community, the reputation of belonging to the dominant race, in this instance the white race, is 'property,' in the same sense that a right of action or of inheritance is property." The court conceded it was for the purposes of the case but argued that the statute did not take his property: either he was a white man who was entitled or a black man who was not. But who decides, and how? The train conductor seemed to have power to make racial classifications, which would result in arbitrary decisions, but the court did not

105

see that issue as properly before it. The state legislatures could guide decisions on racial classifications, but some said "any visible admixture of black blood stamps the person as belonging to the colored race; others, that it depends upon the preponderance of blood; and still others, that the predominance of white blood must only be in the proportion of three-fourths."

Justice Harlan was the sole dissenter, claiming that the decision would prove to be as "pernicious" as the Dred Scott *case, which declared that escaped slaves who traveled north to freedom were still property and should be returned to their southern masters. For Harlan, the statute seemed inconsistent, for example, in allowing black nurses to attend white children but not a white adult in bad health. Harlan also pointed to another group that "is a race so different from our own that we do not permit those belonging to it to become citizens of the United States" and are "with few exceptions, absolutely excluded from our country." But under the law "a Chinaman can ride in the same passenger coach with white citizens," yet blacks, "many of whom, perhaps, risked their lives for the pres-ervation of the Union, who are entitled, by law, to participate in the political control of the state and nation, who are not excluded, by law or by reason of their race, from public stations of any kind, and who have all the legal rights that belong to white citizens, are yet declared to be criminals, liable to imprisonment, if they ride in a public coach occupied by citizens of the white race."*

Harlan wondered whether the court's ruling about the reasonableness of separation would allow a town to assign the races to different sides of the street, a courtroom, or a jury box. Unlike the majority, Harlan argued the purpose of the law was to compel blacks to "keep to themselves" while traveling rather than keep whites out of black areas, and "no one would be so wanting in candor as to assert the contrary." He acknowledged that whites were the dominant race and said that while "every true man has pride of race" that can be shown in appropriate situations, the Thirteenth Amendment abolished slavery and "prevents the imposition of any burdens or disabilities that constitute badges of slavery or servitude." Even though whites were the dominant race and "will continue to be so for all time," he was clear that

> *in view of the Constitution, in the eye of the law, there is in this country no superior, domi-nant, ruling class of citizens. There is no caste here. Our Constitution is color-blind, and nei-ther knows nor tolerates classes among citizens. In respect of civil rights, all citizens are equal before the law. The humblest is the peer of the most powerful. The law regards man as man, and takes no account of his surroundings or of his color when his civil rights as guaranteed by the supreme law of the land are involved.*

The previous chapter reviewed inequalities in income and wealth to establish the foundations for later discussion of how economic bias undermines the ideal of equal-ity before the law such that the poorest is not the peer of the most powerful. This chapter provides an overview of how race influences our view of who our "peers" are to provide a foundation for future discussion of the extent to which racial and ethnic minorities are treated as equals or peers under a criminal justice system that should be color-blind. While the election of a biracial man as president signals progress in overcoming discrimination, claims that the United States is now in a "postracial" era are wildly exaggerated. President Obama (2009) noted:

> There's probably never been less discrimination in America than there is today. But make no mistake: the pain of discrimination is still felt in America. By African-American women being paid less for doing the same work as colleagues of a different color and gender. By Latinos made to feel unwelcome in their own country. By Muslim Americans viewed with suspicion for simply kneeling down to pray. By our gay brothers and sisters, still taunted, still attacked, still denied their rights.

Despite progress in some areas, racial discrimination still persists in the administration of justice as exemplified by racial profiling and is magnified through each step of the criminal justice process to result in serious minority overrepresentation of blacks and Latinos in prison. Michelle Alexander (2012) argues that the impact of criminal laws and their enforcement creates *The New Jim Crow*.

While this chapter makes generalizations about the experiences common to all minority groups within a system in which the whites are the dominant group, it also recognizes the importance of diversity. Each minority group has its own unique history that influences its members' views of, and experiences in, the United States. Indeed, just "as it is presumptuous to consider a Bostonian Irishman, an Anglo-California yuppie, a Jewish Greenwich Village artist, a Texas rodeo star, and a New Age Santa Fe vegetarian as all the same because they are coincidentally 'white,' it is just as unwise to render all 'Latinos' (or Asians or African Americans) as inherently alike" (Burnley et al., 23). Among Hispanics, wide variations exist, with those of Cuban background generally being better situated in terms of income, employment, health, and education than Puerto Ricans or Mexicans or Mexican Americans. Further, women frequently have a different experience than men of a minority group because of *gendered racism*, a term used to reflect the overlapping systems of gender and racial discrimination.

At the same time, members of racially and ethnically diverse minority groups are all victims of ideological racism, in which dominant group traits are overvalued while those of other groups are devalued. Although race is not merely an extension of class, part of the common experiences of most minorities is their overall lower economic status as a result of long-term discrimination in employment, education, and housing, among other significant factors that influence a person's well-being. Occupying a lower economic stratum in a society that confers privilege on people who occupy higher economic strata makes poor minorities vulnerable to exploitation and control by the criminal justice system. Thus, understanding the political economy of an era and the influence that wealth and race have on the perception of a human's value in the United States is where any discussion about privilege should begin. Certainly, the need for cheap labor or a surplus of workers is a key factor in understanding why emphasis is placed on a quasi-caste system—one that is fortified by the belief in natural differences between people but is fundamentally unjust. Historically, for example,

> the African slave trade began in earnest only after large-scale Native American slavery proved impractical in North America. The abolition of slavery led to the importation of low-wage labor from Asia. Legislation banning immigration from Asia set the stage for the recruitment of low-wage labor from Mexico. The new racial categories that emerged in each of these eras all revolved around applying racial labels to "nonwhite" groups in order to exploit them while at the same time preserving the value of whiteness. (Lipsitz 2005, 68)

The criminal justice system has played a significant role in these processes of exploitation and marginalization. After the Civil War, the criminal justice system swept the newly freed slaves off the streets and leased them back to plantation owners for a profit (Oshinsky 1996). After the completion of the transcontinental railroad and the economic recession in the 1870s, the criminal justice system responded to surplus labor and white fears by passing the Chinese Exclusion Act of 1892, outlawing opium use among Chinese but not whites (Lusane 1991, 31). The desire for land and natural resources led to the forced relocation of Native Americans and the wholesale violation of all treaties signed by the US government and sovereign tribes (Lazarus 1991). In each case, minority group entanglement with law and criminal justice was related to changes in the political economy and was justified by an ideology of white supremacy that devalued minority groups. In each case, too, criminal justice served to maintain white privilege by regulating cheap labor, economic competition, and perceived social threats.

The racism that criminal justice both reflects and re-creates is thus part of the "sociology of waste" that squanders the talent and potential of minority groups (Feagin and Vera 1995). People of color pay the heaviest and most direct price because of white supremacy, but "few whites realize the huge amount of energy and talent that whites themselves have dissipated in their construction of anti-black attitudes and ideologies and in their participation in social discrimination" (Feagin and Vera 1995, 2). Racism diverts the attention of whites and causes them to scapegoat minority groups rather than "seeing clearly their own class exploitation and . . . organizing effectively with black and other minority workers" (Feagin and Vera 1995, 15).

The rest of this chapter is divided into three discussions. First, we discuss how race and ethnicity are socially constructed concepts, meaning that an arbitrary set of biological markers is used to signify a racial category that is manufactured for political purposes. We then define key terms such as racism, stereotypes, discrimination, and prejudice. Of particular importance is the idea of privilege and understanding that whites also have race. Finally, we examine the status of minorities in economic, political, and social terms.

One final note on the terminology of this chapter is necessary because so many terms are used to refer to racial groups. Of necessity, we must use the language of resources we consulted for this book. For example, governmental data and authors who follow the government classification system use *black* and *American Indian*. We are aware that many minorities prefer *African American* and *Native American*, and we use these terms as well, both when our sources do and interchangeably with "official" terms. *Native American* refers to American Indians, and the capitalization designates their status as aborigines or First Peoples on the land before it became the United States. Asian Indians are from India. At times, to capture the history of discrimination or someone's prejudice, we include quotations that are intended by the original speaker to be derogatory. We do not endorse these attitudes or the use of racial epithets but believe it is important to accurately portray the attitudes that have been held.

THE SOCIAL CONSTRUCTION OF ETHNICITY AND RACE

Race is socially defined as a collection of physical traits. *Ethnicity* refers to national origin, language, culture, and religion. There is some overlap between race and ethnicity because both categories imply that there are physical characteristics in common among members of some groups, but in general, race more often refers to biological features whereas ethnicity more often refers to behavioral features. Some of this overlap is confusing. For example, in 2010 the Bureau of the Census had five categories of race: White, Black or African American, American Indian or Alaska Native, Asian, and Native Hawaiian or Other Pacific Islander. For respondents unable to identify with any of these five race categories, the 2000 and 2010 censuses included a sixth category—Some Other Race. The census treats race and ethnicity as separate concepts. So for the 2010 census, "Hispanic or Latino" refers to a person of Cuban, Mexican, Puerto Rican, South or Central American, or other Spanish culture or origin regardless of race.

Explaining why we count this way is a political history that highlights the importance of understanding that racial categories are socially constructed—and that the process of manufacturing them carries great social consequences. Back in the 1930s, in response to congressional debate about immigration restrictions, the census created a category of "Mexican." It was an additional racial category, thus officially declaring Mexicans to be nonwhite, even though Mexicans had been slipped in with whites for purposes of school segregation and Jim Crow laws because their blood did not have "negro ancestry." After the census, the Mexican government and Mexican Americans successfully lobbied to have the classification changed: "Although having their whiteness restored did not lessen discrimination, the Mexican government and Mexican Americans fully understood the implication of being officially recognized as a non-White group" (Foley 2005, 60). When Congress again called for the creation of statistics on people of Spanish culture, origin, and descent in the 1970s, political lobbying resulted in the current system of ethnicity being separate from race so that Hispanics would not automatically be nonwhite.

The political lobbying should not be seen as defeating an "objective" system of classification because there are no genetic markers that allow for the identification of race, and geneticists are unable to determine race from a DNA sample. Two randomly selected people from the world's population would have about 99.8 percent of their genetic material in common (Feagin and Feagin 1996). Scientists agree that modern humans originated from a small population that emerged out of Africa and migrated around the globe, so there is a continuum of genetic variation that makes the concept of race meaningless to geneticists. The various racial categories thus represent a social-political construct that reflects a negotiated definition of race recognized in the United States.

Indeed, the 2010 census lists fifteen racial categories and provides space to write in specific "races" not listed on the form. As figure 4.1 reveals, though, much of the new information about "race" is really capturing nationality—and the borders of many countries are arbitrary, constantly changing political compromises. For example, the form lists "Pakistani" under "other Asian," but Pakistan split in 1947 from what was then British India. The borders of British India were based on trade deals originally established by the British East India Company, which gradually came to colonize and rule India before turning it over to the British government. Pakistan's population was largely Muslim (and it is now an Islamic republic) while India's population is mostly Hindu, so there are differences between the countries—just not racial. Other na-

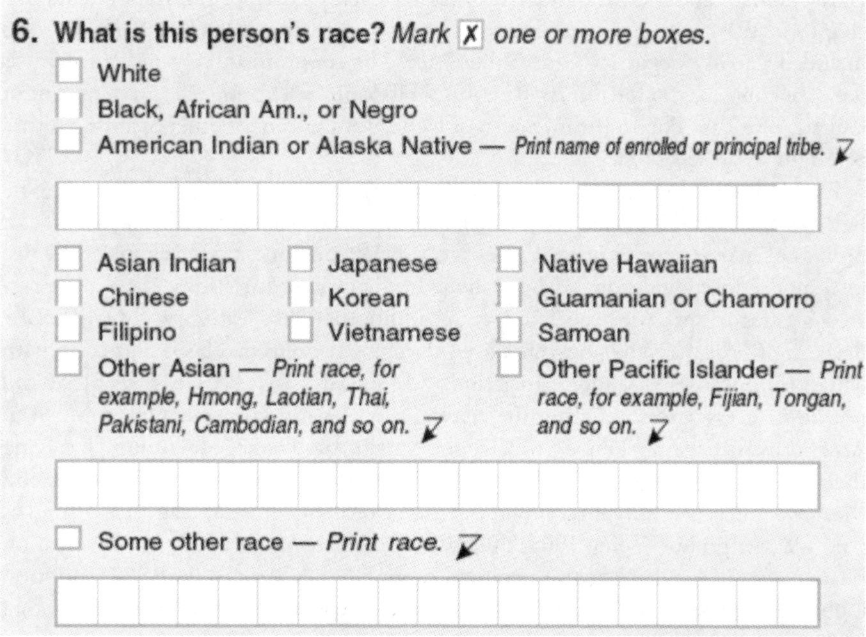

6. What is this person's race? *Mark* ☒ *one or more boxes.*

- ☐ White
- ☐ Black, African Am., or Negro
- ☐ American Indian or Alaska Native — *Print name of enrolled or principal tribe.*
- ☐ Asian Indian
- ☐ Chinese
- ☐ Filipino
- ☐ Other Asian — *Print race, for example, Hmong, Laotian, Thai, Pakistani, Cambodian, and so on.*
- ☐ Japanese
- ☐ Korean
- ☐ Vietnamese
- ☐ Native Hawaiian
- ☐ Guamanian or Chamorro
- ☐ Samoan
- ☐ Other Pacific Islander — *Print race, for example, Fijian, Tongan, and so on.*
- ☐ Some other race — *Print race.*

Figure 4.1. Racial Categories for the 2010 Census

Source: Population Reference Bureau, http://www.prb.org/Census2010/Questionaire.aspx.

tionalities listed on the form are similarly based on political, economic, and military history rather than reflecting "natural" home states for discrete "races."

Still, many people—not just white supremacists—believe race is an objective fact; they see race as part of their essence, inherent to them, even a property of the blood flowing through them (see box 4.1). Physical differences do exist among people, and some of these traits are linked to biology and genetics, but the social construction approach recognizes that selecting the number of racial categories, deciding what characteristics determine the categories, and assigning people to the categories is ultimately an attempt to segregate people based on a manufactured view of their social worth as defined by white supremacy. In reality, there is no such difference. For example, in *Plessy*, the court ducked this very question of what makes a person black—a single drop of blood, half heritage, two-thirds, or any visible trace? All of these have been used by various state legislatures. Up to 1967, many states had antimiscegenation laws that prohibited whites from marrying members of a different race, which required specific definitions of race in order for state registrars to certify a person's racial composition. In Virginia, *white* meant "no trace whatever of any blood other than Caucasian; but persons who have one-sixteenth or less of the blood of the American Indian and have no other non-Caucasian blood shall be deemed to be white persons" (*Loving v. Virginia*, 388 U.S. 1). The fraction of Native American blood was based on the "desire of all to recognize as an integral and honored part of the white race the descendants of John Rolfe and Pocahontas."

The "mixed race" option introduced in the 2000 census is another good example of the social construction of race. The census had previously forced people of multiple races to specify only one, but they now have the option of reporting what they feel are the "important" racial identities in their background or simply focusing on one. One of many who described himself as black has a white Jewish father and an African-Bermudan mother: "Checking more than one race," he contends, "would undermine the influence of blacks by reducing their number as a distinct group and so most likely diluting public policies addressing their concerns" (quoted in Schemo 2000; see also Brune 1999). But others are embracing the option: 3 percent of Americans (nine million people) identified with more than one race in the 2010 census. Indeed, "in the past decade, the U.S. experienced substantial growth among people who reported more than one race. . . . No states had less than 1.0% multiple-race reporting in 2010" (Jones and Bullock 2013). The number of multiple-race people in the United States, then, has increased, thereby blurring the shape of traditional race categories and perhaps rendering them useless.

Further undermining any claim that race is an objective, fixed status is that between 1960 and 2000, the Native American population doubled, mostly because of increased self-identification on census forms. There is less "taint" from being Native American (Brune 1999), and the popularity of genealogy websites has increased "ethnic shifting" or "ethnic shopping" among whites (Hitt 2005). A number of whites go ethnic shopping to see whether there is an ethnic ancestor in their past they can use as a basis for a different identity—and Native American is one of the most popular.

BOX 4.1.   RACE AND BLOOD

Hans Serelman was a doctor in Germany in 1935. His patient needed a blood transfusion, which at the time was done by finding a live donor rather than using stored blood. Unable to find a suitable donor quickly enough, the doctor opened his own artery and donated his own blood. Instead of receiving praise, the Jewish doctor was sent to a concentration camp for defiling the blood of the German race.

In the succeeding years, Germany moved to eliminate the "Jewish influence" from medicine by limiting access to patients and medical school. To bolster claims of Aryan supremacy, the study of blood became a focus for distinguishing Aryans from Jews. The combined effects of these initiatives dealt a self-inflicted wound to the Nazi war effort. Hastily trained and inexperienced paramedics replaced the more than eight thousand Jewish doctors barred from practice. The infusion of mythology and misapplied anthropology set back serious scientific research on blood. The Nuremberg Laws severely limited the availability of blood for transfusions because of the possibility of being charged with "an attack on German blood" if the donor could not prove it was pure Aryan blood (Starr 1998, 26).

In the United States, the topic of "colored" versus "white" blood also stirred up controversy during World War II. The Red Cross knew that "blood was blood" and did not differentiate it by race but nevertheless followed the wishes of the military and refused to collect blood from African Americans. Following the attack on Pearl Harbor and the large demand for blood to treat many wounded soldiers, the Red Cross collected blood from blacks but labeled and processed it separately. As historian Douglas Starr notes, "The policy proved offensive to many Americans because the country was, after all, fighting a racist enemy"(1998, 108). A *New York Times* editorial commented, "The prejudice against Negro blood for transfusions is all the more difficult to understand because many a Southerner was nursed at the breast of a Negro nanny. Sometimes we wonder whether this is really an age of science" (quoted in Starr 1998, 108).

In the late 1950s, Arkansas passed a law requiring the segregation of blood. Louisiana, home of the *Plessy v. Ferguson* case, "went so far as to make it a misdemeanor for physicians to give a white person black blood without asking permission" (Starr 1998, 170). The segregation of blood ended during the 1960s, more because of the civil rights movement than further advances in science.

Research on Latinos and Latinas also finds that their "choice to identify as white or not does not reflect permanent markers such as skin color or hair texture but that race is also related to characteristics that can change such as economic status and perceptions of civic enfranchisement" (Tafoya 2004, 2). Indeed, Hispanics "experience racial identity as a measure of belonging: Feeling white seems to be a reflection of success and a sense of inclusion" (Tafoya 2004, 3).

Further, no other country uses the same categories as the US census. This issue has important consequences for what criminal justice data are collected, how they are analyzed, and what "knowledge" is produced. For example, Canada collects criminal justice data only about "natives" and "non-natives." The government there is concerned that "'black' citizens have originated from many different countries over the last century, including the U.S., the West Indies, India, and Africa" (Lauritsen 2004, 70). Combining this diverse group into a single category makes analysis problematic, especially when there is no record of the country of origin or time of arrival in Canada. Criminologists then try to interpret white-black differences, even as "new 'white' immigrants continue to arrive from places as diverse as Russia or middle-eastern countries" (2004, 70). The broader question is how analysis using official data can provide "objective" knowledge about race if race itself cannot be objectively and consistently defined (Gabbidon and Greene 2005, 40).

Stating that race and ethnicity are socially constructed does not deny that some differences exist among people or that people experience very real oppression based on race and ethnicity. But far from reflecting inherent or essential racial identities, these racial categories reflect the social, economic, and political dynamics of the society that creates them, so there is a hierarchical ordering. Power and privilege are reflected in the schema of racial classification, which shapes people's lives and identities through stereotypes, prejudices, discrimination, and racism.

STEREOTYPES, POWER, AND PRIVILEGE

Stereotypes are preconceived notions about the behavior, attitude, looks, feelings, and motives of a group of people. They serve to further reinforce the categorization of people (often by assuming that a person will behave a certain way because of his or her race, gender, religion, clothing, etc.), but they also have the additional property of being fixed, and they are largely negative generalizations about a group. Many definitions stress the inadequate or problematic basis of stereotypes in personal experience—such as when people hold stereotypes about groups they have never personally encountered but "know" about because of friends, the media, or social institutions that reflect prevailing beliefs. Stereotypes build on people's tendency to look for examples that confirm their beliefs and dismiss those contrary to how they see the world ("that's the exception that proves the rule"). In other words, people cling to their stereotypes as a means by which to quickly identify and prepare them to interact with people they don't know as well as maintain their place in the racial hierarchy

Many Asians are stereotyped as the "model minority," and although this seems like a positive rather than negative evaluation, being "a paragon of hard work and docility carries a negative undercurrent" (Feagin and Feagin 1996, 404) that is meant to tell other minority groups to work harder and complain less. These stereotypes are also negative for Asians because they include unusually high expectations, an unusually low tolerance for deviance, and a reservoir of disappointment, among other debilitating pressures. Other evaluations about "exotic" women tend not to be truly positive but instead reinforce their status as sex objects. These evaluations carry a history of racism and colonial conquest. The term *orientalism* is used to describe these attitudes toward the Middle East and Far East and reflects the values of the colonizing power. It also captures a tendency to focus on differences (from the Western "norm") and refer to other cultures in generalizations that suppress authentic human experience and complexity.

Prejudice refers to a negative or hostile attitude toward another social group. It is an attitude that exists before any action against the social group is performed. Psychologically, people project onto the minority group many of the negative attributes they wish to deny in themselves, such as a propensity toward violence, criminality, promiscuity, or immorality. Prejudice literally means prejudging someone, usually on the basis of a stereotype. While prejudice is a thought or attitude, *discrimination* occurs when people act on the basis of stereotypes and prejudice, such as denying people housing or employment.

Because whites still have the vast majority of the power in society, they have the greatest ability to discriminate, so much of this chapter focuses on the problems associated with white prejudice and discrimination. In other words, people of all races can have prejudices or excessive pride of race, referred to as *individual* or *individualized racism*, and this describes individual people who consciously or unconsciously favor one race over another. Members of racial and ethnic minorities can certainly subscribe to stereotypes and be prejudiced, but they generally do not have the power that can translate attitudes into substantial and recurring discrimination against whites in areas such as employment, business contracts, classrooms, department stores, and housing (Feagin and Feagin 1996). In this way, the election of President Obama is a milestone of sorts in marking declining prejudice, but it does not radically change the overall power of minority groups and their ability to discriminate against the white majority. The term *institutional* or *institutionalized racism* acknowledges that racist behavioral patterns or consequences may have structural aspects that systemically stratify society, shape identity, and produce substantive differences. For example, Stokely Carmichael and Charles Hamilton observed:

> When white terrorists bomb a black church and kill five black children, that is an act of individual racism, widely deplored by most segments of society. But when in that same city—Birmingham, Alabama—five hundred black babies die each year because of lack

of proper food, shelter and medical facilities, and thousands more are destroyed and maimed physically, emotionally, and intellectually because of conditions of poverty and discrimination, that is a function of institutional racism. (1967, 65)

A lack of understanding about race is perpetuated through the belief that race is about people of color and that whites do not have race. Being white or Caucasian involves having a race. That race (being white) affects identity and opportunity, even if whites have little race consciousness: "In the same way that both men's and women's lives are shaped by their gender, and that both heterosexual and lesbian women's experiences are shaped by their sexuality, white people *and* people of color live racially structured lives. In other words, any system of differentiation shapes those on whom it bestows privilege as well as those it oppresses" (Frankenberg 1993, 1).

Because whites are the dominant group, this social position and its privileges are naturalized through ideology so that being white seems neither privileged nor socially constructed. Ideology serves to naturalize the racial hierarchies, along with the prejudice and stereotypes that help re-create them. The ultimate point is not just that white traits come to be valued and minority traits devalued, but further that *white privilege* is created when whiteness becomes the norm, so that white people are not seen as speaking for whites but from and for a universal point of view:

> There is no more powerful position than that of being "just" human. The claim to power is the claim to speak for the commonality of humanity. Raced people can't do that—they can only speak for their race. But nonraced people can, for they do not represent the interests of a race. (Dyer 2005, 10)

Richard Dyer believes whites have race, and he is speaking to the popular perception of whites instead having no race. The point of studying the race of whites is to make that point of view clearer:

> White people have power and believe that they think, feel and act like and for all people; white people, unable to see their particularity, cannot take account of other people's; white people create the dominant images of the world and don't quite see that they construct it in their own image; white people set standards of humanity by which they are bound to succeed and others bound to fail. (2005, 12)

Because the majority group position is naturalized, members do not think of themselves as privileged and have few occasions to reflect on the "property interest" they have in being white. Box 4.2 contains a series of questions to provoke thoughts about naturalized or unrecognized privilege. Also, Ruth Frankenberg's work on white women explores the social construction of whiteness through interviews with women who have had to confront their whiteness through a variety of life experiences (including interracial relationships). Understanding whiteness involves asking many difficult questions, as indicated by a woman interviewed by Frankenberg: "I have an identity that doesn't have to do with my volition, but I've been profiting from it from birth. So what does that make me, and where does my responsibility lie? And where

BOX 4.2.   YOU KNOW YOU'RE PRIVILEGED WHEN . . . (PART 2)

As we noted in box 3.1 on class privilege, Peggy McIntosh's frustration with men who would not recognize their male privilege prompted her to realize that whites "are carefully taught not to recognize white privilege, as males are taught not to recognize male privilege" ([1988] 1997, 292). Her list of forms of white privilege includes the following:

- When I am told about our national heritage or about "civilization," I am shown that people of my color made it what it is.
- I can go into a music shop and count on finding the music of my race represented, into a supermarket and find staple foods that fit with my cultural traditions, into a hairdresser's shop and find someone who can cut my hair.
- Whether I use checks, credit cards, or cash, I can count on my skin color not to work against the appearance of financial reliability.
- I can talk with my mouth full and not have people put this down to my color.
- I can swear, or dress in secondhand clothes, or not answer letters without having people attribute these choices to the bad morals, the poverty, or the illiteracy of my race.
- I can do well in a challenging situation without being called a credit to my race.
- If I declare there is a racial issue at hand or there isn't a racial issue at hand, my race will lend me more credibility for either position than a person of color will have.
- I can take a job with an affirmative action employer without having my coworkers on the job suspect that I got it because of race.
- I can go shopping alone most of the time, pretty well assured that I will not be followed or harassed.
- I do not have to educate my children to be aware of systemic racism for their own daily physical protection.
- I can think over many options, social, political, imaginative, or professional, without asking whether a person of my race would be accepted or allowed to do what I want to do.

Stephanie Wildman ([1996] 1997, 325) suggested some additional conditions specific to dominant cultural white privilege, made with respect to her Latina and Latino friends, acquaintances, and colleagues:

- People will not be surprised if I speak English well.
- People seeing me will assume I am a citizen of the United States. . . . People will never assume that my children or I are illegal immigrants.
- If I am late, people will assume that I have an individual, personal reason for being late. My lateness will not be dismissed as a joke about white time.
- People will pronounce my name correctly or politely ask about the correct pronunciation. They will not behave as if it is an enormous imposition to get the name right.

does my blame lie?" (1993, 175). Tim Wise writes about the willingness of whites to tell racial and ethnic minorities to stop dwelling on past injustices while simultaneously continuing to celebrate the past, as they want to remember it on holidays like the Fourth of July. He describes the origin of white privilege in this way:

> From nearly the second that Europeans first stepped onto the shores of this continent, our identity mattered. It allowed us to feel superior to the native peoples whom we began to kill, subordinate and displace from their land almost immediately. It allowed us to take advantage of land-giveaway programs in the colonies—which we created, of course—like the head right system which provided fifty acres of land to males from England who were willing to settle in the so-called New World. Within a few decades, classification as a white person would become the key to avoiding enslavement; it would determine who could hold office, who could sit on juries, who had rights of due process; and by the time the republic was founded, being considered white would become the key to citizenship itself. (Wise 2012, 4)

In this way, Wise sums up the unearned benefit package that was first bestowed on European settlers and that was subsequently enlarged through generations of human trafficking (slavery) that transferred gifts of land, power, status, money, education, and assumed virtuosity to the descendants of those settlers for the next 350 years. Whites also have the privilege of writing this history, so the contributions of entire races of people to the development of the "American" way of life are ignored in textbooks and omitted from the nation's ongoing history. White privilege allows these kinds of contributions to be deleted from the historical literature, particularly from secondary school textbooks, as if they never existed.

Andrew Hacker (1995) has created a classroom exercise to help students understand the value of being white. In "The Visit," an embarrassed official comes to a white person to say he (or she) was supposed to have been born to black parents. At midnight, he will become black and will have the features associated with African ancestry, so he will not be recognizable to current friends but inside will be the same person he always has been. The white man is scheduled to live another fifty years as a black person, and the official's organization is willing to offer financial compensation, as the mistake is the organization's fault.

Hacker notes that white students do not feel out of place asking for $50 million, or a million dollars a year, which is a good indication of the value—the property interest mentioned in *Plessy v. Ferguson*—of being white. Students who say that because of affirmative action they would be better off as a black still come up with a figure to "buy protections from the discriminations and dangers white people know they would face once they were perceived to be black" (Hacker 1995, 31–32). And social indicators of well-being reveal none in which African Americans or Hispanics occupy a favored position. Indeed, Michael Tonry summarizes the situation as one in which "mountains of social welfare, health, employment, and education data make it clear that black Americans experience material conditions of life that, on average, are far worse than those faced by white Americans" (Tonry 1995, 128; see also Johnson and Leighton 1999).

ECONOMIC, POLITICAL, AND SOCIAL SPHERES

This section summarizes how the various racial and ethnic groups compare to one another. Given the brevity of this section, it is important to remember that diversity within groups is masked by the broader categories. For example, Native American includes 566 federally recognized tribes, although there are actually more because the federal government has stringent requirements for recognition, which is the basis for certain grants, entitlements, and casinos. States and localities recognize a larger number of tribes, and there are also tribes that have no interest in recognition from governments that have systematically treated Natives so badly (see the opening of chapter 7). Likewise, averages for other groups can conceal internal diversity even as they help illuminate the larger picture.

Table 4.1 presents an overview of the US population to highlight the relative size of ethnic and racial groups for 2011. For the 2010 census, a new instruction was added that explicitly stated, "For this census, Hispanic origins are not races." However, many individuals self-identified their race as "Latino," "Mexican," "Puerto Rican," "Salvadoran," or other national origins or ethnicities. Still, over half of the Hispanic population identified as White and no other race, while about one third provided responses that were classified as "Some Other Race alone" when responding to the question on race. Overall, the vast majority of the growth in the total population in 2010 came from increases in those who reported their race(s) as something other than White alone and those who reported their ethnicity as Hispanic or Latino.

Economic Sphere

Chapter 3 mentioned that minorities were disproportionately represented in the early part of the income and wealth distributions. For example, back in 1975, black

Table 4.1.   Population by Race and Ethnicity, 2011

Categories	Population
Not Hispanic	**259,547,000**
One Race	253,712,000
White	197,511,000
Black or African American	38,337,000
American Indian and Alaska Native	2,291,000
Asian	15,064,000
Native Hawaiian and Other Pacific Islander	509,000
Two or More Races	5,835,000
Hispanic	**52,045,000**
One Race	50,595,000
White	45,960,000
Black or African American	2,414,000
American Indian and Alaska Native	1,524,000
Asian	515,000
Native Hawaiian and Other Pacific Islander	183,000
Two or More Races	1,451,000
TOTAL	**311,592,000**

Source: Statistical Abstract of the United States, 2013, table 6.

median income was 60 percent of white median income, while Hispanic median income was nearly 72 percent of white median income (Lynch, Patterson, and Childs 2008, 3–4). In 2012, black median income was 58 percent of white median income, and Hispanic median income withdrew to 68 percent of white median income (DeNavas-Walt, Proctor, and Smith 2013, 5).

Table 4.2 also illustrates the large gap in median income and the disproportionate number of blacks and Hispanics in poverty in 2012. The annual report used for table 4.2 does not include American Indians and Alaska Natives or Native Hawaiian and Other Pacific Islanders. But a separate report, the Census Bureau's 2007–2011 American Community Survey, found that 27 percent of American Indians and Alaska Natives lived below the poverty line, as did 17.6 percent of Native Hawaiian and Other Pacific Islanders (Macartney, Bishaw, and Fontenot 2013, 13). (This

Table 4.2.   Median Family Income and Individual Poverty Rate by Race and Hispanic Origin, 2012

Categories	Household Income	Individual Poverty Rate (%)
All	$51,107	15
White (non-Hispanic)	$57,009	9.7
Black	$33,321	27.2
Asian alone	$68,638	11.7
Hispanic (all race)	$39,005	25.6

Source: DeNavas-Walt, Proctor, and Smith 2013, 5, 14.

survey contains detailed breakdowns of the larger populations in each category.) The differences in income and poverty are a result of lower levels of educational attainment, higher unemployment rates, and lower wage rates that are due, in part, to discrimination. For example, the occupations with the largest number of Hispanics include building/grounds work, cleaning/maintenance, and food preparation/service; occupations with the fewest Hispanics included legal, computer, and health care/medical (Pew Hispanic Center 2005, 10).

Some of the dynamics captured in the table can be understood through the research of Devah Pager and Bruce Western, who sent whites, blacks, and Latinos to apply for real entry-level jobs. Job applicants were matched so that their résumés would show the same basic level of education and work experience, although some whites also presented evidence of a felony conviction. The proportion of positive responses—being offered a job or called back for an interview—"depends strongly on the race of the job applicant. This comparison demonstrates a [clear] racial hierarchy, with whites in the lead, followed by Latinos, with Blacks trailing far behind" (quoted in Reiman and Leighton 2010, 73). In the experimental variation, the "white applicant with a felony conviction appears to do . . . better than his black [and Latino] counterpart[s] with no criminal background. These results suggest that employers view minority job applicants as essentially equivalent to whites just out of prison" (quoted in Reiman and Leighton 2010, 75).

As noted in chapter 3, income and wealth are important indicators of social status because they relate to political power and the ability to shield one from hardships:

> While family or household income supports day to day living expenses, savings and other assets provide a safety net for unexpected expenses and a reserve for special purchases, college tuition, or retirement. Families without this cushion are vulnerable to financial hardships if a family member requires expensive medical care or loses a job. Another major advantage of net worth—even modest amounts—is transferred to the next generation, enabling children to pay off loans, for example, or afford the down payment on a house. One reason that today's African Americans and Hispanics have less net wealth is that they were less likely to inherit assets. The continuing wealth gap perpetuates the financial disadvantage of African Americans and Hispanics. (Kent 2010)

In 2007, the average family net worth of nonwhites or Hispanics was about 33 percent that of white non-Hispanics. If a family's net worth was determined by all of its assets, including ownership of homes, cars, stocks, and/or businesses, and so on, and the average white family had $692,200 in assets, the average non-white or Hispanic family then had $228,500 in assets. (The numbers in chapter 3 were medians, while these averages are of mean net wealth.) About 76 percent of white families owned their primary residence in 2007, while only 52 percent of nonwhite or Hispanic families did. Taken together, these statistics portray a better quality of life, on average, for white families in the United States as compared to nonwhite or Hispanic families in the United States in recent years despite efforts to diversify the nation's schools, neighborhoods, and workplaces. The wealth of minorities is also disproportionately in houses, cars, and checking accounts, as opposed to financial assets such as stocks and businesses (which chapter 3 noted generates the most economic and political power).

Appreciating this diversity within racial and ethnic categories will be crucial to understanding the intersections of class, race, and gender in chapter 6. While the aggregate net worth of the poorest 50 percent of blacks is negative (Kochhar 2004, 9)—the debt of the lowest 33 percent cancels out the small net worth of the other 17 percent—2.4 percent of blacks had net worth above $500,000 (Kennickell 2003, 34) and included three black CEOs of Fortune 500 companies. Some data suggest that there is a little-discussed but sizable black middle class, evidenced by the 16 percent of blacks with net worth between $50,000 and $100,000 (34). Thus, blacks cannot be expected to have a single or unitary point of view but rather one that finds the middle class struggling to care for elderly parents who are living on paltry social security benefits and raising children. Their views about racism and discrimination may be somewhat different from those of their parents' generation, but their renewed interest in maintaining political power stems partly from the realization that many blacks have actually lost ground in this generation compared to when the civil rights movement was at its height.

In her seminal work, *The New Jim Crow,* Michelle Alexander laments that although civil rights were won all over the nation during that movement, one sphere of influence was left untouched: "The Thirteenth Amendment to the U.S. Constitution had abolished slavery but allowed one major exception: slavery remained appropriate as punishment for a crime" (Alexander 2012, 31). She goes on to argue that the Supreme Court of Virginia, in a landmark case, solidified the equivalence of convicts and slaves, which would later become the avenue for backward progress on civil rights.

Political Sphere

Racial and ethnic minorities continue to be underrepresented in politics, although the situation has improved. In the United States, voter registration and participation is lower among minorities, adding to other difficulties in electing minority officials. Table 4.3 highlights voter participation and minority representation at the national level in recent elections. In 2012, the overall voting rate was 61.8 percent in the presidential election, a decrease from 64 percent in both 2004 and 2008 but perhaps a significant increase from the 58.4 percent of 1996.

Not surprisingly, the campaign and election of the first African American president in 2008 and his subsequent reelection in 2012 made a significant difference in voter participation by minorities. For example, black women had the highest voter turnout in history, and overall the electorate was also the most racially and ethnically diverse, with nearly one in four votes cast by nonwhites (Lopez and Taylor 2009). While the nation's three largest minority groups—blacks, Hispanics, and Asians—each accounted for unprecedented shares of the presidential vote, overall, "whites

Table 4.3.   Voting Participation and Members of Congress by Race and Ethnicity, 2012

	% of Electorate Eligible to Vote	% of Total Population Who Registered	% of Total Population Who Voted	No. in US Senate (out of 100)	No. in House of Representatives (out of 411)
White non-Hispanic	71.1	72.4	63	96	359
Black alone	12.5	68.5	62	0	43
Asian alone	10.8	37.2	31.3	2	10
Hispanic (any race)	3.8	38.9	31.8	2	29
American Indian	not reported	not reported	not reported	0	1

Sources: US Census Bureau. *Current Population Survey.* November 2012. Percent of Population Eligible to Register: Thom 2013. Members of Congress: Manning 2012.

made up 76.3% of the record 131 million people who voted in November's presidential election, while blacks made up 12.1%, Hispanics 7.4% and Asians 2.5%. The white share is the lowest ever, yet is still higher than the 65.8% white share of the U.S. population" (Lopez and Taylor 2009).

Representation for minorities is higher at the local level but still low. In state government, 86 percent of legislators are white, as are 90 percent of the legislative staff (Kurtz and Weberg 2009). Because the Hispanic population is relatively young in the United States, Hispanics have great potential for gains in the future, especially if they can increase their voter participation rate. As a result, both parties are actively courting the Hispanic vote, with Republicans in particular hoping to improve minority participation in the party since only 8 percent of eligible blacks register Republican. Indeed, President Obama's nomination of Sonia Sotomayor created difficulties for Republicans who did not want her on the Supreme Court but who did not want to publicly oppose the first Hispanic of the court.

Social Sphere

Educational attainment influences economic status and health. Since 1970, all racial and ethnic groups have experienced increases in their level of educational attainment; increases for blacks have been the most marked, while increases for Hispanics have been relatively small. Non-Hispanic whites and Asians are more likely than blacks, Hispanics, and American Indians to have completed education beyond high school.

Additionally, educational attainment of college graduation or higher for whites increased from 11 percent to 30 percent between 1970 and 2010, while the same category saw increases for blacks from 4 percent to around 20 percent. Hispanics (nonwhite) saw increases from about 5 percent to 14 percent for college graduation or higher. Such marked increases in educational attainment for all race groups might also be expected to improve income levels across all race groups, but there are still large differences between race and gender groups in terms of income. A summary of those findings by Robert McNeely for the National Education Association in 2011 reported:

> The highest earning demographic of participants in the study were White men, who out-earned every other demographic at every educational level below a master's degree, while Asian American men earned the highest amount at the professional degree level. One staggering statistic is that White males who received a professional degree earned $2.4 million more than Hispanic women who were at the same educational level over a 40-year period. (McNeely 2011)

Thus, race and gender still seem to highly influence income levels even when some minorities achieve higher education levels.

Further, black Americans are more likely than whites or any other minority group to live in toxic physical environments. "In 1987 the Commission for Racial Justice of the United Church of Christ reported that three of every five black and Hispanic Americans live in a community with uncontrolled toxic-waste sites" (Austin and Schill 1991, 69; C. Lee 1992). Although poverty is an important factor, "the racial composition of a community was found to be the single variable best able to explain the existence or nonexistence of commercial hazardous waste facilities in a given community area" (Bullard 1990; C. Lee 1992, 14). Another survey indicated that although attention has been focused on the problem of environmental racism, the concentration of toxic waste in low-income communities was *growing*, especially for low-income black Americans. Hazardous wastes were examined because nationally comprehensive data were easily available: "Many other problems in minority communities, such as air pollution, workplace exposure, pesticides, lead poisoning, asbestos, municipal waste and others, are equally or more serious" but not subject to ready assessment (C. Lee 1992, 16; see also Bullard 1994; Kozol 1991; Lynch and Stretesky 1998).

IMPLICATIONS

The United States continues to be marked by a profound and persistent racial divide. This divide exists on numerous dimensions: "as a perception of others or in the form of stereotypes; in vastly different access to health care and education; and in the unequal distribution of economic goods and access to employment. And, despite society's best interests and intentions, there appear to be unconscious processes that continue to facilitate racial bias in criminal justice processes" (Lynch, Patterson, and Childs 2008, 13). The ideology of racism can make it difficult for whites to understand the vulnerability minorities feel, which seems exaggerated to whites who have had few occasions to think about the privileges conferred on them. Even whites who would demand a large sum in exchange for having to live as a black person are aware that being white does give them some protections, but it is a large step to internalizing the sense of social marginality that comes from living every day as a minority in a country controlled by whites, even a highly multiracial country such as the United States.

Unfortunately, even in the face of history and a mountain of social indicators that all illustrate minority disadvantage, many whites are still unable to see their racial privilege. In spite of a wide variety of data on the growing inequality in society and in the administration of criminal justice, politicians and media pundits for the most part support the same old practices that are responsible for these problems. Indeed, there were even calls to bring back the "chain gang" in spite of its long and obvious symbol as a tool of racial oppression (Gorman 1997).

Meanwhile, communities are being destroyed, and the experience of incarceration makes it harder for inmates to be productive community members on release. Even though released inmates have "done their time," the government has been developing increasingly sophisticated computerized records that help ensure that criminal record data are easily and widely available. Thus, "it is not fanciful to worry about the emergence of a sophisticated computer quarantine that had profound implications for social structure" because it isolates and separates and further marginalizes the poor, especially the black and Latino poor (Gandy 1993; Gordon 1990, 89; Lopez 2008).

This chapter should help clarify why many minorities picture themselves as profoundly marginal and expendable, leaving them with a sense of alienation perhaps best captured in Derrick Bell's "Chronicle of the Space Traders" (1989). In this story, blacks as a group are sacrificed to aliens for gold needed to retire the national debt, a chemical to clean up pollution, and a limitless source of clean energy. Following a national referendum and a Supreme Court decision, blacks are lined up and turned over to the aliens—in chains, just as they entered the country hundreds of years ago.

The moral of this story for Bell is that we have made no racial progress; whites would sacrifice blacks for their own gain today just as they did four hundred years ago with the institution of slavery. Among blacks, the chronicle "captures an uneasy intuition" that black Americans "live at the sufferance of whites—that as soon as our [black] welfare conflicts with something they [whites] consider essential, all our gains, all our progress, will turn out to be illusory" (Delgado and Stefancic 1991, 321). Not too many whites share such a "pessimistic" view of the progress made (or not made) regarding racial relations in the United States, especially with the recent election of an African American president, but this is still likely tied to whites' inability to appreciate white privilege and the overall experience of minorities.

REVIEW AND DISCUSSION QUESTIONS

1. What is meant by the social construction of race? What are some of the examples the authors have given to support this point?

2. Highlight the distinctions between the following related terms: stereotypes, prejudice, discrimination, and racism. How are institutional and individual racism different?

3. What is meant by the term *white privilege*? List some examples of *white privilege*.

4. What are some ways that all minority groups share similar experiences in the United States? Drawing on the chapter and your own knowledge, what are some of the differences between the experiences of different groups?

5. What is meant by diversity within a minority group? What are some examples of this diversity, and when it might be important to advancing our social and criminological knowledge?

5

Understanding Gender
and Male Privilege

The 1990s will be remembered for attention to a relatively new kind of violence: "rampage school shootings." During this period, a "wave" of shootings by white males in middle and high schools occurred across the rural and suburban (but not urban) United States. Between 1994 and 1998, there were approximately two hundred violent deaths: 83 percent homicides, 13 percent suicides, and 4 percent combinations of the two (Hammond 1999). In peak years like 1998, forty-two school-related homicides happened. Among the homicides, no particular groups were targeted by the all-male adolescent and preadolescent perpetrators of these killings (Newman et al. 2004). (The 2006 shooting at an Amish school in Lancaster, Pennsylvania, did involve five female victims, but it was done by a man in his thirties and not a student peer.)

While media attention to school violence has declined, preliminary data for 2010–2011 show that among youth of ages five to eighteen, there were thirty-one school-associated violent deaths (twenty-five homicides and six suicides), or about one homicide or suicide of a school-age youth at school per 3.5 million students. Youth homicides at secondary schools remained less than 2 percent of the total number of youth homicides (Robers et al. 2013, 6). This is consistent with other years surveyed as well. There have also been a handful of acts of homicide and suicide on college campuses during the first decade of this century, the most infamous at Virginia Tech.

Those analysts who pay close attention to the wider organizational and societal features of community relations tend to distinguish between the more familiar revenge killings and the rampage shootings. The latter assaults involve a special kind of attack on multiple parties, selected almost at random. "The shooters may have a specific target to begin with, but they let loose with a fusillade that hits others, and it is not unusual for the perpetrator to be unaware of who has been shot until long after the fact" (Newman et al. 2004, 15).

These explosions are not attacks aimed at the popular kids, bullies, athletes, and/or harassers per se, as many commentators and pundits have suggested. Instead, they are attacks on whole institutions—schools, teenage pecking orders, community social structures—and they represent "backlash" or "blowback" effects from male adolescents who are unable to successfully navigate the treacherous waters of doing teenage masculinity. Schools are the selected sites for these culturally played-out scripts of "becoming a man" and performing violence because "they are the heart and soul of public life in small towns" where there are "high levels of background violence, dysfunctional families, chaotic schools, [and] distracted adults too busy with town lives to pay attention to the local teens" (Newman et al. 2004, 15). These rampage school shootings thus contradict our most firmly held beliefs about childhood, home, and community: "They expose the vulnerable underbelly of ordinary life and tell us that malevolence can be brewing in places where we least expect it, that our fail-safe methods (parental involvement in children's lives, close-knit neighborhoods) do not identify nascent pathologies" that may be part and parcel of patriarchy, gender, and coming of age for socially and marginally adolescent males living in the nonmetropolitan United States (Newman et al. 2004, 15).

Many popular explanations for these rural and suburban shootings include mental illness, family problems, bullying, peer support, culture of violence, violent media, availability of guns, and the copycat effect. But most of these explanations on their own do not hold up, while some of these explanations in combination with others and with qualification—such as peer support and culture of violence—are more helpful. But what is missing from these types of analyses is the importance of young adolescent males as the perpetrators. Misfit girls have their problems, too, but they do not resort to rampage or any other kinds of mass shootings. Since all the perpetrators are male, masculinity should be a central part of the investigation—and certainly if all the perpetrators had been girls, the question would be "What's going on with girls?" (or "girls gone wild!") rather than "school violence" and "what's wrong with kids?" (J. Katz 1999).

Of course, both boys and girls seek status, perform for peers, find identities, and cope with their parents and other adults. The point is that the process of finding a workable niche in society is distinctive along gender lines. The all-male club of rampage shooters shares at least in their own eyes and perceptions (if not in the eyes and perceptions of others, too) a dual failure—failing at adolescence and failing at manhood. For adolescent males, demonstrating masculinity is central to what makes a popular boy high on the social pecking order. As the authors of Rampage: The Social Roots of School Shootings *have stated:*

> *To be a man is to be physically dominant, competitive, and powerful in the eyes of others. Real men exert control and never admit weakness. They act more and talk less. If this sounds like Marlboro Man, it is because adolescent ideals of manliness are unoriginal. They derive from cultural projections found in film, video, magazines, and the back of comic books. In-your-face basketball players, ruthless Wall Street robber barons, and presidents who revel in being "doers" and not "talkers" all partake of and then reinforce this stereotype. (Newman et al. 2004, 144)*

The most powerful source of stigma for an adolescent boy coming of age in the United States today is being labeled "gay." The assumption is that being a man means being heterosexual, and even the specter of homosexuality compromises a boy's status and place on the social ladder because "gay" constitutes a failure at achieving masculine gender. "Gay" does not merely refer to a sexual orientation, preference, or reference, but also to a broader connotation now used as a slang term for any form of social or athletic incompetence and an array of other mistakes and failures. One fifteen-year-old girl explained: "Boys have a fascination with not being gay. They want to be manly, and put each other down by saying 'that's gay'" (quoted in Newman et al. 2004, 146). Thus for boys, "the struggle for status is in large part competition for the rank of alpha male, and any kind of failure by another boy can be an opportunity to insult the other's masculinity and enhance one's own. It's a winner-take-all society, and any loss one boy can inflict on another opens up a new rung on the ladder that he might move into" (146).

As for those socially marginal and psychologically distressed youth who end up at the bottom of the social pecking orders as a result of their real or imagined failure to do masculinity, a few of them ultimately find themselves trapped in a limited repertoire of cultural scripts or strategies of action that resolve their feelings of shame, humiliation, and inadequacy. Various rampage school shooters all felt at the moment of crisis that they had no other options but to come forth and fire their weapons. They had all considered suicide, but that wasn't the manly thing to do. Going out in a blaze, perhaps shooting it out with the police, would certainly allow them to go down in school infamy as full of machismo. In carrying out these scenarios of killing, these adolescent males are not simply reacting to glorified violence but rather are immersing themselves in violent roles that they believed were powerful and would thus enhance their status as men.

In short, having violence, aggression, and domination as cultural norms for masculinity provides a framework for their behavior. These gendered rampage shootings provide these young males with a way to demonstrate their "anger with an entire social system that had rejected them. . . . For this purpose, any target [will] do just as well as any other, so long as the shootings [occur] on a public stage for all to see" (Newman et al. 2004, 152). In the process, these truly rare rampage killers, characterizing the extreme end of trying to do masculine gender, are able in a "twisted" way to claim the power and status their peers had denied them.

As with class and race, discussions of gender raise controversy. There's the *F* word—feminism—that many men and women resist even as they endorse basic tenets of treating women with dignity, respect, and equality. Discussing sex and gender means exploring what we mean by *equality* when men and women are different biologically in ways that go far beyond racial differences like skin color or hair texture. This problem is most evident in issues around human reproduction and biology, but it is also present in debates about whether men and women are "similarly situated" and thus deserve equal treatment as a matter of law. Women are 51 percent of the population but are considered a minority and part of affirmative action plans. Should equality be based on what men were getting? Are both sexes to be treated equally based on what women are getting? Or is there another alternative?

One flashpoint in these ongoing debates was the comments of Harvard's former president and former economic advisor to President Obama, Lawrence Summers, about diversifying personnel in science and engineering. The reasons he suggested for the small number of women in these fields were, in order of importance: (1) women do not put in the long workweeks over the long run because they value family and want to have children; (2) innate differences between men and women lead men to outperform women; (3) discrimination and socialization (Summers 2005b). The comments created a great deal of dissent and discussion, much of it focused on the issue of innate differences—and much of it noting that since Summers became president at Harvard in 2001, the percentage of women getting a permanent tenured professorship at Harvard had declined by half, to 12 percent.

Critics pointed out that the number of women in science and engineering had climbed from 3 percent to about 20 percent in thirty years, and the female genome and DNA had not changed that much in a few decades, so innate difference could not be a major factor. Indeed, later research based on a test given in sixty-five developed countries around the world found that fifteen-year-old "girls generally outperform boys in science—but not in the United States" (Fairfield 2013). A major culprit is "the stereotype threat," which means that at around age four, children start to understand gender roles in occupations from an unequal society. This trajectory is reinforced by "stories of the lone girl in the AP physics class, ostracized by her male classmates. The girl on the FIRST Robotics team who is assigned marketing duties when there's nothing she'd like to do more than work on engineering. The counselor who recommends not taking an advanced math class because it would make the student's schedule too rigorous. The science teacher who never seems to call on the girl in the front row" (Cutler 2012). The same study, based on extensive interviews with experts in the STEM (science, technology, engineering, and math) fields, notes that the problem did not end with high school: "Unfortunately, gender discrimination is still a persistent and pernicious problem in higher education as well, as is made frightfully clear in a recent Yale study that showed both male and female science faculty exhibiting gender bias against female job candidates" (Cutler 2012).

Still, the chair of the sociology department at Harvard, when asked about the views of Lawrence Summers, inquired, "Has anyone asked if he thinks this about African-Americans, because they are underrepresented at this university?" (Bombardieri 2005). Deborah Blum, a Pulitzer Prize–winning science writer, felt a sense of déjà vu: "Spend any time at all studying the biology of behavior and you will find it riddled with similar, nature-based defenses of the often less-than-perfect status quo. In the days before women were admitted to college, male scientists insisted that girls were born too fragile and emotional to even handle higher education" (Blum 2005). Critics also reported many studies showing the impact of socialization—women being steered away from a field, told they would not be good or interested, and finding no role models—and wished someone as educated as Summers and speaking from a place of such prominence had not reinforced the idea that "women were, well, dumb" when it came to math and science (Blum 2005).

In spite of supporters claiming he was the victim of political correctness, Summers (2005b) wrote a series of apologies in which he said he never meant to suggest "that girls are intellectually less able than boys, or that women lack the ability to succeed at the highest levels of science." He was just trying to be provocative, he claimed, and certainly did not wish to discourage talented girls and women, especially after all he learned about "the very real barriers faced by women in pursuing scientific and other academic careers" (2005b). Lost in the discussion was Summers's comment about women's willingness to put in the hours and sacrifice that it takes to get to the top, not only in engineering but in American corporations as well. At least in this respect, his comments were similar to the analysis in a cover story of *Fortune* magazine, which noted some reluctance of women to make sacrifices for power and who instead looked for jobs that were satisfying or personally meaningful. Still, in 2013 there were twenty Fortune 500 companies headed by women, including Ursula M. Burns (the first African American woman to spearhead a Fortune 500 company like Xerox, which is ranked at no. 131), Indra K. Nooyi (an Indian American woman named one of the ten most powerful women in the world by the Forbes corporation in 2013), and Marissa A. Mayer, who runs Yahoo, which ranks at no. 494.

While this discussion has been about women in science and corporations, much of the same themes and lessons apply to criminology and criminal justice as well. One letter, signed by more than a hundred scientists in response to Summers's comments, noted: "If society, institutions, teachers, and leaders like President Summers expect (overtly or subconsciously) that girls and women will not perform as well as boys and men, there is a good chance many will not perform as well" (Anita Borg Institute 2005). Criminology recognizes the same phenomenon in labeling theory, and more generally the chapters in the third part of this book will review how stereotypes and expectations affect the treatment of men and women as both victims and offenders. Beliefs about women being too emotional and unable to handle the rigors of logic kept women out of law school and the practice of law for many years. Concerns about women's weakness continue to exert influence on women in policing and positions as correctional officers. Gender discrimination shapes opportunities in legitimate criminal justice work and also shapes the opportunities in crime, where women tend to be at the lower end of criminal organizations and immersed in typically female-dominated crime, that is, sex work.

In taking up the task of analyzing gender, we recognize that within the criminal justice system, men are the majority of offenders and victims. This may be due, at least in part, to the fact that women and girls have gone mostly understudied in these areas. "Criminology theories were constructed 'by men, about men' and explain male behavior rather than human behavior" (Belknap 2007, 3). Hence, many women may have simply avoided detection in areas of crime that do not relate solely to the sex industry. Nevertheless, theoretical understandings of crime and violence up until recently did not consider why men have such high rates of offending relative to women, nor were theorists giving much attention to the roles of gender, socialization, and doing masculinity in decisions about crime. Women are certainly still a small minority of the criminal justice caseloads, but females are the fastest-growing incarcerated population (Belknap 2007, 5). As a consequence, until recently not much attention was paid to the differential treatment of male and female offenders, including the different needs of female inmates.

Because people's treatment within the administration of justice is shaped by what takes place outside the criminal justice system, this chapter, like the previous two, locates its discussion—this time on gender—in terms of the larger economic, political, and social spheres of interaction. Before turning to a comparative discussion of the relative positions of men and women, we first address the relevant gender terminology. The point from the previous chapter about racial privilege is revisited in terms of male privilege—and in terms of how racial privilege impacts feminism. Finally, the implications of these relations to the whole concept of equal justice are examined as well as the study of crime and social control.

GENDER AND SEX IN SOCIETY

Sex generally refers to "biological differences, including differences in reproductive organs, body size, muscle development, and hormones" (Belknap 2007, 8). While sex tends to be thought of as limited to male and female, *gender* typically refers to those traits that are "ascribed by society and that relate to expected social roles" such as "clothing, wages, child-care responsibilities, and professions." Gender thus refers to the set of expectations or roles that males and females are expected to fill in order to be masculine and feminine. Both masculine and feminine gender roles are based on heterosexual expectations, with some allowance for women to be sexual with each other when done for male pleasure. Beyond heterosexuality, gender role expectations vary by class and race.

Masculinity and femininity involve *social* processes through which people learn and are socialized into acting according to the notions of what an appropriate role is for men and women in our society based on their social location. For example, Victor Rios, in an ethnographic study aptly titled *Punished: Policing the Lives of Black and Latino Boys* (2011), found that violence and aggression are an integral part of demonstrating masculinity for some boys who perceive themselves to have no access to traditional avenues of success:

> Whereas race determined how a young person was treated in the criminal justice pipeline, masculinity played a role in whether they desisted or recidivated as they navigated through the system. One of the outcomes of pervasive criminal justice contact for young Black and Latino men was the production of a hyper-masculinity. Angela Harris defines hyper-masculinity as an "exaggerated exhibition of physical strength and personal aggression," which is often a response to a gender threat "expressed through physical and sexual domination of others." Drawing on this definition, I contend that the criminal justice system encourages expressions of hyper-masculinity by threatening and confusing young men's masculinity. This, in turn, leads them to rely on domination through

violence, crime, and school and criminal justice counterculture. In essence, detrimental forms of masculinity are partly developed through youths' interaction with police, juvenile hall, and probation officers. (Rios 2010, 130)

Today, women are actually taught subservient roles held in place by social processes that stigmatize women for nonconformity. That is, women who are unapologetic about sexual pleasure and who try to control their own sexuality are called "sluts" and subject to slut shaming; women who are not married or mothers by a certain age are ridiculed; women who are ambitious and aggressive at work are derided by a society that inculcates young men with the ideology that, as boys, they have a natural right to control and dominate their spheres of influence.

Understanding these social processes is crucial because it is both easy and convenient to attribute differences to biology ("innate") when the focus should be on socialization and factors that relate to how someone "becomes" a woman or man in our society. For example, people customarily identify women as being more in touch with feelings and more nurturing than men. One explanation would be biological, attributing those qualities to women's reproductive functions in having a child. An alternate explanation would highlight the importance for women of understanding the feelings of others when society is male dominated because women frequently earn less than men and are taught to become dependent on men economically. Further, many women are subject to a great deal of male violence or oppression because boys have been taught to control and manipulate women (and other boys) as a demonstration of masculinity that is sometimes modeled in sports, video games, and other forms of popular culture. In such a context, being attuned to the feelings of those in a dominant position and having the ability to provide comfort would arise out of necessity and become part of the gender role.

Essentialism is the belief in inherent qualities, an unchanging and indispensable quality. With gender, the debate is over *biological* essentialism, which refers to some innate and distinguishing qualities or personality traits that would exist in each sex that goes beyond cultural conditioning. The issue here is not to point to biological differences in, say, reproductive function, but to find out whether men or women have inherent traits that exist across cultures and throughout time. Feminists are generally skeptical about claims of essentialism because they tend to be used to justify inequality and male privilege. Just as Lawrence Summers (above) tried to point to innate differences when it comes to the hard sciences, Blum pointed to earlier justifications that women were innately unable to deal with the rigors of college-level education. Similar thoughts have been behind denying women the right to vote and the ability to get a number of professional licenses (including law and medicine) because women were viewed as too emotional and/or seen as unable to handle the rigor of the field. Further, essentialism (whether based on sex, race, class, or anything else) homogenizes a group of people; that is, it denies differences and diversity within a group of people (e.g., women, blacks, the poor). Just as with racial stereotyping, this process is dehumanizing and normalizes the power relations so that inequality is not questioned because it appears to be the result of natural differences. It is important to remember here the references made to the fallacy of this argument in the previous chapter (chapter 4) about "natural" differences by race. Simply put, there are none.

Gender is thus a social construction, a process through which gender is "done" (or "performed") through routine interactions with other people. By being aggressive and not displaying feelings, males can assert claims to masculinity; attacking gays reinforces the heterosexual aspect of masculinity, as does sexual aggression and domination of women. By making themselves up to look attractive to men and being sensitive to others, quiet and nonassertive, women perform femininity. In both cases, men and women "do gender" by handling situations in such a way that the outcome is considered gender appropriate and therefore heterosexual. Still, masculinity and femininity are never accomplished and secure in a final way; they are something that must be continually "done" and (re-) accomplished; that is, men and women are expected to continuously demonstrate "gender" throughout their lives.

Gender roles are the socially scripted or appropriate behaviors for males and females, and they have traditionally reflected patriarchal values that have reserved for men public power and control of women (see box 5.1). Gender roles for women, for example, until recently have included those values and attitudes that often placed "women on a pedestal," representing "the idea that women need male protection and that they should be more virtuous than men, for example, by not telling dirty jokes, getting drunk, or paying their share of the cost of a date" (Scully 1990, 79). Indeed, historically, "the pedestal" prevented women from working outside of the home, participating in sports and/or athletics, and voting as well as many other privileges reserved for men. Men were expected to deal with the "public sphere" outside the home, which could be competitive and corrupt. Women were expected to seek protection and guidance from men as their lawful husbands and to make the home (the "private sphere") a pleasant refuge for men.

BOX 5.1.   YOU KNOW YOU'RE PRIVILEGED WHEN . . . (PART 3)

**A poem for men who don't understand
what we mean when we say they have it**

privilege is simple:
going for a pleasant stroll after dark,
not checking the back of your car as you get in, sleeping soundly,
speaking without interruption, and not remembering

dreams of rape, that follow you all day, that woke you crying, and
privilege is not seeing your stripped, humiliated body
plastered in celebration across every magazine rack, privilege
is going to the movies and not seeing yourself
terrorized, defamed, battered, butchered
seeing something else

privilege is
riding your bicycle across town without being screamed at or
run off the road, not needing an abortion, taking off your shirt
on a hot day, in a crowd, not wishing you could type better
just in case, not shaving your legs, having a decent job and
expecting to keep it, not feeling the boss's hand up your crotch,
dozing off on late-night buses, privilege
is being the hero on the TV show not the dumb broad,
living where your genitals are totemized not denied,
knowing your doctor won't rape you
privilege is being smiled at all day by nice helpful women, it is
the way you pass judgment on their appearance with magisterial authority,
the way you face a judge of your own sex in court and
are overrepresented in Congress and are not strip-searched for a traffic ticket
or used as a dart board by your friendly mechanic,

privilege is seeing your bearded face reflected through the history texts
not only of your high school days but all your life, not being relegated to a paragraph
every other chapter, the way you occupy
entire volumes of poetry and more of your share of the couch unchallenged,
it is your mouthing smug, atrocious insults at women
who blink and change the subject politely—
privilege is how seldom the rapist's name appears in the papers
and the way you smirk over your PLAYBOY

it's simple really,
privilege means someone else's pain, your wealth
is my terror, your uniform
is a woman raped to death here or in Cambodia or
wherever your obscene privilege
writes your name in my blood, it's that simple,
you've always had it, that's why it doesn't
seem to make you sick at stomach,
you have it, we pay for it, now
do you understand

Source: Clarke, D. A. 1981. *Banshee.* Portland, ME: Peregrine.

However, these traditional notions of how proper ladies behave never included women of color. Women of color have always worked outside of the home, for example, in the rice fields of Asia, on the plantations of the Old South in the United States for African Americans, or on the fruit and vegetable farms of the United States for Latina migrant workers. Women of color have always been expected to protect and defend themselves and their children in the absence of a man in the home as in times of slavery or in homes where migrant/seasonal workers left home for long periods of time. White women who fell off of the pedestal or whose social position never occupied a pedestal because of their nationality, religion, or economic standing were seen as "legitimate victims" who deserved hostility and contempt—even vigilante punishment—whether in the form of harassment, domestic violence, or sexual assault. Beth Richie, in her most recent book, *Arrested Justice: Black Women, Violence, and America's Prison Nation* (2012), lamented that one of the biggest reasons why the women's anti-violence movement slowed at the height of its build-up in the 1980s is that white men co-opted the movement and provided a new structure for service delivery that involved hierarchies for service providers and clients. As a result, "clients" were redefined as women who possessed certain qualities (such as being white, married, heterosexual, chaste, and having middle-class social standing) rather than just any women who needed treatment for violence suffered at the hands of men. By redefining who qualified for services, the number of women helped and the kind of women who provided the help changed dramatically.

Patriarchy refers to those societies organized around male privilege or hierarchy. Patriarchal societies vary in form and expression, depending on whether they are agricultural, industrial, or service societies. The totality of their oppressive and exploitative uses of male authority and female subordination also varies. *Sexism*, which can be present both at the individual and institutional level, describes the beliefs and social relations holding that men are superior to women. Sexism includes *paternalism*, the view that women need protection and are not fully responsible for their actions, and *chivalry*, the reluctance to inflict harm on a woman accompanied by unwillingness to believe that a woman could possess criminal intent (Moulds 1980). Adrienne Rich has defined *misogyny* "as organized, institutionalized, normalized hostility and violence toward women" (quoted in Humm 1990, 139). Interestingly, the word for hatred of men, *misandry*, rarely appears in print or public discourse. *Phallocentrism* refers to social constructs that make men the focus of law and meaning (Gamble 1999). Taken together, these values, norms, and beliefs of patriarchy devalue women in society, setting them up for all kinds of unequal treatment.

One area in which patriarchy impinges on women through social, economic, and political forces is reproductive rights, as women's bodies have historically been subjected to control through control of their reproductive processes. According to the World Health Organization, *reproductive rights*

> rest on the recognition of the basic right of all couples and individuals to decide freely and responsibly the number, spacing and timing of their children and to have the in-

formation and means to do so, and the right to attain the highest standard of sexual and reproductive health. They also include the right of all to make decisions concerning reproduction free of discrimination, coercion and violence. (2005)

While reproductive rights in the United States are often associated with the right to abortion, they encompass a much wider array of women's (and men's) reproductive processes and a woman's right to choose or refuse treatments: abortion, sterilization, contraception, family planning, infertility treatment. Reproductive rights also include the right to be free from illnesses or other conditions that might interfere with sexual and reproductive functions. They encompass the right to provide for healthy children by meeting not only their physical needs but also their educational, emotional, and social needs (Flavin 2009).

Reproductive rights are "fundamental rights" that should receive the highest level of protection because they are related to "the right to bodily integrity, the right to privacy (including the right to an abortion), and the right to procreate" (Flavin 2009, 39). The right to privacy is frequently explained as "the right to be let alone" or "have government off our back" and establishes a personal sphere free from government intrusion. The right to bodily integrity is strong enough that organs cannot be taken from the dead without their prior permission. Indeed, "if a person cannot be forced to have criminal evidence removed from his body, or a father cannot be compelled to donate an organ to [save] his child['s life], then it follows that forcing a woman to be sterilized or take contraceptives similarly violates her right to bodily integrity" and privacy (Flavin 2009, 40).

Further, while it is important to think about individual rights, central concerns also include how the social, economic, and political conditions affect a woman's autonomy over her own body and her reproductive health. Thus, any analysis of these relations should look at not only a woman's (or man's) decision but also the role of poverty, racial discrimination, gender violence, abuse of technology, pharmaceutical and/or medical coercion, and family planning programs. For example, the United States has a history of coerced sterilization, particularly of women of color, and several states in the early 1990s considered mandating the use of Norplant or Depo-Provera (a type of long-acting contraceptive implant) to control younger, inner-city women on welfare and poorer women of color. "The consequences of this extend beyond the biological question of 'Who procreates?' It speaks to the question of 'Who matters?'" (Flavin 2009).

In the years leading up to the *Roe v. Wade* Supreme Court decision legalizing abortion, most white, middle-class feminists advocated for abortion and birth control. The radical feminists focused on the pursuit of sexual pleasure without fear of being forced into a marriage or getting pregnant; they fought for sexual liberation and voluntary motherhood. In addition to this group, minority women who joined the women's movement hoped to procure these reproductive and amatory rights, but they also sought to destroy racial stereotypes of sexual deviance while seeking equal protection under the laws against domestic violence, forced sterilization, and racism in employment, health care, and housing, among other threats to their families.

Sexuality may be thought of as combining elements of sex and gender as well as a person's subjective sense of himself or herself, or what is usually referred to as gender identification. Sexuality is an important site for patriarchal control as it has often been tied to men's control over female reproduction and reproductive rights, standards of beauty and body objectification, and attempts to ensure sexual access or availability. Part of the gender role for both men and women assumes heterosexuality, with modest allowances for female same-sex activity when done for the enjoyment of men. *Homosexuality*, male or female, refers to the sexuality of people who are characterized by a sexual interest in persons of the same sex. Gays and lesbians are frequently seen as "unnatural" because their sexual desire and gender orientation call into question aspects of masculinity, femininity, and gender roles that people would like to see as innate ("natural") but that are really socially constructed. Lesbians are frequently depicted in mass media as killers because the "unnaturalness" of their sexuality is seen as explaining the "unnaturalness" of the weaker and gentler sex committing violent crime. In reality, most women who kill direct their violence against a chronic male abuser. According to the National Institute of Justice Violence Against Women Survey, "intimate partner homicides make up 40–50 percent of all murders of women in the United States according to city or State specific databases. In 70–80 percent of intimate partner homicides, no matter which partner was killed, the man physically abused the woman before the murder" (Campbell et al. 2003).

In patriarchal societies, homosexuals are often represented or viewed as a threat to heterosexuals, especially by those who are "homophobic." The general prejudice against being gay is so strong that it affects many social interactions among men. Guys who have a deep friendship and intimate connection run the risk of being seen as gay, creating a problem for male bonding and *homosociality* (friendship with the same sex). Members of fraternities, sports teams, and sometimes those in the military have significant bonds with other men and thus pursue excessive heterosexual conquests to disavow the label of gay. A focus on scoring, using women, and being a player keeps the masculine heterosexual identity intact while allowing for close male friendships. Gang rapes can be a more extreme version of this phenomenon, where groups of men bond by using a woman (or series of women) and still maintain the masculine heterosexual identity (Jody Miller 2008).

Feminism comprises both a basic doctrine of equal rights for women and an ideology for women's liberation from patriarchy. Feminism's basic tasks are consciousness raising about oppression and encouraging actions that undo the exclusions of women's opinions, experiences, and accomplishments. As discussed and elaborated on in chapter 1, a wide diversity of perspectives are contained under this umbrella term, indicating that *feminisms* is more appropriate by not suggesting a singular woman's point of view. As stated previously, women of color do not always have the same concerns and perspectives as white feminists. Hillary Potter, author of *Battle Cries: Black Women and Intimate Partner Violence* (2008) puts it this way: "Because the multicultural interventions and programming that are based on middle-class women do not typically meet the needs of women of color, a similar adage can be applied to address the admonitions of women activists of color in the antiviolence movement: We cannot simply 'add women of color and stir'" (Potter 2008, 7). Still, there are additional segments of feminisms. Liberal feminism, for example, tends to seek equality for women within much of the existing political and economic system. In contrast, socialist and more radical feminisms tend to seek equality for men and women but under a different system, usually one that is less hierarchical and stratified than currently exists. Third-world feminism adds another layer of diverse women's viewpoints from developing countries, although that goes beyond the scope of this book.

Chapter 4's discussion of race noted that people of all races could be prejudiced and have stereotypes, but discrimination implied a position of power to act on those prejudices, so the chapter emphasized discrimination against minorities by the white majority. Similarly, while men and women can both buy into stereotypes and harmful gender role expectations, men will be the primary initiators of sex discrimination because they tend to have the positions of power and decision-making ability. Further, while both men and women can engage in sexual harassment, male perpetrators are more of a problem because of the greater economic power of men combined with the prevalence of violence against women.

MALE PRIVILEGE

The chapter on race quoted Richard Dyer about how whites had power because they could claim to speak for all people while people of color were normally considered to speak for their race. The same concept applies to gender, with men being seen as having no gender—and thus speaking for all ("mankind")—while women are seen as speaking only for women, a "special interest group." To further illustrate this point, substitute "men" for "whites" in Dyer's quote: "Men have power and believe that they think, feel and act like and for all people; men, unable to see their particularity, cannot take account of other people's; men create the dominant images of the world and don't quite see that they construct it in their own image; men set standards of humanity by which they are bound to succeed and others bound to fail" (based on Dyer 2005, 12).

Men do not usually see this privilege (see box 5.1) because it is the purpose of gender roles and stereotypes to rationalize the inequality so that the status quo appears natural, inevitable, and just. But

> men's physiology defines most sports, their needs define auto and health insurance coverage, their socially designated biographies define workplace expectations and successful career patterns, their perspectives and concerns define quality in scholarship, their experiences and obsessions define merit, their objectification of life defines art, their military service defines citizenship, their presence defines family, their inability to get along with each other—their wars and rulerships—defines history, their image defines god, and their genitals define sex. (MacKinnon, quoted in Forell and Matthews 2000, 5)

And law tends to see women as men see them because most laws are written, enforced, and judged by men.

Critiques of the "reasonable man" standard in law are a good illustration of male privilege. The standard arose initially because women were not allowed to sue in court or sign contracts, so questions about negligence or duties of care were based on a "reasonable man." But the standard remained even after women achieved more civil rights and were better integrated into the workforce, where the development of sexual harassment law exposed the problem of applying the reactions of a "reasonable man" to behavior that victimizes a woman. For example, one of the early cases involving a hostile work environment involved a female manager in an office with widespread pornographic pictures and a coworker the court majority described as "extremely vulgar and crude" who "customarily made obscene comments about women" (Forell and Matthews 2000, 37).

The majority, applying a "reasonable person" standard, found the environment to be "annoying" but not hostile in a way that raised sex discrimination issues. In the court's view, the pornographic posters had minimal effect "when considered in the context of a society that condones and publicly features and commercially exploits open displays of written and pictorial erotica at the newsstands, on prime-time television, at the cinema, and in other public places" (Forell and Matthews 2000, 37). For the majority, that such environments existed was a given, and the woman had "voluntarily entered" it; by showing intolerance of such conditions, the court implied that the woman was being hostile—not the environment. Besides, the law was "not meant to—or can—change" such workplaces, nor did the majority think it was "designed to bring about the magical transformation in the social mores of American workers" (37).

Critics of the decision point out that the neutral-sounding "American worker" is "men who hold values allowing them to talk crudely about women and look at degrading pornography whenever they want to, including at work" (Forell and Matthews 2000, 38). In short, the majority opinion of the court (comprising men exclusively) chose not to include, adopt, or give credence to the standard of a "reasonable woman" in determining what the standard of a "reasonable person" requires in a co-ed office setting. Instead, they chose to maintain the standard of a "reasonable man" to represent the standard of a "reasonable person" for setting the tone for co-ed office space.

The dissenting judge was one of the first to recognize that the appropriate standard was the reaction of a "reasonable woman." In addition to widespread pornographic posters, he noted that women in this office were "routinely" called "whores" and "cunts" (Forell and Matthews 2000, 40). The issue was not the personality of the woman bringing the suit, but the behavior of men in the office: "No woman should be subjected to an environment where her sexual dignity and reasonable sensibilities are visually, verbally or physically assaulted as a matter of prevailing male prerogative" (42). For this judge, the male perspective was disguised as "reasonable person." He suggested, "Unless the outlook of the reasonable woman is adopted, the defendants as well as the courts are permitted to sustain ingrained notions of reasonable behavior fashioned by the offenders" (42).

One commentary on this case noted that the dissenting judge is an African American, "and his experiences as a black man may have made it easier for him to recognize discrimination—and that in certain situations the law needs to empathize with those who are viewed as the outsiders" (Forell and Matthews 2000, 42). While this example does help illustrate how men can be feminists and develop feminist sensibilities, it is also unfortunately the case that many men with the same experience as the dissenting judge focus on race to the exclusion of gender (sometimes arguing that race is more important). Further, Dyer's quote about white privilege applies to feminism in that white women experience white privilege, even as they are discriminated against as women. Thus, there has been a tendency to write about white women's experience as "women's experience," while women of color speak only for their race and gender. Nonwhite feminists critiqued the feminist movement, especially its earlier phases, as being about the issues of middle-class white women. White feminists need to resist the urge to create white images and standards of humanity, even as they urge men to examine male privilege.

ECONOMIC SPHERE

Women make up slightly more than half of the total US resident population and are thus a numeric majority in this country. However, because of their unequal position in the economic, political, and social spheres of American life, women are still considered a "minority group" on par with minority racial and ethnic groups. Women who worked full-time all year in 2010 earned eighty cents for every dollar that men earned for their full-time, year-round work (Census Bureau 2012, 421). The median earnings of full-time, year-round men were about $42,848, compared with $34,788 for women (Census Bureau 2012). In explaining this discrepancy, the authors of the thoroughly researched book *The Cost of Being Female* noted that women

> are excluded from many good jobs. We are discriminated against in pay. More and more of us are supporting ourselves and our children with or without a husband's help. If we try to climb the corporate ladder, we bump our heads on a "glass ceiling," beyond which we cannot climb. (Headlee and Elfin 1996, xiv)

Because of discrimination, child care costs, and deadbeat dads, many women are unable to work full-time and year-round, so other economic comparisons show women to be more economically disadvantaged than the comparisons above. For example, in 2012, the median earnings of a female householder with no husband present were $34,002 compared to an income of $48,634 for a male householder with no wife present (DeNavas-Walt, Proctor, and Smith 2013, 6). Such disparities in wages mean that women are disproportionately in poverty: In 2012, 17.4 percent of households with a male head and no wife present were in poverty, but 33.9 percent of female-headed households with no male were in poverty (Census Bureau 2013). The economic situation of single, female-headed families (no male) with children under age eighteen is particularly grim. Overall, nearly half of all such households live below the poverty line, compared with one-quarter of single male-headed households (no female). These findings hold for white, black, or Hispanic families, although white families generally are better situated than black or Hispanic families: "Among children living in single female-headed families, more than half of black children (53.3%) and Hispanic children (54.7%) were poor; in contrast, over one-third of non-Hispanic white children (36.5%) were poor" (Gabe 2013, 7). The situation of older, retired women tends to be worse than their male counterparts because lower earnings over a woman's lifetime mean less money for retirement, along with fewer assets.

In addition to glass ceilings that prevent the advancement of women, a large amount of occupational segregation with "sticky floors" keeps women in low-paying occupations such as secretaries and typists—jobs that are seen as "women's work" and devalued accordingly. Even women in higher-level jobs and professions earn less than their male counterparts. A common explanation for this discrepancy is that women have less education and work experience than men. However, women "in their thirties actually have more education than men in that age group, and are still paid less" (Headlee and Elfin 1996, 7). Other studies show that additional years of experience do not have the same rate of salary return for women as they do for men.

Hence, women remain severely overrepresented in clerical and service occupations, making up over 90 percent of those employed as registered nurses and licensed practical nurses, secretaries and receptionists, kindergarten teachers, and child-care workers. Meanwhile, men are disproportionately employed in craft and laborer jobs; around 90 percent of all mechanics, construction workers, metal workers, truck drivers, and other motor vehicle workers are men, as are 90 percent of all architects and engineers, clergy, airplane pilots, police officers, and firefighters. In 2013, there were twenty-one women CEOs at Fortune 500 companies, including the first African American woman.

Chapter 3 noted that determining social class for women can be difficult, especially where they are dependent on men for income while they disproportionately perform unpaid domestic labor such as raising children. The especially difficult aspect of figuring class is determining the separate wealth and assets of men and women, but estimates indicate that never-married women working full-time have a median wealth that is only 16 percent of never-married men working full-time (Chang 2010, 7). Further, "the median wealth owned by non-married women is only 36% of the median wealth owned by non-married men" (Chang 2010, 15). Not surprisingly, the sex differences for accumulated wealth are larger than differences in income. Women's "smaller nest eggs are subject to depletion in crisis situations," so women invest in less risky assets that have lower rates of return (Chang 2010, 16). Current public policy also imposes a motherhood wage and tax penalty because "for every year a woman is a full-time caregiver, she must work five extra years to make up for the lost income and pension benefits" (2010, 16). Of course, many women have zero or negative wealth, including more than half of all single Hispanic women, 26 percent of white single women, and 36 percent of black single women (Chang 2010, 15). These differences are important in terms of women's security, health, retirement, and overall economic power.

POLITICAL SPHERE

Final ratification of the Nineteenth Amendment occurred in 1920 and finally gave women the right to vote, fifty years after the Fifteenth Amendment granted former (male) slaves the right to vote. African Americans used their political voice to pursue a federal antilynching law, while white women pursued issues related to child labor and laws about women's working conditions. Women were united in the goal of getting the right to vote, but once they had it, "the lines that divided women—class, race, age, ideology—became more significant" (DuBois and Dumenil 2005, 483). The National Women's Party introduced an equal rights amendment in 1923, which immediately exposed different views of equality. At a time before a minimum wage law and a mass of New Deal legislation that many now take for granted, women had worked to pass laws that protected them from exploitation in the workplace before unions, collective bargaining, and occupational health and safety laws. They feared equality would mean that hard-won protections would be repealed, while others "countered that such legislation treated women as invalids and could limit their economic opportunity" (DuBois and Dumenil 2005, 483).

In 1986 the historical pattern of higher voter turnout rates for men than for women was reversed. Ever since then, the proportion of eligible female adults who voted has exceeded the proportion of eligible male adults who voted. But increased participation in voting has not led to proportionate representation, especially at the national level. When the 113th Congress convened in January 2013, women held 20 of 100 Senate seats and 78 of 435 seats in the House of Representatives (plus three nonvoting positions representing Washington, D.C., Guam, and the Virgin Islands). Of these congressional women, fourteen are African American, seven are Asian Pacific Islanders, nine are Latino, and the representative from the Virgin Islands is a Caribbean American. On the state level in 2013, women accounted for five governors and ten lieutenant governors; 24 percent of state legislators were women (Center for the American Woman and Politics 2013). While women do not all see issues the same way, the shortage of women's voices in national politics hinders attempts to alter the status quo and effect lasting changes in social and criminal justice legislation and policy.

SOCIAL SPHERE

Women tend to live longer than men in almost every country of the world. In the United States, the gender gap is due largely to gender differences in smoking behavior, traumatic deaths (such as car accidents, suicides, and murder), heart disease, and cancer, according to a cross-national study in *Social Science Quarterly* (Clark and Peck 2012). The authors measured the level of modernization and development, women's status, and economic inequality and found that "income inequality widens the gender gap in life expectancy. . . . When females occupy a greater share of the legislature, the welfare state expands, serving as a cushion for impoverished groups, a condition that disproportionately helps males. . . . Democratization positively affects female life expectancy but has no significant impact on male life expectancy" (Clark and Peck 2012). Overall, the authors conclude that political equality is good for women and economic inequality is bad for men. Also, whereas initially there may be a widening of the gap of life expectancy when women's status improves, continued rises in women's political and economic efficacy ultimately narrows the gap of life expectancy between men and women.

Troubling, however, is the continued reliance on white males as the primary subject for medical and biological research in the United States. Specifically, "outside the specialized realm of [women's] reproduction, all other health research concerned men's bodies and men's diseases. Reproduction was so central to women's biological existence that women's nonreproductive health was rendered virtually invisible" (Kreiger and Fee 1994, 16). Some argue that "the lack of [medical] research on white women and on men and women in nonwhite racial/ethnic groups resulted from a perception of white men as the norm" (16), while others argue that "for the most part, the health of women and men of color and the nonreproductive health of white women were simply ignored" (16).

In challenging this bias, whether it is based on false universalism or male-centered practice of medical science, the women's health movement since the 1960s has demanded that the medical community pay more attention to biology and illnesses specific to women and to conduct more research using women as subjects. It has also promoted women's empowerment through self-education and has lobbied for governmental changes on the local and national levels (e.g., establishment of governmental women's health organizations such as the Office on Women's Health under the US Department of Health and Human Services). While these efforts have led to some social change, the gap in the knowledge about women's health remains.

While the female gender role is increasingly accepting of female athletics, the cultural notion of ideal feminine beauty still emphasizes being thin, young, quiet, and pleasing—an image from mainstream mass media that causes a much higher rate of eating disorders linked to poor body image and low self-esteem among women than men. Indeed, Jean Kilbourne (known for her videos titled *Still Killing Us Softly*) notes that women's magazines are "an invitation to pathology":

> A typical woman's magazine has a photo of some rich food on the front cover, a cheese-cake covered with luscious cherries or a huge slice of apple pie with ice cream melting on top. On the back cover, there is usually a cigarette ad, often one implying that smoking will keep women thin. Inside the magazine are recipes, more photos of fattening foods, articles about dieting—and lots of advertising featuring very thin models. There usually

also is at least one article about an uncommon disease or trivial health hazard, which can seem very ironic in light of the truly dangerous product being glamorized on the back cover. (Kilbourne 2000)

The impact of these messages is different across race, and the culture of thinness falsely universalizes the eating disorder experience of women of color. For example, one study found that minority women who suffer from "acculturative stress," which occurs when members of a minority group try to "fit in" with the cultural beauty standards of the dominant group, are more likely to have an eating disorder (Gordon et al. 2010). But minority women who do not have significant levels of "acculturative stress" may not suffer from an eating disorder. Instead, many black and Latino girls and women subscribe to their own group's beauty standards that do not require thinness. So while black and Latino women are certainly aware of the thin body image to which the dominant group subscribes, many of them do not adopt that body image for themselves. One important implication of this research is this: "The fact that Latinas selected significantly thinner ethnic group body ideals than Black women suggests clustering all 'non-White' women together is not appropriate because it obscures ethnic group differences in putative risk factors for eating pathology" (Gordon et al. 2010, 141). Further, black and Latino women should be measured for "acculturative stress" before any attempts are made to diagnose them with an eating disorder.

Beyond eating disorders, media messages and low self-esteem lead to very different rates of cosmetic surgery for men and women. Body image is a much more salient aspect of the female gender role than the male, so women are encouraged to take physical beauty and weight much more seriously. Thus, according to the American Society for Aesthetic Plastic Surgery (2013), 90 percent of the cosmetic procedures and surgery in 2012 were performed on women. The top surgical procedures, in order of popularity, were breast augmentation, liposuction, and abdominoplasty ("tummy tuck"). While cosmetic procedures are also increasing for men, the overall level is still quite low because the male gender role emphasizes achievement, especially in the areas of wealth and power.

IMPLICATIONS

Studying gender, or how men and women accomplish masculinity and femininity, entails a consideration of how social structures constrain and channel behavior, which, in turn, may influence a person's criminal or law-abiding behavior or his or her actions in the workplace (Martin and Jurik 1996; Messerschmidt 1997; West and Zimmerman 1987). While some success has been realized, there is much ground yet to be covered in achieving gender equality and justice. After reviewing the economic, political, and social evidence, it is apparent that most power is concentrated in the hands of men; the United States is still a male-dominated society. Men (particularly white men) still control all of the key institutions of power, such as the military, government, business, academic, and financial institutions of the United States.

Increasingly, scholars are challenging the treatment of gender in existing theory and research, moving away from treating women as anomalies toward locating women at the center of research. This research also increasingly wrestles with the exploration of how race and ethnicity, class, and other social characteristics such as age intersect with gender to shape one's experience, as will be explored in the next chapter. But as long as victims from either gender are stigmatized, blamed, or ridiculed for their situations, as long as women and men are harmed by purportedly "gender-neutral" policies, as long as workers are sexually harassed in the workplace, as long as women and minority men are treated as "problems" or "anomalies," as long as the institutions governing the treatment of men and women in the legislature, law enforcement, adjudication, or incarceration continue to be dominated by one sex, the fields of crime and justice will not progress.

REVIEW AND DISCUSSION QUESTIONS

1. What helps to explain why only male students have committed "rampage school shootings," and what helps to explain why these killings have occurred only at rural and suburban, not urban, high schools?
2. Distinguish between the terms *sex* and *gender*.
3. What is male privilege? What are some examples from the chapter and from your experiences?
4. How does privilege relate to feminism? Who benefits from male privilege?
5. In the context of economic, political, and social spheres, how are men still privileged in relation to women in American society?

6

Understanding Privilege and the Intersections of Class, Race, and Gender

The reciprocal and intersecting relations of class, race, gender, and crime are captured in the ethnographic examinations of two recent books written by former gang members who have become university professors and high-profile gang researchers. Both of these books are informed by critical race theory and by these authors' personal experiences, which are incorporated into their otherwise historical and contemporary analyses of life in the barrios and ghettos of several cities across the United States, including Ogden, Utah, Denver, Colorado, and Oakland and Santa Barbara, California. The second of these accounts, published in 2012, is Gang Life in Two Cities: An Insider's Account, *written by Robert J. Duran. Duran has adopted a colonization framework that explains how structural and socioeconomic conditions have helped to shape physically and psychologically threatening and insecure environments for both males and females born or raised in these communities of oppression. Duran also explains how ethnic gangs from the barrios and ghettos emerge as forms of resistance and self-protection to communities of marginal political, social, and economic oppression that end up ironically reproducing similar forms of oppression.*

The first of these accounts, published in 2011, was Victor Rios's book Punished, *referred to in the previous chapter. It is a nuanced treatment of the criminalization of urban and marginalized male street youths and their resistance to the cultural mainstream, inside and outside of the criminal justice system. In one of Rios's anecdotal reflections, he tells the story of an encounter between a white female potential employer-manager and a young black man seeking unsuccessfully to bridge the cultural gap and find legitimate work. Rios writes:*

> *Ronny was called in for a job interview at Carrows, a chain restaurant that served $9.99 sirloin steak and shrimp. He called me up, asking for help. I lent him a crisp white dress shirt, which I had purchased at a discount store when I worked as a server at a steak house*

147

during my undergraduate years. I convinced Ronny to wear fitted khakis, rather than his customary baggy jeans. He agreed, with the condition that he would wear his white Nike Air Force Ones, a popular basketball shoe at the time . . . famous basketball players such as Kobe Bryant wore these shoes during games and advertised for Nike. Black and Latino youths in Oakland gravitated to these shoes, sometimes even wearing them to more formal events such as high school proms and weddings. I asked Ronny why he insisted on wearing these shoes in a professional setting. He replied, "Because professionals wear them."

Many of the boys believed that they had a clear sense of what courteous, professional, and "good" behavior was. Despite their attempts to present themselves with good manners and good morals, their idea of professional behavior did not match mainstream ideas of professional behavior. This in turn created what I refer to as misrecognition. When the boys displayed a genuine interest in "going legit," getting a job or doing well in school, adults often could not recognize their positive attempts and sometimes interpreted them as rude or malicious acts and therefore criminalized them.

With these observations, Rios describes some of the traps within which many poor black and Latino boys become ensnared by a society that closely resembles a caste system of immobility based on ranks of class, race, and gender. The boys' socialization in poor urban neighborhoods has taught them to survive by being aggressive and charismatic, by being willing (and able) to fight at a moment's notice, by being able to run from danger, and by maintaining a stylish appearance at all times.

For that reason, Air Force One shoes by Nike are part of an inner-city uniform—some might even call it a cloak of protection or power signifying elite status. So when these boys think about trying to get respect from the mainstream society while maintaining readiness and respect in their own neighborhoods (which is where they will have to return after working a shift at a restaurant), their first inclination is to wear their best sneakers to a job interview. And although the message received by employers might be one of disrespect, the employers usually don't understand the life that these boys have to navigate.

In short, living in a poor neighborhood and being Latino or black and being male is an intersectional problem: the difficulties that some people face just for being poor (indecent housing, inadequate clothing, poor diet, crowded living conditions, limited transportation, etc.) are compounded by the difficulties of being black or Latino (prejudice, discrimination, stereotypes, police brutality, mass incarceration, hopelessness, etc.) and with being males (hypermasculinity standards, toughness, independence, the role of sexual aggressiveness, etc.). So with all of this stacked against them, it is very hard for a young man like Ronny to believe that he should wear a pair of wing-tip shoes to a job interview at a restaurant when the people in his neighborhood will think he is "soft" or "ripe" for victimization while he is walking to and from his job. Besides, Ronny already believes that "professionals" wear Air Force Ones because highly paid rappers such as Nelly and sports figures such as Kobe Bryant wear them. Rios continues:

The boys attempted to use the resilience skills they had learned on the streets, their organic capital, in spaces that could not value the respectability and morals that they brought to the table. These morals and values were often rendered deviant, and the boys were excluded or criminalized. Ronny's story is indicative of how many of the boys attempted to tap into main-

stream institutions but failed. As they encountered rejection, they returned to the resilience and survival strategies that they had developed in their neighborhoods.

The day of the interview, Rios prepared Ronny for his interview, helping him to develop the "acceptable" cultural capital. He also located himself in the restaurant and ordered a meal so that he could observe the interaction between Ronny and his potential manager. During the interview, "Ronny tried to use his charisma to connect with the manager, but she kept her distance and did not look at Ronny the entire time he answered questions, seemingly uninterested in what he had to say. At the end of the interview, Ronny abruptly stood up and walked away from the manager, with no handshake or smile. He went outside."

Rios had decided to take his food to go, and as he was leaving the restaurant to meet up with Ronny, he noticed that the manager "was greeting a White male youth. She smiled, gave him her hand, and offered him a place to sit down. Ronny's first contact with her was not this friendly."

At the debriefing following the interview, Ronny told Rios that "he had a good feeling and that the manager had seemed to like him." In turn, Rios asked Ronny to walk him through the interview, confirming that Ronny followed the plan flawlessly. Rios wrote:

> I was proud of him. "You followed the plan. You did a great job," I told him. "Why didn't you shake her hand when you left?" I asked. "Cause," Ronny replied. "Why not?" I scolded. "Because it was a White lady. You not supposed to shake a White lady's hand. They be scared of a nigga. They think I'm a try to take their shit or fuck 'em. I just said thanks and walked out." Ronny did not get the job.

Rios captures the drive that many black and Latino boys have in trying to gain legitimate employment by being willing to enter into work spaces as low-level employees, showing enthusiasm for the job and seeking out mentors to help to prepare them for the interview. But the stereotypes abounding in the United States that criminalize black and Latino boys are brought into the interview, not from the mainstream side (in this case) but from the outsider's point of view. Ronny is well aware of the stereotypes of people who look like him, and his knowledge of those stereotypes all but compelled him to practically sabotage his own attempt to gain employment. Certainly, it is unclear whether Ronny didn't get the job because of his shoes or his unwillingness to shake the manager's hand, but Rios is purposeful with his description of the job candidate who came in after Ronny, that is, making a point to mention the welcoming behaviors that were absent during Ronny's interview and yet so obvious to Rios at the beginning of the second boy's interview. Such are the kinds of "niceties" that many whites face in interviews with people of their same race, where they may take for granted that someone will be welcoming to them when they appear for an interview. This is, in part, one example of the unearned benefit package that exists in white privilege and class privilege: not having to wonder whether interviewers will view you as someone who will try to rob or rape them.

Imagine standing in the middle of an intersection with a view down several streets that run in different directions. If a friend stands at the end of one of those streets, she can share some of the same view, but her perspective will also be different: the features that are closest will be different, and she will have a view down different side streets. Now think of those streets as being social dimensions such as class, race, ethnicity, gender, age, and sexual orientation. To add to the analogy, imagine class as being represented by the height of the buildings and the floor one is standing on (including, perhaps, being in a basement). The view of those streets represents a person's life experiences, worldview, and "social location." Describing a person's social location based solely on race, for example, would be incomplete and possibly confusing; it would be like saying "Main Street" or "Third Street" in a large, diverse city without specifying a cross (intersecting) street. An indication of whether the location was in a penthouse or lower floor would also have value in describing both the location and the view (perspective). Thus, an accurate description requires other markers, such as gender and class, to get a "fix" on the location.

This chapter is about recognizing that all people are at the center of multiple inter-sections of power, inequality, and privilege as shaped by their class, race/ethnicity, and gender. Nobody fits into any one category alone; instead, everyone exists at the inter-section of many categories that shape not only their view of the world and the actions they take but also other people's view of them (Wildman [1996] 1997). The overlap-ping of two or more of these classifications (e.g., race, class, and gender), however, is often unobserved in discussions about any one of these individual classifications. So when researchers talk about "Latinos" or "women" or "poverty" they very rarely acknowledge the large number of people who experience the world as all three! That is, poor Latina women experience the disadvantages of all three groups simultaneously.

As straightforward as this perspective seems, scholars of crime and justice have been slow to embrace the idea of "intersectionalities" applying to all groups of people. Researchers tend to focus on one social dimension at a time, independent of others. Even the widely used phrase "women and minorities" does not take into account that approximately 15 percent of the population are *both* women *and* racial or ethnic minorities (see box 6.1). Women of color cannot choose to be treated as a

BOX 6.1.   ASK A SIMPLE QUESTION . . .

Facts: Men are more likely than women to be murdered in their lifetime. Blacks are more likely than whites to be murdered in their lifetime.

Question: Who is more likely to be murdered, a white man or a black woman?

Fact: Blacks constitute about 13 percent of the US population but make up nearly 1 million of the total 2.3 million people who are currently incarcerated in the United States (NAACP 2009–2013). Women make up over half of the US population, and around 7 percent of those incarcerated in state or federal prisons.

Question: Are black women overrepresented or underrepresented in correctional facilities?

Having trouble answering these questions?

Answers: To take the first example, logic probably made it relatively easy to figure out that black men face the highest likelihood of being murdered relative to black women and whites. The conclusion that white women face the lowest likelihood of being murdered relative to white men and blacks was probably also straightforward. But to answer the question posed with any degree of confidence requires more information on race and gender combined—for example, for black women, white men, and so on. This information ultimately reveals that black women actually face a higher likelihood of being murdered than white men.

The second question is probably best answered "Both." Black women are both overrepresented (as blacks) and underrepresented (as women) in prisons. Of course, black women incarcerated in state or federal prison have more at stake than simply a choice of words. While the disproportionate incarceration of blacks has received a great deal of attention in the media, most of this attention has been focused on black men. Similarly, a typical discussion of "women's experiences" has all too often assumed that black women share the experiences and needs of white women.

It was this situation that the editors of a classic text were addressing when they named their book *All the Women Are White, All the Blacks Are Men, but Some of Us Are Brave* (Hull, Scott, and Smith 1982). This seminal work set the foundation for creating black women's studies as an academic discipline for university students. The authors meant the book to serve as a "reference text and pedagogical tool" for people interested in creating a discipline that would reduce the "extremely negative ways in which Afro-American women have been portrayed in literature, scholarship, and the popular media" and would expand "opportunities for Black women to carry out autonomously defined investigations of self in a society which through racial, sexual, and class oppression systematically denies our existence" (1982, xviii).

The issues raised by these two questions go beyond mere semantics and wordplay. This exercise speaks in a small way to the importance of considering characteristics such as race and gender not as separate constructs but as interlocking ones.

member of the oppressed sex one day and a member of the oppressed racial group the next. They are—and will always be—both, although race may be more important in some situations and gender in others. Being both, however, frequently leads to invisibility, which came up during the 2004 vice-presidential debates. Moderator Gwen Ifill asked both candidates about AIDS, "and not about AIDS in China or Africa. But AIDS right here in this country, where black women between the ages of twenty-five and forty-four are thirteen times more likely to die of the disease than their counterparts." Between Dick Cheney and John Edwards, the candidates talked about AIDS in Africa, health insurance, and genocide in Sudan, but "nary a word about Ifill's original question. The ball dropped, and bounced, and rolled away as if it were invisible" (Talvi 2004).

It is important to acknowledge these layers of identity and experiences, though, because examining them reveals differing opinions about crime and justice. For example, "whites, wealthier people, males, Republicans, and westerners have tended to support the death penalty more than Blacks, poorer people, females, Democrats, and Southerners," but also "diversity within group racial and ethnic identity does lead to diversity in death penalty opinions and justifications for support" (Mallicoat and Brown 2008). The authors go on to report that the Hispanic/Latino and Asian American participants in their study show greater variance in support of the death penalty compared with whites.

Further, even when research does try to discuss more than one dimension, it still lacks an understanding of privilege. Many studies that look at race differences do not acknowledge white privilege and how that can shape patterns of behavior, research questions, methods, and conclusions. Likewise, many studies of gender differences do not acknowledge male privilege and how that can shape patterns of behavior, research questions, methods, and conclusions. Many criminologists, in other words, still assume that gender is relevant only when discussing women, race is relevant only when discussing blacks and other people of color, and class is relevant only when talking about the very rich or the very poor. Similarly, many people assume that sexual orientation is relevant only when applied to gays and lesbians. The point is, on the contrary, that everyone is a member of a social class and an ethnic/racial group, and all people also bring their sexuality and gender construction to their presentation and reception of self in everyday reality.

The intersections of class, race, and gender thus describe a way of viewing social inequalities or privileges as interrelated and interacting. So, for example, sometimes black and Latino women make decisions about how to respond to abusive intimate partners based on how they believe the police will treat their abusive partner because he is a poor black or Latino male. Sometimes, "multicultural interventions and programming that are based on middle-class White women do not typically meet the needs of women of color" (Potter 2008, 6). Researchers, policymakers, and others should not *essentialize* groups by assuming that all women or all blacks or all poor people are a certain way; there is a great deal of diversity within class, race, and gender groups. But in dealing with the complexity of differences, it is also a mistake to become so focused on differences that one misses the larger patterns of class, race, and gender privilege that are present in crime and social control.

One way to begin working on incorporating the various dimensions of race, class, and gender is to view these categories as worthwhile and impactful. Since the study of racial minorities is ongoing, why not add a dimension or two to broaden the perspective in the same way that some scholars have begun to do? In the introduction to a special issue of *Feminist Economics*, the authors make the case for intersectional exertion:

> Intersectionality gives us at least three ways to think about women as distinguished by color, caste, and class. One way is to consider the particularity of each group. The experiences of African American women are distinct from those of Chinese American women. . . . Another way is to examine how each group is ideologically defined by elements of another's characteristics . . . [such as] the sexing of race, or class, or caste. And we know all too well the third aspect of intersectionality, which is the common attribution of inferiority made on all of these bases. (Brewer, Conrad, and King 2002, 13)

Maxine Baca Zinn and her colleagues use the analogy of a prism to capture this idea: light is made up of many colors that appear to be the same, but it "is not an infinite, disorganized scatter of colors. Rather refracted light displays an order, a structure of relationships among the different colors—a rainbow" (2005, 1). As we discuss more below, currently there are quite a few studies of individual groups, and the next major task is to build better understandings of the larger structure of relationships so that the "patchwork" of studies can be transformed into something even more understandable.

Thus, this chapter explores some of the challenges to understanding intersectionality, a term used to capture the many dynamics involved in studying how the pieces of class, race, and gender "abrade, inflame, amplify, twist, negate, dampen and complicate each other" (quoted in Baca Zinn, Hondagneu-Sotelo, and Messner 2005, 7). Toward this end, the rest of the chapter is divided into three sections followed by a section on the implications. The first section examines the question of whether one factor is more important than others, which would simplify the conceptual challenge if class or race or gender were always the most significant influence. The next section examines privilege, which may blind people to parts of their location and thus the dynamics involved in other situations. Finally, there is a section on the available data and techniques for modeling social phenomena that present another challenge to the development of knowledge about intersectionality.

NO "MASTER STATUS"

Attempting to examine the interacting effects of class *and* race *and* gender is difficult, so a logical step to getting a handle on it is to ask which is the most important. If, for example, gender consistently had the most significant impact, then it could be described as the *master status*. Unfortunately, though, neither class nor race nor gender is always the most important consideration. In some situations, one may be more important than the others in shaping the social reality of a situation, but existing theory is not sufficiently developed to predict which factor will be most important under which conditions. While this knowledge gap is frustrating, the less-than-perfect knowledge about how class, race, and gender interact does not undermine the advantages of trying to examine all of them rather than settling for a simpler, inaccurate analysis.

Theorists who focus primarily on class or race or gender can make a strong claim about the importance of the attribute they study. Marxists, for example, point to class and argue that history is defined by the struggle between the rich and poor, the haves and have-nots. Law is a tool used by the rich, who make the law in this class warfare. Some feminists see "the battle of the sexes" as more fundamental and point to the failure of much traditional class analysis to examine women's unpaid household work and reproductive labor (which makes it difficult to place them in the class structure, as noted in chapters 3 and 5). Law tends to have a patriarchal bias because men tend to make the law and are the majority of judges. Others would argue that race is fundamental because it has been the basis of genocide in the United States (see chapter 7), slavery, and the Nazi Holocaust; chapter 4 noted that American history has included a succession of exploited minorities—blacks, Asians, Native Americans, and so on. Laws made by the white majority defined the slave owner's property rights, reaffirmed segregation, and established the basis for the criminal justice system to police minorities—especially to maintain social control over excess labor. All three positions make an important and strong claim, which is why this book highlights class, race, and gender. Yet, when combined, the arguments do not support a claim that one factor is *always* the most important, so the emphasis must be on understanding how they work together.

To take a concrete example, consider the case of a minority congressman, Representative Harold E. Ford from Tennessee. Under many circumstances, being a member of Congress is the most important aspect of his interactions, so class would be the primary status (remember that class includes status as well as actual salary). But when he was stopped by a police officer at the airport in Washington, D.C., race was the important factor as even the congressman was affected by a version of "driving while black." Ford said the officer "demanded to see identification, and when I showed it to him, he couldn't believe it was my car and that I was a member of Congress. . . . Finally, he let me go. No apology or nothing. It really hurt me. If I'm treated like this, I can imagine how folks who don't have access to the things I do as a member of Congress are treated" (Samborn 1999). In this situation, race was the reason for the stop and was so significant that the officer did not feel an apology was necessary, even after discovering he had stopped a member of Congress. To his credit, though, Ford is aware that intersections are important and that in other situations, being a member of Congress provides a privilege and access to power that other minorities do not have.

Privilege

As pointed out in each of the chapters on class, race, and gender, privilege makes inequalities seem "natural" and blinds people to many social dynamics. The rich are less likely to appreciate structural barriers to class mobility; male privilege will affect how men view gender equality; and white privilege will affect how whites view and understand racial issues. An intersectional example of rich, white, male privilege is from the 2012 presidential election, when candidate Mitt Romney, who was reported to be worth $230–$250 million, advised a group of students about how to get ahead: "Borrow money from your parents if you have to, start a business." He did not seem to realize that most students do not come from families with large amounts of disposable income. One website reported that "the advice fits right into the characterization that Romney is 'out of touch' with regular people" (Strasser 2012).

Further, class, race, and gender are only the starting point for understanding privilege. For example, the Social Work Code of Ethics requires those engaged in the provision of services to understand their clients in ways that include but are not limited to "race, ethnicity, national origin, color, sex, sexual orientation, age, marital status, political belief, religion, and mental or physical disability" (quoted in Leighton and Killingbeck 2001). This statement is part of a larger requirement to understand diversity and oppression, so the National Association of Social Workers recognizes that privilege can potentially exist in all those areas.

Box 6.2 elaborates on the notion of privilege by examining some of the overlapping class, race, and gender privileges for a middle-class white male. Readers who do not fall into this category can still identify aspects of privilege they may share. The focus of attention should be on the idea of *privilege* rather than classism, racism, and sexism (Krisberg 1975; McIntosh [1988] 1997; Wildman and Davis 1997). These "isms" and other forms of systematic discrimination would not exist if some people in the social order and hierarchy did not benefit from them. Also, discussions of the "isms" are much more common than candid discussions of privilege, but they may contribute to the very problems they identify by individualizing what is a systemic problem of power and inequality. For example, calling someone a racist or a sexist lays the blame on the individual rather than the cultural, social, and legal mechanisms that support and reinforce these expressions of racism and sexism.

As a consequence, instead of being concerned about institutionalized racism and sexism, whites and men tend to focus on how to avoid the respective labels of racist and sexist while simultaneously benefiting from their privileged position in relation to these "isms" the labels refer to. An example of this is the way that sexual harassment cases are viewed in the United States. Women are more likely to file sexual harassment complaints against men: in fact, "men rarely report being victims of sexual harassment . . . and when they are, its effects are comparatively inconsequential" (Sheets and Braver 1999). But women are "9 times more likely to have quit a job, 5 times more likely to have been transferred, and 3 times more likely to have lost a job because of sexual harassment." Still, rather than deal with the overall culture of male dominance that allows women to be harassed by men in the workplace, each

BOX 6.2.   YOU KNOW YOU'RE
PRIVILEGED WHEN . . . (PART 4)

In keeping with this section's focus on intersectionality, we have expanded on the forms of white privilege discussed in chapter 4 and male privilege discussed in chapter 5. This list attempts to identify some of the specific characteristics of middle-class white male privilege:

- People who meet me for the first time will assume that I have a regular job and no criminal record.
- I get praise from women friends and colleagues when I demonstrate that I can cook, clean, or care for small children.
- The schools I went to as a child had relatively new textbooks, computers, and solid teachers.
- When I wear expensive clothing or jewelry or drive an expensive car, I will be treated as though I obtained these goods through the fruits of my own legitimate labor rather than through illegal activity or my association with a sexual intimate.
- If I am a parent of small children who works long hours outside the home, people will perceive me as a good provider who only wants the best for my family rather than as someone who puts career above family or is otherwise a faulty, absentee parent.
- In the event I am assaulted while walking home at two in the morning, no one will assume I was involved in an illicit business transaction that went bad or blame me for being out late at night.
- At work, no one will imply that I got my job based on my race or sex.
- I can think over many options, social, political, imaginative, or professional, without asking whether a person of my race would be accepted or allowed to do what I want to do.
- If I have low credibility as a leader I can be sure that my sex and race are not the problem.

Jewel Woods (2008) notes that because of white privilege, many black males do not see themselves as privileged. But he notes many ways that black men have privilege when compared to black women:

- When I learn about the civil rights movement and the black power movements, most of the leaders that I will learn about will be black men. I will be taken more seriously as a political leader than black women.
- I can easily imagine that most of the artists in hip-hop are members of my sex. I can easily imagine that most of the women that appear in hip-hop videos are there solely to please men.

- I have the privilege of consuming and popularizing the word *pimp*, which is based on the exploitation of women, with virtually no opposition from other men.
- I can believe that the success of the black family is dependent on returning men to their historical place within the family rather than in promoting policies that strengthen black women's independence or that provide social benefits to black children. My "strength" as a man is never connected with the failure of the black family, whereas the strength of black women is routinely associated with the failure of the black family.
- If I am a coach, I can motivate, punish, or embarrass a player by saying that the player plays like a girl.
- I do not have to worry about being considered a traitor to my race if I call the police on a member of the opposite sex.

case continues to be decided individually where issues of sexism, classism (including the relative statuses of the individuals in the organization who are parties to the complaint), and sometimes racism or ageism continue to be central to the harassment complaint.

To the extent the "isms" discourse remains necessary, people should realize that patterns of domination and subordination are not interchangeable. In other words, someone subordinated under one form of discrimination or oppression is not similarly situated to someone under another form. This would mean, for example, that there is a difference between a black or brown male subject to racial prejudice and a white, a black, and a brown female subject to sexual stereotypes; white women who view themselves as oppressed under sexism are in a privileged position based on heterosexism and racism. Drawing attention to a matrix of privilege and oppression is more complex but also more potentially productive because it highlights the benefits of the current system for different groups as well as the ideological blinders that may prevent individuals from seeing those benefits.

As one of many examples, while there is still some public debate on "affirmative action" and admission to colleges and universities, there is relatively no mention of "legacy admissions." A study of all law school admissions found that twice the number of whites as blacks got into law schools on the basis of alumni preference, an elegant essay, or recommendations from powerful people (Wightman 1997). These students—largely white and of higher class—would not have been admitted on grades and test scores alone. These legacy admissions favor children of influential alumni or donors over other applicants—sometimes twice as many students were admitted through legacy admissions than through affirmative action (Padilla 1997, 2). Significantly, legacy students are perceived as deserving rather than unfairly privileged. However, many view students admitted under affirmative action as having received an undeserved advantage. In the case of legacies, nobody shouts "continued discrimination"; in the case of affirmative action, many shout "reverse discrimination."

Being aware of privilege is an important first step. Going further requires reading and seeking out knowledge "from the margins," that is, created by the marginalized groups. This material relates experiences that more privileged groups do not have and may include theorizing about those experiences that were not previously recognized as valid "knowledge" or "truth." As Dorothy Smith discusses in her chapter "Women's Experience as a Radical Critique of Sociology" (1990), the insider's experience—"an experience distinctively of women, though by no means the experience of all women"—furnishes the basis for a critical standpoint. It can expose privilege in the existing bodies of knowledge, in the creation of new languages, and in the methods, practices of knowing, and political strategies. Ideally, this knowledge should not be collected into a sociology of women but should "bring us to ask how a sociology might look if it began from a woman's standpoint and what might happen to a sociology that attempts to deal seriously with that standpoint" (D. Smith 1990, 12).

With criminology and criminal justice, it is important to incorporate the views of these marginalized groups into theories, policies, and procedures because the point of law enforcement, for example, is to protect and serve all the people within a particular jurisdiction. A view that incorporates the perspective of only one group in that jurisdiction is simply inaccurate and cannot serve all the interests of a diverse community, even though some people in privileged strata may prefer (and even advocate for) the more simple (and traditional) view from their social location. Returning to the analogy that opened this chapter, problems arise when policy is made for a whole city based on the view from a skyscraper in a wealthy neighborhood. This view captures the details of only their reality to the exclusion of many others who may be viewing the world from the windowless basement floor of a building at a different intersection of the city. "Justice" requires a more balanced approach, an approach that considers the view of people from several floors in different buildings that sit on several different intersections in a city simultaneously. The point of such discussions and writing should not be to make people feel guilt over privilege, because that is rarely the basis for a productive reaction or sustainable change. Rather, the point should be to raise awareness about privilege so that the person is in a better position to participate in the creation of a more equal and inclusive society through individual and collective actions.

DATA AND MODELING

A final challenge to studying intersections relates to the lack of complete data for systematic comparisons and the limitations of many models used to study social dynamics. Even when race data are fully collected, some of the five categories are relatively small, so they get collapsed into the category of "other" or even completely omitted. Various chapters have already noted how internally heterogeneous racial categories can be, and adding together Native Americans, Pacific Islanders, and nonwhite Latinos creates a category so diverse that it defies interpretation. Reports from governmental agencies typically use panethnic/racial categories such as black, Hispanic, and white (occasionally Asian and Native American) that mask great variations along generational, class, language, gender, and ethnic lines within each group. Also, government agencies tend to treat race and gender as separate variables rather than as overlapping social locations. Even reports published by the Bureau of the Census, the Department of Labor, and the Department of Justice seldom present breakdowns by race and gender simultaneously that would permit readers to compare, for instance, the offenses committed by white men to those committed by white women.

Another barrier to understanding intersections in relation to crime and justice is that most academic and government sources on criminal justice information reduce the social relations of class, race, and gender to static categorical variables. With the widespread availability of computers and statistical software, researchers increasingly attempt to isolate specific effects of class, race, and gender on, say, a person's likelihood of being arrested or incarcerated. These mostly quantitative attempts to disaggregate effects come at the expense of understanding how these structuring factors interact with one another to yield, for example, *gendered racism* in a myriad of forms and shapes.

Furthermore, the emphasis on quantitative methods and statistical analyses has resulted in a tendency among academics to conduct research from the assumption that we can "hold all else constant." But even though it is common knowledge that racial discrimination means blacks have lower income, researchers "control" for income to estimate the amount of racial discrimination, and the results of this sophisticated statistical control end up minimizing the amount of discrimination under the assumption that race and class are not related.

Using interactive terms and additional variables and incorporating nonlinear or reciprocal dynamics has assisted quantitative analyses, but the fundamental problem is conceptual, not statistical. Whereas master statuses may have previously been thought of as fluid in many ways, today researchers might be better able to appreciate that being a "black woman" is more constant than previously thought. To wit, "black women" are always black women in a society that tends to stereotype both "blacks" and "women." And

> empirical studies support this simultaneity of race-gender experiences. Whites' prejudice against Black women is a stronger predictor of their opposition to affirmative action than their prejudice against Blacks in general. . . . Similarly, Black-women's joint race-gender identity is more salient for their mental health than either the identities Black or woman alone. (Vespa 2009, 366)

So although those traditional categories might have been separated, perhaps future research will continue to put them together. Much of the scholarship that best helps us understand how intersections play out in the social world tends to be qualitative, descriptive, and narrative, emphasizing the contextual aspects of people's day-to-day existence. Adding variables like "black women" and "Hispanic men" to social surveys as categories of demographic import is not only structurally possible but also increases the sensitivity of those instruments. And while efforts have been made to expand racial categories to allow multiracial comparisons on the census, for example, and to include homosexuality as a preference in the literature as denoted by "same sex" variables in recent years, there is a greater need to continue trying to capture the interplay between some of these dualities.

Some literature insists that "from an intersectional framework, race and gender are not reducible to individual attributes" and that they instead form a "mutually constituted system of relationships" that provides a unique location of inequality within which people are forced to navigate the world. Hence, we believe that qualitative studies, in combination with quantitative data, are best suited for demonstrating the nuanced meanings of class, race, gender, and their intersections. Here, the task is to go beyond what Baca Zinn and colleagues (2005) call the "patchwork quilt" phase of study, in which difference is acknowledged as important but done by "collecting together a study here on African American women, a study there on gay men, a study on working-class Chicanas, and so on." Some researchers have already begun to use an intersectional approach to studying criminality. For example, April Bernard (2013), in a case study of criminality, argued that an intersectional approach was necessary to understanding why one young Afro-Caribbean woman was incarcerated for a drug-related crime. Bernard purposefully moved away from Robert Merton's original strain theory of adaptation to one that viewed the woman from an intersectional lens: "Rather than seeking results that can be generalized to broader populations, the purpose of the methodology is to ground the findings in the standpoint of the women interviewed, and ultimately, to demystify and humanize their lived experiences and perspectives while providing a range of practical explanations of the choices and behavior of women involved in drug-related crimes" (Bernard 2013, 9). Hence, the particularities of the respondent's experience (physical and sexual abuse by family members, anger, depression, isolation, poverty, and invisibility) can be understood only inside the framework of a theory that seeks to understand it. Bernard concludes that

> the challenge is for theorizing on female criminality to complicate malestream perspectives on women's criminality by including more empirical studies that seek to deconstruct one-dimensional and essentialist understandings of women's lives while intentionally exploring the interconnected, constraining, and multiple, yet unique, manifestations of power and oppression. The praxis of feminist criminology serves as a reminder that alternative theorizing, policy, and programmatic provisions in support of innovative interventions designed to nurture the development of each member of society are needed. An intersectional approach to feminist criminology functions to confront the collective culpability of all members of society in perpetuating oppressive ideologies and structures that favor the progress of the elite over those who, like Angelique, have limited means to escape the margins. (2013, 16)

IMPLICATIONS

A challenge remains to sort out the complex ways in which class, race, and gender simultaneously structure people's actions and others' reactions to them and to understand the complex ways in which these hierarchies are used to either sustain or resist the prevailing systems of inequality and privilege. The theoretical frameworks and orientations are still works in development that make sense of these situations both in general and in criminology. These attempts are further impeded by the shortage of official information that describes the distribution of social benefits and harms along class, race, and gender combined, not separately. Even with the limited information available, though, indicators of political, economic, and physical well-being indicate that social goods are not evenly distributed but rather are concentrated among the upper-class white men while poor racial and ethnic minority women incur the greatest social costs.

Nonetheless, the intersections of class, race, and gender in relation to inequality, privilege, and wealth or poverty may be further complicated by additional variables such as sexuality and marital status or household living arrangements, including cohabitation, once married, and serial marriages. For example, a nationally representative panel survey from 1979 to 2004 and a life course of different group experiences revealed that whites generally had the most accumulated household wealth and that Hispanics also had more wealth than blacks (consistent with the information from chapters 3, 4, and 5). This study revealed that whites' unadjusted average net worth was considerably more than that of blacks or Hispanics regardless of whether the cohabitation history was one of "directly married" ($160,000), "spousal cohabitation" ($160,000), "one-time cohabitation" ($162,000), or "serial cohabitation" ($158,500). But Hispanics' net worth was a bit more than blacks' with respect to both spousal cohabitation ($60,000 to $58,000) and serial cohabitation ($61,000 to $57,000) and significantly more when directly married, $100,000 to $57,500. Yet conversely, the net worth of one-time cohabitating blacks was $60,500 compared with $57,500 for Hispanics (Painter and Vespa 2008, 10). The authors conclude "that race and ethnicity are associated with qualitatively different cohabitation experiences due to marriage markets, attitude, and non-marital childbearing" (Painter and Vespa 2008, 2).

In other words, cohabitation and marriage serve to boost the quality of life for both whites and, to a lesser degree, Hispanics ("direct marriage" more than cohabitation), but it may not serve to boost the quality of life of those people who are concentrated at the bottom of the economic strata, that is, mostly blacks. If that is the case, whites may seek to marry more often and Hispanics may seek to marry or cohabit more often because they see it as a benefit to their economic situation that will further improve their quality of life. In contrast, some blacks may seek to remain single and to have children as single people not because they reject traditional family values (e.g., love, commitment, fidelity, upward mobility) but because they may have experienced marriage or cohabitation as an exacerbation of their economic inequality; that is, when poor individuals cohabit with other poor individuals or with precariously situated middle-class individuals, the average level of goods and services available to both individuals in the cohabitation may decrease rather than increase—sometimes suddenly if a couple experiences sickness, accidents, arrests (with or without conviction for a crime), or the loss of a job. There may be fewer examples of such a situation that raises both individuals to middle-class standing as it might do for solidly middle-class individuals or even solidly working-class individuals in other races. This is a different way of viewing marriage, cohabitation, and public policies than from privileged vantage points. This view may not have gained traction in public discourse. Indeed, low-income minorities are still decidedly ostracized for having children outside of wedlock and for having a lower marriage rate and an older average age for first marriages. This set of facts has typically been viewed as disdain for those traditional family values in mainstream society, but it is well understood to be the result of mostly social, political, and economic factors outside the control of the minority individuals who experience it. Intersectionality, then, again serves to provide interpretations of data that have previously been overlooked.

While criminology has had a long-standing interest in class, only in the past thirty to forty years has this interest in social difference and privilege been extended to include race and gender; some argue that now the previous interests in class have almost been forgotten. In any event, the attention to the intersections of these social dimensions is an even more recent development. Since the late eighties, increasing numbers of scholars have recognized the problems inherent in assuming that all women or all members of a particular race or sex, for example, stand on a similar footing.

Among the most promising developments has been a focus on the ways in which class, race, and gender are not only social constructs but also are processes involving creative human actors. Structured action theory in particular highlights the ways in which our dominant cultural conceptions of doing masculinity and femininity intersect with the physical body, racial category, and social class, and how these relations, in turn, shape crime and justice. Hence, whether addressing the needs of victims, offenders, or criminal justice workers, we must not assume that "same" treatment is "fair" treatment because too often, equal treatment is defined by a male norm or reflects white middle-class biases and ignorance of the challenges faced by poor men and women of color.

In evaluating proposed policies and legislation, for example, we should take care to consider their impact on people occupying a range of social locations rather than, for instance, assuming that all women face the same challenges in leaving an abusive partner. We should ask: What is this program, policy, or law supposed to accomplish? How will it actually be implemented? What are the ramifications for historically marginalized groups? On what assumptions is it based? Who is included, and who is left out? What can be done to improve on this effort (S. Miller 1998; Renzetti 1998)?

REVIEW AND DISCUSSION QUESTIONS

1. In the opening narrative, how did class, race, and gender play into Ronny's experience with trying to get a job at Carrows?
2. Explain how the intersectionalities of class, race/ethnicity, and gender apply to everybody, including men and women, whites, people of color, straights, and gays.
3. What is meant by "master status"? Explain how a "master status" can be intersectional.
4. How does privilege impact the study of intersections? Specifically, what privileges do you think are most important for you to understand in approaching the study of class, race, and gender? What other types of privilege discussed in the chapter may also be important? Why?
5. What are the advantages of viewing society, crime, and/or criminal justice from an intersectional perspective? What are the disadvantages of failing to view society, crime, and/or criminal justice from an intersectional perspective?

III

LAW AND CRIMINAL JUSTICE

7

Victimology and Patterns of Victimization

Because the deprivations of some minorities have been so extensive, some argue that these conditions amount to genocide, a powerful word used to describe extreme cases of mass violence and victimization that blends the Greek genos *(race or tribe) with the Latin-derived* -cide *(kill). The underlying concept of genocide involves an attempt to exterminate a group that shares common characteristics. Hence, charging genocide is claiming great harm and victimization; it not only indicts the perpetrators but also bystanders for doing nothing in the face of mass violence, and it confers a moral authority on the victims to be heard and to demand change.*

The study of genocide has been confounded by a long and pervasive history of denial (Chalk and Jonassohn 1990). For example, traditional criminology takes great interest in serial killers and mass murderers but typically ignores genocide and other violations of human rights; there's even little interest in understanding a political mass murderer like Osama bin Laden. In the context of victimology and victimization, such denial is a good reason to review claims that the majority population of the United States has committed genocide involving both Native Americans and African Americans.

Many citizens of this nation consider charges of genocide by minority populations to be overstated at best. They tend to associate genocide with the Holocaust in Nazi Germany, which has created a distorted standard because it is an extreme case rather than a more typical one. The core concept, however, is "an attempt to exterminate a racial, ethnic, religious, cultural, or political group, either directly through murder or indirectly by creating conditions that lead to the group's destruction" (Staub 1989, 8). Such destruction encompasses "not only killing but creation of conditions that materially or psychologically destroy or diminish people's dignity, happiness, and capacity to fulfill basic material needs" (25).

Every year on Columbus Day signs protest "five hundred years of genocide." Like many claims of genocide, this one is met with much denial. Indeed, for the five hundredth anniversary of Columbus's arrival in North America, the National Endowment for the

Humanities refused to fund any film that proposed to use the word genocide. *Rather than look at events from the Natives' point of view, people refuse to discuss whether Columbus himself was an "agent of genocide" and whether the colonization he set in motion has resulted in genocidal processes. Whether genocide is a fair characterization of the next five hundred years revolves around Staub's definition of genocide as involving indirect murder through the creation of conditions leading to a group's social destruction. Raphael Lemkin (1900–1959), the man who coined the term* genocide, *understood it to be the "destruction of the essential foundations of the life" of the group and the undermining of the integrity of the group's basic institutions, which produces the "destruction of the personal security, liberty, health, dignity, and even the lives of the individuals belonging to such groups" (quoted in Kuper 1985, 9). Moreover, very few instances of mass murder that have been acknowledged to be genocide involve the actual elimination of a group. Thus, the state of Israel and the presence of Jews worldwide today do not undermine a claim that the Holocaust was genocide.*

With Native Americans, the low point of the population was down 90 percent from the level before the time Columbus arrived. Some population fluctuation was inevitable, but the drastic decline here is related to a number of practices that involved direct murder as well as indirect attacks on the well-being and cultural integrity of Native Americans. Consider, for instance, the aggressive appropriation (theft) of land that included forced marches—such as the Trail of Tears—that had a high death toll because hunger, exhaustion, and exposure to inclement weather killed many women, children, and elderly people. The removal of Native Americans from land that was sacred and that had cultural significance eroded their cultural integrity, and their placement on desolate land further undermined the essential foundations of life. This process of forced relocation recurred multiple times with increasing numbers of white settlers or the discovery of mineral wealth on what was thought to be wasteland earlier designated for Native Americans (Lazarus 1991; Weyler 1992). Today, many reservations are still located on inhospitable land that can also be sites for toxic and radioactive materials (Eichstaedt 1994).

To control the Native American population in the 1800s, settlers intentionally gave them disease-infested blankets that would kill large numbers who did not have immunity to European diseases. In addition, children were taken—sometimes at gunpoint—and put into boarding and reform schools, where they were deprived of access to their culture and native language. Indeed, children were punished for doing anything "Indian" and were taught to be ashamed of their heritage. Even today, many Native Americans in prison are denied access to culturally appropriate practices such as the sweat lodge and are coerced into Christian-based programs such as Alcoholics Anonymous, which further erodes their cultural integrity (Little Rock 1989).

The US government—the representative of the American people—has broken every treaty it has made with the Native Americans (Lazarus 1991). The government's refusal to honor treaties negotiated in good faith by the Native peoples has denied them rights to land, resources, and sovereignty in many ways that have, both historically and currently, imposed hardship and destroyed their personal security, liberty, health, and dignity. Although several cases involving broken treaties have resulted in symbolic reparations for

Native Americans, the ongoing problems remain. Indeed, most tribes, even on reservations, have little in the way of sovereignty and are subject to state and federal control. The tribal decision-making bodies are not always the same as those tribal members officially recognized as the leaders by the federal government. In addition, the Bureau of Indian Affairs has come under scathing criticism for being corrupt and not having the best interests of Native Americans at heart in administering their affairs (Lazarus 1991; Weyler 1992). In the latter part of the twentieth century, the FBI and other law enforcement agencies met activism on the part of Native Americans, such as the American Indian Movement (AIM), with illegal surveillance and at times violent repression (Churchill and Vander Wall 1990a, 1990b).

Although most of the direct killing of Native Americans is part of the past, the place accorded them by the white majority is one that destroys the essential foundations of their life. While the ongoing effort to undermine the integrity of Native Americans' basic institutions has occasionally met with spirited and creative acts of resistance to domination and colonization, these demonstrations have failed because of the unaltered structural relations of inequality between the majority of whites and marginalized minorities. What the National Advisory Commission on Civil Disorder noted about inner-city ghettos applies equally well to reservations: "What white Americans have never fully understood—but what the Negro can never forget—is that white society is deeply implicated in the ghetto. White institutions created it, white institutions maintain it, and white society condones it" (quoted in Pinkney 1984, 78).

In each case, whatever the intentions or consciousness of white society, both the inner city and reservations are places of extreme social deprivation and violence. Indeed, as African American Harvard sociologist Sidney Willhelm (1970, 304) noted, "The Black ghetto evolves into the equivalent of the Indian reservation." Obvious questions thus arise as to whether the history or current conditions of blacks can be described as genocide as well.

Charges related to genocide of blacks start with the institutions of slavery and the forced removal of Africans from Africa to work in involuntary servitude on southern plantations, a process that resulted in fifty to one hundred million premature deaths (S. Anderson 1995; Gorman 1997; Oshinsky 1996; Tolnay and Beck 1995). In 1951, black scholar William Patterson wrote a 240-page indictment against the United States called "We Charge Genocide" that he deposited with the United Nations (Patterson 1970, 1971). Interestingly, US delegates argued that the treatment of blacks was an economic rather than racial dynamic and therefore that the genocide convention did not apply. In other words, the delegates maintained that it was an issue of social class rather than race because what had been done to poor blacks happened because they were poor—which ignores the obvious fact that it did not happen to poor whites.

Although the class dynamic is in operation with blacks, it is also racism that keeps blacks disproportionately in poverty. Furthermore, class cannot explain the history of lynching or of segregation that consistently condemned blacks to inferior accommodations. Blacks have certainly made gains since the 1950s in terms of civil rights, income, and political representation. Despite these gains, however, the "mountains" of data discussed in chapter 4 demonstrate pervasive social, economic, and political disadvantages. Blacks are still much more likely to live in poverty and in inner-city neighborhoods that are places of concentrated poverty (Mandle 1978, 1992; Massey and Denton 1993; W. Wilson 1987).

The concentrated poverty and social disorganization of inner-city black communities function to compromise many essential foundations of life and the integrity of local institutions. The consequences of this racial stratification can be seen in a study of life expectancy done by Johnson and Leighton (1999) that compares the observed number of deaths for a race with the number that would be expected if it had the death rate of the other race. If blacks had the same death rate as whites in 1991, the expected figure would be 78,951 fewer untimely deaths of blacks that year (45,693 men and 33,258 women). If whites had the death rate of blacks, the expected figure would be 647,575 more premature deaths each year (376,992 men and 270,583 women).

The relatively shortened black lives are not always the result of direct intervention by whites but also reflect black-on-black violence and self-destructive behavior. The debate about genocide does not deny the personal responsibility blacks have for their actions, although it does take note that such behavior reflects adaptations to a broader social context marked by a "socioeconomic predicament which is itself profoundly antisocial" (Rubenstein 1987, 206). This theme was first articulated in 1899 by W. E. B. Du Bois in his classic study, The Philadelphia Negro, *where he argued that Negro crimes were adaptations to a "lack of harmony" with their surroundings. Almost a century later, Chancellor Williams linked Du Bois's lack of harmony (similar in kind with Durkheim's anomie) to both black-on-black crime and white genocide:*

> *They, the so-called criminals and their youthful followers, expect nothing beneficial from the white world, and they see no reason for hope in their own. Hence, like caged animals, they strike at what is nearest them—their own people. They are actually trying to* kill *a situation they hate, unaware that even in this, they are serving the white man well. For the whites need not go all out for "genocide" schemes, for which they are often charged, when blacks are killing themselves off daily on such a large scale. (1987, 325; emphasis in the original)*

In the case of both blacks and Native Americans, white society has created conditions that undermine the essential life foundations and integrity of the group. Genocide still entails a certain—and unspecified—level of destruction and white involvement in those destructive processes. These elements are very much a subject of contention and cannot be resolved in this chapter. The goal here is to overview the claim of genocide and to indicate why it should not be dismissed as "mumbo jumbo" or paranoia of "wild-eyed conspiracy mongers" (J. White 1990, 20). Beyond the specific debate about genocide, Hacker (1995, 54) raises questions and uses logic that deserves further consideration:

> *Can this nation have an unstated strategy for annihilation of [black] people? How else, you ask yourself, can one explain the incidence of death and debilitation from drugs and disease, the incarceration of a whole generation of [black] men, the consignment of millions of women and children to half lives of poverty and dependency? Each of these conditions has its causes. Yet the fact that they so centrally impinge on a single race makes one wonder why the larger society has allowed them to happen.*

Finally, the issue of genocide should lead into asking about the future of marginal groups, especially as technological developments and global capitalization make them increasingly expendable and their labor of decreasing value (Aronowitz and DiFazio 1994; Rifkin 1995; W. Wilson 1996). Sidney Willhelm first raised the question in his 1970 book, Who Needs the Negro?, *which argued that impersonal forces and processes such as automation make the unskilled, uneducated poor expendable. Thus, even those who do not believe genocide is currently happening might be able to see the vulnerability felt by blacks, especially when more young black males end up in prison than in college.*

Victimology is the scientific study of victims and victimization. The field can be traced back to 1937, when Benjamin Mendolsohn began gathering information about victims for his law practice. He subsequently conducted research on victims, including a rape study in 1940. Initially, Mendolsohn and others "formulated a broad-based victimology that considered not merely crime victims, but all victims, including those produced by politics, by technology, by accidents, as well as by crime" (Elias 1986, 18). In 1948, Hans von Hentig provided the first landmark victimological study, *The Criminal and His Victim,* followed in 1954 by Henri Ellenberger's "Psychological Relations between Criminals and Victims."

The field, research, and applications of victimology have continued to develop, as evidenced by numerous victimization studies, typologies, many international conferences on victimology, the emergence of *Victimology: An International Journal* in 1976, the creation of the World Society of Victimology in 1979, and the establishment of victim compensation programs in the United States and most of the developed nations of the world. Still, the struggle to maintain the broader perspective (beyond formal victims of street crime) envisioned by Mendolsohn has been a difficult one. Indeed, victimology has tended to follow the leads of Hentig and Ellenberger, narrowly focusing on criminal victimization, victim-offender relationships, and victim precipitation (the contribution the victim makes to his or her victimization) without examining the larger social, cultural, political, and economic relations that establish power arrangements between "offenders" and "victims." Thus, much victimology is limited to victims based on existing criminal law—especially street crime rather than corporate crime—and is focused on individual-level (microlevel) analysis that excludes structural sources and context for better understanding victimization.

In his treatise, *The Politics of Victimization,* Robert Elias captures the dilemma in victimology caused by scarce acknowledgment of victimization:

> Americans are a frightened people. We anticipate victimization even more than we experience it, although much actual victimization does occur. We mostly fear being robbed, raped, or otherwise assaulted, or even killed. Yet, while these crimes have captured our imaginations, they comprise only part of the victimization we suffer. We face not only the danger of other crimes, but also countless other actions that we often have not defined or perceived as criminal, despite their undeniable harm. We may have a

limited social reality of crime and victimization that excludes harms such as consumer fraud, pollution, unnecessary drugs and surgery, food additives, workplace hazards and diseases, police violence, censorship, discrimination, poverty, exploitation, and war. We suffer victimization not only by other individuals, but also by governments and other social institutions, not to mention the psychological victimization bred by our own insecurities. (Elias 1986, 3–4)

He suggests that the pathway to a more comprehensive victimology lies in the wedding of victimology with human rights, which can

dissolve the "mental prison" that often characterizes how we think about victimization, and substitute a . . . broader conception that considers not only common crime but also corporate and state crime, that examines not only individual criminals but also institutional wrong-doing, and that encompasses not merely traditional crime but all crimes against humanity. (Elias 1986, 7)

As indicated by the opening narrative on genocide and by our discussion of sociological contributions to crime and victimization, this chapter and book adopt a broader conception of victimization. This conception is also consistent with our concerns about social justice rather than just the narrow traditional focus on legally defined equal protection and criminal justice. The connection between these disparate types of victimization—the personal and the structural—is captured by Gregg Barak (2003, 116) when he writes about a sense of the collective experience of victimization and the nature of violence in the structural orders of the ghetto, the slums, poverty, and other forms of oppression: "All of those persons who inhabit impoverished environments, even if they have never been mugged, raped, or robbed by others living in their victimized neighborhoods, have been structurally violated every day of their lives."

Nevertheless, this type of structural violence is rarely, if ever, given official recognition or taken into account by the administration of justice. Chapters 2 and 8 in particular underscore the inherent problems and biases associated with the criminal law's role in shaping people's beliefs about crime. In a parallel fashion, the criminal law also limits the boundaries of victimization and the scope of those who are considered victims. In other words, the "criminal law may provide the first narrowing of our consciousness of both crime and victimization, a process that continues in enforcement and subsequent stages of the criminal process" (Elias 1986, 32). Elias (33) continues that the penal code may "create an 'official' or 'social' reality of victimization which, among those harms it defines as criminal, stresses acts mostly committed by less privileged people, de-emphasizes and softens the acts committed by more privileged people, and then excludes from its definition other, extensive, and (usually more) harmful acts altogether, such as corporate crimes, state crimes, and what human rights advocates would call 'crimes against humanity.'"

While the criminal law, for example, excludes Quinney's "crimes of domination" (discussed in chapter 2), other examples that need to be included in studying victimology are actions committed with the authority of the state involving torture and other crimes against humanity (see box 7.1), those state-corporate crimes committed at the intersection of business and government, and those acts of commission and omission by agents of the criminal justice system in violation of the rule of law.

BOX 7.1. TORTURE AND THE BUSH ADMINISTRATION'S ABUSE OF POWER

In 2009, five years after the photographs of detainees being abused at Abu Ghraib aired, *New York Times* columnist Frank Rich wrote that it is important that we as a society "acknowledge that our government methodically authorized torture and lied about it" (Rich 2009a). He continues:

> We also must contemplate the possibility that it did so not just out of a sincere, if criminally misguided, desire to "protect" us but also to promote an unnecessary and catastrophic war. Instead of saving us from "another 9/11," torture was a tool in the campaign to falsify and exploit 9/11 so that fearful Americans would be bamboozled into a mission that had nothing to do with Al Qaeda. The lying about Iraq remains the original sin from which flows much of the Bush White House's illegality.

Rich is referring to a combination of events post-9/11 that led up to the second Iraq War, including the torture of the al-Qaida operative Ibn al-Shaykh al-Libi in 2002, whose testimony became the centerpiece of Secretary of State Colin Powell's speech before the UN Security Council in 2003 to justify the invasion of Iraq. Libi was left unnamed, but Powell devoted nine paragraphs to "a senior terrorist operative" that linked al-Qaida terrorists with Saddam Hussein and his weapons of mass destruction. Subsequently, Libi disavowed his torture-induced testimony, and the facts on the ground totally discredited the existence of any connections between al-Qaida and Iraq or any weapons of mass destruction.

Four interrogation memos released by the Justice Department in the spring of 2009 revealed in dispassionate legal prose that the Defense Intelligence Agency, with authorization from the White House, engaged in brutal interrogation techniques—including waterboarding, an act for which the United States prosecuted the Japanese after World War II. An editorial in the *New York Times* about the released memos stated: "The language is the precise bureaucratese favored by dungeon masters throughout history. They detail how to fashion a collar for slamming a prisoner against a wall, exactly how many days he can be kept without sleep (11), and what, specifically, he should be told before being locked in a box with an insect—all to stop just short of having a jury decide that these acts violate the laws against torture and abusive treat-ment of prisoners" (*New York Times* 2009b). Other passages described forced nudity and the dousing of detainees with water as cold as forty-one degrees (Mazzetti and Shane 2009).

What these memos do not disclose is the number of detainees who were killed by these and other torturous measures. Proof, however, of at least eight detainee deaths was documented in the 2007 Academy Award–winning film, *Taxi to the Dark Side*. Regrettably, as Rich (2009a) states, most Americans would rather:

> cling to myths that quarantine the evil. If our country committed torture, surely it did so to prevent Armageddon, in a patriotic ticking-time-bomb scenario out of "24." If anyone deserved blame, it was only those identified by President Bush as "a few American troops who dishonored our country and disregarded our values": promiscuous, sinister-looking lowlifes like Lynndie England, Charles Graner and the other grunts who were held accountable while the top command got a pass.

Those scapegoated "grunts" whom the US military tried, convicted, and punished were only carrying out orders for which their military and civilian superiors had previously praised them. After all, the White House, the Justice Department, and the Pentagon had each authorized all those practices of torture.

It does not look as though there will be any criminal prosecutions, inde-pendent investigations, or truth commissions involving the architects of these crimes of torture. The architects and high-level perpetrators of these crimes will never have to publicly face up to their violations of domestic and interna-tional law. The insistence by the Obama administration that we concentrate on the future and not dwell on the past, as well as the complacency of the American people to confront the truth of these crimes, are consistent with a long tradition of the United States of avoiding and denying its numerous crimes against humanity. The continuation of denial does not bode well for building either peace or justice in the future because the wounds from these assaults run much deeper than most people realize:

> Even as the torturer shatters the world of his victim, he assaults the foundation of his own world, although he does not know it. Indeed, his blindness is a con-sequence of the torture, even a condition for it. The torturer and his victim are close to each other. There is physical contact. Yet in every other respect they are as distant as it is possible for one person to be from another. In the moral and affec-tive vacuum that has been generated, sympathy, empathy, pity, understanding—every form of fellow-feeling—have been reduced to absolute zero. That is why

One form of state-sanctioned victimization comes in the form of a lack of action on the part of state agencies to investigate, charge, and prosecute suspects for criminal law violations. For example, some research has uncovered that rape cases are sometimes "exceptionally cleared" because law enforcement officials (i.e., police and prosecutors) decide not to pursue them. When such decisions are based on gender stereotypes, discretion is abused and "the misuse of the *exceptional clearance* raises the possibility that individuals who may in fact be guilty of rape are not arrested, prosecuted, and punished" (Spohn and Tellis, 2011).

Another way in which citizens may be victimized by the state is when a jury fails to convict a person accused of a crime based on shared but inaccurate stereotypes. Such was the general feeling of many African Americans in the outcome of the case involving Trayvon Martin. Trayvon Martin, an African American teenager, was shot and killed by a man who thought of himself as a "white" person but whose actual heritage was half-white, half-Peruvian. George Zimmerman, a neighborhood watchman, claimed that Martin looked suspicious because he was wearing a hoodie (hooded sweatshirt). At first, police refused to arrest the neighborhood watchman after he shot and killed Trayvon Martin, even though no evidence was produced that showed the victim was out of place in his own neighborhood nor that he was carrying a weapon of any kind. In fact, Trayvon Martin was found to have been holding a cell phone and carrying a bag of candy and an iced-tea drink. Eventually, George Zimmerman was arrested, tried, and acquitted of second-degree murder and manslaughter charges.

In an article titled "We Are All George Zimmerman," Victor Rios argues that Zimmerman "represents mainstream America. We schools, law enforcement, the media, intellectuals, politicians, and everyday citizens—are all involved in a system that creates and perpetuates fear and outcaste of a vulnerable, marginalized segment of our population" (2013). Unlike others, Zimmerman

> pulled the trigger. We simply continue to mundanely mete out punitive treatment, stigma, and systematic stripping of dignity to young people of color, slowly killing their soul and their right to pursue happiness. By the time we sit in a courtroom to determine whether Trayvon Martin's life is worth imposing a sanction on George Zimmerman, five white jurors have already been socialized and acculturated to criminalize young racialized bodies and to view the victim as a culprit. (Rios 2013)

Similarly, Allison Cotton, in her book *Effigy: Images of Capital Defendants*, asserts that the trial process itself is designed to pit prosecutors against defense attorneys in a battle to define the defendant for jurors where jurors are subsequently asked to reconcile contradictory images and to place one in permanent record as a verdict. And in cases involving a poor African American male, the outcome is likely to be predetermined by racial stereotypes. "Race and SES, particularly the stereotypes surrounding poor, black men, may predispose jurors to internal attributions of guilt for certain crimes. Put another way, poor minorities are viewed as people who simply choose to be violent instead of being viewed as people who can be *provoked* to violence by their situations" (Cotton 2008, 94).

Other forms of state-sanctioned victimization involve acts by the police or correctional officers, not necessarily with the backing of the state but often with the
implicit or explicit approval of the larger society (Nelson 2000). (If these police or
correctional personnel are private rather than public employees, then the victimization may be thought of as state-corporate crime.) These acts are the most common
types of state victimization, even though the data surrounding police and penal
victimization are sparse. Still, enough evidence of the use of excessive force and
institutionalized violence exists to conclude that such behaviors do systematically
occur, although not uniformly, across the United States. For example, Amnesty
International (AI) documented patterns of ill treatment across the nation, including
police beatings, unjustified shootings, and the use of dangerous restraint techniques
to subdue suspects (Amnesty International 1999b). Moreover, although only

> a minority of the many thousands of law enforcement officers in the USA engage in
> deliberate and wanton brutality, [AI] found that too little was being done to monitor
> and check persistent abusers, or to ensure that police tactics in certain common situ-
> ations minimized the risk of unnecessary force and injury. The report also noted that
> widespread, systemic abuses had been found in some jurisdictions or police precincts.
> It highlighted evidence that racial and ethnic minorities were disproportionately the
> victims of police misconduct, including false arrest and harassment as well as verbal and
> physical abuse. (Amnesty International 1999b, 1)

Abuse of police authority and discretion ranges from verbal slurs and racial profiling to physical brutality and murder; reports are widely circulated about the misuse
of pepper spray, tasers, and police dogs; deaths resulting from dangerous restraint
holds; and police shootings in disputed circumstances. Officers tell black youth:
"We want you to kill each other off, that way we don't have to deal with locking you
up" (Rios 2013). Rogue officers may commit these acts alone or in small teams, or
they may be endemic to a police force. Some of this behavior is spontaneous and
personal in response to a specific incident, such as a high-speed chase. Some of it is
more planned and organizational, such as the Rampart scandal, involving the Rampart Division of the Los Angeles Police Department (LAPD), where a federal judge
ruled in 2000 that the government's antiracketeering statute—known as the RICO
(Racketeer Influenced and Corrupt Organization) law and created for the purpose
of dealing with drug bosses and organized crime figures—could be applied to the
LAPD (Cannon 2000).

Penal violence, associated with incarceration and punishment for criminal convictions, is yet another significant and common experience besides police violence. The
range and variety of penal abuse is much broader. Common concerns involve the
physical and sexual abuse of inmates as well as the excessive use of batons and electro-
shock weapons. Each year, dozens of inmates kill other inmates, and thousands are
injured seriously enough to require medical attention. Many of these acts, including
some instances of prison rape, are indirectly state crimes because they are facilitated
by and/or overlooked by the correctional workforce.

Further, mentally ill inmates are not adequately treated for their conditions and are then punished when they act out. A study by the Bureau of Justice Statistics found "more than half of all jail and prison inmates had a mental health problem" (2006c, 1). In state prisons, 73 percent of female inmates had mental health problems, as did 75 percent of female inmates in local jails. Unfortunately, only one-third of state prison inmates and one in six jail inmates who had a mental health problem had received treatment since their admission (2006c, 9)—and proper community treatment might have prevented the incarceration altogether. Instead, prison conditions and poor services can often make mental health problems worse. For example, administrative lockdowns or policies of segregation and isolation can hurt inmates with and without mental health problems. Prisoners deemed to be particularly disruptive and dangerous (such as those with untreated mental illness) are secured in small, often windowless cells for twenty-three hours a day. At any given time in the contemporary United States, tens of thousands of prisoners are subjected to this modern solitary confinement, "a form of numbing mental torture that drives about one-third of them psychotic, induces irrational anger in 90 percent, and ups the likelihood they will commit violent crimes upon release" (Ross 2009, 1).

Whether the victimization is accomplished by police force or penal violence, the victims of these acts are in the vast majority of persons with little power, status, or stake in American society. These same groups, unfortunately, tend to be disproportionately victims of street crime, especially violent victimization. Just as the state can victimize with relative impunity because of its power, class-, race-, and gender-based inequality lead to greater levels of victimization of the powerless. The argument, summarized by John Braithwaite (1992) and noted in chapter 2, is that inequality increases crimes of "need"—people motivated to commit property crimes to satisfy basic needs as well as culturally constructed material "needs." Poor people and minorities (and poor people who are also minorities, as discussed in chapter 6) also find the inequality structurally humiliating, which can lead to property or violent crime. Braithwaite writes that "the propensity to feel powerless and exploited among the poor and the propensity of the rich to see exploiting as legitimate both . . . enable crime" (1992, 94).

Similar dynamics apply to race (Unnever and Gabbidon 2011), but gender inequality plays out in a different way. The key variable of humiliation, which turns to violence and victimization through rage, is less likely in women because of gender socialization: "Women, instead of feeling humiliation and rage, feel guilt and shame" (Braithwaite 1992, 95). This can lead to self-destructive behaviors as well as victimization by the privileged. Gender inequality or degradation of women "enables rape and violence against women on a massive scale in patriarchal societies, not to mention commercial exploitation of the bodies of women by actors who might ambiguously be labeled white-collar criminals" (1992).

In each of the four sections that follow, we try to report both what is known about victimization and some of the missing elements in this official picture of the "reality" of victimization. The data for the tables in these sections come mostly from the National Crime Victimization Survey (NCVS), one of the largest victimization surveys and based on a nationally representative sample of almost 100,000 households. Because the survey, done by the Bureau of the Census, is nationally representative, researchers can draw some conclusions about the distribution of victimization across income, race, gender, and several aspects of intersections. The picture is still not complete—for example, there is no data on wealth (only annual income), and intersectional data are seldom available. The survey also uses the criminal law as its basis for asking about victimization, so it does not measure the incidence of corporate crime or workplace harms, let alone crimes by the criminal justice system, the state, or various types of environmental or structural violence. Thus, the amount of actual victimization recorded by the survey is small in relation to the harms suffered by people each year in the United States. We do try to comment on several notable exclusions and ask readers to become aware of the *analogous social harms* discussed in chapter 8.

VICTIMIZATION AND CLASS

Researchers have found that the overall level or amount of victimization in rates of urban criminal violence is due largely to the differences in racial inequality and socioeconomic conditions. For example, a classic study by Judith Blau and Peter Blau in the early 1980s found that increases in the rates of criminal violence were positively associated with the socioeconomic inequality between races as well as with economic inequality generally. In making a case for *relative* rather than absolute deprivation, Blau and Blau (1982, 114) concluded, "If there is a culture of violence, its roots are pronounced economic inequalities, especially if associated with ascribed position." A quarter of a century later in a replication of Blau and Blau's classic study, Lisa Stolzenberg, David Eitle, and Steward D'Alessio concluded that the overall data support the "relative deprivation thesis," which holds that increases in economic inequality, particularly race-based inequality, result in increases in violent criminality: "Cities with large income disparities between Whites and Blacks had higher rates of violent crime, controlling for other factors" (Stolzenberg, Eitle, and D'Alessio 2006, 303). Thus, from a sociological perspective, making sense out of criminality or victimization involves more than understanding individual behavior. From an integrated or holistic perspective, it is also about understanding the structural conditions, the institutional arrangements, and the social and cultural relations of a society—and how these impinge on individual and group adaptations.

Unfortunately, victimization data from the NCVS, whose results are distributed by the Bureau of Justice Statistics, reveal little about the structural context of victimization in terms of income, wealth, class, or even home ownership. The NCVS does have several tables on victimization by income level, but the top income category is $75,000 and above, which includes a third of the income. Even this limited information was discontinued with the report on the 2011 victimization statistics. More general publications such as the *Sourcebook of Criminal Justice Statistics* use data from a number of sources, but nothing on class, income, or wealth.

Table 7.1 reports the effect of income on property crime victimization. The clear conclusion is that those who have less than $7,500 are victimized more than those making more than $75,000. Table 7.2 reports the effect of income on violent victimization. The clear conclusion again is that those who have less than $7,500 are victimized more than those making more than $75,000.

Even if the victimization survey restored the two tables on victimization by household income, they would still present incomplete pictures of victimization in several respects. For example, many harmful acts of business and government are not part of the criminal law, so many types of injury are excluded from official data. Jeffrey Reiman and Paul Leighton (2013) recalculate figures from the FBI's *Uniform Crime Reports* on how Americans are murdered to include workplace hazards, occupational diseases, and preventable medical errors to arrive at "How Americans Are Really Murdered." While the FBI reports information on about 13,000 murders where the weapon is known, "How Americans Are Really Murdered" includes information on almost 170,000 murders (2013, 95). The category of "Occupational Hazard and Disease" contributes significantly to the revised estimate, and because the victims in this category work in blue-collar manufacturing and industrial jobs, these victimizations are disproportionately located in the lower-income groups. As noted in chapter 4, toxic waste facilities also tend to be in poor and especially minority areas, increasing the victimization for a range of diseases.

In a similar vein, businesses and other institutions are excluded from estimates of victimization. However, because of their concentrated wealth and social organization, businesses are able to publish supplementary statistics on the victimization they suffered from, say, employee theft or credit card fraud. Insurance companies may also produce additional information on fraud related to false claims by patients and doctors. But there is a profound lack of data in criminology and elsewhere about the fraud and theft done by businesses to consumers—and some of this could easily be picked up if the NCVS added survey questions on white-collar victimizations, such as those the National White Collar Crime Center periodically uses (Reiman and Leighton 2013). Credit card companies inappropriately charge fees or charge for services and then do not provide them; insurance companies deny proper claims to boost their profits. In addition, there is no accounting of victimization related to medical services that are denied and/or exceedingly difficult to obtain because of the health insurance industry's desire to secure greater profits. People who have no dental insurance and pull their own teeth out with pliers (Gladwell 2005) are not part of the discussion of victims.

Further, the victimization for any year would not pick up the mass financial victimization caused by corporate frauds at Enron, WorldCom, Tyco, and many others. Most of these losses would be to middle- and upper-income, largely white victims. They have generally been neglected by the victim's rights movement even though the impact of these losses includes people delaying retirement, rejoining the workforce,

Table 7.1. Property Crime Rates by Household Income, 2010 (per 1,000 Households)

Type of Crime	<$7,500	$7,500–$14,999	$15,000–$24,999	$25,000–$34,999	$35,000–$49,999	$50,000–$74,999	$75,000+
Property crimes	172.1	187.3	148.2	141.6	134.6	115.4	123.8
Completed household burglary	47.7	57.2	32.8	30.5	25.8	19.1	17.4
Theft	120.4	124.1	107.1	103.8	102.9	90.4	101.3

Source: Statistical Abstract of the United States 2013, table 326.

Table 7.2. Violent Crime Rates by Household Income, 2009 (per 1,000 Age Twelve and Older)

Type of Crime	<$7,500	$7,500–$14,999	$15,000–$24,999	$25,000–$34,999	$35,000–$49,999	$50,000–$74,999	$75,000+
Crimes of violence	47.7	40	22.3	18.6	16.6	12.6	11.5
Completed violence	NA by income	NA by income	NA by income	NA by income	NA by income	NA by income	NA by income
Rape/sexual assault	3.9*	1.8*	0.9*	<0.05*	0.3*	0.2*	0.2*
Robbery	7.3	5.7	3.8	2	2	0.9*	1.1
Aggravated assault	15.5	6	4	3.9	4.5	2	2.1

Source: Statistical Abstract of the United States 2013, table 322.

* Based on ten or fewer sample cases.

and scaling back on college education for their children (Leighton and Reiman 2002). Enron has been found guilty of illegal activities related to California's power crisis, and on audiotapes made by Enron employees, "traders joked about stealing money from California grandmothers and about the possibility of going to jail for their actions." But the grandmothers would have nothing to report to the victimization survey. Neither would all those persons who had their mortgages foreclosed and lost their homes in 2007–2009 as a result of fraudulent lending practices. The exclusion of these types of victimization from crime surveys and most discussions in criminology adds to the sense that these harms do not amount to "real" crime. To help counter this absence of victimization or a false sense of a lack of victims, some insight into the harms done by corporate and white-collar criminals is reproduced in box 7.2.

BOX 7.2. VICTIM IMPACT STATEMENTS ABOUT CORPORATE AND FINANCIAL FRAUD

The many financial frauds exposed in 2001–2002 resulted in mass victimization. One example of the harm done by financial fraud is this victim impact statement that was prepared for submission at the sentencing of Scott D. Sullivan, former chief financial officer of WorldCom. It has been edited for brevity.

My name is Henry J. Bruen Jr. I am former shareholder, and former employee of WorldCom's NYC National Sales Group. I requested the opportunity to address this court out of a sense of duty, honor, and an obligation to give voice to individuals that have suffered as a result of the fraud perpetrated primarily by Scott Sullivan and Bernard J. Ebbers. I represented the working professional . . . and the average investor that has suffered indescribable trauma financially as a result of the criminal activities of Scott Sullivan and his co-conspirators. I want to take this opportunity to be a witness to justice being done in this matter.

I have never met Scott Sullivan personally but the effect of his activity of being the principal architect of this scheme, and implementer of this heavy-handed fiscal fraud, [has] affected me deeply and personally. On June 28, 2002, articles began appearing in newspapers which depicted Sullivan's palatial hideaway in Boca Raton, Fla. There were descriptions of the then 40-year-old being the financial brain of a devastating profit-rigging scheme to cook up nearly $4 billion in cash flow that never existed.

The pictures alone of his "palatial villa" had at best a chilling effect on World-Com business in Manhattan. I was forced to defend to my customer how a 40-year-old executive was able to afford such a monstrosity of a home. The next comment from my customers was "obviously the rates that you are charging for your service are far too high . . . I need to look at renegotiating my contract with your company." This turned out to be the tip of an ongoing escalating death spiral of revenues and new business opportunities. Not to mention the obliteration of any personal credibility, trust and goodwill that I may have built with a customer. As the amount escalated by the billions so did the intensity of abuse and skepticism that I experienced on a daily basis. Not to mention the fact that my retirement funds and bonuses were tied up in stock options which eventually became worthless.

I was a member of the National Accounts Group that was the most profitable sales channel of all six WorldCom sales channels dealing with global, multinational and national size enterprises. I had brought in major new accounts resulting in over $5 million in new business. I had become a top 5 percent Presidents Club winner four consecutive times in a row and had been recognized in my branch over 15 times for outstanding sales performance with an average income of $180,000. After the fraud announcement on June 26, 2002, my commission income dwindled to next to nothing due to an inability to attain new business from customers that was previously committed and contracted with WorldCom.

Over the next six months after the fraud announcement, I was saddled with the stigma of being a legacy WorldCom employee in addition to being tasked with explaining the accounting fraud and subsequent scandals that unfolded in the media daily to customers and personal friends alike. Rounds of layoffs began immediately starting at the senior management levels and worked their way down. Finally I was laid off in the sixth company-wide layoff in early 2003. During my tenure at WorldCom I experienced the agony of watching over 30,000 co-workers get laid off while each day wondering when my name would be on the list. The psychological effect of finding out what new disaster awaited you at work each day from the media coverage was both savage and demoralizing. The daily pounding and constant assault of improprieties in the newspaper was mind-numbing and debilitating. This experience embodied the definition of hell on earth if there ever was one.

Over the last two years I have suffered the loss of all my personal savings, medical benefits, retirement funds, stock market investments, and personal property assets as a result of my inability to replace my personal income due to no fault of my own. I was just one of thousands of hard-working professional employees that put their faith and belief in what was a great company, which was destroyed solely by the greed and avarice of Scott Sullivan and his co-conspirators. What happened to me as a result of Scott Sullivan is representative of tens of thousands of other employees and investors who had their careers, retirement and livelihoods literally destroyed by the layoffs and bankruptcy of WorldCom Inc.

My only hope and prayer is that this sentencing proceeding reflects to Scott Sullivan the severity of his crimes, which led to the disintegration of WorldCom, and demonstrates that this type of activity will not be tolerated in corporate America[,] for he can never repay me or the tens of thousands of people like me[,] whose lives disintegrated before them in the blink of an eye. I hereby respectfully submit this statement to be entered into the record which reflects my personal feelings, and the sentiment of many people like me trying to piece back the broken pieces of our lives in the wake of this disaster. (*New York Times* 2005).

The subprime mortgage fraud of 2007–2009 had a more devastating and widespread impact than the earlier fraud. But the deregulation causing the crisis meant that there were few laws to break, so there have been almost no criminal charges filed against those who caused a global economic meltdown (Barak 2012). But this time period involved the discovery of another unrelated fraud: the Ponzi scheme of Bernard Madoff. Account statements at the time of the collapse of Madoff's empire showed that losses could be as high as $65 billion.

Ponzi schemes essentially involve using the money from new investors to pay back earlier investors and to support the perpetrator's lifestyle. Paying back earlier investors and meeting requests from people who want to take some of their money out establishes the façade of legitimacy. Madoff seems to have started the scheme to cover losses that he thought would be fleeting. Though Madoff did not look directly at any of the victims when they spoke of their pain and suffering in US district court during the sentencing phase, he did turn to them during his remarks before the sentence was announced and simply uttered: "I'm sorry. I know that doesn't help you." He added:

> I cannot offer you an excuse for my behavior. How do you excuse betraying thousands of investors who entrusted me with their life savings? How do you excuse deceiving 200 employees who spent most of their working life with me? How do you excuse lying to a brother and two sons who spent their entire lives helping to build a successful business? How do you excuse lying to a wife who stood by you for 50 years? . . . I will live with this pain, with this torment, for the rest of my life . . . I have left a legacy of shame . . . to my children and grandchildren. (Frank and Efrati 2009a, A1)

The thousands of victims who knowingly and unknowingly invested with Madoff came from all walks of life; they included the world's largest banks and wealthiest people as well as folks of modest means. However, just 113 of them filed letters with the federal court, and only nine victim statements were recorded live on the day of sentencing. The victims who spoke that day, with one exception, were not wealthy. They were ordinary people with median incomes, including a physical therapist, a retired correctional officer, and an accountant. Collectively, their stories of financial devastation where life savings were lost lasted about one hour.

Tom Fitzmaurice, sixty-three, who was working three jobs to make ends meet, stated, "There will be no retirement, no trips to California to visit our one-year-old grandson." He also read from a statement by his wife, Marcia, who stood by his side: "I cry every day when I see the pain in my husband's eyes. . . . I cry for the life we had." In a letter shared by Judge Chin from one widow who had gone to see Madoff two weeks after the death of her husband to invest their life savings, he was quoted as saying, "Your money is safe with me," as he put his arm around her. Another victim, Miriam Siegman, stated, "I now live on food stamps. . . . I scavenge in dumpsters at the end of the month." On the other hand, Burt Ross, a former mayor of Fort Lee, New Jersey, having lost $5 million in retirement funds and trusts for his children, stated that he was not in bad shape personally but was speaking on behalf of other victims. He noted that renowned Holocaust survivor and author Elie Wiesel had invested millions of dollars on behalf of nonprofit charities. Ross commented, "As if Mr. Wiesel hasn't suffered enough in his lifetime" (Lattman and Lobb 2009, A12).

Recognizing that sentencing a seventy-one-year-old man to 150 years is largely symbolic, Judge Chin explained that "symbolism is important for victims" because a "substantial sentence may in some small measure help the victims in their healing process." Similarly, Jayne Barbard, a law professor, was in attendance at the sentencing and reflected: "The proof of the value of the process is exactly what we saw in the courtroom today. The victims were eloquent, they were dignified, and they told very powerful stories" (Lattman and Lobb 2009, A12). They also referred to Madoff as a "monster" and a "low-life" (and who can argue?). The victims present at the sentencing also burst into applause and cheers when the tough sentence was given (Frank and Efrati 2009a).

VICTIMIZATION AND RACE

As the previous section indicated, according to self-report data, crime victims are disproportionately from the lower economic classes. While whites make up the majority of the poor, minorities are disproportionately poor and disproportionately victims of crime. The figures that follow illustrate some of the racial differences, but official statistics, as noted earlier, do not capture the structural violence experienced by marginal folks, minorities in particular, day in and day out (Barak 2003; see also Brown 1987). Nor do they expose the impact racial inequality has on the level of patterns of victimization.

For example, William J. Wilson, in *The Truly Disadvantaged* (1987), wrote about the "cycles of disadvantages" and how the deindustrialization of the United States and the associated economic and social changes eliminated hundreds of thousands of manufacturing and other jobs from urban areas by the 1980s. This created a permanent underclass of residents, especially African Americans. Subsequently, other researchers also linked the costs of social inequality, urban poverty, and racial discrimination to social problems generally, including violence and other forms of victimization as well as conspicuous drug consumption and trafficking often found in marginal, distressed communities (J. Hagan 1994; Sampson and Wilson 1995). Similar lines of inquiry have also developed from the sociological schools of social disorganization and social ecology as well as from neighborhood studies, all of which link crime and victimization to "kinds of places" rather than "kinds of people." For example, Rodney Stark's "theory of deviant places" explains why urban areas, with more dense housing and poor neighborhoods, are more likely to facilitate conspicuous crime than suburban and rural areas, where communities are more spread out (Stark 1987).

In one of the most comprehensive and imaginative analyses of the contradictions of capitalism in relation to marginally oppressed African Americans, victimization, and crime, Becky Tatum has provided a hybrid formulation that employs social psychology and Marxist notions of oppression in her "neocolonial model of adolescent crime and violence." In particular, "the theory examines the relationship between structural oppression, alienation, and three adaptive forms of behavior—assimilation, crime and deviance, and protest" (Tatum 1996, 34). Building on models of colonialism and internal colonialism, Tatum's model shifts the study of crime "from the victims of oppression to exploitative structural systems" (48). Tatum's model assesses behavioral adaptations to blocked structural opportunity from the perspective of race as the primary variable, followed by class. By specifically combining the perspective of racial conflict and anomie, she argues that African American and lower-class youth experience greater structural exclusion than white or middle-class youth. At the same time, the social psychology of a lack of bonding interacts with perceptions of oppression and feelings of alienation so that crime and violence are also viewed as dependent on the local environment. Ultimately, Tatum suggests a dynamic reciprocal model, where lower-class youths, especially African Americans, experiencing structural exclusion, perceived oppression, and fewer systems of community support result in higher levels of alienation and in higher inter- and intrapersonal levels of crime, violence, and victimization.

Probably the most provocative thesis that links social inequality, racism, and biology to socioeconomic and racial/ethnic group victimization is the "weathering framework" by Arline Geronimus, a professor of health behavior and a social epidemiologist. Her approach is based on studies of African Americans and whites living in Detroit and demonstrates "that blacks are, biologically speaking, older than whites of the same chronological age" (Blitstein 2009, 56). Geronimus argues that victimization occurs when a combination of racism and stress weathers or erodes the systems of the human body, fueling the progression of disease, aging, and death. As stressors ranging from environmental pollution to high crime to racism-induced anger accumulate and feed on one another, they alter the culture and behavior of a community, which can lead, for example, to higher rates of smoking, drinking, and drug use.

Geronimus and her colleagues have already shown that blacks having experienced repeated exposure and adaptation to the above types of stressors are also experiencing earlier health deterioration. These racial differences are not explained by poverty because "poor and nonpoor Black women had the highest and second highest probability of high [stress] scores, respectively, and the highest excess scores compared with their male or White counterparts" (Geronimus et al. 2006b, 826; see also 2006a). Other similarly focused research has "established that the health of Latino immigrants declines as they stay in America longer and improve their lots in life, and that South Asian Indian mothers, who have socioeconomic profiles comparable to whites, suffer from birth outcomes as poor as those of low-income blacks" (Blitstein 2009, 53).

Finally, as discussed earlier in the chapter, there is a relationship between health disparities and racial inequality. Consistent with the Geronimus thesis, there are some very revealing comparative data on the disparities between blacks and whites living in the United States. For example, the following figures illustrate the health differences between African Americans and whites:

- black residents of high-poverty areas are as likely to die by the age of forty-five as American whites are to die by sixty-five;
- the disability rates of black fifty-five-year-olds approach the rates of seventy-five-year-old whites;
- in impoverished urban areas such as Harlem, one-third of black girls and two-thirds of boys who reach their fifteenth birthdays don't reach their sixty-fifth— a rate that is almost three times higher than among average Americans;
- in 2009, blacks were dying at rates comparable to that of whites from 1979; and
- in 2000, cancer death rates for blacks were 30 percent higher than among whites; a half century earlier, in 1950, black rates were slightly less than whites (Blitstein 2009, 49–51).

All of these health disparities in accelerated rates of mortality, including the findings by Geronimus and her colleagues regarding comparative rates for teen pregnancy, motherhood, and infant mortality, strongly support the argument that this victimization is a byproduct of social disadvantages and racial inequality (Kaufman, Geronimus, and James 2007).

While the research noted above finds victimization for rich and poor minorities, it is also important to remember that these racial health disparities exist in a nation that has restricted access to health care by income. So when racial minorities are concentrated at the bottom of the economic pyramid, access to preventive health care, such as early detection for cancer and heart disease, prenatal care, and nutrition information, is also limited. For example, one study of "health care centers in a Detroit tri-county metropolitan area" was conducted where "75% of blacks reside in the central city and over 90% of whites reside in suburbs" (Dai 2010). The researcher concluded: "It is evident that living in areas with higher black segregation, higher socioeconomic disadvantages, higher sociocultural barriers, and poorer mammography access is associated with a higher likelihood of late-stage presentation of breast cancer" (Dai 2010, 1050).

In 2010, the US Congress passed the Affordable Health Care Act (known as "Obamacare"), which will expand access to health insurance for millions of additional Americans and provide for many preventive services without copays or deductibles. That should help reduce some of the disparities in health care outcomes, although other forms of discrimination and barriers to quality health care also need to be remedied.

As with official data on class and victimization, BJS data do not mention or measure contributions from the larger social context. Table 7.3 presents victimization rates of violent crime by race. These data are from 2010, which is the last year BJS published fuller breakdowns of the types of victimization before deciding to report only total violent victimization and what it calls "serious violent victimization." All the data, though, point to the same conclusion: blacks were more likely than whites to be victims of overall violence. Native Americans have the overall highest rate of violent victimization, with the exception that those who identify as being two or more races have the highest victimization rates. Less than 1 percent of the population self-identified as being of more than one race (multiracial), so that category is small and heterogeneous (comprising people of all races in various mixtures), which makes meaningful analysis difficult. (However, the violent victimization rates are twice as high as those for blacks, so something dramatic is happening with the statistics or in the lives of mixed-race people that deserves further investigation.)

Most victimization involves offenders and victims of the same race and are thus *intraracial* crimes, although American Indians are the most likely of any racial group to experience a violent victimization by someone of a different race (BJS 2004a, 14). The pattern of intraracial offending for whites and blacks is consistent with strong patterns of racial segregation (Krivo and Peterson 2009; Massey and Denton 1993). For 2012, out of the homicides for which the FBI had data on the race of victims and offenders, 2,614 homicides were white on white, and 2,412 were black on black (UCR 2012, table 6). The absolute number of black-on-black homicides is lower than that for whites, but blacks make up about 13 percent of the population, so the proportion is very high, and the problem is compounded because the homicides are concentrated among black men (as victims and perpetrators).

Still, these data destroy the concern many whites have that the biggest threat to them comes from minorities. Troubling, however, is the continued overrepresentation in the media of minorities as the perpetrators of violence against whites with the simultaneous overrepresentation of whites as victims of all crimes. A study of 3,712 Californians about random acts of violence portrayed in the media and its relationship to the amount of fear it raises in consumers of that media, for example, suggested "crime-related media elevated the fears of white respondents who perceived that they were living in a community with a large percentage of blacks" (Callanan 2012, 98). The author noted, "Local television news elevated perceptions and fear of crime irrespective of race/ethnicity. Since it focuses on violent street crimes, especially among strangers, a stable and pervasive message may be of violent suspects/offenders as non-white." The truth of the matter in victimization data, however, is

Table 7.3. Victimization Rates of Violent Crime by Race/Ethnicity, 2010 (per 1,000 Age Twelve and Older)

Types of Crime	White Non-Hispanic	Black Non-Hispanic	Hispanic	American Indian or Alaskan Native	Asian or Pacific Islander	Two or More Races
Crimes of violence	13.6	20.8	15.6	42.2	6.3	52.6
Rape/sexual assault	0.7	1.1*	0.8*	<0.05*	0.6*	1.2*
Robbery	1.4	3.6	2.7	4.3*	1.1*	8.0*
Aggravated assault	2.6	4.7	2.3	19.5*	0.5*	8.5*

Source: BJS. "Criminal Victimization, 2010," table 9.

Notes: Other race includes American Indians, Alaska Natives, Asians, Native Hawaiians, and other Pacific Islanders.

* Based on ten or fewer sample cases.

that blacks and other minorities commit fewer crimes than whites overall and that the overwhelming majority of victims in the United States tend to be minorities rather than whites.

One subset of crimes involving different races, or *interracial* crimes, is "hate crimes," or bias-motivated offenses. Box 7.3 covers some of the controversy about these acts and their punishment. The FBI defines hate crimes or "bias crimes" as crimes against persons or property motivated at least in part by the perpetrator's bias against a "particular race, religion, sexual orientation, ethnicity/national origin, or physical or mental disability" (UCR 2012). The 2009 Matthew Shepard Act expanded the definition to include some narrow instances of gender-based hate crimes, but rapes generally do not count as hate crimes. Terrorist acts are not included in hate crime statistics, although some (like the bombing of the federal building in Oklahoma City) appear in the homicide section of the Uniform Crime Reports. The three thousand deaths from 9/11 were excluded from the New York homicide figures of the Uniform Crime Reports for 2001 (Leighton 2002) and were also not recorded as hate crimes, which was consistent with the Bush administration's efforts to define terrorism as a war rather than a crime.

BOX 7.3.   THE CONTROVERSY OVER HATE-CRIME LEGISLATION

Hate speech typically involves actual speech or writing that expresses hostility to a group, and it may also include symbolic speech such as burning a cross. In *R.A.V. v. St. Paul* (507 U.S. 377 [1992]), the Supreme Court decided to invalidate a law making it a crime to display objects such as a burning cross that "arouses anger, alarm or resentment in others on the basis of race, color, creed, religion or gender." In addition to other problems with the ordinance, the majority of the court found it was an impermissible regulation on the content of free speech guaranteed by the First Amendment. On the other hand, in a subsequent case, *Virginia v. Black* (538 U.S. 343 [2003]), the court modified its position somewhat by upholding a Virginia law prohibiting the burning of crosses where it was done with an attempt to intimidate.

Sentencing enhancement laws for bias-motivated crimes, by contrast, go much further than merely prohibiting hate speech or symbolism, by adding additional penalties to personal or property crimes because of the bias or hate shown in victim selection. For example, the Supreme Court unanimously upheld sentencing enhancement for bias-motivated assaults in *Wisconsin v. Mitchell* (508 U.S. 476 [1993]). In that case, Todd Mitchell, a black teenager, had been watching the civil rights film *Mississippi Burning* with friends. When they were outside later, the group saw a young white boy, and Mitchell asked the group whether they felt "hyped up to move on some white people." He added: "You all want to fuck somebody up? There goes a white boy; go get him" (quoted in *State v. Mitchell* [485 NW2d 807, 809, 1992]). The court held that the Wisconsin statute was not aimed at punishing protected speech or expression and that motive could be a consideration of the sentencing judge. Likewise, previous speech and utterances by defendants are frequently admitted into evidence in court to establish motive.

Interestingly, those who oppose sentencing enhancement penalties for hate crime do so, among other reasons, because "crimes against some type of victims will incur greater penalties, with this injustice spurring resentment" (Cockburn 2009a, 9), the point being that such laws—based on a victim's actual or perceived race, color, religion, and national origin—value some victims over other victims, creating disparate or unequal treatment of victims. But much current law punishes bias against the majority as well as the minority (anti-white and anti-black, anti-Christian as well as anti-Islam). Valuing other victims thus could mean expanding the types of bias that result in punishment. Indeed, the 2009 Matthew Shepard Act, which was signed into law by President Obama, was controversial because it added federal penalties for bias-motivated crimes based on the victim's actual or perceived sexual orientation, gender, gender identity, or disability. (Although the FBI collects data on some of the categories based on state law offenses, federal law had no provisions to enhance penalties for these types of bias-motivated crimes before the 2009 act.)

Opponents also argue that these types of laws create thought crimes. The difference between a regular assault and a bias-motivated one is the perpetrator's thoughts about some characteristic of the victim. Instead of creating new categories of crime, opponents maintain that "federal and state hate crime laws are unnecessary and dangerous" because the object of criminal adjudication should be "to apply existing laws in a manner that constitutes justice, no matter who the victim may be" (Cockburn 2009a, 9). In contrast, the Supreme Court in *Mitchell* found that the state provided an adequate basis for singling out bias crimes for enhanced penalties because they are "more likely to provoke retaliatory crimes, inflict distinct emotional harms on their victims, and incite community unrest" (508 U.S. 476 [1993]).

In 2012, race and ethnicity/national origin combined accounted for almost 60 percent of bias crime incidents (UCR 2012, table 1). Of the offenders for whom race was known, 55 percent were white and 23 percent black, with the other racial groups comprising the rest (UCR 2012, table 9). The FBI does not report offenders by ethnicity, only race. Even though race is frequently dichotomized into "white" and "minority" (or just "black"), not all crimes by minorities involve antiwhite bias, because members of some minorities have prejudice and antipathy toward other minorities. For 2012, the largest category of hate-crime incidents was antiblack (1,805 incidents), followed by anti-Jewish (674), antiwhite (657), and anti–male homosexual (605) (UCR 2012, table 1).

Hate-crime statistics should be interpreted with caution. First, the number does not reflect all hate crimes but simply those that were recorded as such by the police. For 2012, the state of Alabama officially recorded six hate crime incidents and Louisiana recorded four (UCR 2012, table 12). Any biases present in the police force will affect the likelihood of officers being willing to record the offense as bias motivated and fill out the additional paperwork. For example, white privilege may make some white officers more sensitive to aspects of bias in crimes involving white victims and minority offenders; at the same time, they may be less likely to see bias in crime involving minority victims and white offenders. Also, future increases in the number of reported hate crimes might be viewed cautiously as they could be due to more complete reporting practices as well as greater sensitivity on the part of police. Increases in *reported* hate crime may or may not reflect trends in the actual occurrence of hate crimes.

VICTIMIZATION AND GENDER

Braithwaite's analysis (discussed at the end of the introduction) indicates that some victimization caused by gender inequality will not be seen as crime and will thus be excluded from official statistics. And making sense of official statistics requires going beyond his analysis to draw in the critique of masculinity and the problematic values—aggression, domination, and so on—that comprise it (chapter 5). With this background, it makes sense that men make up the majority of officially defined offenders; the majority of male and female victims involve a male perpetrator. Certainly, violent women do exist, and some women batter some men, although these examples are exceptions to main trends despite their cultural prevalence in media and culture.

The clearest indication of this pattern is the homicide data reported in table 7.4. The largest category is male offender and male victim, and the next largest is male offenders and female victims. The third-largest category is female offenders and male victims, although some of these are battered women killing abusive men. This general pattern holds for other types of violent crime. According to the Bureau of Justice Statistics: "Between 1998 and 2002, nearly 4 out of 5 violent offenders were male. Males accounted for 75.6 percent of family violence offenders and 80.4 percent of nonfamily violence offenders. Among violent crimes against a spouse, 86.1 percent of the offenders were male; against a boyfriend or girlfriend, 82.4 percent; and against a stranger, 86 percent of the offenders were male" (BJS 2005b, 14). In 2012, the NCVS reported that the rate of violent victimization (per one thousand persons age twelve and older) was 29.1 for men and 23.3 for women (BJS 2013c,

Table 7.4.   Race and Sex of Victim by Race and Sex of Offender, 2012

	Sex of Offender	
Sex of Victim	Male	Female
Male	3,725	421
Female	1,609	124

Source: FBI. Uniform Crime Reports, 2012. Expanded homicide data table 6.

Note: For single victim/single offender homicides.

table 7). For all categories except rape/sexual assault, men experienced higher levels of victimization. Overall, males were victims of violent crime, robbery, and aggravated assaults at rates higher than females.

Besides men's greater risk of most types of victimization, the most striking differences between men's and women's victimization patterns emerge when we consider the victim-offender relationship. Men are more likely to be victimized by another male who is a stranger, while women are more likely to be victimized by a male known to them. According to findings from the National Crime Victimization Survey, 32 percent of women's violent victimization occurred at the hands of strangers, including 30 percent of rapes recorded by the survey. In contrast, 54 percent of men's violent victimization involved a stranger, including 58 percent of aggravated assaults (BJS 2004b, 9). In 2010, 39 percent of female homicide victims were killed by an intimate, compared with less than 3 percent of male homicide victims (BJS 2013d, 3). A separate survey of college women revealed that about 90 percent knew their attacker: "For both completed and attempted rapes, about 9 in 10 offenders were known to the victim. Most often, a boyfriend, ex-boyfriend, classmate, friend, acquaintance, or coworker sexually victimized the women" (BJS 2000, 17).

Historically, the law has been reluctant to define women as victims when the crimes committed against them take place in their homes or as part of a relationship. For centuries, men benefited from not being held accountable for their crimes against women. The failure to recognize domestic violence as criminal behavior reinforced the patriarchal idea that "a man's home is his castle." Since the 1970s, however, violence against women in the home has been considered a crime. Likewise, over the ensuing twenty years, what was originally viewed as a "private matter," such as acquaintance rape, marital rape, and stalking, is now being treated as a criminal offense. Nevertheless, while women are gaining the right to be treated like any other assault victim and to have their battering husband, for example, arrested and punished, the reality is that many women still face social, economic, and cultural barriers that further victimize and humiliate them when they seek equal protection under the law. The question of why women stay in an abusive relationship is in part a reflection of male privilege in criminology if it is not also accompanied by a searching examination of why men batter. Chapter 5 on gender noted the sexual harassment case in which the male judges decided that sexist environments were a given and decided that women had "voluntarily" entered into it. With battering, the violent behavior of men is taken for granted, so the question has been focused on the woman's behavior. The assumption seems to be that she "voluntarily" stays, with the mistaken idea that she enjoys it (or at least accepts it) more implicit than in the past but still present. Box 7.4 further discusses this issue to clarify that a variety of social and other factors are important in understanding the dynamics of women staying in abusive relationships.

BOX 7.4. WHY BATTERED WOMEN SOMETIMES STAY

Asking "Why does she stay?" rather than "Why does he batter—and why doesn't he let her leave?" ultimately privileges men and oppresses women. The question about women's behavior invites scrutiny and finding fault while treating the man's behavior as unremarkable. This is similar to sexual assault, where drinking privileges men and oppresses women: "He was drunk" tends to excuse sexual violence, and "She was drunk" invites blame. So the questions people should be asking are "Why is he violent? Why does the community not intervene? And how can we all stop men from abusing women and better support women who are abused by men?"

Still, the question about barriers to women leaving abusive relationships is important. So the first point is that most battered women do leave several times and work to minimize the violence that they—and their children and pets—face. Second, leaving is the most dangerous time period. Batterers do not need anger management; they want control of their partners, and leaving the relationship threatens that control, so it is met with increased violence.

Susan McGee (2004) notes that "battered women sometimes stay for their children." They do not want the abuser to get custody and "reason that they will sacrifice themselves so their children can have a father, good schools, a safe neighborhood, or financial security." They may not have the money for divorce and a custody battle. Battered women are typically in a catch-22 situation: they get blamed for breaking up the family if they leave and blamed for endangering the children if they stay.

Further, "Some battered women stay because there is no place for them to go" (McGee 2004). Shelters do not exist in all parts of town, and some areas, especially rural, may not have a shelter at all. Funding for shelters and domestic violence services is precarious. Abusers frequently try to isolate a woman from her friends and family—and difficult economic times mean people are working harder to survive and have less capacity to help. After staying at a shelter, a woman must get an apartment, which requires money for a security deposit and a credit rating (both of which an abuser may prevent her from having). Also, "women face discrimination in the rental market, and landlords are often reluctant to rent to formerly battered women, believing that their assailant will show up and cause property damage or physical harm."

Some battered women also stay "because they are not given accurate information about battering. They are told that they are codependent or enablers of his behavior—if they would change, their assailant would" (McGee 2004). Women keep trying to change their behavior and themselves, only to be blamed for not trying harder. They may believe that therapy will stop the violence because they want to believe in him and hope "the violence will end and their relationship can resume. All women want the violence to end; many do not want the relationship to end." Indeed, sometimes battered women stay because "they believe in love and they still love their partners." McGee (2004) emphasizes that "women may love their partners and at the same time hate their violent and abusive actions." She notes that "many people have been in difficult relationships (or jobs) that they should leave but couldn't, or needed time to be able to depart." Further, "Love is glorified in our culture. Popular songs and movies reinforce the idea that love is the most important thing in life and that people (especially women) should do anything for it."

In addition, some battered women stay "because they believe what most people in our society think about battered women: that they imagine or exaggerate the violence" and "that they provoke or are to blame for the violence" (McGee 2004). They may believe that abuse does not happen to women like themselves (Weitzman 2000), in families like theirs, and/or in communities like theirs. Friends, family, clergy, and professionals may also believe myths about domestic violence and/or make excuses for the abuser ("he's under a lot of stress"). The result is that she will feel blamed and be labeled as "hysterical" or selfish for wishing to escape abuse, and she is offered ideas that will not help her situation and that may actually make it more difficult to escape.

Some battered women also stay "because their assailants deliberately and systematically isolate them from support" (McGee 2004). An abuser desires control, so he tries to isolate a woman from friends and family—as well as trying to get her to become his ally. Abusers "accuse the partner of infidelity every time she speaks to someone" and pick fights when she contacts people, so she gradually gives up communicating with them. Abusers take car keys and phones and even nail windows shut and/or lock women in the home. They may also threaten her ("if I can't have you, no one will"), her family, friends, and pets if she escapes; they may threaten suicide. Some assailants may even "play on homophobia and tell their partners that shelters are lesbian recruiting stations, are staffed by lesbians, or are places where she will be attacked by lesbians or become one." An abuser may also harass her at work, make her late, or engage in other activities so that she loses her job—and the ability to support herself. Economic resources are an important predictor of not just leaving but achieving a permanent separation, so inequality in income (see chapter 5) and the disproportionate number of minority women in poverty (see chapter 6) are real barriers to escaping abusive relationships.

Finally, "some battered women stay because they are addicted and their addiction prevents them from taking action" (McGee 2004). Women may drink or take drugs to deal with the physical and emotional pain caused by the relationship. An abuser may encourage the consumption or even coerce her into doing it and then sabotage efforts at recovery. "Doctors may prescribe tranquilizers for a battered woman's 'nerves.'" Drinking and drug use, even short of addiction, "make the woman less able to act on her own behalf and give the assailant a handy tool for discrediting and blaming her" (McGee 2004).

Simply because there are real and substantial barriers to leaving does not mean that a battered woman should stay in a relationship. As McGee (2004) notes:

> Although leaving may pose additional hazards, at least in the short run, the research data and the experience of advocates for battered women demonstrate that ultimately a battered woman can best achieve permanent safety and freedom apart from the batterer. In sum, leaving requires strategic planning and legal intervention to avert separation violence and to safeguard survivors and their children.

Still, the most powerful change in the thinking around why women stay in abusive relationships may be to redirect the question to inquire, "Why do men abuse women?" This focuses the attention on the person committing the crime—the man who abuses a woman—rather than the victim's response. Other crimes do not invite such scrutiny and blame for the victim, and it is especially misplaced where batterers are unlikely to abuse only one woman; repeat abusive behavior in subsequent relationships should be expected. The fruitful inquiry is thus about why the batterer was not effectively dealt with the first time that he abused a woman. How do we deter men from abusing women? What cultural changes can we make to ensure the safety of women who live with men? These are questions that get at the root of the problem because if abusive men did not batter women, women would not have to leave abusive men.

One of the other crimes with a distinct gendered pattern is stalking, which is "a course of conduct directed at a specific person that would cause a reasonable person to feel fear" (BJS 2009f, 1). Legal definitions vary widely from state to state in the activities they consider harassing, in threat and fear requirements, and in how many acts must occur before the conduct can be considered stalking. Both men and women can be victims and offenders of stalking, but data from a 2006 BJS survey indicated women are almost three times more likely to be stalking victims (20 per 1,000 females age ten and over) than men (7.4 per 1,000 males age eighteen and over) (BJS 2009f, table 3). In general, no difference was found in stalking prevalence between white women and minority women, but some evidence suggests that American Indian/Alaska Native women report proportionately more stalking victimization than women of other racial and ethnic backgrounds (BJS 2009f, table 3; BJS 1998c). People who identified as being more than one race had noticeably higher rates of victimization (BJS 2009f), indicating (again) that something dramatic is happening with the statistics or in the lives of mixed-race people that deserves further investigation.

An earlier study found that nearly 95 percent of female victims and 60 percent of male victims identified their stalker as male (BJS 1998c), while the more recent one found that "female victims of stalking were significantly more likely to be stalked by a male (67%) rather than a female (24%) offender" (BJS 2009f, 4). The earlier survey found that some type of intimate partner stalks most women, while men tend to be stalked by strangers and acquaintances (BJS 1998c). The more recent survey did not break down the victim/offender relationship by gender but noted that "about a tenth of all victims were stalked by a stranger, and nearly 3 in 4 of all victims knew their offender in some capacity" (2009f, 4). Also, a strong link exists between stalking and other forms of violence in intimate relationships. Four out of five women who were stalked by a current or former husband or cohabiting partner were also physically assaulted by that partner, and nearly one-third were also sexually assaulted by that partner.

VICTIMIZATION AND INTERSECTIONALITY

In chapter 6 on privilege and intersections, box 6.1 asked about the relative rates of victimization for white men and black women. Men have higher victimization rates than women, but the rates for blacks are higher than for whites, so the question reinforced the importance of understanding intersections. Indeed, while the data in the previous sections are accurate, examining intersections reveals some exceptions and important variations that are not clearly visible with more limited comparisons. For example, official statistics support the contention that men are more likely to be victimized than women, but this will vary by racial/ethnic and class backgrounds. In particular, young black men—especially those who are poor—are at a greater risk for homicide victimization. Their risk of being murdered is four to five times greater than that of young black women, five to eight times higher than that of young white men, and sixteen to twenty-two times higher than that of young white women. Furthermore, a breakdown of official victimization rates by both race and sex reveals that some groups of men are less likely to be victimized than some groups of women.

Table 7.5 displays victimization rates broken down by race, ethnicity, and gender. The men in each category have higher victimization rates than women in the same racial or ethnic category. Black men have higher victimization rates than men of other races, and black women have higher rates of victimization than other women. But black women have generally higher rates of violent victimization than white men, with the exception of robbery. Indeed, the category of completed violence (as opposed to "threatened and attempted violence") shows black men having the highest victimization rate, followed by black women and Hispanic men.

Given the strong pattern of people with low income experiencing greater victimization, part of this dynamic may be class based because minority women have the least income of all those who are poor. Unfortunately, the data are not published in a form that breaks down gender by income. However, table 7.6 presents victimization rates by race and selected levels of income. Conclusions need to be carefully drawn because numbers marked by an asterisk (*) are based on less than ten cases and the reliability is problematic. The poorest blacks in the survey (income less than $7,500) have higher rates of overall violent victimization, and it seems likely that blacks have higher levels of victimization from completed violence than whites at the same income level. Blacks experience more burglaries than whites of the same income and are probably the victims of theft of more than $250 more than whites of similar incomes. Previously, it was stated that whites are more likely to be victimized by whites and blacks are more likely to be victimized by blacks. With higher rates of victimization reported by whites in higher income categories, then, it appears that this initial statement is affirmed with victimization data.

Using data beyond income may be helpful in spotting criminal victimization trends. For example, credit ratings can impact what apartments and rental opportunities are available, thus presenting different neighborhoods to blacks and whites who have the same income. For blacks and whites who have the same income and have bought a house, accumulated savings and wealth (chapter 3) influence opportunities in different regions of cities and suburbs.

While the National Crime Victimization Survey data provide a snapshot of the amount of victimization, the data do not capture the cumulative lifetime chances of being a victim. Being at higher risk of victimization is rarely a one-year event, but it means that one's overall chances of being a victim of a certain crime are greater, as well as the chances of being a victim of multiple crimes. Indeed, the lifetime chances of criminal victimization need to be added to the probability of victimization from other acts not formally labeled as crimes as well; to the likelihood of criminal assault should be added, for example, the chances of increased exposure to toxic waste, unsafe work places, and brutality at the hands of the criminal justice system (to name just a few). For women, the victimization rate for, say, acquaintance rape needs to be added to the likelihood of a relationship involving domestic violence, sexual

Table 7.5. Victimization Rates by Race, Ethnicity, and Gender, 2008 (per 1,000 Age Twelve and Older)

Types of Crimes	Male White Only Rate	Male Black Only Rate	Male Hispanic Only Rate	Female White Only Rate	Female Black Only Rate	Female Hispanic Only Rate
Crime of violence	20.2	29.2	17.9	16.1	23	14.8
Completed violence	4.3	11.6	5.5	4.9	8.9	4.8
Rape/sexual assault†	0.3*	0.6*	0.4*	1	2.9	0.9*
Robbery	1.8	7.3	4.4	1.3	3.9	2.3
Aggravated assault	3.6	5.7	3.9	2.5	4.7	3

Source: BJS 2011. *Criminal Victimization in the United States, 2008—Statistical Tables,* tables 6 and 8.

* Estimate is based on ten or fewer sample cases.

† Includes verbal threats of rape and threats of sexual assault.

Table 7.6. Victimization Rates by Race and Income, 2008 (per 1,000 Age Twelve and Older)

	White Only, <$7,500	Black Only, <$7,500	White Only, $25,000–$34,999	Black Only, $25,000–$34,999	White Only, $75,000+	Black Only, $75,000+
Crime of violence	40.9	57.1	25.1	24.3	12.4	11.7
Completed violence	18.3	19.7*	7.8	12.3*	3	8.4*
Rape/sexual assault†	6.8*	0.0*	0.4*	0.0*	0.4*	1.5*
Robbery	2.7*	12.5*	2.2*	9.7*	1.2	2.5*
Aggravated assault	8.5	14.8*	3.5	4.6*	2	0.0*
All household burglaries	55.7	74.7	29.7	57.2	15.6	23.3*
Theft	132.6	147.3	107.9	122.8	112	105.5
Less than $50	36.3	17.8*	27.4	28.2	26.1	13.8*
$250 or more	25	41.2	25.6	18.7*	32.5	39.3

Source: BJS 2011. *Criminal Victimization in the United States, 2008—Statistical Tables*, tables 15, 21, and 22.

* Estimate is based on ten or fewer sample cases.

† Includes verbal threats of rape and threats of sexual assault.

harassment at work, catcalls on the street, and unwanted exposure to pornography in a variety of settings. Women of color will have additional factors beyond those articulated for white women and also include victimizations that relate to racial stereotyping, such as the likelihood of being accosted by offensive messages in degrading music videos, the lack of women of color being used as a standard of beauty and health in the United States, and stereotypical portrayals of family life in "reality" television shows and police dramas that depict "ghetto" images as normative in the black community.

Further, perceptions of the victim and his or her "worthiness" will shape the reaction to these individual and lifetime profiles of victimization in ways that vary by class, race, gender, and their combinations. For example, when a black man is assaulted, many people may be more inclined to assume he was doing something that precipitated the violence, perhaps by being involved in the drug trade or some other illicit business. The same misguided assumptions hold true for minorities who go missing in the United States—that is, the assumption is that minority women and girls are runaways or prostitutes or that minority men and boys are somehow involved in illegal activities. Consequently, missing persons cases involving racial minorities rarely receive national media or federal law enforcement attention, thereby making it less likely that the abducted minorities (least of all minority men and boys) will be located and their abductors brought to justice. Hence, a white, middle-class woman may be seen as the ultimate "victim," deserving of the most sympathy, especially when her behavior was consistent with the "pedestal values" (described in chapter 5). These constant assumptions about who is a "true victim" of crime and, by extension, who deserves intervention or help are harmful, stereotypical, and wrong. Again, black men constitute a disproportionate number of the victims of crime, yet they receive very little attention in the media as such.

A final limitation of the survey data is that they do not reveal the experience of victimization, the barriers to getting help, or many aspects of life related to the victimization. For example, while the physical experience of being battered is the same for all women, a victim's ability to obtain help in escaping the abuse is strongly related to class, race, and ethnicity. Box 7.4 noted this dynamic in general, and Rivera's work ([1994] 1997) on the experiences of battered Latinas offers some more specific insights, some of which hold true for other racial and ethnic minorities. She observed that a shortage of bilingual and bicultural criminal justice workers creates a system ill prepared to address many battered Latinas' claims—a problem that exists for many immigrant women. Racial and ethnic minority women must decide whether to seek assistance from an outsider who "may not look like her, sound like her, speak her language, or share any of her cultural values" ([1994] 1997, 261). Frequently stereotyped, minority women such as Latinas are often seen as docile and domestic or sensual and sexually available. This kind of racial and ethnic stereotyping devalues some minority groups of women in particular and may place even more social distance between these women and those assigned to handle their complaints.

Similar problems exist within the Asian/Pacific Islander community. In addition, "the low status they hold in the traditional Asian/Pacific family hierarchy as children and as females, compounded with a culturally based emphasis on maintaining harmony even if it is at the cost of the individual's well being, continues to discourage these teenagers from asserting their rights and needs" (Yoshihama, Parekh, and Boyington 1998, 192). It can also be a barrier for adult women, and it combines with shame and guilt to further increase the barriers to reporting and to receiving help. Thus, when the Bureau of Justice Statistics (2009a, table 5) reports that Asian females are less likely than non-Asian females to be victimized by an intimate (and more likely to be victimized by a stranger), caution is warranted in interpreting the results. It is not clear how much of this difference is based on the woman's place in the family hierarchy, maintaining harmony, and so on, and how much reflects real differences in victimization.

The economically marginalized position of many women of color also means they have limited resources to fill the gaps in available support services to assist them (e.g., by procuring an attorney, seeking counseling, hiring a translator, or telephoning family and friends who reside outside the United States). An immigrant woman may face additional challenges to seeking help. If she doesn't speak English, police officers may rely on the batterer to provide the translation. Immigrant women's families may be far away, contributing to the experience of isolation. Or, as Tina Shum, a family counselor at a social service agency, observed, many battered Asian immigrant women share a house with extended family members where there is no privacy on the telephone and no opportunity to leave the house. Some immigrant women are basically held hostage by their boyfriends or husbands, who threaten the women with deportation if they report their abuse. Even if such threats are unfounded, they may still intimidate women with no independent access to information. Many women do not realize that even if they are not US citizens, they are still entitled to police protection from abuse.

Some minority women are reluctant to seek help from the police. They may fear the police will do too little and not take their victimization seriously. Or they may fear the police will do too much and deal with the abuser too harshly, thus compounding the problem of minority overrepresentation in prison (see chapter 10). Many women of color have had experiences with police—either in the United States or in their country of origin—that led them to distrust or place little confidence in the police. Interviews with operators of domestic violence shelters in Harlem, for example, revealed that police brutality was the dominant issue in minority communities, while violence against women was not even a close second. "Women of color fear that the protections they seek could result in their men being beaten or even killed by cops. And if the batterer, often the sole source of support for the victim and her children, is charged with a felony, he could spend his life behind bars under the 'three-strikes-and-you're-out' mandate" (Swift 1997).

Responses to battered women need to acknowledge not only that women of color experience sexual and patriarchal oppression at the hands of their male partners but also that they "at the same time struggle alongside them against racial oppression" (Rice 1990, 63). For black women in particular, the emphasis on racial solidarity and not "airing dirty laundry" has often meant placing the needs of collectivity (family, church, neighborhood, or race) over their own individual needs. This emphasis on in-group survival often "promotes a paradigm of individual sacrifice that can border on exploitation" and that may have dire consequences in terms of their need for help in escaping abuse (Collins 1998, 29).

IMPLICATIONS

The US government has been well aware of racial disparities in crime, violence, victimization, criminal justice, and health care for decades. As far back as 1984, the Department of Health and Human Services established its Task Force on Black and Minority Health. In 2000, Congress elevated the National Institutes of Health Office of Minority Health, turning it into the higher-profile National Center on Minority Health and Health Disparities. Nevertheless, no major legislation on the problem was ever submitted by Congress to George W. Bush for his signing, even though most health disparity measures were either stagnant or getting worse during the Bush administration.

As noted earlier, the comprehensive health care law called the Affordable Care Act (or "Obamacare") has some potential to help because it prevents insurance companies from charging women higher health-care premiums, covers mammograms, and improves coverage for birth control, among other advantages for women. In addition, the reauthorized Violence Against Women Act has "expanded protections for gays and lesbians, Native Americans and illegal immigrants" (Lederman 2013). Overall, these measures start to address some of the many inequalities facing women and minorities in the United States today.

Structural victimization is difficult to separate from institutional and individual forms of victimization as each of these three spheres of intersection becomes consumed with emotional issues of self-esteem and social respect. At the same time, the issues of shame, humiliation, and anger associated with institutionalized abuse are less about individual behavioral characteristics and more about group cultural characteristics associated with variables of class, race, gender, and age. These variables and other social indicators of value or status serve to differentiate the forms of abuse and nonabuse that are socially constructed as appropriate for men, women, boys, girls, heterosexuals, homosexuals, whites, African Americans, Asians, Hispanics, the rich, the poor, the homeless, immigrants, the mentally ill, and so forth.

Furthermore, what differentiates institutionalized expressions of victimization from interpersonal and structural expressions is that the former are often interwoven with the normative practices of socialization found in the home, at school, in the street, at the workplace, and in the criminal justice system. In the case of crime control, the institutional forms of victimization carried out by the administration of justice are part and parcel of the cultural attitudes, social identities, and relations of power and conflict that parents and children, teachers and students, adolescents and adults, and agents and enemies of the established order occupy. At the same time, victimization by agents and agencies of the criminal justice apparatus is supported by ideologies that rationalize, justify, or excuse such behavior by helping to blur the distinctions between abuse and discipline, harassment and teasing, assault and defense, and punishment and reform.

Finally, acts of victimization—interpersonal, institutional, and structural—do not survive because the majority formally or overtly endorses these kinds of behavior. On the contrary, most of these acts are denied, ignored, or dismissed as exceptional events rather than seen as general patterns of structural and cultural interaction. Accordingly, most attempts at criminal justice reform are "reformist" rather than "structural" in nature. They do not upset or challenge existing power relations, nor do they address the larger social and cultural roots of these patterns of victimization. Instead, these efforts in criminal justice reform or victimization reduction are aimed almost exclusively at controlling and/or changing the individual perpetrators ("bad apples") of excessive abuse. Services for victims are still secondary concerns. What are called for, in contrast, are much wider strategies of recovery that include an array and diversity of services, programs, and resources that revolve around "restorative" and redemptive practices of justice. Such policies strive to reconcile the collective interests of perpetrators, victims, and bystanders alike in the processes of rehabilitating, reaffirming, and reconstructing the personal and social sense of well-being. These strategies of intervention are also aimed at strengthening community, and they are designed in the spirit of establishing community efficacy (Barak 2003).

REVIEW AND DISCUSSION QUESTIONS

1. What is meant by the term *genocide*, and how is it accomplished? Based on your answer, what are the important arguments for and against the position that "the majority population of the United States has committed genocide involving both Native Americans and African Americans"?
2. What is the difference between the "narrower" and "broader" approaches to victimology? Which approach does this book take, and why?
3. Explain how victimization occurs for people by (a) class, (b) race, and (c) gender. How do these different kinds of victimization overlap and create issues of intersectionality that have previously been ignored?
4. What are the other important conclusions you can draw about the patterns of victimization in relationship to class, race, and gender? Please answer in terms of official and unofficial data.
5. What are the barriers to women leaving an abusive situation? How many of these—and what other barriers can you think of—apply to minority women, abused heterosexual men, and gays and lesbians abused by their partners?

8

Lawmaking and the Administration of Criminal Law

In 1964, a court sentenced William Rummel to three years in prison after he was con-victed of a felony for fraudulently using a credit card to obtain $80 worth of goods. Five years later, he passed a forged check in the amount of $28.36 and received four years. In 1973, Rummel was convicted of a third felony—obtaining $102.75 under false pretenses by accepting payment to fix an air conditioner that he never returned to repair. Rum-mel received a mandatory life sentence under Texas's recidivist statute. He challenged this sentence on the grounds that it violated the Eighth Amendment's prohibition of cruel and unusual punishment by being grossly disproportionate to the crime.

In Rummel v. Estelle *(445 U.S. 263 [1980]), the Supreme Court affirmed Rum-mel's life sentence for the theft of less than $230 that never involved force or the threat of force. Justice Lewis Powell's dissent noted, "It is difficult to imagine felonies that pose less danger to the peace and good order of a civilized society than the three crimes committed by the petitioner" (445 U.S. 263, 295). However, Justice William Rehnquist's majority opinion stated there was an "interest, expressed in all recidivist statutes, in dealing in a harsher manner with those who by repeated criminal acts have shown that they are simply incapable of conforming to the norms of society as established by its criminal law" (445 U.S. 263). After "having twice imprisoned him for felonies, Texas was entitled to place upon Rummel the onus of one who is simply unable to bring his conduct within the norms prescribed by the criminal law" (445 U.S. 284).*

Now consider the case of General Electric, which is not considered a habitual crimi-nal offender despite committing diverse crimes over many decades. In the 1950s, GE and several companies agreed in advance on the sealed bids they submitted for heavy electrical equipment. This price-fixing defeated the purpose of competitive bidding, cost-ing taxpayers and consumers as much as a billion dollars. GE was fined $437,000—a tax-deductible business expense—the equivalent of a person who earns $175,000 a year getting a $3 fine. Two executives spent only thirty days in jail, even though one defendant *had commented that price-fixing "had become so common and gone for so many years that we lost sight of the fact that it was illegal" (quoted in Hills 1987, 191).*

In the 1970s, GE made illegal campaign contributions to Richard Nixon's presidential campaign. Widespread illegal discrimination against minorities and women at GE resulted in a $32 million settlement. Also during this time, three former GE nuclear engineers—including one who had worked for the company for twenty-three years and managed the nuclear complaint department—resigned to draw attention to serious design defects in the plans for the Mark III nuclear reactor because the standard practice was "sell first, test later" (Hills 1987, 170; Glazer and Glazer 1989).

In the 1980s, GE pled guilty to felonies involving illegal procurement of highly classified defense documents, and in 1985, it pled guilty to 108 counts of felony fraud involving Minuteman missile defense contracts. In spite of a new code of ethics, GE was convicted in three more criminal cases over the next few years, plus it paid $3.5 million to settle cases involving retaliation against four whistleblowers who helped reveal the defense fraud. (GE subsequently lobbied Congress to weaken the False Claims Act that protects whistleblowers.) In 1988, the government returned another 317 indictments against GE for fraud. In 1989, GE's stock brokerage firm paid a $275,000 civil fine for discriminating against low-income consumers, the largest fine ever under the Equal Credit Opportunity Act. A 1990 jury convicted GE of fraud for cheating on a $254 million contract for battlefield computers, and journalist William Greider reports that the $27.2 million fine included money to "settle government complaints that it had padded bids on two hundred other military and space contracts" (1996, 350; see also Clinard 1990; Greider 1994; Pasztor 1995; Simon 1999).

GE is also one of the prime environmental polluters and is identified as responsible for contributing to the damage of fifty-two active Superfund sites in need of environmental cleanup in this country alone. In 1999, the corporation agreed to a $250 million settlement to clean up the Housatonic River in Massachusetts. GE is responsible "for one of America's largest Superfund sites, the Hudson River, where the company dumped more than a million pounds of toxic wastes including cancer-causing polychlorinated biphenyls over a period of decades, according to the EPA" (Center for Public Integrity 2007). Instead of cleaning up its part of the 197-mile site, the company mounted an eight-year challenge to the Superfund law that requires polluters to remedy toxic situations they created. (GE's corporate environmental counsel during part of this time, Ignacia Moreno, was appointed by President Obama to be assistant attorney general for the Environment and Natural Resources division in the Department of Justice.)

GE created a number of finance arms to help people and companies buy its products, and those activities account for nearly half of its earnings (Gerth and Dennis 2009). Most people know GE "for light bulbs and home appliances, but GE Capital is one of the world's largest and most diverse financial operations, lending money for commercial real estate, aircraft leasing and credit cards for stores such as Wal-Mart. If GE Capital were classified as a banking company, it would be the nation's seventh largest" (Gerth and Dennis 2009). GE is one of the entities sued by the Federal Housing Finance Agency over "securities law violations or common law fraud" in the sale of mortgage-backed securities to Fannie Mae and Freddie Mac (FHFA 2011).

Even though felons usually lose political rights, GE donated almost $18 million to candidates in federal elections between 1989 and 2009 (Center for Responsive Politics 2009b), and it spent $191 million for lobbying between 1998 and 2009 (Center for Responsive Politics 2009a). In spite of having been convicted of defrauding every branch of the military multiple times, GE is frequently invited to testify before Congress. Until 2013, GE also had the ability to shape public opinion through its ownership of NBC Universal, which owns NBC television (and A&E, USA, and others), MSNBC, and the financial news outlet CNBC.

In 2010, GE made profits in the United States of $5.1 billion and paid no taxes (Kocieniewski 2011). The story ran on several networks but not on the GE-owned NBC Nightly News or the NBC public affairs program Meet the Press. GE's CEO was then appointed to chair President Obama's Council on Jobs and Competitiveness. With this kind of political, economic, and social power, it is easy to understand why "three strikes and you're out" does not apply to "big hitters" like GE.

The pattern outlined by these examples was reinforced in 2003, when the Supreme Court upheld a fifty-year sentence for two acts of shoplifting videos from Kmart. Under California's "three strikes" law, Leandro Andrade's burglary convictions from the 1980s counted as the first two, and the prosecutor decided to charge the shoplifting incidents as strikes, which carry a mandatory twenty-five years each. The Supreme Court, citing Rummel v. Estelle, held that the sentences were neither disproportionate nor unreasonable (Lockyer v. Andrade, 538 U.S. 63 [2003]).

At the same time, Enron's chief financial officer, Andrew Fastow, negotiated a plea bargain for not more than ten years in prison and was subsequently sentenced to six years based on his cooperation with prosecutors. (He is eligible for "good time" reduction in sentencing and a one-year reduction for undergoing drug treatment for his dependence on antianxiety medicine, so Fastow could serve as little as four years.) Fastow had been instrumental in the fraud, which resulted in the largest bankruptcy in US history at that time. He had worked the deals to launder loans through allegedly independent entities to make them appear as revenue for Enron, and he helped push the accountants to approve the deals and used the massive banking fees Enron paid to silence Wall Street analysts who asked questions about Enron's finances. Fastow was originally charged with about a hundred felony counts, including conspiracy, wire fraud, securities fraud, and falsifying books, as well as obstruction of justice, money laundering, insider trading, and filing false income tax returns. And the sentence was negotiated in the environment where getting tough on corporate crime was seen as a high priority (Leighton and Reiman 2004).

Contemporary legal scholar Donald Black states: "Law itself is social control, but many other kinds of social control also appear in social life, in families, friendships, neighborhoods, villages, tribes, occupations, organizations, and groups of all kinds"

(1976, 6). However, law is a special form of social control because it represents "governmental social control" (Radcliffe-Brown [1933] 1965) over the citizenry. The government has a monopoly on the "legitimate" use of coercion—detention, arrest, incarceration, and execution—and the law serves to identify the acts (crimes) and actors (criminals) that power is to be used against. Robin Miller and Sandra Lee Browning capture this sentiment in their introduction to *For the Common Good*:

> Law is a structural force that, at least theoretically, reaches everyone. It can be powerful in its scope, its frequency, and its intensity. . . . And a law that is not commonly accepted by the people still has the power to shape behavior through sheer force of the punishments handed down for violations of it. (2004, 6)

The criminal law thus represents the first stage at sorting through annoying, troublesome, harmful, and deviant behavior to see what acts should be crimes and subjected to formal social control. The criminal law, by what it includes as well as the seriousness of the punishment, signals to the police how to prioritize their efforts. It does the same for prosecutors. Sentencing guidelines, while advisory, shape the behavior of judges by indicating which defendants should be sent to prison (and for how long) and which can be subject to execution.

The criminal law not only shapes the priorities of those in the criminal justice system but also plays an important role in shaping people's attitudes about what is dangerous and harmful behavior. In this sense, not only does the criminal law reflect consensus that rape, robbery, and street crime are serious harm, but it also helps create consensus that these are the worst harms and that many white-collar and corporate behaviors are not really crimes. This effect is magnified through the media, which uses the criminal law as the basis for reporting on crime, including story frames about the "crime problem" and "crime waves."

For example, Rummel was convicted of three property crimes and received a life sentence, while Andrade was convicted for four property crimes over the course of decades and received a mandatory fifty years. But the criminal law seemingly has no provisions to penalize those who cause a global financial crisis that wipes out trillions of dollars in wealth. The reporting of the crisis, even on those who profited handsomely from billions of dollars in bonuses paid for from a taxpayer-funded bailout, was not from the framework of crime. In general, the corporate-owned media did little to expose massive problems before the economic collapse, and they have tended to expose a few "bad apples" rather than systemic problems that require a systemic overhaul to protect people from future property losses caused by the behavior of the powerful.

This chapter examines the ways in which law and lawmaking are shaped by class, race, and gender. The foundation of this chapter is that criminal law is not a "natural" or "objective" reflection of harm but the result of a political process where money and privilege matter. While some laws reflect widespread consensus of what conduct should be prohibited, other laws reflect the interests of powerful groups with special access to and influence over lawmakers. In pursuing this topic, this chapter elaborates on many ideas introduced in chapter 2, such as the importance of examining the types of harms written into the criminal law.

The next section of this chapter provides many examples of how class—and thus wealth and ownership of the economic power—shapes the law. At times, this influence means harms done by the rich and powerful are not part of the criminal law, or they receive sentences that are much less harsh than comparable street crimes. At other times, laws have been passed to help big business avoid paying taxes on their profits and to enable corporate fraud.

Comparatively, the topic of class presents striking examples of bias in the law because most of the obvious racial examples, such as Jim Crow, have slowly been erased from the books, and laws now look facially neutral (there are no acts on the books where the wording of the text indicates that they apply only to blacks or minorities). So the section on race in this chapter reviews some of the history of race-based law and then turns to an examination of race and differential treatment in the administration of justice. Although traffic laws are facially neutral, they are applied differentially and create the problem of "driving while black" (DWB) that we will discuss in chapter 9 on law enforcement. This section on race also builds on the earlier discussion of classical criminology and provides a foundation that will be explored further in the chapters on law enforcement, criminal adjudication, punishment, sentencing, and imprisonment.

This chapter's section on gender examines the many ways of trying to make sense of equality, given that men and women have important differences (including, but not limited to, reproductive functions). Feminist analyses differ on where they locate the sources of inequality and what they see as the goal of change; they question whether women should direct themselves to equality with men based on a male standard within the current economic system. While feminism does make gender inequality a primary question, the diversity of analysis and goals suggests that the discussion should be about *feminisms* rather than a singular feminism. Such an understanding is important for subsequent chapters that will discuss gender inequality in relation to specific practices and policies of criminal justice administration.

CLASS, CRIME, AND THE LAW

The rich and powerful use their influence to keep acts from becoming crimes, even though these acts may be more socially injurious than those labeled criminal. The concept of *analogous social injury* "includes harm caused by acts or conditions that are legal but produce consequences similar to those produced by illegal acts" (Lanier and Henry 2004, 19). Much of the harmful and illegitimate behavior of the elite members of society has not traditionally been defined as criminal, but nearly all the harmful and deviant behavior perpetrated by the poor and the powerless, the working and middle classes, is defined as violating the criminal law. Thus, basing crime control theory and practice on a neutral criminal law (as discussed in chapter 2) ignores the fact that the legal order and the administration of justice reflect a structural class bias that concentrates the coercive power of the state on the behaviors of the relatively poor and powerless members of society.

This observation is consistent with the analysis in Donald Black's highly acclaimed book, *The Behavior of Law* (1976). Black sought to discover a series of rules to describe the amount of law and its behavior in response to social variables such as stratification, impersonality, culture, social organization, and other forms of social control. When it comes to issues of class, the variables of stratification and social organization are the two most relevant. Black proposed that the law varies directly with hierarchy and privilege such that the more inequality in a country, the more law. He also applied his proposition to disputes between two parties of unequal status and wealth. Based on a wide variety of cases, Black concluded there is likely to be "more law" in a downward direction, such as when a rich person is victimized by a poorer one. This means the use of criminal rather than civil law, for example, and a greater likelihood of a report, investigation, arrest, prosecution, and prison sentence. In contrast, when the wealthier harms the poorer, Black predicted there would be less law—meaning civil law, monetary fines rather than jail, and therapeutic sanctions rather than punitive ones. Further, Black argued that there is likely to be "more law" in the downward direction when an individual victimizes a group high in social organization, such as a corporation or the state. Conversely, "less law" and a pattern of differential application are likely to be the result of a corporate body or the state victimizing individuals or groups of individuals that have lower levels of social organization, such as poor communities.

Two class-based systemic operations in the administration of criminal justice are "selective enforcement" and "differential application" of the law. Selective enforcement of harms by the law refers to the fact that most harms perpetrated by the affluent are "beyond incrimination" (M. Kennedy 1970) and not part of the criminal law. When harms committed by the politically and economically powerful are part of the criminal law, differential application means that the police, prosecutors, and other agents of the criminal justice system use their discretion to ignore or minimize the consequences. In these ways, Jeffrey Reiman and Paul Leighton argue that the processing of offenders serves to "weed out the wealthy." Many harmful acts will not come within the realm of criminal law, "or, if technically criminal, not prosecuted, or, if prosecuted, not punished, or if punished, only mildly" (2013, 61).

Criminologist Stephen Box suggests that one of the most important advantages of "corporate criminals" lies "in their ability to prevent their actions from becoming subject to criminal sanctions in the first place" (quoted in Braithwaite 1992, 89). Although certain behaviors may cause widespread harm, the criminal law does not forbid abuses of power in the realm of economic domination, governmental control, and denial of human rights (Simon 1999). Great Britain, for example, has a corporate manslaughter law that makes criminal manslaughter provisions applicable to companies where a gross failure of supervision leads to a worker's death; Canada and Australia have similar laws, but not the United States (Leighton and Reiman 2014).

As described in the opening narrative of this chapter, being a habitual offender is against the law in most areas, where "three strikes and you're out" applies to street criminals. But habitual offender laws do not apply to corporate entities (such as GE), which can repeatedly commit serious crimes without being subjected to these statutes or to the legal possibility of a state revoking a corporation's charter to exist (Hartmann 2002).

In some cases, harmful actions will be civil offenses rather than criminal ones, but the difference is significant because civil actions are not punishable by prison and do not carry the same harsh stigma. A plea to civil or administrative charges usually does not require an admission of guilt and thus cannot be used against a business in other related litigation. Other destructive behavior may not be prohibited by civil law or regulations created by administrative agencies. In this respect, the tobacco industry produces a product that kills about 440,000 people a year, but its actions are not illegal and are not a substantial part of the media campaign of the Office for National Drug Control Policy or Partnership for a Drug-Free America.

In general, getting tough, wars on crime and drugs, and "zero tolerance" have characterized lawmaking for harms done by the poor. Legislators have imposed mandatory minimum sentences, toughened penalties, and appropriated money for police and prisons. In contrast, the general approach to business activity—even harmful and dangerous acts—has been deregulation. This has involved legislators rejecting new laws to punish corporate crime, trying to reduce the power of enforcement agencies, and reducing the budgets of enforcement agencies so that they have fewer resources with which to write new regulations, fight for them in court against challenges by business, and investigate wrongdoing.

The Rich Get Richer and the Poor Get Prison suggests that the result of these relations is that law is like a carnival mirror. It distorts our understanding of the harms that may befall us by magnifying the threat from street crime because it criminalizes more of the conduct of poor people. At the same time, it distorts our perception about the danger from crime in the suites by downplaying and not protecting people from the harms perpetrated by those above them in the class system. As a consequence, both the criminal law and the administration of justice do "not simply *reflect* the reality of crime; [they have] a hand in *creating* the reality we see" (Reiman and Leighton 2013, 61; emphasis in the original). Thus, to say that the criminal law appropriately focuses on the most dangerous acts is a problematic statement because the criminal law shapes our perceptions about what is a dangerous act.

Corporations and those with economic power are also able to use mass-mediated communication to shape the public discourse and moral outrage about "crime" (Barak 1994). In short, the corporate elite's relative monopoly over the "free" airways allows them to act as "transmission belts" for creating consensus over what is and is not a crime. For example, Reiman and Leighton (2013) note that multiple deaths that result from unsafe workplaces tend to get reported as "accidents" and "disasters," while "mass murder" is reserved exclusively for street crime. While there are differences between the two, it is not clear that one should be a regulatory violation and the other should be a crime—especially since the criminal law recognizes harms done knowingly, recklessly, and negligently.

In spite of the influence of the criminal law and media in shaping beliefs about harm, the American public occasionally regards white-collar crimes as being at least as serious as street crime and determines that corporate criminals are treated too leniently for the harms they do to workers, consumers, and the environment (Grabosky, Braithwaite, and Wilson 1987; see also Lanier and Henry [2004]). For example, respondents in polls have supported stiffer sentences than had been handed down under the Food, Drug, and Cosmetic Act. People in other surveys favor incarceration for false advertising, unsafe workplace environments, antitrust offenses, and the failure of landlords to make repairs, resulting in the death of a tenant. The offense of "knowingly manufacturing and selling contaminated food that results in death" was ranked in seriousness behind assassination of a public official and killing a police officer during the terrorist hijacking of a plane; the selling of contaminated food was considered more serious than "killing someone during a serious argument" and the "forcible rape of a stranger in a park" (Grabosky, Braithwaite, and Wilson 1987, 34–35). Even though people do see some corporate crimes as being as serious as street crime and as deserving of punishment, these sentiments are not reflected in the mass media or criminal law because such rules would adversely affect the interests of the rich and powerful, who have better access to lawmakers.

The remainder of this section discusses various harms committed by the poor and the powerful to illustrate the class bias in the criminal law and administration of justice. The starting point is injuries and violations of bodily integrity, some of which are analogous to violent street crime. Later in the section, we review fraud, the economic crisis, and acts analogous to theft because they involve an illegitimate appropriation of resources.

Not all injuries committed by corporations are analogous to violent crime, but consider that as far as the criminal justice system was concerned, there was no crime committed in the 2005 deaths of twelve miners in West Virginia, even though

> time and again over the past four years, federal mining inspectors documented the same litany of problems at central West Virginia's Sago Mine: mine roofs that tended to collapse without warning. Faulty or inadequate tunnel supports. A dangerous buildup of flammable coal dust. (Warrick 2006)

In the two years before this explosion, the mine was cited 273 times for safety violations, one-third of which were classified as "significant and substantial," and "16 violations logged in the past eight months were listed as 'unwarrantable failures,' a designation reserved for serious safety infractions for which the operator had either already been warned, or which showed 'indifference or extreme lack of care'" (Warrick 2006). This state of affairs seems to fit within the criminal law categories of knowing, reckless, or negligent, but most matters like this stay within the realm of administrative sanctions and the civil law. Despite the obvious importance of human decisions, events like this tend to be reported as "disasters" or "accidents."

Outside of mining, the situation is the same. From 1982 to 2002, the Occupational Safety and Health Administration (OSHA), which has primary responsibility for the nation's workplace safety, identified 1,242 deaths it concluded were related to "willful" safety violations. But only 7 percent of cases were referred for prosecution, and "having avoided prosecution once, at least 70 employers willfully violated safety laws again, resulting in scores of additional deaths. Even these repeat violators were rarely prosecuted" (Barstow 2003). One of the many barriers is that causing the death of a worker by willfully violating safety laws is a misdemeanor with a maximum sentence of six months in jail, so such cases are of little interest to prosecutors. This level of punishment was established in 1970 by Congress, which has repeatedly rejected attempts to make it tougher, so currently, harassing a wild burro on federal lands carries twice the maximum sentence of causing a worker's death through willful safety violations (Barstow 2003).

Compare the lack of change in the punishment for a worker's death with the escalating toughness for all types of street crime, where Congress continued to be "tough on crime" even during the height of the war on crime and enacted three-strikes laws, expanded the number of "strikeable" offenses, increased the number of criminal acts covered by a mandatory minimum sentence, increased the mandatory minimum sentences, and made more offenses eligible for the death penalty. During the same period and into the present, Congress has voted down all laws to increase penalties for workplace deaths that result from willful behavior, even modest proposals to increase the maximum penalty to ten years (Barstow 2003). Likewise, the level of fines was increased only once (in 1990) from the levels set in 1970 and thus has not kept pace with inflation. In congressional testimony on the Protecting America's Workers Act (which did not become law), Assistant Secretary of Labor for Occupational Safety and Health David Michaels noted how "currently, serious violations—those that pose a substantial probability of death or serious physical harm to workers—are subject to a maximum civil penalty of only $7,000" (quoted in Reiman and Leighton 2013, 81).

The analysis provided here also applies to financial crimes, including several episodes of massive and widespread fraud. For example, Representative Frank Annunzio, who was chair of the House subcommittee on financial institutions that investigated the prosecution of criminals involved in the savings and loan (S&L) wrongdoings of the late 1980s, makes the same points in his opening remarks to one congressional hearing:

> Frankly, I don't think the administration has the interest in pursuing Gucci-clad white-collar criminals. These are hard and complicated cases, and the defendants often were rich, successful prominent members of their upper-class communities. It is far easier putting away a sneaker-clad high school dropout who tried to rob a bank of a thousand dollars with a stick-up note, than a smooth talking S & L executive who steals a million dollars with a fraudulent note. (US Congress 1990, 1)

These comments highlight how hard it is to prosecute upper-class criminals, even though the harm done is much greater than that of street crime, and how reluctant the system is to prosecute them. Some S&L executives personally stole tens of millions of dollars, and others were responsible for the collapse of financial institutions that needed government bailouts to the tune of $1 billion (Binstein and Bowden 1993; Calavita, Pontell, and Tillman 1997; Pizzo, Fricker, and Muolo 1991). The total cost of the S&L bailout ultimately climbed to about $500 billion (Day 1993), yet few S&L crooks went to prison (Pizzo and Muolo 1993), and the ones who did received an average sentence of two years compared with an average of nine years for a bank robber (US Congress 1990).

After such expensive and widespread fraud, Congress briefly decided to "get tough" but soon removed all the regulations put in place to safeguard against similar fraud taking place. These actions set the stage for the 2002 financial scandals involving Enron, WorldCom, Global Crossing, Tyco, and others. The *New York Times* captured the subsequent situation with the headline: "Now Who, Exactly Got Us into This? Enron? Arthur Andersen? Shocking Say Those Who Helped It Along" (Labaton 2002; see also Leighton and Reiman 2004). With respect to the economic meltdown and Great Recession of 2008–2010, the same types of questions were raised and the same types of financial offenders appear to be avoiding criminal culpability. They also were able to keep their million-dollar corporate bonuses for helping to run the US and global economies into the ground, necessitating trillion-dollar bailouts that dwarf the bailouts associated with the earlier savings and loan scandals from twenty years ago. While some of the bailout money has been repaid, other loans and investments will result in losses, and the government has had to spend large sums for economic stimulus, meaning taxpayers have had to pay a substantial "Wall Street incompetence tax" (Ritholtz 2008a).

Barry Ritholtz, CEO of a financial research firm and author of *Bailout Nation* (2009a), stated that a consistent element of the problem has been "an abdication of responsibility from the various entities assigned to supervise and regulate" our financial system (2008c). He suggests that we would not allow the Super Bowl to be played without referees because "we *know* that players would give in to their worst impulses" (2008d, emphasis in the original) and the financial system is the same. In an article explaining the crisis, Ritholtz (2008b, 100), in "A Memo Found in the Street: Uncle Sam the Enabler," writes: "D.C.: We could not have done it without you. We may be drunks, but you were our enablers: Your legislative, executive, and administrative decisions made possible all that we did. Our recklessness would not have reached its soaring heights but for your governmental incompetence." But the result was less from incompetence than from industry lobbying to deregulate the activities of financial institutions.

At the root of the financial crisis are complex securities based on mortgages originated because lax underwriting standards encouraged lenders to give mortgages to borrowers who were without the resources to repay them (unless housing prices continued to increase indefinitely). The Federal Reserve had power to regulate mortgage underwriters but failed to do so. At any point in time, the Fed could have imposed tighter lending standards or prohibited mortgages where borrowers did not have to verify income or assets (a "liar's loan"). Mortgages were in great demand by investment banks that made large profits pooling and reselling them as mortgage-backed securities. Mortgage underwriters were paid if the borrower made the required payment for the first several months, so they invented numerous mortgages that had low interest rates and payments for the first year or so and then reset to higher rates that the borrowers could not afford.

In spite of underwriters giving hundreds of thousands of dollars to people so poor "they did not have a pot to piss in" (*This American Life* 2008), underregulated credit-ratings agencies such as Standard & Poor's and Moody's gave the securities high credit ratings, which encouraged investors all over the world to buy them (Barak 2012). Lawmakers were not concerned about the obvious conflict of interest inherent in the credit ratings agencies' business model of being paid by the investment banks to rate their products. Ratings agencies that gave out anything less than the best credit ratings lost business and were not used by the investment bank for rating other mortgage-backed securities.

To make matters worse, the Securities and Exchange Commission (SEC) waived its leverage rules for five big Wall Street firms. "Leverage" is essentially how much a firm can borrow for the amount of assets it has. Before 2004, the permitted debt-to-capital ratio was 12 to 1, but after lobbying by investment banks, the SEC allowed these firms to use whatever leverage they wanted. Firms increased their leverage to 30 to 1 and even 40 to 1, essentially borrowing $30 and even $40 for each dollar of assets (Ritholtz 2008b, 101). Further, many companies were involved in buying or selling "credit default swaps," which can be thought of as insurance against a company's inability to pay its debt. But unlike insurance, no federal or state agencies regulate the trillions of dollars of swaps, and there is no centralized clearinghouse to keep track of what parties have sold, how much protection, and whether they would be able to pay if the situation required it. Thus, as Wall Street firms started to run into financial trouble, no one knew who might run into problems caused by their exposure to credit default swaps. The lack of transparency caused a lack of trust that froze up the credit system because no one wanted to lend money in case the borrower turned out to be in deep financial trouble.

The financial institutions that previously posed "systemic risk" because they were "too big to fail" are now even larger because of government policy to provide financial support for combining weaker institutions with stronger ones. The financial crisis did produce sweeping legislation—the Dodd-Frank Wall Street Reform and Consumer Protection Act of 2010. It is too early to assess the impact of this legislation because it is a "framework" that calls for almost one hundred studies and for agencies to write hundreds of rules (Barak 2013). But the coauthor, Congressman Barney Frank, says the bill is "facing a death through a thousand cuts" because of lobbying—$1.3 billion in 2009 and the first three months of 2010 (quoted in Reiman and Leighton 2013, 149). The strategy involves not just putting loopholes in new rules but also reducing the budgets of enforcement agencies. Congress cut the proposed SEC budget for 2012 to the same level it had for 2011, even though Dodd-Frank gave the agency more responsibilities. The smaller budget does not save taxpayers anything because fees paid by the firms it regulates fund the SEC. Thus, financial institutions pay less to government and have a weaker watchdog on the beat. Ritholtz rightly calls this keeping the SEC "defective by design." Former SEC chairman Harvey Pitt agrees: "It's almost as if the commission is being set up to fail" (Reiman and Leighton 2013, 149).

In summary, the massive systemic fraud with the S&Ls is followed by massive systemic fraud of Enron, WorldCom, and so on, which is followed by a fraudulently based financial services industry driven by the banking cartels of Wall Street that lead to a global economic crisis (Barak 2012). Most of the people who caused this are not only still in place at their jobs but also received bonuses, and the companies that required bailing out because they were "too big to fail" are now even bigger. These same financial institutions, such as Goldman Sachs, Bank of America, and AIG, who receive taxpayer bailouts are undercutting serious financial reform. The stage is being set for bigger problems and a more expensive taxpayer bailout. To understand this frustrating situation, consider that banks and securities firms spent $193 million to fund political campaigns for the 2008 elections—and they raised additional money through trade groups (Ritholtz 2009b). The more general problem is with corporate power, discussed in chapter 3. As Braithwaite notes, "Power corrupts and unaccountable power corrupts with impunity" (1992, 89).

Finally, because the government (the state) makes the laws, many of its own abuses of power are not considered to be crime. Government-sponsored genocide of Native Americans in order to secure their land and its mineral wealth violated basic human rights and treaties, but these acts were never subject to criminal law, nor were the victims ever counted in terms of the numbers of people murdered in this nation (Barak 1998). Following 9/11, Congress passed the Patriot Act as part of the effort to fight the "war on terrorism" and removed some of the legal rights that had protected US citizens from invasion of privacy by government agents—some laws requiring search warrants, for example.

One of the classic statements on this topic, first referred to by President Dwight Eisenhower as the "military-industrial complex," is a book by C. Wright Mills called *The Power Elite* (1956). He contended that an elite composed of the largest corporations, the military, and the federal government dominates life in the United States. Mills argued that these three spheres of power are highly interrelated, with members of each group coming from similar upper-class social backgrounds, attending the same private and Ivy League universities, even belonging to the same social or political organizations. In addition to their mutual "ruling class interests," corporate elites also make large political donations to both the Republicans and Democrats to ensure their access to the lawmaking process.

RACE, CRIME, AND THE LAW

The classic analysis of "punishment and social structure" by Georg Rusche and Otto Kirchheimer ([1939] 1968) revealed the relationship between the type and form of punishment in society and the changes in the political economy. Important aspects of the analysis are the notion of surplus labor and the costs of production. While the idea of surplus labor can be used in a class-based analysis, frequently minorities are the labor pool that is regulated through punishment. One striking example is the rise of black imprisonment following the Civil War—which some would argue applies to the rise of black imprisonment rates today through the developments in a changing industrial-service and global economy (see chapter 4).

The Civil War abolished involuntary servitude and freed the slaves, although "the transition from bondage to freedom was more theoretical than real" (Gorman 1997, 447). Millions of blacks were "suddenly transformed from personal property to potential competitors" (Tolnay and Beck 1995, 57). Southern whites in particular had to compete with blacks for jobs, and plantation owners would now have to compete with one another for good help with higher wages. In addition, many whites feared "domination" by the newly freed blacks, who outnumbered the whites, and they feared black men in regard to white women, especially since many young white men were killed or wounded in the war. Some whites, on the other hand, "believed that blacks would perish in freedom, like fish on the land. The Negro's 'incompetence,' after all, has been essential to the understanding—and defense—of slavery itself" (Oshinsky 1996, 19). One southerner summed up the situation:

> I think God intended the niggers to be slaves. Now since man has deranged God's plan, I think the best we can do is keep 'em as near to a state of bondage as possible. My theory is, feed 'em well, clothe 'em well, and then, if they don't work whip 'em well. (Quoted in Oshinsky 1996, 11)

In the latter part of the nineteenth century, actual imprisonment was not much of an option as there were few prisons, and the Civil War had destroyed many buildings in the South. The solution lay in leasing inmates out to the plantations from which they had just been freed. After all, the economic base of the South was the same, involving labor-intensive crops such as tobacco and cotton. Leasing the former slaves to plantation owners meant the owners had cheap labor, the blacks were back under control, and—as a bonus—agents of the criminal justice system took a share of the money involved in the leases. Blacks were the ultimate losers of the new system of criminal laws and the administration of justice, and many were returned to the plantation so quickly that they hardly noticed emancipation. The threat of plantation prisons kept many other blacks in servitude under labor contracts that re-created the conditions of slavery: "The horror of the ball and chain is ever before [blacks], and their future is bright with no hope" (quoted in Gorman 1997, 71).

Worse still, under the lease system, owners no longer had the same economic interest in blacks as property, which removed some restraints against brutality. If a slave died, the owner had to buy another, but leased blacks who died were easily and cheaply replaced. One employer of leased convicts noted in 1883 that with "these convicts we don't own 'em. One dies, get another" (quoted in R. Johnson 2002, 43). The situation is summarized by the title of David Oshinsky's book, *Worse Than*

Slavery, and he notes that in Mississippi in the 1880s not one leased convict lived long enough to serve a sentence of ten years or more (1996, 46). However, because of the social control, cheap labor, and fees generated by the leases, the system expanded. Blacks were put to work not only on plantations but in a variety of grueling and dangerous jobs that included mining, building roads, clearing swamps, and making turpentine.

The nominal basis for arrests was laws based on slave codes: "The slave codes of the antebellum period were the basis of the black codes of 1865–1866 and later were resurrected as the segregation statutes of the period after 1877" (in Gorman 1997, 447). When able-bodied black men had not actually done anything wrong, the police would falsely charge them with crimes. When the men could not pay off the court fees, they were forced to go to work to "pay back their debts." These bogus arrests were sometimes orchestrated by "employers working hand-in-glove with local officials to keep their [work] camps well stocked with able-bodied blacks" (Oshinsky 1996, 71).

The picture that emerges is of black convicts as slaves and the state functioning as slave master (Gorman 1997). Understanding black "criminality" at this juncture involves the perspective Darnell Hawkins (1995, 34) described in which arrest is "less a product of their conduct than their social standing" (similar to the contemporary "driving while black" issues discussed in chapter 9). The folk song "Standin' On De Corner" captures this dynamic:

> Standin' on the corner, weren't doin' no hahm,
> Up Come a 'liceman an' he gab me by d'ahm.
> Blow a little whistle an' ring a little bell;
> Heah come 'rol wagon a-runnin' like hell.
> Judge he call me up an' ast mah name
> Ah tol' him fo' sho' Ah weren't to blame.
> He wink at 'liceman, 'liceman wink too;
> Judge he say, "Nigger, you got some work to do."
> Workin' on ol' road bank, shackle boun'.
> Long, long time fo' six months roll aroun'.
> Miserin' fo my honey, she miserin' fo me,
> But, Lawd, white folks won't let go holdin me.
> (Quoted in Franklin 1989, 104–5)

Variations on this pattern occur for other minorities at different points in history. For example, after the transcontinental railroad was completed, Asian (Chinese mostly) labor was no longer needed. To control this surplus population, the United States passed new criminal laws that selectively prohibited "Orientals" from possessing drugs (e.g., the Chinese Exclusionary Act of 1882 outlawed opium use among Chinese but not whites) or differentially applied existing drug laws against them. At the same time, both moral panics and the criminalization of minorities could occur for reasons other than political economy; bigotry and racism on their own were enough.

For example, the use of racism and drug laws to further the social control of minorities is revealed in a 1910 report that detailed "the supposed superhuman strength and extreme madness experienced by Blacks on cocaine, and explained that cocaine drove Black men to rape" (Lusane 1991, 33). Rumors circulated that cocaine made blacks bulletproof. In fact, an article in the *New York Times* ("Negro Cocaine 'Fiends' Are a New Southern Menace") reported that southern police were switching to larger-caliber weapons to protect themselves from drug-empowered blacks (Lusane 1991, 34). Just to be sure, Georgia kept its pre–Civil War statutes where black men faced capital punishment when convicted of the rape or attempted rape of a white woman (however, for white men convicted of raping black women, the penalty was a fine, prison, or both [Scully 1990]).

For much of the nation's history, laws like the one at issue in *Plessy v. Ferguson* explicitly required differential treatment for minorities in the form of "separate but equal." Of course, separate facilities were never equal to those that whites had, and the recognition of this inequality led the Supreme Court to strike down segregated systems. For example, separate law and medical schools for blacks were never equal to white institutions, so the court struck down these arrangements and forced integration in a series of cases that would culminate in the famous *Brown v. Board of Education* case. In *Brown*, the court finally recognized not just that separate was unequal, but that it was contrary to the majority holding in *Plessy* (see the opening of chapter 4), that separation stamps a badge of inferiority on those segregated.

After *Brown* and the 1960s civil rights legislation, these laws had made racial classifications largely disappear. However, "facially neutral" statutes can still have a disproportionate impact on minorities, and that is the current problem. Such laws may or may not be racist in their intent, but they are in their effects and impact. Traffic laws are racially neutral, but one important controversy is about DWB and the large number of black men who are pulled over. The other significant example is the federal sentencing guidelines that have penalized the possession of crack cocaine more heavily than powdered cocaine. Originally, federal law required a mandatory five-year sentence for possession of five hundred grams (about a pound) of powder cocaine or five grams (about one-sixth of an ounce) of crack cocaine. The sentence for first-time crack offenders (without possession of a weapon or other aggravating factors) is longer than the sentence for kidnapping and only slightly shorter than the sentence for attempted murder. About 85 percent of those sent to prison under the crack provisions of the original and amended laws have been black (Bureau of Justice Statistics 2001, 11), so this sentencing pattern contributes directly to problems of disproportionate minority confinement.

Whatever the intent of lawmakers, if arrests had been proportionate to use, then the ratio of black to white arrest and incarceration rates would have been very different, suggesting that there is an additional differential application of this allegedly neutral law. Indeed, as former drug czar William Bennett acknowledged during his reign, the typical crack smoker is a white suburbanite despite the urban stereotypes of crack houses filled with blacks (Lusane 1991). As the US Department of Health and Human Services reported, 2.6 percent of whites, but only 0.2 percent of blacks, ages eighteen to twenty-five had done crack cocaine during their lifetime; 0.6 percent of whites and 0.1 percent of blacks had done it in the previous year, according to the 2012 survey (SAMHSA 2012, table 1.36B).

In many ways, establishing actual racial intent is beside the point and should not be necessary for remedial action. In the areas of employment and housing discrimination, for example, evidence of patterns of discrimination or disparate impact is sufficient. Further, Congress knew the impact of this law from protests, reports, and recommendations from the US Sentencing Guidelines Commission itself to end the disparate penalties. In 1995, 1997, and 2002, the US Sentencing Commission recommended ending the 100 to 1 disparity between powder and crack penalties, and, in an unusual display of bipartisanship, Congress rejected their recommendation and kept the 100 to 1 disparities (Hinojosa 2008; Smothers 1995). In 2007, the Chair of the Sentencing Commission stated: "The Commission believes that there is no justification for the current statutory penalty scheme" and it "remains committed" to its 2002 recommendation that any ratio "be no more than 20 to 1." The Fair Sentencing Act of 2010 did not eliminate the disparity but reduced the 100:1 disparity to 18:1. Says sociologist Nikki Jones (2011), "What the Act suggests is that it's better for our criminal justice system to be somewhat racist rather than very racist." The disparity between coke and crack will continue to fuel the problem of disproportionate minority confinement because of differential application of the law. As a candidate, Barack Obama (2007) said, "Let's not make the punishment for crack cocaine that much more severe than the punishment for powder cocaine when the real difference between the two is the skin color of the people using them."

The most powerful contemporary indictment of the racial effect of legislation is Michelle Alexander's *The New Jim Crow* (2012). She argues that the illegal discrimination against blacks in the Jim Crow era has been replaced by legal discrimination against (black) "criminals." Once the criminal justice system labels blacks as "criminals," then whites can "engage in all the discriminatory practices we supposedly left behind," because blacks with criminal records are subject to "legalized discrimination in employment, housing, education, public benefits and jury service, just as their parents, grandparents and great-grandparents once were" (2012, 1–2). Laws in many states strip convicted felons of the right to vote as well as minor criminals whose poverty makes it impossible to repay fines and court costs. Alexander notes the case of Clinton Drake, who had $900 in fines due after being in prison for five years because of two marijuana possession charges. As a Vietnam veteran, "I put my life on the line for this country," he notes—and his two sons have also served in the military: "But I'm not able to vote" (2012, 159). To him, the fines "are like a poll tax. You've got to pay to vote," just like with the Jim Crow laws that restricted black voting after the Fifteenth Amendment gave the freed male slaves the right to vote.

A final issue related to lawmaking and race is the imposition of state and federal criminal justice systems on Native American reservations. The Indian Law and Order Commission noted, "Because the systems that dispense justice originate in

Federal and State law rather than in Native nation choice and consent, Tribal citizens tend to view them as illegitimate; these systems do not align with Tribal citizens' perceptions of the appropriate way to organize and exercise authority" (2013, 4). Tribes generally focus on "restoring balance and good relations among Tribal members," which is usually not the focus of state and federal criminal justice systems. Because of stereotypes,

> prosecutors may be more skeptical of Indian victims. Judges might award harsher sentences to Indian defendants because of assumptions they make about Indian country crime and those individuals involved. In the case of Federal courts, criminal sentences for the same or similar offenses are systemically longer than comparable State systems. (2013, 5)

Further, trials—usually in courthouses far from reservations—do not involve a jury of the Native Americans' peers.

Such systems are thus seen as lacking legitimacy and generate distrust, so victims do not come forward, and witnesses may be reluctant to cooperate. Under these conditions, public safety suffers. The Indian Law and Order Commission, created by the Tribal Law and Order Act of 2010, argued that respecting Native sovereignty and self-determination on issues of tribal justice can best attain public safety on reservations. This means allowing tribes to select whether to have a system of federal law or state law or use their "inherent authority" to create a system of tribal justice that reflects all defendants' constitutionally guaranteed rights (2013, 23).

Contemporary issues of race and law are rooted in an obvious degree of complacency on the part of legislators with disproportionate minority imprisonment, the "closed circuit of perpetual marginality" (Alexander 2012, 95) and the "institutional Illegitimacy" (Indian Law and Order Commission 2013, 4) of legal systems imposed on Native Americans. Rather than trying to debate the character of legislators and whether or not they are personally racist, we believe it is important to understand the moral status of such complacency by applying the distinction between direct and oblique intention that moral philosopher R. M. Hare (1990, 186) has articulated:

> To intend some consequence directly one has to desire it. To intend it obliquely one has only to foresee it. . . . We have the duty to avoid bringing about consequences that we ought not bring about, even if we do not desire those consequences in themselves, provided only that we know they will be consequences. I am to blame if I knowingly bring about someone's death in the course of some plan of mine, even if I do not desire his death in itself—that is, even if I intend the death only obliquely and indirectly . . . this is very relevant to the decisions of legislators (many of whose intentions are oblique), in that they have a duty to consider consequences of their legislation that they can foresee, and not merely those that they desire.

While Hare highlights the moral responsibilities of legislators for the foreseeable results of laws, the larger point for purposes of this book is that disparities can arise from facially neutral legislation because of the administration of justice. This includes the police, courts, and especially sentencing. Laws are written in categorical language that calls for arrest and processing of persons engaged in legally prohibited acts, but police officers and other agents of crime control do not apply these laws uniformly. Rather, when deciding whether or not to give a traffic violator, for instance, a warning, a ticket, or an intensive search, law enforcement will exercise a certain amount of discretion. The question becomes to what extent discretion is exercised as a reflection of institutionalized (rather than individualized) racial bias against nonwhites, over and above any bias created by enforcing laws that have a disproportionate impact on minorities.

GENDER, CRIME, AND THE LAW

One of the main themes of this text is examining inequality, which is easiest to do along the lines of class and race. With gender, analysis requires attention to the ways that men and women are different—which goes beyond the physical differences that are included in constructions of race and ethnicity and beyond the material differences that are included in the constructions of class. Remedying gender inequality also requires addressing the question of whether equality in the current system, which is based on male norms, is the appropriate measure. What does equality look like when women (but not men) can get pregnant and society treats all women of childbearing age as if they were "pre-pregnant" (Flavin 2009)? Feminists have contributed different perspectives on these questions, making it more correct to discuss *feminisms* rather than a monolithic feminism. At times, "feminism" tends to refer to a privileged white, middle-class liberal feminism, but just as we have encouraged readers to be aware of the diversity within gender, we now consider the diversity of feminism—itself reflective not only by women's different economic classes and ethnic locations in society but also by their sexual orientations or lifestyle practices.

What feminisms have in common is a concern with women's oppression and marginalization; all feminism makes women's experiences central to the social, political, and economic analysis. But feminisms differ in where they locate the source of oppression, what they consider to be the most salient issues, and thus what the central policy implications are. Thus, there is no single analysis of gender discrimination or of how to reconcile sexual differences with equal protection and gender equality. So this section reviews the main strands of feminist legal thinking and politics of change that are helpful in understanding gender issues related to law and the administration of justice. While it attempts to identify and articulate core beliefs of different feminisms, they have overlap. Also, individuals may think in terms of liberal feminism on one issue but be more radical or socialist on another.

Liberal feminism has focused on discrimination and considers legal and customary restraints to be the main barriers to women getting their fair share of the pie. Thus, the goal is to ensure that women and men have equal civil rights and a level playing field when it comes to economic opportunities. Liberal feminists concentrate on discrimination against female offenders, prisoners, and workers as well as on the criminalization of deviance among women for behaviors such as prostitution. Their project for change revolves around achieving sexual and gender equality vis-à-vis equal opportunity programs such as affirmative action and antidiscrimination policy.

Critical feminists of whatever strain—Marxist, socialist, radical, and postmodern—object to liberal approaches not only for failing to question the existing legal and economic system but also for wanting equality in it. As Colette Price framed the issue more than thirty years ago: "Do we really want equality with men in this nasty competitive capitalist system? Do we want to be equally exploited with men? Do we want a piece of the pie or a whole different pie?" (Redstockings 1978, 94). As a diversified group, critical feminists differ in the emphasis they place on economic, biological, racial, and sexual sources of oppression, privilege, and inequality.

Marxist feminism has been concerned with the way the criminal justice system under capitalism serves the interests of the ruling class at the expense of the lower classes. Marxist feminists view the oppression of women as an extension of the oppression of the working class. They argue that it is impossible for anyone to obtain genuine equal opportunity in a class society in which the wealth produced by the powerless mainly ends up in the hands of the powerful few. These relatively few powerful are disproportionately male, which makes it even harder for women, as the privileged have a vested interest in maintaining their higher status, especially as reflected in the laws and capitalist legal order. Moreover, Marxist feminists argue that women are at a disadvantage in general and in relation to the law specifically because they are less likely than men to be lawmakers, attorneys, judges, and other types of criminal justice workers. Hence, they maintain that if *all* women are to be liberated—not just the middle class and affluent—then the capitalist system and its "bourgeois laws" must be replaced by a system of "people's laws."

Socialist feminism argues that women are oppressed not only because of their subordinate economic position but also because of their "class" as women. Social feminists were among the first of the feminist theorists to recognize exploitation rooted in racism, ageism, and heterosexism. Like Marxist feminism, socialist feminism clarifies how economic conditions alter labor market demands for women. In addition, socialist feminism highlights how sexist ideology legitimates women's exclusion from higher-paying men's jobs and their dominance in the domestic sphere. Patriarchal ideologies and exclusionary practices produce pools of marginal women who resort to crimes of survival, such as transporting drugs or exchanging sex for money or other goods and services. Hence, socialist feminists call for widespread economic and cultural changes to dismantle the twin evils of capitalism and patriarchy. They place special emphasis on the needs of the poor and working women—women who suffer the consequences of a system that not only exalts men over women but also exalts those who have over those who do not. They advocate equal work opportunities for men and women as well as policies that would alleviate women's "second shift" by increasing child-care and family-leave programs while at the same time increasing men's involvement in domestic work.

Radical feminism tends to focus on female victims, particularly survivors of gendered violence such as domestic violence and sexual assault. Radical feminists argue that the source of the problem is male-dominated society. They criticize liberal and Marxist feminists for not going far enough. It is not sufficient to overturn society's male-dominated legal and political structures; transformation must also happen to all the social and cultural institutions (such as the family, the church, and the educational system) that reinforce women's roles in devalued activities such as childbearing and nurturing—as well as devaluing women's activities. (Teaching and nursing, for example, are important professions, but the vast majority of workers are women, so those professions are "feminized" and devalued.) Radical feminists focus attention on how men attempt to control females. They argue that one of the pathways to women's liberation involves self-determinism inside and outside their sexual and parental roles. That includes, for example, permitting each woman to choose for herself when to use or not use reproduction-controlling technology (i.e., contraception, sterilization, abortion) and reproduction-aiding technologies (i.e., artificial insemination, in vitro fertilization, surrogate and/or contract motherhood).

Postmodern feminism questions both the essentialism of other feminisms and the absolutism of truth. Postmodern feminists argue for multiple truths that take context into account, so they emphasize the importance of alternative accounts or narratives to show the privilege embedded in dominant social constructions. Postmodern feminists, for example, examine the effects of language and symbolic representation, especially how legal discourse constructs different "types of woman" such as "prostitute," "bad mother," or "worthy victim." Postmodern feminism may be divided into two camps: *skeptical* and *affirmative*. The skeptical postmodernists embrace a more extreme relativist perspective, where there are no objective truths, and therefore they do not adopt policy stances and remain noninterventionist, relying on critique and deconstruction alone. By contrast, affirmative postmodernists address the possibilities of reconstruction, of rebuilding through policies based on contingent truths. They tend to emphasize the power of agency, self-determinism, and how humans actively build and rebuild their social worlds rather than being merely passive subjects or legal objects of external forces only (Henry and Milovanovic 1999). Postmodern feminist scholars tend to recognize a responsibility to build legal bridges across diverse groups in order to work collectively—not to arrive at a universal understanding of justice, but "to do our best to make judgments that make the world a good place to be" for everyone (Wonders 1999, 122).

The feminisms reviewed above adopt three approaches to gender inequality: the sameness perspective, the difference perspective, and the dominance perspective. Each of these perspectives has its strengths and weaknesses. Advocates of the *sameness perspective*, also referred to as the "gender neutral" or "equal treatment" perspective, support a single standard governing the treatment of women and men. Take, for instance, the lack of vocational and educational programs in women's prisons relative to those found in men's prisons. One solution is to give women the same programs that men have. If men have programs designed to rehabilitate sex offenders, then these programs should be available to women prisoners as well. However, few women prisoners (less than 2 percent) are rape and sexual assault offenders (Greenfeld 1997). In other words, women prisoners on the whole do not have the same need for sex-offender programs as men prisoners do. In contrast, many women—but few men—were primary caretakers for children before incarceration, so setting policies and programs about children based on men's prisons is also problematic.

Our analysis and others' suggest caution in equating equality with justice. The sameness approach may actually harm women, as the approach is not neutral but tends to be based on the treatment of men. "Equality with a vengeance" is a real concern if sentencing for women is based on the "get tough" standard that applies to men. Further, gender bias in sentencing cannot be eliminated simply by stipulating (as is done in the US Federal Sentencing Guidelines) that gender is not to be considered. Gender neutrality, in other words, cannot be legislated because society is not gender neutral. In the area of purportedly gender-neutral training, for example, Dana Britton (1997) observed that the rhetoric of correctional officer training in her study was explicitly gender neutral, yet closer examination revealed that the training model was based on the experiences of male officers, particularly those working in male-dominated institutions. Similarly among women and employment, the gender-neutral framework is most likely to benefit those women whose biographies and class backgrounds most resemble those of successful white males.

Advocates of the *difference perspective* call for differential treatment of women and men. After all, some very real differences exist in the situations of men and women, such as women's capacity to bear children. Some critics of this perspective, such as Catharine MacKinnon ([1984] 1991), view it as both patronizing and necessary. Others talk about how women might be seen as getting "special treatment" or receiving "special rights," while other critics raise concerns about reinforcing gender stereotypes. For example, a policy of permitting single parents to receive a "downward departure" from sentencing guidelines would primarily benefit women and would likely be seen as a special right for those playing a traditional gender role.

Both the sameness and the difference approaches to gender equality do not measure up for two reasons. First, they both assume a male norm. As MacKinnon has argued, "gender neutrality" is simply the male standard and the "special protection" rule is simply the female standard, "but do not be deceived: masculinity, or maleness, is the referent for both" ([1984] 1991, 83). Second, both perspectives reflect a preoccupation with gender differences while ignoring the role of power and domination. An alternative to the sameness and difference perspectives is the dominance perspective that takes up the neglected aspect of the other two approaches, namely *power*.

The *dominance perspective* recognizes that men and women are different and that the sexes are not equally powerful. Most differences between men and women can be attributed to a society in which women are subordinate and men are dominant. Advocates of the dominance perspective maintain that the solution to gender inequality is not to create a single standard (sameness) or a double standard (difference) but to address the inequality in power relations between the sexes. For example, proponents

of the dominance approach have exerted pressure on the US legal system to abandon its "hands-off" attitude toward domestic violence, to redefine wife battering
and marital rapes as crimes on the same level as injuries caused by strangers, and to
expand the meaning of and protection from sexual harassment.

The dominance approach is not without weaknesses, too. It has also been criticized for its overconfidence in legal recognition and its failure to acknowledge that
"legal rights are sometimes overshadowed by social realities" (Chesney-Lind and
Pollock 1995, 157). For instance, while women have the legal right to be treated like
any other assault victim and to have their battering husband arrested and punished,
the reality is that women also face social, economic, and cultural barriers that may
impede or prevent them from taking full advantage of their legal rights. The dominance perspective along with the other feminist perspectives on gender equality have
all been critiqued for being "essentialist" and "reductionist" in their approaches. In
short, each of these perspectives assumes one monolithic "women's experience" that
can be described independent of other characteristics such as race, class, age, and
sexual orientation.

Essentialism and reductionism occur when a "representation" or a "voice"—
mostly white, straight, and socioeconomically privileged—claims to embody or
speak for everyone (see chapter 5). In a one-dimensional or essentialist world, for
example, "black women's experience will always be forcibly fragmented before being subjected to analysis, as those who are 'only interested in race' and those who
are 'only interested in gender' take their separate slice of our lives" (David Harris
1999, 295). However, critical race feminism attempts to simultaneously address the
importance of an anti-essentialist and intersectional approach to race, gender, crime,
and the law.

Despite these divergent and multiple perspectives on inequality and gender, all
would agree that in 2014 men still control the most important industries, from
technology to crime control and the administration of justice, from Wall Street to K
Street. While the curtailment of male entitlements has occurred and the expansion
of women's legal and economic rights has helped to transform American life, these
have hardly produced the absence of patriarchy or anything like matriarchy. Despite
the relative improvement, over the past fifteen years in many arenas the progress of
women has actually stalled, their average earnings are still lower than men's, and they
are more likely to be poor than men. Less powerful than men generally and with
respect to their class and race more specifically, women still find themselves marginal
to lawmaking and the administration of criminal and civil law.

INTERSECTIONALITY, CRIME, AND THE LAW

In understanding the larger processes of criminal justice, many aspects of the class
analysis and race analysis overlap. The idea is that the criminal justice system does
not criminalize crimes of the rich, described by Quinney as many of the crimes of

domination (see chapter 2). In contrast, the crimes of the poor become the main focus of criminal law, and the processes of criminal justice become a tool in class warfare to control the poor, especially the unemployed surplus labor pool that contains a disproportionate number of minorities. The class analysis focuses on the poor, while the race analysis equates the controlled "dangerous classes" with racial minorities. Given that most minorities are disproportionately poor, the class and race analyses are similar, though the race analysis would consider minorities more vulnerable to entanglement in systems of control because of prejudice and stereotypes. Racism and racist assumptions are frequently involved in creating "moral panics" or other situations thought to justify increased social control (e.g., drug and immigration laws) of the *other*.

The current widespread perception that black men are engaged in criminal activity, for example, is facilitated by the inundation of images of black criminals that not only contributes to what Katheryn Russell (1998) refers to as the *criminal blackman* but also to an uncritical acceptance of different punishments for the same crimes. Russell (1998, 71) argues, "Crime and young Black men have become synonymous in the American mind" (see also Alexander 2012, 106).

The impact of class and race can also be seen in Cathy Shine and Marc Mauer's (1993) research on the discrepancies in punishment between drug users and drunk drivers. According to the Uniform Crime Reports, there were 8.5 million arrests for criminal offenses nationwide for the year the researchers analyzed. Of those, drug abuse violations accounted for 1,101,302 arrests, and driving under the influence (DUI) accounted for 971,795 arrests. Shine and Mauer report that drug use resulted in an estimated 21,000 deaths a year (through overdoses, diseases, and violence associated with the drug trade) at an estimated annual cost of $58 million. Alcohol was associated with 94,000 deaths annually, with estimated societal costs of $85 million.

Although the criminal uses of illicit drugs and alcohol both cause great harm to society, the responses to these crimes are strikingly different. In particular, the criminal justice system punishes the possession of illicit drugs much more severely than it punishes drunk driving. While persons convicted of drug possession are typically charged with felonies and are likely to be incarcerated, drunk drivers are typically treated as misdemeanants and receive nonincarceration sentences. In New York State, for example, persons convicted of drug possession are twenty-four times more likely to be sentenced to prison as those convicted of drunk driving.

Shine and Mauer suggest that this differential response to similarly harmful behavior may stem from the different profiles of the perceived "typical" drug offender and drunk driver. For both drug abuse and DUI offenses, the overwhelming majority of arrestees are male (over 80 percent). However, nearly 90 percent of all those arrested for drunk driving are white, compared to less than two-thirds of those arrested for drug abuse violations. Blacks made up approximately one in ten of all those arrested for driving under the influence but over one in three of all persons arrested for drug abuse violations. Shine and Mauer note that DUI offenders are typically white, male, blue-collar workers, while persons convicted of drug possession are disproportionately low income or indigent African American and Hispanic males. The authors conclude, "Although substantial numbers of deaths are caused by drunk drivers, our national approach has emphasized prevention, education, and treatment. . . . For drug abuse, particularly among low-income people, treatment initiatives have lagged behind the move to 'get tough'" (Shine and Mauer 1993, 35). Even if states have made some progress in increasing penalties, there is still a large discrepancy in public opinion about the problems and flow of offenders through the system.

A more recent analysis of arrests and forced interventions on pregnant women reinforces Shine and Mauer's (1993) conclusions. Lynn Paltrow and Jeanne Flavin review "413 cases from 1973 to 2005 in which a woman's pregnancy was a necessary factor leading to attempted and actual deprivations of a woman's physical liberty" (2013, 299). They found that 52 percent of the women were black, 59 percent were women of color, and 71 percent were represented by an indigent-defense attorney, meaning that they were poor (2013, 310–11). Rationales for arrest included drug use (even where treatment was not provided), alcohol, cigarettes, being the victim of abuse (which had health implications for the fetus), failure to obtain prenatal care, having HIV, refusal to undergo cesarean surgery, "or gave birth at home or in another setting outside a hospital" (2013, 316). While many state actions were ultimately overturned by courts, the basis for these actions was that feticide or unborn victims of violence laws "make it a crime to cause harm to a 'child in utero' and recognize everything from a zygote to a fetus as an independent 'victim,' with legal rights distinct from the woman who has been harmed" (2013, 323). These laws, "generally passed in the wake of a violent attack on a pregnant woman," are supposed to protect pregnant women but are used against poor and/or minority women in ways that undermine their dignity and health.

Paltrow and Flavin note a comprehensive analysis in the *Journal of the American Medical Association* finding that concern about prenatal exposure to cocaine resulted in "irrational" policies because the harm done was no greater than a number of other risk factors that normally do not justify criminal intervention (2013, 334). Paltrow and Flavin note (2013, 334):

> As has been compellingly argued by historians, sociologists, legal scholars, and others, the willingness to believe that cocaine, and especially crack cocaine, required uniquely punitive responses was derived in large measure from racist assumptions about African Americans in general and African American mothers in particular. The harsh treatment imposed on the pregnant women in our study, including being taken straight from their hospital beds and arrested shortly after delivery, being taken in handcuffs, sometimes shackled around the waist, and at least one woman being shackled during labor, is consistent with a long and disturbing history of devaluing African American mothers.

Similarly, Meda Chesney-Lind (2006, 10) argues in "Patriarchy, Crime, and Justice" that "to fully understand the interface between patriarchal control mechanisms and criminal justice practices in the United States, we must center our analysis on the race/gender/punishment nexus." She explains how media demonization, the masculinization of female offenders, and the criminalizing of women's victimization—all part of the feminist backlash starting in the 1980s—have resulted in greater increases in rates of arrests and incarceration for both women and girls compared to those of men and boys. And this increased incarceration rate has disproportionately and negatively affected girls and women of color. Between 1994 and 2003, the arrests of adult women increased by 30.8 percent whereas male arrests for the same offense fell by 5.8 percent; between 1989 and 1998, girls' detentions increased by 56 percent compared with a 20 percent increase for boys' detentions. Similarly, a joint study by the American Bar Association and the National Bar Association published in 2001 found that nearly one-half of the girls in detention were African American girls, and they constituted about 12 percent of the girl population, and conversely, white girls, who constituted 65 percent of the girl population, accounted for 35 percent of those in detention (Chesney-Lind 2006).

A final important example of intersections is fetal protection laws, through which the criminal law enhances punishment for harms to pregnant women. Although many states have chosen enhanced penalties for assaulting a pregnant woman, the federal Unborn Victims of Violence Act of 2004 "and most state fetal homicide laws treat the fetus as an independent second victim that has legal rights distinct from the pregnant woman harmed by the criminal act: that is, when a pregnant woman is murdered or injured, two victims are claimed—the woman and her fetus—not one" (Flavin 2009, 99). The concern about these laws is that they have been passed based on concern about domestic violence to pregnant women, but those who support the laws have little concern for the Violence Against Women Act or related initiatives. In addition, the laws are used as a back door to prosecute pregnant women for drug addiction, when drug counseling is not available to many poor pregnant women. Fetal protection laws have not been applied against men, even though studies find a correlation between men's exposure to certain chemicals (pesticides, solvents, etc.) and increased risk of miscarriage or fetal defects.

The recognition of fetal "rights" has important implication for women's bodily sovereignty by giving fetuses a legal cause of action against mothers and turning them into "baby carriers" or "bystanders to their own bodies" (Flavin 2009). Thus, not only does the criminal law erode women's rights, but the differential application of such laws targets poor and minority women. Rather than more directly confronting domestic violence, universal health care, or a drug war that has not made treatment a priority, attention is focused on "bad" pregnant women.

IMPLICATIONS

Ideally, the study of lawmaking, criminal law, and the administration of justice should take the intersectionality of class, race, gender, sexuality, and age into consideration. This is difficult on the one hand because the law does not take into account or define crimes based on the class, race, and sex or gender of the offender. The criminal law is most obviously biased in a class-based way, while it is more race- and gender-neutral on its face. But what the law regards as a crime and whom society sees as the criminals reflect the statuses of class, race, and gender. Indeed, the problem is that facially neutral laws still result in disparate treatment because of the administration of criminal justice.

For example, while blacks are overrepresented in street crime and underrepresented in suite crime, Blumstein (1995) found that 20 to 25 percent of the black incarceration rate (representing about ten thousand blacks annually) is not explained by disproportionate offending. As the *Harvard Law Review* noted: "Substantial underenforcement of antidiscrimination norms" and "increasingly sophisticated empirical studies indicate disparities in the treatment of criminal suspects and defendants that are difficult to explain by reference to decisional factors other than racial discrimination" (1988, 1476). This finding applies to both men and women, with the absolute number of minority men involved in the criminal justice system at very high levels and the number of minority women at relatively lower levels but increasing at the fastest rates.

This disparate treatment is corrosive of justice and generates the very different perceptions of the justice system held generally by whites and minorities. A biased law enforcement like pretextual stops (DWB), for example, can "undermine the legitimacy of the use of coercive power and can make the criminal justice system no better than the criminals it pursues. In the process, such stops based on racial bias erode trust in the system of justice, create public cynicism and hostility, and make police work more difficult and dangerous" (Cole 1999; see also D. Harris 1999). As the New York State Office of the Attorney General (1999) reported, civil rights do not exist unless the personal safety of all citizens is secured lawfully; policing without respect for the rule of law is not policing at all.

Legislators, policymakers, and criminal justice practitioners alike argue that they cannot foresee all the consequences of proposed and enacted laws. One way to assist them and to provide constant feedback on the fairness and justness of the administration of justice would be to implement class, race, and gender "impact statements" modeled after current environmental and financial impact statements. These types of analyses of the impact of new laws and the enforcement of old laws on class, race, and gender in relationship to the practices of crime control would specifically collect the relevant data necessary for evaluation.

Lawmakers could still pass laws that would make the situation worse for victims and/or offenders based on class, race, and/or gender, and criminal justice practitioners could continue to make exceptions to the "rule of law," but neither the makers nor the enforcers of law could maintain any longer that they did not know the consequences of their actions, especially if impact reports continued to be updated to reflect the actual changes related to the law's taking effect. Moreover, public officials would have to dialogue with and answer to an empowered community armed with the knowledge of how class, race, and gender impact the differential administration of justice in the United States.

REVIEW AND DISCUSSION QUESTIONS

1. How do class, race, and gender affect lawmaking and the administration of criminal law and justice? What were the best examples from the text, and are there others you can think of?
2. What is meant by the concept of *analogous social injury*? What are some examples, and why are these acts when done by elites "beyond incrimination"?
3. How has the treatment of ethnic and racial minorities by the administration of justice both improved and not improved over the past century?
4. Discuss the differences between both the various types of feminism and the various feminist approaches to addressing law and gender inequality. Which of these models/approaches do you ascribe to, and why?
5. Using the examples of drunk driving and drug possession, discuss the relationship between the different profiles associated with each and the intersectionality of class, race, and gender.

9

Law Enforcement
and Criminal Prosecution

The movie review headline in the entertainment section read in bold and large type:
Racism, raw and modern. *The subtitle read: "Crash bravely admits that prejudice*
isn't a thing of the past." This critically acclaimed and controversial film takes place in
cosmopolitan Los Angeles in 2005, not in the Deep South in 1955. In a documentary-
like day-in-the-life montage of overlapping racist explosions, the audience watches as
over the course of two days cars—and lives—begin to collide. "There's a traffic stop. A
fender-bender. A fiery car crash. A carjacking. And as the accidents mount, the accidental
collisions of different people build, and the result is always some ugly, revelatory racism"
(Whitty 2005, E2). All of the scenarios that unfold convey a sense of equal-opportunity
racism: black, brown, red, yellow, and white, male and female, rich and poor, powerful
and powerless, nobody has yet escaped the prejudices, biases, and stereotypes of the other.

While it is true that every group has prejudices, chapter 4 noted that an important
difference was in the power whites generally had to act on their biases and create dis-
crimination. There's the issue of white privilege, which makes conscious and unconscious
racism "an amalgam of guilt, responsibility, and power—all of which are generally known
but never acknowledged" (quoted in Bell 1998, viii). The protection of white privilege
in turn has important consequences for the treatment of minorities. In this vein, Laura
Fishman (1998) writes about "the black bogeyman and white self-righteousness" by which
she and other authors of color such as Derrick Bell are commenting on how "whiteness"
or white racism continues to serve as "a connector spanning the gargantuan gap between
those whites at the top of the economic ladder and most of the rest scattered far below"
and how "politicians and others can so easily deflect attention from what they are not
doing for all of us to what whites fear" people of color might do to them (Bell 1998, viii).

Only the white racism analysis, and not the "equal opportunity racism" view presented
in Crash, *recognizes the differential treatment and consequences of racial power. The*
very concrete and tangible consequences for those who lack the necessary privilege include

233

aspects of the administration of justice such as racial profiling. While built on myths about the alleged propensity for blacks and browns to be involved with drugs and carry weapons, police scholars and the courts largely discredit such findings. For example, like other criminal justice research that has found burdens associated with being young, minority, and male (Spohn and Holleran 2000), Robin Engel and Jennifer Calnon's (2004, 84) very thorough examination of racial profiling found that after relevant legal and extra-legal factors were controlled, young minority males were "at the highest risk for citations, searches, arrests, and use of force during traffic stops." Yet those same black and brown drivers were no more likely to be carrying contraband than white drivers.

This chapter will present additional data later about driving while black (DWB), but consider for the moment a study done by New York's attorney general based on 175,000 "UF-250" forms, the "Stop, Question and Frisk Report Worksheet" that NYPD officers are required to complete after a wide variety of encounters. These data go beyond driving to include a wider range of stops related to the Supreme Court's decision in Terry v. Ohio (392 U.S. 1 [1968]), under which a police officer can detain a civilian if the officer can articulate a "reasonable suspicion" that criminal activity is "afoot." The attorney general's report found the following:

> Blacks comprise 25.6 percent of the city's population, yet 50.6 percent of all persons "stopped" during the period were black. Hispanics comprise 23.7 percent of the city's population, yet 33.0 percent of all "stops" were of Hispanics. By contrast, whites are 43.4 percent of the city's population, but accounted for only 12.9 percent of all "stops." (NYSOAG 1999)

The Office of the Attorney General, with the aid of Columbia University's Center for Violence Research and Prevention, also performed a regression analysis to see whether differing rates of street crime for minorities could explain the increased rate of stops of minorities. But even after accounting for the effect of differing crime rates, the analysis showed blacks were stopped 23 percent more often than whites and Hispanics were stopped 39 percent more often (NYSOAG 1999). A more recent analysis of data on 4.4 million stops between 2004 and 2012 found that 83 percent of those stopped by the NYPD were black or Hispanic, even though these groups made up about 50 percent of the population (Goldstein 2013). In response to police arguments that these groups committed a disproportionate amount of crime, a federal judge noted, "Nearly 90 percent of the people stopped are released without the officer finding any basis for a summons or arrest." Further, the judge found that "weapons were seized in 1.0% of the stops of blacks, 1.1% of the stops of Hispanics, and 1.4% of the stops of whites. Contraband other than weapons was seized in 1.8% of the stops of blacks, 1.7% of the stops of Hispanics, and 2.3% of the stops of whites" (Floyd v. City of New York, 08 Civ. 1034 [2013], 7).

While disproportionate focus on minorities is a problem, national evidence also indicates that many traffic stops involved extensive searches. Police would start by looking under seats and in the trunk but continued by deflating tires, prying off door panels, and taking apart sunroofs. The belongings of blacks have been strewn on the highways, blown around by passing trucks, and urinated on by dogs sniffing for drugs. Other stops involved officers who were quick to unholster firearms. Some of these stops happened to rich or famous blacks, including politicians. *The judge in the NYPD case found that "once a stop is made, blacks and Hispanics are more likely to be subjected to the use of force than whites, despite the fact that whites are more likely to be found with weapons or contraband"* (Floyd v. City of New York, *08 Civ. 1034 [2013], 13*). *The overall picture is that minorities are disproportionately targets of police power and "vulnerable to the whims of anyone holding a criminal justice commission"* (Doyle 1992, 75.) *The situation is better than, but still reminiscent of, the problem described by the song "Standin' on De Corner" in the previous chapter. Indeed, "One NYPD official has even suggested that it is permissible to stop racially defined groups just to instill fear in them that they are subject to being stopped at any time for any reason—in the hope that this fear will deter them from carrying guns in the streets"* (Floyd v. City of New York, *08 Civ. 1034 [2013], 14*).

These incidents amount to abuses of police discretion because of prejudice and stereotypes, which may be unconscious and shared with wider society. But unjustified stops and unjustifiable interventions harm not only the individual but also damage the rule of law, which helps protect individual liberties by demanding clearly articulated law and due process, applied equally to all. The notion of a rule of law is contrasted with a rule of men, which can be arbitrary and unclear; it is frequently used to benefit the ruler and differentially applied at the whim, caprice, or prejudice of those who hold power. Thus, violations of the rule of law can undermine respect for the law and institutions of criminal justice, which can come to be seen as exercising an arbitrary or discriminatory power—and are consequently seen as unjust.

More specifically, David Harris (1999) addresses the question of why DWB matters and points out that it has substantial impact on the innocent. "The great majority of black people who are subjected to these humiliating and difficult experiences but who have done absolutely nothing to deserve this treatment—except to resemble, in a literally skin-deep way, a small group of criminals." Because the majority of those stopped are innocent, but the stops themselves are legal, blackness is, in effect, criminalized. Further, while most profiles are based on flawed data and assumptions, the profile focuses increased police attention on the group, which can uncover additional wrongdoing that becomes evidence in support of the profile. Discrimination is rationalized through a self-fulfilling prophecy that denies the presence of drugs in white suburbia and, without a profile, does not deploy massive resources there to investigate.

In addition, Harris contends that DWB distorts the legal system by fostering deep cynicism of its fairness, both because of its impact on the innocent and because the increased scrutiny of blacks means disproportionate numbers of them end up in prison—so black communities "bear a far greater share of the burden of drug prohibition" (1999). DWB matters further, he says, by distorting the social world, by which he means that it imposes a "spatial restriction on African-Americans, circumscribing their movements" and basically ensuring that blacks stay out of areas where whites and the police feel they "do not belong" (see also J. Lee 2000; Withrow 2006). Finally, DWB undermines community policing, which requires mutual trust of police and the citizens they patrol. In the end, Harris notes, "aside from the damage 'driving while black' stops inflict on African-Americans,

*there is another powerful reason to change this police behavior: it is in the interest of police
departments themselves to correct it" (1999).*

Like other institutions of social control, a primary role of criminal justice administration—law enforcement, adjudication, and punishment—is to persuade people to abide by the dominant values of society. As noted in the previous chapter, the criminal justice system is different in being able to exercise coercive power. Police can stop, detain, arrest, and use deadly force; courts can imprison, order execution, or sentence people to intensive regimes of surveillance through probation or parole. While the politicians play an important role in defining crime, police are more visible because of their presence on the streets and the numerous television shows devoted to their work.

In the United States, "criminal justice" is administered by a loose confederation of more than fifty thousand agencies of federal, state, and local governments, each carefully limited by law or subject to *jurisdiction*—"the right or authority of a justice agency to act in regard to a particular subject matter, territory, or person" (Bohm and Haley 2005, 147). Beyond the statutes that create and direct law enforcement and other criminal justice agencies, the procedural law (derived mainly from US Supreme Court decisions) also imposes limitations on the authority of those agencies, as do civilian review boards, ombudsmen, departmental policies and procedures, and civil liability suits.

An individual enters the criminal justice system first as a suspect, next as a defendant, and finally as a convicted criminal. The criminal justice response to crime typically begins when a crime is reported to the police, or far less often, when the police themselves discover that a crime has been committed. Solving a crime is sometimes easy, for example, when a victim or witness knows who the perpetrator is or where to find him or her. In these situations, an arrest supported by either victim and/or witness statements and by crime scene evidence is sufficient to close the case. More often, however, the police must conduct an in-depth investigation or engage in a manhunt to find suspects. In either situation, if the investigation is successful, a suspect is arrested and then brought to the police station for booking.

The court subsystem consists of four basic stages: charging, pretrial, trial, and sentencing. Soon after the suspect is arrested and booked, a prosecutor reviews the facts of the case and the available evidence. The prosecutor decides whether to charge the suspect with a crime or crimes. If no charges are filed, the suspect must be released. When it comes to the less serious crimes such as misdemeanors or ordinance violations, the prosecutor prepares a *complaint* specifying that the named person has committed an offense. If the offense is a felony or a more serious crime for which a person may be confined in a prison for more than one year, then either the prosecutor prepares an *information* or the grand jury issues an *indictment*. Both the information and the indictment, each used in about 50 percent of the jurisdictions, consist of a formal charge or written accusation of the crime or crimes committed.

After the charge or charges have been filed, the pretrial stages begin, when the suspect, who is now the defendant, is brought before a lower-court judge for an *initial appearance*. The defendant is presented with the formal charge(s) and advised of his or her constitutional rights. For a misdemeanor or an ordinance violation, a *summary trial* without a jury may be held. For a felony, a *probable cause hearing* is held to determine whether or not there is enough evidence to make a "reasonable person" believe that, more likely than not, the proposed action is justified and to decide whether or not *bail* is appropriate. If there is sufficient evidence, the suspect is next subject to a *preliminary hearing*, whose purpose is for the judge to determine whether or not there is probable cause that the defendant committed the crime or crimes. If the judge finds probable cause, then an indictment or information is filed with the court, and the defendant is scheduled for an *arraignment*. The primary purpose of the arraignment is to hear the formal information or indictment, ensure that the defendant knows the charges, and allow the defendant to enter a plea. Upwards of 95 percent of criminal defendants plead guilty to some of the charges against them, based on a *plea bargain* arrangement between the prosecutor, the defense attorney, and the defendant. It typically occurs between the time of the preliminary hearing and the time of the arraignment, but it can occur up to and even after the trial has begun.

If the defendant pleads not guilty or not guilty by reason of insanity, a trial date is set. Of these cases, a mere 10 percent actually go to trial, with about half being a jury trial and about half consisting of a bench trial because the defendant has decided to waive his Sixth Amendment right to a jury trial. If the jury or the judge finds the defendant guilty as charged, the judge and/or the jury, depending on the jurisdiction, participate in the *sentencing process*. Of course, if acquitted (found not guilty), the person is set free; if the jury is "hung" and cannot reach a decision, then the defendant may be released but could be subject to retrial.

Those who are convicted of a crime will be sentenced based on statutory law and philosophical as well as political considerations. After sentencing, the convicted person then becomes subject to the penal-correctional subsystem. Options here usually consist of *incarceration* in prison (for sentences greater than one year), jail (for sentences less than one year), or community *probation*. In some jurisdictions, incarcerated criminals may be eligible for *parole*, in which they finish their sentences outside of prison and are subject to special conditions of behavior, violations of which may result in reimprisonment. Once offenders have served out their whole sentence in one form or the other, they are formally released from criminal justice authority. However, "invisible punishments" may still affect them, including the exclusion from public housing, denial of student loans, and loss of the right to vote (Mauer and Chesney-Lind, 2002).

This descriptive overview of the criminal justice system highlights the formal workings of law enforcement, prosecution, adjudication, and punishment bureaucracies according to the formal rules of law. Embedded throughout this system, however, at literally every decision-making point, are numerous informal opportunities for discretion that create variations in police, prosecutorial, and judicial behavior that often result in unequal treatment for many. The exercise of "discretion" (S. Miller 1999; Skolnick [1967] 1996; J. Wilson 1972) is explored in this and the next chapter as a means of trying to appreciate the relationship between the formal and informal practices of law enforcement and criminal adjudication. More specifically, in each of the next three sections we examine the identification of criminals and labeling of crime in the context of class, race, gender, and their intersections.

CRIME, CRIMINAL IDENTIFICATION, AND CLASS CONTROL

On November 20, 1993, the front page of the *New York Times* carried two stories about crime. The first was about the US Senate approving what would become the 1994 Omnibus Crime Bill. That legislation provided $8.9 billion for hiring 100,000 police officers, $6 billion for prisons and boot camps, and increased federal penalties for a variety of gang-related activities. The second story's headline read: "Anti-Drug Unit of CIA Sent Ton of Cocaine to U.S. in 1990." This pure cocaine was sold on the streets of the United States, where federal penalties at the time were a five-year mandatory minimum for possession of five hundred grams of powder cocaine or only five grams of the cheaper crack cocaine. (There are 907,000 grams in a ton.)

The Omnibus Crime Bill and the unprosecuted crimes of the CIA not only serve to selectively enforce and differentially apply laws against illegal drug distribution, but together they also help to reproduce various stereotypes associated with drug-related behavior. For example, the new police officers paid for by the crime bill were among those out on the streets searching for gang members and busting numerous poor people with small amounts of cocaine, who ended up in the prisons built with an influx of federal dollars. Meanwhile, little comparable effort was invested in law enforcement's going after the more affluent consumers of powder cocaine, who rarely ended up in prison and, when busted, often found their way into detoxification or drug treatment facilities (Humphries 1999). At the same time, the CIA was not identified as a drug trafficker, nor were any officials arrested. One CIA officer resigned and a second was disciplined in what was called "a most regrettable incident" that involved "instances of poor judgment." Nothing ever came of this political scandal in the "drug war" waged against the gangs of East Los Angeles.

This episode in law enforcement reflects a larger pattern in which police focus their efforts on controlling the behavior of the poor, identifying criminals as predominantly members of the lower economic classes. Similarly, investigative tools such as the use of "profiles" are constructed around street criminals and gangs rather than on corporate criminals, even though the recidivism rates of offenders like "citizen GE" are habitual in practice (see the opening narrative in chapter 8). As Edwin Sutherland found in his classic study of corporate crime in the United States more than a half-century ago:

The records reveal that every one of the seventy corporations had violated one or more of the laws, with an average of about thirteen adverse decisions per corporation and a range of from one to fifty adverse decisions per corporation. . . . The "habitual criminal" laws of some states impose severe penalties on criminals convicted the third or fourth time. If this criterion were used here, about 90 percent of the large corporations studied would be considered habitual white-collar criminals. (Quoted in Reiman and Leighton 2013, 122)

More recent studies confirm the high prevalence of repeat criminality and habitual corporate crime, even after they successfully prevent many of their harmful actions from becoming categorized as crimes. For example, a Justice Department study examining the years 1975–1976 found that more than 60 percent of six hundred corporations had at least one enforcement action initiated against them, and half of the companies were charged with a serious violation. A later study by *U.S. News & World Report* found that during the 1970s, 20 percent of the Fortune 500 had been convicted of at least one major crime or paid a civil penalty for serious illegal behavior. From 1975 to 1984, almost two-thirds of the Fortune 500 "were involved in one or more incidents of corrupt behavior such as price fixing, bribery, violation of environmental regulations and tax fraud" (Etzioni 1990, C3). As one observer of corporate crime noted, the "corporate structure itself—oriented as it is toward profit and away from liability—is a standing invitation to such conduct" (quoted in Hills 1987; see also Bakan 2004).

While it is often noted that in the area of elite deviance hardly anyone ever goes to prison, less attention is given to the law enforcement reality that the US regulatory and judiciary systems "do little if anything to deter the most damaging Wall Street crimes" (Leaf 2005, 38). Such a situation exists for several reasons: (1) most state regulators and prosecutors do not make white-collar crime a priority; (2) the FBI does not make white-collar and corporate crime a priority, leaving substantial aspects of the problem to underfunded regulatory agencies that work in an environment encouraging deregulation and industry self-regulation; and (3) corporate resources result in substantial legal talent and an array of tactics that help force settlements favorable to the corporation. (Self-regulation frequently involves a minimal effort to promote good behavior in order to prevent stricter outside regulation.)

First, state regulators and prosecutors, with exceptions like some New York attorneys general, shy away from complicated cases involving financially powerful entities. Resources and training are issues; so are politics. Corporations and wealthy individuals can be large campaign contributors and exercise substantial political influence. Regulators also know that if they cooperate with industry, they have a better chance of landing a lucrative job with the industry after they finish working for the government. After getting industry experience, they are valued as regulators, which then increases the chance they can land a better-paying job with the industry. This revolving door is described as *agency capture*, which refers to the process by which regulatory agencies—the police on many white-collar crime beats—come to be dominated (from the inside) by the industries they regulate through the revolving door of personnel. Prosecutors typically enter private practice or politics after government service and do not want to make enemies of the wealthy and powerful who could be a source of campaign donations, an employer, or a lucrative client.

Second, white-collar task forces of the FBI are stretched too thin and tend to focus on such wide-ranging schemes as Internet, insurance, and Medicaid fraud. Further, white-collar crime includes acts where middle- and upper-class perpetrators victimize those who are more powerful, as well as perpetrators (including corporations) who victimize those who are less powerful. As Henry Pontell, coauthor of *Big-Money Crime: Fraud and Politics in the Savings and Loan Crisis*, has stated: "I've seen welfare frauds labeled as white-collar crimes" (quoted in Leaf 2005, 38). Consistent with the discussion (above) of Black's *Behavior of Law*, the FBI and other policing agencies have been more involved with sanctioning middle managers who embezzle from institutions and executives of small companies than with executives of large companies that cause mass victimization. According to the *U.S. Attorney's Annual Statistical Report*, for the year 2012, there were 5,964 white-collar or business crimes filed against 8,927 defendants, but there were only 52 cases of corporate fraud filed against 77 individuals.

While this pattern has been long-standing, it was made worse by the reassignment of agents from white-collar crime to the war on terror. But the percentage of inmates in federal prisons for drugs has continued to increase, indicating that the war on terror has been used to justify reducing the forces fighting white-collar crime but not the drug war. Thus, the "limited resources for white-collar crime" mask a decision to make fighting the drug war a higher priority than costly white-collar crime that has destabilized the economy and thus national security, as explored in box 9.1. The shift in priorities reflects a lack of will to combat white-collar crime even as the nation was experiencing the impact of Enron and the frauds of other "criminal enterprises" that shook the confidence of the nation's securities markets when the share prices of affected companies collapsed, cost investors billions of dollars, and affected the entire economy. At the close of the George W. Bush presidency, the FBI was devoting so few resources to white-collar crime that companies had to turn to private investigators to prepare "courtroom-ready prosecutions" that they could take to the FBI because they were unable to get the agency's attention, even in cases of multimillion-dollar cases of loss (Lichtblau, Johnston, and Nixon 2008).

While popular opinion and political rhetoric blames regulatory agencies for stifling business and killing jobs, underresourced regulatory agencies are ineffective at protecting investors, consumers, workers, and communities from a variety of harms. For example, between 1990 and 2007, the number of federal OSHA inspectors declined from 1,300 to 1,100, and "it is estimated that OSHA actively regulates [the work conditions of] only about 20% of the American workforce" (Friedman and Forst 2007, 459). Dr. David Michaels, assistant secretary of labor for Occupational Safety and Health, noted that in 2011, federal OSHA had 1,200 inspectors and "state plans have around the same, so there are less than 2,500 inspectors to cover 7.5 million workplaces employing more than 130 million workers" (quoted in Reiman and Leighton 2013, 81).

BOX 9.1.   ECONOMIC CRISIS
AND THE WAR ON STATE-CORPORATE CRIME?

Immediately after the terrorist attacks of 9/11 a common expression was that "everything is different now." In fundamental ways, many things are different in relation to counterterrorism strategies and the enforcement and administration of criminal justice, both at home and abroad. More importantly, what has fallen below the radar are the connections between these changing legal-crime fighting operations and their effects on the missing war on white-collar and state-corporate crime. It is these omissions in controlling many financial practices that may be linked to this country's recent economic crisis.

The primary response to 9/11 and to the larger war on terrorism by the United States had been the passage of the Homeland Security Act of 2002, which created the Department of Homeland Security (DHS). According to the legislation, the DHS was created for seven purposes, and the one that is most often ignored by public and private conversations alike is the legal charge that the DHS will "ensure that the overall economic security of the United States is not diminished by efforts, activities, and programs aimed at securing the homeland."

Although the DHS has had its share of failures (the recovery in New Orleans in the wake of Hurricane Katrina), Homeland Security's most serious failure to date has been to bulk up its war on terror and remain heavily invested in a war on drugs while failing to replace those agents engaged in the fight against white-collar crime. The issue is not a choice between fighting terrorism or white-collar crime but of placing a higher priority on a questionable drug war while white-collar and corporate crime control become "nonpriorities."

For example, following the September 11 attacks, the FBI shifted more than 1,800 agents, or nearly one-third of all agents, from law enforcement to terrorism and intelligence duties. So depleted were the ranks of the investigators in the areas of white-collar and corporate crimes that many executives in the private sector were complaining that they had difficulty attracting the bureau's intervention in even those cases that potentially involved frauds in the hundreds of millions of dollars. Moreover, since late 2003 and early 2004, the FBI had been requesting additional resources to the tune of $1 billion as well as eight hundred more agents so that they could go after the perpetrators of mortgage fraud and other economic crimes that they viewed at the time as posing a looming threat to the financial markets.

While the agency did receive $50 million, or 5 percent of its request for the "war on white-collar crime," in 2008 the number of investigators for these crimes was down 625 agents, or 36 percent, from 2001. Finally, after trying to acquire the necessary resources and person power for more than four years, the FBI has recently launched more than 1,500 criminal investigations into this nation's mortgage-related business practices, including those financial and institutional transactions of such corporate giants as Fannie Mae, Freddie Mac, the American International Group, and Lehman Brothers.

Before another economic crisis of global proportions occurs, perhaps the United States will learn, once and for all, the powerful lessons of the adverse effects of antiregulation policies and nonenforcement of upper-world white-collar and corporate crime on the wider society and world as a whole. Historically, that was not the case with either the savings and loan scandals of the late 1980s or the corporate frauds perpetrated early in the twenty-first century by those CEOs in charge of Enron, HealthSouth, Adelphia, WorldCom, Global Crossing, Xerox, and Waste Management, to name the most conspicuous offenders. And when the US Congress has acted to reform the situation by passing legislation such as the Sarbanes-Oxley Act in an attempt to regulate "corporate fraud gone wild," it was only a matter of time before those legal efforts were stripped of their enforcement teeth by lobbyists working on behalf of powerful antiregulation forces.

Even former Federal Reserve chairman Alan Greenspan, who did nothing to regulate in the face of a real-estate fraud bubble, has finally come to the realization that "free enterprise" without regulation is no way to run the economy. In fact, it is criminal to run an economy that way, and having done so is now costing the American taxpayers almost a trillion dollars as part of a plan to rescue the nation's financial system from a Wall Street–orchestrated, federally enabled, multibillion-dollar pyramid scheme.

Source: Adapted from Barak (2008).

The advisory system for notifying consumers about dangerous or defective products is weak, and Congress refuses to fully fund all the mandates it passed in the FDA Food Safety Modernization Act (FSMA) passed into law in 2011. A Department of Health and Human Service's Office of Inspector General (OIG) study in 2010 "found that more than half of all food facilities have gone 5 or more years without an FDA inspection and that FDA does not always take swift and effective action to remedy violations found during inspections" (Department of Health and Human Services 2011, 6). An editorial in the *Journal of the American Medical Association* harshly critiqued the system of checking on the safety of drugs once they were on the market. In an article called "Postmarketing Surveillance—Lack of Vigilance, Lack of Trust," the authors conclude that without a "long overdue major restructuring," the United States will be "far short of having an effective, vigilant, and trustworthy system of postmarketing surveillance to protect the public" from problematic prescription drugs or contaminated food products (Fontanarosa, Rennie, and DeAngelis 2004, 2650). These examples are merely illustrative rather than a comprehensive review of the policing of business.

Third, corporate financial resources mean corporations can retain top legal talent and employ a host of strategies that frequently result in settlements favorable to the corporation. Criminologist James Coleman (1985) did an extensive study of the enforcement of the Sherman Antitrust Act in the petroleum industry and identified four major strategies that corporations employ to prevent full application of the law. First is endurance and delay, which includes using expensive legal resources to prolong the litigation and obstruct the discovery of information by raising as many motions and legal technicalities as possible. Second is the use of corporate wealth and political connections to undermine the will of legislators and regulators to enforce the law's provisions. Third is secrecy and deception about ownership and control to prevent detection of violations and make them more difficult to prove. Fourth are threats of economic consequences to communities and the economy if regulations are passed and/or fully enforced.

Attorney general Eric Holder acknowledged these concerns in 2013 congressional testimony when he said that financial institutions have become "so large" (see chapter 3) that it is "difficult for us to prosecute them" (quoted in Douglas 2013). The specific concern for Holder was that criminal charges could "have a negative impact on the national economy, perhaps even the world economy. . . . It has an inhibiting influence, impact on our ability to bring resolutions that I think would be more appropriate." Senator Charles Grassley described Holder's comments as stunning because "big bankers know that if they commit financial crimes, they can expect a passive response from the Justice Department" (quoted in Douglas 2013). No doubt in areas outside of finance, the equivalent of "too big to fail" also means "too big to jail."

Thus, despite the impressive record of habitual criminality on the part of the corporate United States, the Reagan, Bush I, Clinton, and Bush II administrations have all consistently worked to get government "off the backs" of (e.g., to deregulate) corporations as they ratcheted up their war on the crimes of the poor. Such strategies of crime control (actually policies of class control) are the equivalent of removing police from a high-crime area because the free will of criminals is being interfered with. Rather than "get tough," deregulation of business affairs has produced an environment of expanding criminal activity as it has reduced enforcement and penalties.

This pattern can be clearly seen in the area of financial crimes. An investigative report of the SEC found that regulators, "while determined and well trained, are so understaffed that they often have to let good cases slip away." Even when referrals are made, "prosecutors leave scores of would-be criminal cases referred by the SEC in the dustbin, declining to prosecute more than half of what comes their way" (Leaf 2005, 38). Investigation using TRAC data (Syracuse University's web data clearinghouse, which has been tracking prosecutor referrals from virtually every federal agency) from 1992 to 2001 revealed that SEC enforcement attorneys referred 609 cases to the Justice Department for possible criminal charges. Of that number, US attorneys decided what to do on about 525 cases, declining to prosecute just over 64 percent of them; of the 195 remaining cases, prosecutors successfully convicted 76 percent of those, with only some 20 percent, or eighty-seven of those criminals, finding their way into prison (Leaf 2005, 39).

The situation did not change dramatically after Enron and the slew of other corporate financial scandals. In the immediate aftermath of the scandals, President Bush created a new corporate fraud task force, although critics pointed out that the official responsible for this "financial SWAT team" directed a credit card company that had paid more than $400 million to settle consumer and securities fraud suits. The Corporate Fraud Task Force issued reports on corporate fraud in 2003 and 2004, but they were lists of cases and settlements, with no effort to summarize data, discuss larger problems, make policy recommendations, and so on. After 2004, the task force did not issue another report until early 2008, which included a substantial number of cases from the 2003 and 2004 reports. Although this report was issued just before the financial crisis, it did not detect or note any patterns that forewarned an imminent global crisis. The Department of Justice ultimately disbanded Bush's Corporate Fraud Task Force for a more narrowly focused Financial Fraud Enforcement Task Force that quickly lost focus on corporations and investigated individuals who victimized financial institutions (Barak 2012).

In the wake of Enron, the Department of Justice did convene a number of specialized task forces, the Enron task force being one of the better known. They secured dozens of convictions, starting with lower-level employees who struck plea bargains in exchange for information about the activities of those higher in the company. The task force ultimately secured the conviction, at trial, of CEOs Ken Lay and Jeffrey Skilling. As these trials were winding down, FBI officials in 2004 said that mortgage-related problems had "the potential to be an epidemic" (Schmitt 2008), but they were ignored.

At the same time, then SEC chair Christopher Cox (2005–2009) said, "We've done everything we can during the last several years in the agency to make sure people understand there's a strong market cop on the beat," but he required staff to get approval for an increased number of actions from SEC commissioners. According to former SEC chair Arthur Levitt, this has effectively "handcuffed" the inspection and enforcement division (Paley and Hilzenrath 2008). An SEC press release claimed that under Chairman Cox, the percentage of staff working on enforcement has increased, but the actual number of enforcement staff declined from 2005, and the percentage increased only because other SEC divisions had bigger cuts. (*New York Times* columnist Floyd Norris asks, "Is there anyone at the commission with the nerve to tell Mr. Cox that the enforcer of disclosure laws ought to be particularly careful to avoid misleading hype?" [2008b]). Further, "the commission delayed settlements while commissioners negotiated to impose smaller penalties than the companies had agreed to pay" (Norris 2008a). (Imagine a chief prosecutor who delayed a plea bargain to try to impose a smaller penalty than requested by the defense lawyer for a drug dealer!)

By 2008, federal officials brought fewer prosecutions of securities fraud than in 2000, the year before Enron. They were either profoundly ignorant of the widespread fraud about to crash the global economy, or the people who knew were prevented from taking action. In either case, the former lead prosecutor of Enron's Ken Lay and Jeffrey Skilling commented that "most sitting U.S. Attorneys now staring at the subprime crisis find scant resources available to pursue sophisticated financial crimes" (Schmitt 2008). The FBI found a small number of additional agents and resources to look into mortgage fraud and investigate firms at the center of the financial crisis after the crisis happened, but then attorney general Michael Mukasey repeatedly rejected calls for an equivalent of the Enron task force that was used to prosecute earlier widespread complex financial crime (Lichtblau, Johnston, and Nixon 2008). If there are no investigations, there can be no prosecutions—and there have been no criminal prosecutions of big financial institutions or the executives at the center of the financial crisis.

Some of the civil suits against financial companies have had large-sounding fines that are in fact a small percentage of revenues and profits for the companies. A number of the settlements involved a deferred prosecution agreement, or an agreement that the government will not prosecute a company if it pays a fine, agrees to certain conditions, and does not commit further criminal acts. Both of these issues came to light when Judge Jed Rakoff rejected a proposed settlement in a case in which the SEC claimed Citicorp sold investors a product it was betting would lose value and did not disclose that information, causing investors $700 million in losses. In the settlement, Citigroup did not admit guilt but agreed to pay $285 million and said it would not violate this provision of the law again. The judge noted that the penalty was "pocket change" to Citigroup and would have no deterrent effect or make up for investor losses. Further, the promise not to violate the law in the future was the kind of relief that "Citigroup (a recidivist) knew that the S.E.C. had not sought to enforce against any financial institution for at least the last 10 years" (*U.S. Securities and Exchange Commission v. Citigroup Global Markets* 2011, 11). Indeed, a *New York Times* investigation found that Citigroup "agreed not to violate the very same antifraud statute in July 2010. And in May 2006. Also as far as back as March 2005 and April 2000" (Wyatt 2011). The *Times* found nineteen companies were repeat offenders who had promised not to do it again.

In sum, when it comes to crime, criminals, and class control, the old legal axiom still stands: while rich people don't hold up Dairy Queens and poor people don't price-fix or swindle the consumer, police and prosecutors seem to pursue only those who do, in fact, hold up DQs—namely, the poor and marginal. As for the rich, like in the game of Monopoly®, they seem to have no need for the "get out of jail free" cards, since very few resources in law enforcement are earmarked for the task of reducing white-collar and corporate crime. But even when they are arrested, they can hire attorneys to help escape or minimize the charges.

Consider the situation described by the authors of *Dorm Room Dealers*, who report on the "antitargets" of the drug war—a network of affluent, mostly white college students who supplied marijuana and other drugs to several Southern California colleges. One informant, for example, sold five to ten pounds of marijuana a week, making $80,000 to $160,000 a month in sales and $10,000 to $20,000 in profit. Almost all the dealers were from "middle-upper class to affluent/upper class" and "had parents of considerable economic standing"—mayors, businesspeople, doctors, and accounting executives for major firms (Mohamed and Fritsvold 2011, 11–12). Because of their class status, they operated with relative impunity despite "the near absent or, perhaps more accurately, pathetic risk-minimization strategies employed by most of the dealers" (2010, 6). The authors, while fully aware of class biases in the criminal justice system, write, "We were still taken aback by the lack of criminal justice and university administration attention paid these dealers, despite the brazenness, incompetence, and general dearth of street smarts that tended to characterize the dealers' daily practices" (2010, 7).

Indeed, the authors said, "It almost seemed as if our network's dealers were deliberately trying to draw attention to themselves or test social and legal boundaries" (Mohamed and Fritsvold 2011, 137). One dealer had "a forest" of marijuana growing in his dorm room; others had pungent-smelling packages mailed directly to them. Many dealers described encounters where police were in houses used to grow marijuana and where the dealers' wealth and status served not as a "get-out-of-jail-free" card, but as a "never-go-to-jail-in-the-first-place" card (2010, 132).

In spite of their "brazen" illegality, only a few dealers did end up in the criminal justice system (Mohamed and Fritsvold 2011, 173). One large-scale marijuana dealer, who described himself as "untouchably wealthy," was charged with what the authors call "relatively serious drug and weapons offenses." He ended up with a "possession ticket" and no weapons charges because "I got real good lawyers [laughs]" (2011, 159). Another dealer was caught with over one hundred marijuana plants and $30,000 in growing equipment, but his parents hired a "high-profile private defense attorney" and horticultural and biological sciences experts plus "various psychiatrists." He ended up with an eighteen-month "diversion program" that resulted in no jail time, and all records were expunged when he successfully completed the program, so someone running a criminal history check would find nothing about this incident (2011, 161, 167).

For drug offenses, these students had better representation than poor people facing murder charges. For example, in 2004, Johnny Lee Bell was convicted of second-degree murder and received an automatic mandatory sentence of life in prison despite his public defender's admission that she had spent only eleven minutes preparing for his trial. The National Association of Criminal Defense Attorneys (2004) notes that the "case is egregious, but not unsymptomatic given the trend of substandard legal representation that has become common in many states."

CRIME, CRIMINAL IDENTIFICATION, AND RACE CONTROL

After reviewing an extensive number of studies, the *Harvard Law Review* (1988, 1496) stated: "The argument that police behavior is undistorted by racial discrimination flatly contradicts most studies, which reveal what many police officers freely admit: that police use race as an independently significant, if not determinative, factor in deciding whom to follow, detain, search, or arrest." Because most people, then and now, violate the law at some points during their lives, this heightened scrutiny continues to result in higher levels of arrests and creates a picture of the "typical criminal" as being young, black, and inner-city (Reiman and Leighton 2013). The racially based profile of the typical criminal is then used to justify the belief that "race itself provides a legitimate basis on which to base a categorically higher level of suspicion" (*Harvard Law Review* 1988, 1496). In turn, the cycle becomes a self-fulfilling prophecy as the criminal justice system often operates on stereotypes and profiles that define some groups "as having a propensity to be morally depraved, thus endorsing a view of those who share in that culture as unworthy of equal respect" (*Harvard Law Review* 1988, 1514).

That pattern is still very much relevant today. The single biggest issue involving minorities and law enforcement has been DWB, a topic introduced in the opening of this chapter. A number of lawsuits have been filed against the police for a variety of abusive and discriminatory behaviors. Beyond the lawsuits, this topic generates heated debate and helps account for some of the different attitudes whites and minorities have toward police and the criminal justice system. Many of the early complaints about this practice were ignored or discounted by many whites (see the discussion of privilege in chapter 4). Some settlements for lawsuits alleging discrimination and civil rights violations during the 1990s included requirements to collect more extensive data, which became a practice in numerous jurisdictions with racial tensions.

Other researchers also undertook to find ways to see whether minority overrepresentation in traffic stops was related to race or simply worse driving. The first data were anecdotal but indicated that police targeted black, brown, and other nonwhites frequently for minor violations—no seat belt, tilted license plates, or illegible (dirty) plates. For example, one of the earliest studies to demonstrate racial profiling was a 1988 study of vehicles on the New Jersey Turnpike, which showed that African American motorists with out-of-state plates accounted for fewer than 5 percent of the vehicles but 80 percent of the stops. A decade later, in Illinois, Hispanics made up less than 8 percent of the population and took fewer than 3 percent of the personal vehicle trips, but they made up approximately 30 percent of the motorists stopped for discretionary offenses, such as the failure to signal a lane change or driving one to four miles over the speed limit (D. Harris 1999).

Two studies conducted at the end of the 1990s, one on "driving interventions" and the other on "stop-and-frisk" practices, both revealed significant adverse consequences for minorities. In the state of Maryland, observers who watched an interstate near Baltimore and recorded information on 5,741 cars over 42 hours reported that 93.3 percent were violating traffic laws and thus were eligible to be stopped by the state police. Of the violators seen by the study's observers, 17.5 percent were black and 74.7 percent were white. However, the Maryland State Police reported that 72.9 percent of the vehicles they stopped had black drivers (D. Harris 1999). (The New York stop-and-frisk study was discussed in the opening narrative of this chapter.)

More recent research from Robin Engel and Jennifer Calnon (2004, 69–72) concluded that

- the odds that black drivers would receive a citation were 47 percent higher compared with the odds for white drivers, and the odds for Hispanic drivers were 82 percent higher;
- the percentage of minority drivers who reported having their person or vehicle searched was double that of white drivers—5.4 percent of white drivers were searched, compared with 10.9 percent of blacks, 11.2 percent of Hispanics, and 6.5 percent of other races and ethnicities;
- only 2.6 percent of white drivers reported being arrested, compared with 5.2 percent of black drivers, 4.2 percent of Hispanic drivers, and 2.1 percent of drivers of other races and ethnicities; and
- 2.7 percent of whites reported having force used against them, compared with 6.7 percent of blacks, 5.4 percent of Hispanics, and 1.7 percent of drivers of other races and ethnicities.

While a study for the Bush administration found no evidence of blacks being disproportionately pulled over, the report "Contacts between Police and the Public" supports the general findings above about the *consequences* of the stop. The Bureau of Justice Statistics reviewed evidence from across the nation and found "evidence of black drivers having worse experiences—more likely to be arrested, more likely to be searched, more likely to have force used against them—during traffic stops than white drivers" (Bureau of Justice Statistics 2005a, 9). While the final report still contains the information quoted in the previous sentence, the *New York Times* reported that "political supervisors within the Office of Justice Programs ordered Mr. Greenfeld [head of the Bureau of Justice Statistics] to delete certain references to the disparities from a news release that was drafted to announce the findings, according to more than a half-dozen Justice Department officials with knowledge of the situation." Greenfeld refused and "was initially threatened with dismissal and the possible loss of some pension benefits," an event that the *Times* notes "caps more than three years of simmering tensions over charges of political interference at the agency." Greenfeld ultimately moved to a lesser position, and the report was posted to the BJS website without a news release or congressional briefing, leading to charges that the results were being buried (Lichtblau 2005).

Many traffic stops, especially for concerns such as dirty license plates and minor violations such as failing to signal a lane change, are really a pretext for searching for drugs or weapons: "A classic pretext stop is a traffic stop motivated not by any desire to enforce traffic laws, but instead motivated by a desire to hunt for drugs in the absence of any evidence of illegal drug activity" (Alexander 2012, 67). But the Supreme Court upheld their validity in *Whren v. U.S.* (517 U.S. 806 [1996]), saying that as long as the police saw a violation for which they could stop a car, it did not matter that the stop was a pretext. But *Whren* did not decide any racial discrimination issues raised under an equal protection challenge based on other precedents, such as *Yick Wo v. Hopkins* (118 U.S. 356 [1886]), in which the court held that even if "the law itself be fair on its face and impartial in appearance, yet if it is applied and administered by public authority with an evil eye and an unequal hand the denial of equal justice is still within the prohibition of the Constitution."

Pretextual stops based on racial bias erode trust in the system of justice and create the cynicism and hostility that was discussed in the opening narrative of this chapter. David Harris, for example, contends that "pretext stops capture some who are guilty but at an unacceptably high societal cost" because they "undermine public confidence in law enforcement, erode the legitimacy of the criminal justice system, and make police work that much more difficult and dangerous" (1999). In addition, "pretextual traffic stops fuel the belief that the police are not only unfair and biased, but untruthful as well" because if the stop was about enforcement of the traffic code, there would be no need for a drug search:

> Stopping a driver for a traffic offense when the officer's real purpose is drug interdiction is a lie—a legally sanctioned one, to be sure, but a lie nonetheless. It should surprise no one that those who are the victims of police discrimination regard the testimony and statements of police with suspicion. If jurors don't believe truthful police testimony, crimes are left unpunished, law enforcement becomes much less effective, and the very people who need the police most are left less protected. (D. Harris 1999)

Unfortunately, lawsuits challenging racial profiling have largely disappeared because of a Supreme Court ruling that denies standing to private parties suing under the Civil Rights Act of 1964. "Only the federal government can sue to enforce Title VI's anti-discrimination provisions—something it has neither the inclination nor the capacity to do in most racial profiling cases due to its limited resources and institutional reluctance to antagonize local law enforcement" (Alexander 2012, 138).

Concerns about racial profiling and DWB help reveal why blacks have much less confidence in police than whites. Table 9.1 provides the data for 2012. These con-

Table 9.1. Reported Confidence in Police by Race, 2012

Race	Great Deal/Quite a Lot of Confidence (%)	Very Little Confidence (%)
White	57	14
Black	32	23

Source: Sourcebook of Criminal Justice Statistics 2012, table 2.12.

cerns are reinforced by other tactics related to the war on drugs that target blacks in a discriminatory way. While many people think of black men when asked to imagine a drug dealer (Alexander 2012, 106), this is largely the result of patterns of policing that reinforce the profile:

> How police departments distribute police officers among and within precincts will play a significant role in determining the demographic profile of arrestees. . . . If specialized undercover narcotics units are concentrated in minority neighborhoods, those units will generate arrests and intelligence regarding minority narcotics activity. This may create the impression that minorities inordinately engage in narcotics activity, which, in turn, may impel even more minority arrests. (Sekhon 2011, 1171)

So whereas police resources are deployed to certain areas for certain reasons, they may produce more arrests there, but it does not mean that there is more crime—just a greater likelihood of arrest for those crimes in those areas. The police could just as easily have "seized televisions, furniture and cash from fraternity houses based on an anonymous tip that a few joints and a stash of cocaine" were there, or white "suburban homemakers could have been placed under surveillance and subjected to undercover operations to catch them violating laws regulating the use and sale of prescription" drugs (Alexander 2012, 124).

On the other hand, the opposite of pretextual stops and aggressive policing may be referred to as underenforcement. Some, such as Victor Rios (2011), note a paradox of overenforcement and underprotection. Police have a high visibility in minority neighborhoods and are quite willing to stop, frisk, detain, harass, and arrest young black males—but police are less likely to respond to residents' calls for help in these same neighborhoods. When legal protection fails, marginalized urban males rely on self- and group or gang protection from violence as a means of indigenous social control.

While police are frequently considered the gatekeepers of the criminal justice system, prosecutors also make important decisions about who is released from the system and who gets processed further into it—and for which crimes. Prosecutors have wide discretion about which cases to pursue, the charges to make, whether to use statutes that have mandatory minimums, whether to use "three-strikes legislation," and what bargains to offer in exchange for guilty pleas. These decisions become all the more important in relationship to the federal and state sentencing guidelines. Even where guidelines are advisory, they remove a great deal of discretion from sentencing judges and have made prosecutorial decisions more important.

However, there is virtually no independent review of prosecutorial decisions as there are with judicial decisions or rulings, so bias at this stage of the criminal justice system is the least likely to be evaluated for "equal justice." Michelle Alexander notes that "immunizing prosecutors from claims of racial bias and failing to impose any meaningful check on the exercise of their discretion . . . has created an environment in which conscious and unconscious biases are allowed to flourish" (2012, 117). This is contrary to prosecutorial discretion in countries such as France, Italy, and

Germany, where in the latter nation, for example, judges, victims, and defendants may legally challenge the prosecutor's discretion in individual cases (Ma 2008).

Decisions about the severity of a crime can easily reflect conscious or unconscious stereotypes and racism that relate to dangerousness, moral depravity, and so on to nonwhite defendants. As the *Harvard Law Review* (1988) article concluded, a variety of studies indicate that black-on-white crime is most likely to be seen and treated as more serious in contrast to white-on-black or black-on-black crime. For example, in an analysis of 53,000 homicides, John Roman (2013) found that "between 2005 and 2010, there were 1,210 homicides with a black shooter and a white victim—the shooting was ruled to be justified in just 17 of them (about 1 percent)." During the same five years, "there were 2,069 shootings where the shooter was white and the victim black. The homicide was ruled to be justified in 236 cases (11 percent)."

Further, both empirical data and mock trial experiments indicate that minority defendants face a greater risk of receiving unjust verdicts when their jury does not adequately represent minorities. That is, when the defendant was a minority, "white jurors [are] less likely to show compassion, and are less likely to be influenced by group discussion," so the defendant is more likely to be "found guilty and to be punished severely" (*Harvard Law Review* 1988, 1560). The same review also found that nonminority defendants who have had minority attorneys to represent them have not fared as well as those who have nonminority attorneys.

Further, as Harris noted with respect to pretextual stops, minorities' experience with racism and a greater distrust of the police, based partly on a history of excessive use of force and partly on a history of racial profiling, make minorities more suspicious of the prosecution's case, especially when based substantially on police testimony. In contrast, whites' more favorable or benign interactions with police lead to less skepticism about the latter's testimony, which hence is given greater weight.

CRIME, CRIMINAL IDENTIFICATION, AND GENDER CONTROL

Chapter 7 noted that most offenders and victims are male, so much of the law enforcement and adjudication involves largely male criminal justice employees processing mostly male perpetrators for crimes against other men. According to the FBI's Uniform Crime Reports, in 2012, 73.8 percent of all arrests were men, including 80.1 percent of arrests for violent crime. Women were arrested more frequently only for "prostitution and commercialized vice." While the exact numbers and percentages change over time, the basic proportions have held constant for many years.

In some ways, UCR arrest data understate gender differences because the offense categories are broad and derived from a wide variety of criminal acts. For example, as Darrell Steffensmeier (1995) points out, "fraud" includes shoplifting a ten-dollar item, stealing a radio from a parked car, stealing merchandise from one's workplace, and theft of cargo worth thousands of dollars. Even though larceny-theft is considered a "serious crime" according to UCR definitions, most of the crimes women commit tend to fall at the lower range of offense seriousness. Most arrests of women are for shoplifting, passing bad checks, credit card fraud, and welfare fraud—not serious corporate frauds, let alone physically injurious acts such as manufacturing and selling defective products, industrial pollution, or maintaining unsafe workplaces. Crimes women commit have tended to be extensions of women's domestic and consumer role activities (i.e., paying family bills and obtaining family necessities) rather than evidence of women becoming more like men in committing violent crimes.

In the 1970s, explanations of women's lower level of criminal involvement were often based on an assumption that women have benefited from police officers' and judges' paternalistic and/or chivalrous attitudes. As a result, the argument went, women were less likely to be arrested, convicted, or incarcerated. Over the past quarter century or more, assumptions of paternalism have been criticized on a number of grounds. First, most studies asserting paternalism have not empirically evaluated whether it is in fact responsible for the differences (Daly 1994). Further, "expectations that girls behave obediently, modestly, and cautiously" were

> behind the proliferation of training schools for immigrant girls who were perceived to be immoral and in need of guidance that would enable them to marry and to become responsible mothers. In the mid- and late twentieth century, these expectations supported detention and incarceration of girls for status offenses, for technical probation violations, and particularly for running away. Now, these same expectations result in the detention and incarceration of girls who fight back at home or in intimate relationships and who are victims of sexual exploitation. (F. Sherman 2012, 1586)

Second, there is ample reason to question whether black women and minorities have *ever* benefited from judicial paternalism (Raeder 1993; Young 1986). Dorie Klein ([1973] 1995) notes that chivalry is "a racist and classist concept . . . reserved for the women who are least likely ever to come in contact with the criminal justice system: the ladies, or white middle-class women" (10, 13). Historical evidence of the lack of chivalry toward black women includes the fact that they were placed in chain gangs with men while white women offenders were placed in reformatories (Rafter 1990). Similarly, white women's rebellion against gender roles may lead to psychiatric treatment, while black women are more likely to wind up in prison (Hurtado 1989). Moreover, black women have been characterized by larger society and popular culture as "welfare queens," "Mammys," and "Jezebels," tough, masculine, "black Amazons," and castrating, dangerous "sinister Sapphires"—not the sorts of women on which chivalry is generally bestowed.

In contrast to the widely held but false belief in chivalry is the long-standing denial of police services to female victims of male domestic violence by the mostly male police force. Indeed, chapter 7 noted the historical reluctance to define women as victims who have crimes committed against them in their homes or as part of a relationship, and the police have had a key role in using their discretion to not hold men accountable for their crimes against women. For example, Carol Jordan notes,

"Historically, studies have shown low rates of arrest of domestic violence offenders, ranging from 5% to 18% of cases" and "low arrest rates are documented even when victims have received physical injury from the abuse" (2004, 1416).

In response to widespread concerns and lawsuits claiming that policies denied women equal protection, jurisdictions passed mandatory arrest policies or preferred-arrest policies. Such policies reinforce the message that battering is a serious crime and aim to encourage police action, sometimes by creating conditions where the police should arrest even if the victim does not want to press charges. Although such actions taken against a woman's wishes may further disempower her and cause economic problems if the family is dependent on the batterer's income, the strategies were in response to police claims that they did not arrest because the battered women would not follow through and the case would be dropped anyway. Many jurisdictions also added prosecution "no drop" policies to ensure that police arrests would be matched by activity in the prosecutor's office.

The unfortunate result of these policies has been greater arrest rates of battered women because the police go into a situation and simply arrest both parties if there is evidence each side has hit the other. In this sense, "it is ironic to note, but holding the state accountable for women's safety through changes in law enforcement practices, many victims of ongoing battering have ended up with less protection and fewer services and have been labeled as a defendant. The consequences of mandatory arrest policies may be exacerbated for women of color, in part, because they are more likely to fight back" (Miller and Meloy 2006, 92; F. Sherman 2012). The perceived gender neutrality of the policy hurts domestic violence victims who need to contend not just with the abuse but also with an arrest and subsequent problems that may include denial of access to shelters because of an assault conviction, child custody issues, victim assistance, difficulties with employment or housing, and being mandated to attend a batterer intervention program (Miller and Meloy 2006).

Susan Miller and Michelle Meloy note the problem is also partly caused by a criminal justice system based on incidents and not understanding the long-standing patterns of systemic—physical, sexual, and verbal—abuse that are frequently the context for the woman's actions. They further note that women are disadvantaged in the system because "women are not socialized to use violence, so they remember every incident" and thus "more readily admit their violence than do men" (2006, 92). Women also are "less savvy" about the criminal justice system, and all "these tendencies backfire for women but may fuel the perspective that women are mutually combative and violent in relationships" (2006, 92). (The Bureau of Justice Statistics reported that "among violent crimes against a spouse, 86.1% of the offenders were male; against a boyfriend or girlfriend, 82.4%" [2005b, 14].)

One recent trend has involved trying to train police to identify a primary aggressor as a way to cut down on the number of victims who get arrested. However, advocates for battered women who do trainings with police report frustration in dealing with "the prevalence of sexism in the larger culture and the persistence of hegemonic masculinity in police departments in which women are denigrated and excluded" (Huisman, Martinez, and Wilson 2005, 795). Women represent a little more than

12 percent of all sworn officers, and even fewer are in upper-level management, so there are few counters to male privilege (*Stat Abs* 2013, table 626). Trainers who pointed out the basic fact that most batterers are men were "accused of being sexist or man-hating" and questioned, "sometimes belligerently," about resources for battered men (Huisman, Martinez, and Wilson 2005). Female trainers seemed to be judged by their appearance and received feedback about being "man-hating lesbians with an agenda" (Huisman, Martinez, and Wilson 2005).

Some scholars have suggested that prosecutorial discretion has made it likely that women (particularly white, middle-class women) will be pursued less than men because women's crimes are typically less serious than men's and women do not present as great a threat to society as men do. In some cases, however, the reverse is true, and women may actually be subjected to more vigorous prosecution than men, such as with the criminal prosecution of pregnant, drug-using women. For example, beginning in the late 1980s and continuing throughout most of the 1990s, despite the harms associated with legal drugs, efforts to criminalize pregnant women's drug use had singled out cocaine users—particularly crack or rock cocaine users—for prosecution (Flavin 2009). "Drug-addicted pregnant women" tend to conjure up an image—not of a suburban, white, middle-class woman who smokes, drinks, and takes prescription medications but rather of a poor, urban-dwelling, crack-addicted black woman trading sex for drugs. Few images generate less compassion than the latter, even though an article in the *Journal of the American Medical Association* reviewed seventy-four studies of prenatal cocaine exposure and found that while maternal cocaine use does increase risk, concerns have been exaggerated (Flavin 2009, 107). Moreover, the response has been an increased willingness to criminalize the woman's behavior rather than expand the availability of drug treatment and prenatal care, particularly for women who have small children or are infected with HIV. As a result, most of the women prosecuted have been low-income women of color.

In sum, in subtle and not-so-subtle ways, gender helps to shape the type of crime a person commits and the forms it takes as well as the responses of the criminal justice system, such as crimes involving domestic violence assaults, police behavior, and nonenforceable restraining orders for abusers to stay away. "Equality" is not the point as much as crafting gender-responsive strategies that recognize differences between males and females (and boys and girls) who are identified as violating laws. Females and girls generally need some type of trauma-informed care because "girls in the justice system are more likely than boys to have experienced sexual assault, rape, or sexual harassment, and early sexual abuse is common among girls victimized by commercial sexual exploitation" (F. Sherman 2012, 1601).

INTERSECTIONALITY AND THE IDENTIFICATION OF CRIMINALS

As previously discussed, men disproportionately commit crime, with black men overrepresented in many offense categories and women overrepresented in a few.

And even though a variety of studies have indicated that black-on-white crime and white-on-white crime are most likely to be seen as serious in contrast to white-on-black and black-on-black crime, Michael Radelet (1989), for example, has shown that the key dynamic involved was class, not race. Radelet reviewed the records of almost sixteen thousand executions that occurred in the United States between 1608 and 1989 to look for cases in which whites had been executed for killing blacks. He was able to find only thirty cases—less than two-tenths of 1 percent. Some of these cases occurred during the era of slavery, indicating that class was of more importance than race. In the remaining cases, Radelet found examples where defendants had killed whites but could not be prosecuted because of lack of evidence, where defendants had long records or previous sentences to life imprisonment, and where the occupational status of blacks "clearly surpassed that of the white assailant," including cases "in which the defendants were marginal members of the community, perhaps being labeled as 'white trash'" (Radelet 1989, 534–35).

Discussions of crime and offender characteristics have focused to such an extent on black men that, as noted earlier, "criminal" has almost become a synonym for black men. While official statistics that fail to combine race and gender make the task of criminal identification awkward, certain crimes seem to qualify as "white men's crimes" on the basis of their overrepresentation compared to women in general and minority males in particular. At the federal level in 2012, men were the majority of offenders in all crimes except embezzlement. Of particular note, they were the offenders in 95 percent of sexual abuse cases, 94 percent of racketeering and extortion cases, 96 percent of gambling/lottery cases, 99 percent of child pornography cases, and 100 percent of antitrust cases (US Sentencing Commission 2012, table 5). Whites make up the largest group of offenders for sexual abuse, racketeering and extortion, gambling/lottery, and child pornography (US Sentencing Commission 2012, table 4).

Of course, the serious underrepresentation of women and minority men as CEOs and in other executive positions of large corporations effectively blocks them from the access necessary to engage in large-scale white-collar crimes. Hence, it is not surprising, for example, that all forty-six of the individuals convicted in Operation Ill Wind, a large-scale defense procurement fraud investigation, were white males (Pasztor 1995), and the vast majority of those convicted in the Enron-style corporate frauds also have been white men. A review of 436 defendants from work done by the Corporate Fraud Task Force from 2002 to 2009 found only 37 women, about 9 percent (Steffensmeier, Schwartz, and Roche 2013). "Paralleling gendered labor market segmentation processes that limit and shape women's entry into economic roles, sex segregation in corporate criminality is pervasive, suggesting only subtle shifts in gender socialization and women's opportunities for significant white-collar crimes" (2013, 448). While 156 men were identified as ringleaders, only three women were—and two were married to another ringleader.

A fundamental point of this and other chapters is that the intersections of class, race, and gender shape not only perceptions of crime but also the nature of criminal behavior itself and the responses of the criminal justice system. In short,

opportunities to engage in legal and illegal behavior and to be pursued for the latter
are shaped or framed by relations of class, race, and gender. Drawing on interviews
from women cocaine users, Sheigla Murphy and Marsha Rosenbaum (1997) identified ways in which race and class interact to profoundly influence the type of cocaine
(powder versus crack/rock), patterns of use, and consequences of drug use for different categories of women. Murphy and Rosenbaum consider two young women
"who used cocaine too much": Monique, a poor underclass black woman living in
an impoverished inner-city neighborhood, and Becky, a white, middle-class woman.
Although there were similarities between the two women's experiences (e.g., both
first snorted cocaine in a mixed-gender group with friends, and both continued to
use cocaine not because of the high but to be part of a social scene), several factors
differentiated Monique and Becky's experiences with cocaine.

Monique, growing up in housing projects, was exposed to powder cocaine in early
1985 and was shown how to smoke crack within a year. The availability of crack in
the neighborhood (with less risky drugs being harder to find) and the prevalence of
crack use or dealing among her friends contributed to the escalation of Monique's
crack use. By contrast, Becky lived in a white, middle-class neighborhood. Her first
cocaine source was someone at an upscale rock and roll club. During the first two
years, Becky's cocaine use was limited to the one night a week she worked at the club,
though her cocaine snorting increased once she began to work more steadily at the
club and as more of her friends used powder cocaine. Becky, with her own private
room at work and at home, was able to conceal her drug use, whereas Monique's
crack use kept her outside her house and on the streets. While Becky's avoidance of
detection helped her to avoid the criminal justice system and the label of "deviant"
despite her increasing drug use, Monique was arrested, was stigmatized both formally
and by her family, and suffered many losses.

As the example of Becky and Monique illustrates, being black and poor places a
person in closer geographical proximity to opportunities to buy and/or smoke cocaine and to become a criminal subject of the administration of justice. By contrast,
class and race help to structurally protect someone who is a white, middle-class
person with a stake in conformity from serious consequences of drug use. Such privileges as those shared by Becky and other white, middle-class drug users can make a
"period of heavy [drug] use a mere detour on the road to a solid future" (Murphy
and Rosenbaum 1997, 109). This type of complex and institutionalized selective
enforcement and differential application of the law once again reflects the dynamic
interactions of class, race, and gender.

Understanding the working of class, race, and gender requires an appreciation
of structural inequalities embedded in society, which runs counter to the focus on
individual acts, individual deviants, and individual pathologies. This is the focus
that characterizes many media depictions as well as what the police do in evaluating
potential violations of the law. Further, "without an understanding of institutional
aspects [of inequality], students decontextualize social interactions; they equate
prejudice with oppression and argue that members of privileged groups are also op-

pressed" (quoted in Huisman, Martinez, and Wilson 2005, 802). The decontextual-ized understanding sees society in terms of the "equal opportunity racism" described in the opening narrative of this chapter. The contextualized understanding sees the inequalities of class, race, and gender—dynamics that shape the attitudes and choices of the perpetrators, the treatment of victims, and the power that the criminal justice system can both reflect and re-create.

Finally, the combined differential application and selective enforcement of law by class, income, and racial composition are reflected in the reported confidence that these groups have for the criminal justice system and the police. Not surprisingly, data about public trust in the police tend to reflect different sentiments by income, as reported in table 9.2. For 2012, as income increased, people had more confidence in the police. While the category of a "great deal/quite a lot" of confidence shows increasing numbers as income goes up, the category of "very little" confidence shows very strong movement through the income distribution. For example, only 7 percent of those in the top income category had very little confidence in police, while those in the lowest income category were almost four times more likely to express very little confidence in police.

As with many issues, disentangling income and race is difficult because there are no tables presenting those breakdowns. But such information would be useful in evaluating police and the criminal justice system. For example, how much does whiteness by itself protect people from abuse by the criminal justice system, and how much of this effect is based on income? How much confidence do middle- and upper-class blacks have in the police and criminal justice system? Evidence demon-strates that they are likely to be stopped by police disproportionately to whites of the same income, but they are less likely to be arrested and find their way into prison. There is a class-based process of "weeding out the wealthy" that applies to them as well as to higher-income whites (Reiman and Leighton 2013, 121–22).

IMPLICATIONS

A history of nonregulation of illegitimate white-collar and corporate behavior over the past three decades is the major reason for the current economic recession that

Table 9.2. Reported Confidence in Criminal Justice and Police by Income, 2012

Income Level	Great Deal/Quite a Lot of Confidence (%)	Very Little Confidence (%)
>$75,000	66	7
$50,000–$74,999	58	10
$30,000–$49,999	55	17
$20,000–$29,999	48	24
<$20,000	36	27

Source: Sourcebook of Criminal Justice Statistics 2012, table 2.12.

came to a head in the United States at the end of 2007 and quickly spread around the world as the first serious global downturn in the new age of globalization. Whether we are talking about the US economy, the economies of the developed G-20s, or the global economy as a whole, unless all of these develop regulatory systems with teeth and confront the key structural issues of protectionism and international coopera- tion, we lose some of the important benefits of globalization, according to Joseph E. Stiglitz, a recipient of the Nobel Prize in Economics. Stiglitz chairs the UN Com- mission of Experts, which was given the task by the General Assembly of preparing an interim report for the G-20 summit in June 2009. Stiglitz (2009, 13) and the commission identified ten policies that needed to be implemented immediately and "ten deeper reforms to the global financial system on which work needs to begin."

The point is there are more than a few experts out there who understand how these economies work and what needs to be done to restructure the economies of developed, developing, and underdeveloped countries in the context of both global- ization and the world economy itself. Unfortunately, neither the United States nor the other members of the G-20 are willing to make the required substantive changes because these essentially hurt the interests of the privileged few from these countries. Domestically, the only way that special interests will not continue to dominate the US political and economic policies is for the transmission belts of power (e.g., the lobbyists) to be neutralized through campaign finance reform. Otherwise, it will be "business as usual," where the rich and the powerful financial corporations they run will remain beyond incrimination. Hence, these white-collar and corporate acts of questionable and fraudulent intent will continue unabated. We are not calling for stiffer penalties for the unlucky few who end up facing criminal prosecutions, but in- stead, we seek real regulation, control, and oversight of the various financial empires and of their accountants, feeders, and those private investors involved in securitiza- tion. We are also calling for the restructuring of an economic system that works to the advantage of the few at the expense of most everybody else.

Unlike the underpoliced, privileged world of white-collar and corporate crime that victimizes virtually all members of society, the overpoliced, disadvantaged world of marginalized offenders victimizes mostly other poor people, especially those of color. In these differential processes of enforcement and in the context of class and race control, violations are often commonplace. For example, the Detroit, Los An- geles, and New York police departments have been under recent federal investigation for systematic human rights abuses, especially related to members of minority groups and to cases involving mentally or emotionally disturbed individuals who were killed under questionable circumstances. Other reports document police ill treatment of demonstrators, including those protesting against global capitalism and in support of Occupy Wall Street.

Some of the violence in police-citizen encounters and police shootings may be attributed to disturbed officers, alcohol abuse, the game of "cops and robbers," and especially the role of fear. But the bulk of this behavior has more fundamentally to do with issues of respect. As Hans Toch (1990) notes, police violence is often in response to taunts, because

> the officer's self-love is gauged by "respect" from others. "Respect" for law, when a man feels he embodies the law, inspires private wars under color of law. Few officers may be violent, but these are backed by others—by peers who see police bonds as links to survival . . . violent suspects often tend to be counterparts of violent officers. These suspects also prize respect, and view it as a measure of self-esteem. This suggests that much police violence comes about when either party to a confrontation engages the other in a test of respect. Violence becomes probable where issues of self-esteem are mobilized for both contenders. (230)

Where police forces are obsessed with real and imagined dangers and where various communities are in fear of the police, polarization and distance between the two are inevitable. Fear on both sides increases in-grouping and/or protective behavior among police and increased alienation and distrust among citizens, which leads to further isolation, cynicism, and police abuse or violence. Across the United States, for example, the evidence is quite consistent that African Americans represent a disproportionate share of police shooting victims.

There is also evidence that police behavior can change to reduce the discrimination experienced by minorities and other marginal members of society compared with whites and other middle-class people. In the area of racial profiling, for example, media and public scrutiny resulted in changed leadership and in stronger commitments to fairness, the first steps toward reducing biased behavior in policing. One study of racial profiling involving traffic stops and searches in Rhode Island between 2001 and 2005 found that disparities between whites and blacks were "significantly reduced when news media coverage [put] more pronounced pressure on police organizations and police departments" (Warren and Farrell 2009, 52).

While nobody can expect the police to engage in full enforcement of the criminal law and few expect that every observed and reported infraction of the legislative statutes could be formally prosecuted and adjudicated, the selective enforcement and differential application of the rule of law should nevertheless be carefully examined and officially monitored at all times, because individual and organizational discretion by police, prosecutors, and judges have historically reproduced patterns of crime control that adversely affect the poor and marginal members of society while they positively benefit members of the middle and upper classes. These patterns of law enforcement and prosecutorial discretion reflect not only the relations of class, race, and gender but also other factors as well, including but not limited to: the nature of the crime, departmental policies, the relationship between the victim and the offender, the amount of evidence, the preference of the victim, the demeanor of suspects, the legitimacy of the victim, and local politics (Bohm and Haley 2005).

REVIEW AND DISCUSSION QUESTIONS

1. With respect to class control, street and suite crime, and the administration of criminal law, discuss the workings of selective enforcement and differential application. Provide examples.

2. What are some of the reasons for inadequate prosecution of corporate or executive crimes?

3. In terms of race control, how does the criminal justice system work to the disadvantage of minorities and to the advantage of nonminorities? Provide examples.

4. Regarding gender control, use examples to describe the different ways in which men and women offenders are responded to by the administration of criminal justice.

5. How has the identification of criminals been affected by the intersections of at least two of any combination of the three variables—class, race, and gender? Provide examples.

10

Punishment, Sentencing, and Imprisonment

Sentencing guidelines are a grid judges use to calculate an appropriate sentence. The crime a defendant is convicted of is translated into an offense score, and the defendant's criminal history provides another score. The intersection of these scores on the guidelines grid is the appropriate sentencing range. Individual factors about the case and defendant can provide reasons for the judge to sentence in the lower or upper part of that range as well as provide a rationale for more extensive upward or downward departures. In the federal system, the resulting sentence should, among other concerns:

(a) reflect the seriousness of the offense, promote respect for the law, and provide just punishment for the offense;
(b) afford adequate deterrence to criminal conduct; and
(c) protect the public from further crimes of the defendant.

The question for the Eighth Circuit Court of Appeals in U.S. v. Deegan *(08-2299, 2010) was whether the ten-year sentence of Dana Deegan for second-degree murder should be upheld. Deegan is a Native American and gave birth to a live baby in her home on a reservation. According to the court:*

> Deegan fed, cleaned, and dressed him, and then placed him in a basket. She then left the house with her three other children, intentionally leaving the baby alone without food, water, or a caregiver. Deegan did not return to her home for approximately two weeks. When she returned, she found the baby dead in the basket where she had left him.

The sentencing court heard testimony from Dr. Resnick, an expert in "neonaticide," or killing a newborn in the first twenty-four hours after birth. His report noted that Deegan suffered from extensive abuse and depression. He argued that Deegan, like other women who committed neonaticide, presented a low risk of reoffending and that harsh punishment was unlikely to deter others from committing the offense because women who commit this type of offense are usually overwhelmed and have few resources. Also, similar cases in state court typically resulted in probation or a sentence of not more than three years.

The sentencing judge remarked that he had "spent many, many days and nights thinking about the case" and read Resnick's report "at least three times." He noted that Deegan's life had not been "easy." An appeals court, in upholding the ten-year sentence, noted the sentencing court had said he had "'real compassion for [her] and [her] family and what [she had] gone through,' including the fact that she had three children and that her brother had been murdered. The court said that it 'underst[ood] why [Deegan] took the steps that she did.'"

But both courts felt ten years was necessary to "ensure that justice is done," "reflect the seriousness of the offense, to promote respect for the law and to provide just punishment for the offense." The guidelines in effect were "reasonable": "The sentencing guidelines have been in effect for almost 20 years, and they are designed to provide some honesty in sentencing and to achieve some consistency in the federal system, and they're based upon an analysis of hundreds of thousands of cases."

Because Deegan's crime occurred on a reservation, she was subject to federal sentencing guidelines (see chapter 8), so the appeals court did not see the relevance of state court sentences, including a neonaticide by a North Dakota State University student who received probation. The concern about "sentencing disparities among defendants with similar records who have been found guilty of similar conduct" refers "only to disparities among federal *defendants*" (emphasis in the original). The court would have committed an "error" in considering disparities between federal and state sentences.

Judge Bright dissented, saying this "represents the most clear sentencing error that this dissenting judge has ever seen." He provided a fuller account of Deegan's "history of extensive and cruel abuse," starting with the fact that "her alcoholic father beat her on an almost daily basis." Some of the beatings were so bad that she was kept from school to avoid reports to Child Protective Services, although all the children were eventually sent to foster homes, "where she experienced physical abuse from some of her foster family members." Further,

> At five years of age, her father's drinking buddies began sexually abusing her. By age nine, five or six perpetrators had forced her to participate in oral, vaginal, and anal sex. One of the perpetrators held her head under water several times to make her submissive.

In spite of this abuse, Deegan cared for and protected her siblings, even if it meant she suffered additional abuse.

Deegan began a relationship with the son of one of her foster parents. Instead of being a refuge from abuse, the relationship continued it: "Mr. Hale acknowledged in an interview with the FBI that he had physically, emotionally and verbally abused Ms. Deegan on a regular basis." After their third child was born, Deegan became depressed. Hale was abusing her "two to three times per week, forcing her to have sexual intercourse with him, and refusing to care for their children." When she became pregnant with a fourth child—the victim in this case—she was "so depressed that she could barely take care of herself and her three children." They were poor, unemployed and "when Ms. Deegan obtained any money, Mr. Hale took it and bought methamphetamine."

The dissent noted that Resnick, the neonaticide expert, described the mothers who commit this crime as having poor coping skills and inadequate resources. For example, the reservation had few resources, no outreach services, and no domestic violence shelters. North Dakota had no "safe haven law"—allowing parents to drop off babies at hospitals or police stations without question or criminal punishment. (In the years after North Dakota passed such a law, more than one thousand babies were dropped off; all states now have such a law.)

While Deegan's situation was typical for neonaticide, the dissent noted that neonaticide was not a crime that was included in the sentencing guidelines for second-degree murder—and the guidelines were to create a standard for similar cases and similarly situated offenders. The guidelines "carve out a 'heartland' of typical cases" and provide an approach for sentencing ordinary cases that falls within that heartland. But, in response to his query, the US Sentencing Commission did some research, and of 157,000 cases it could examine electronically, the only case of neonaticide was Deegan's. The dissent's own research went back to federal cases since 1975 and found only one other case. "This case falls so far from the heartland of guidelines sentencing that it is a complete stranger to crimes ordinarily charged and considered as second-degree murder." Thus, any presumption of reasonableness that ordinarily applied to a guidelines sentence did not apply here, the judge argued.

Further, Deegan was not likely to reoffend because she had had her tubes tied and thus could not have another baby. Resnick's testimony was that women who committed neonaticide go on to marry and be good mothers, making this a crime "based on circumstances as opposed to bad character." And her circumstances had changed. Indeed, in the nine years between the act and the trial, "she has got her life together, been a good mother and not been a risk to the community."

While the sentencing judge noted he had considered testimony from Deegan's family, the dissent reproduced a letter from Deegan's sister, noting that "our childhood home was a war zone." Further,

> our family has taken great lengths to reconcile the pain and scars that have been left on our souls. Understanding the intergenerational historical trauma of our American Indian Grandfathers and Grandmothers that came before us, has helped my family to forgive and love our father, knowing that he too suffered. Non-Indian people may not easily internalize this sense of loss and powerlessness so deeply ingrained by American Indian people still today. The cultural deprivations and discriminations of our people merely because of our heritage has contributed to the psychological deficits that Dana, at that particular low time in her life, was unable to overcome. I fear that these same cultural factors may also contribute to harsher penalties of an already oppressed woman.

If neonaticide is understood in the state court—and in twenty-six other countries that have infanticide laws that cover neonaticide—as deserving probation or less than three *years in prison, then "the sentence here is unjust, excessive, and treats a woman on the reservation disparately with a woman off the reservation. Does this disparity not indicate another example of unfair treatment of an American Indian living on a reservation?"*

Because of the sentence, Deegan's children will be removed from her care. The prosecutor said this was Deegan's fault—"basically, it was her choice that caused all of this"—and should not be considered when sentencing. But the dissent noted, "There is plenty of blame to go around. Ms. Deegan's father is dead. But what blame should be placed on Mr. Hale who did not support the children he fathered and consistently abused Ms. Deegan? And what about the failures of society to assist Ms. Deegan in her travail?" A number of modest interventions could have prevented the crime. As this dissenting judge argued: "Ms. Deegan has suffered immense cruelty at the hands of her father, his male friends, and the father of her children. Now her lifetime of travail becomes magnified by an unjust and improper prison sentence."

Punishment is an important aspect of the administration of justice in the United States and the effort to control crime. Historically, there have been several rationales or justifications for punishment, based in very different (even contradictory) approaches. Today, basically five rationales are used to explain or justify the various punishments imposed by the criminal courts: retribution, deterrence, rehabilitation, incapacitation, and restoration.

From biblical times through most of US history, the dominant justification of punishment has been retribution, whose essential idea is that the punishment should fit the harm done by the crime. Retribution implies some kind of repayment for an offense committed, with variations in terms of the more emotional *revenge* and the more rational *just desserts*. The former refers to paying the offender back by making him or her suffer; the latter to the proportional punishment deserved for the harm inflicted. Unlike the other rationales for punishment, retribution is the only one that focuses exclusively on the past criminal offense without consideration given to future criminality.

The classical school of criminology (see chapter 2) introduced the rationale of deterrence in the late eighteenth century. Classical theorists such as Beccaria believed that retribution by itself was a waste of time and that the only legitimate purpose for punishment was the prevention (or deterrence) of crime. Other classical theorists such as Bentham were informed by a utilitarian philosophy of "the greatest good for the greatest number," under which the pain of punishment was morally valid if it produced a larger good, such as a reduction in criminal victimization through deterrence or rehabilitation. Sentencing actual offenders so that the punished individual will not engage in future crime involves *specific* deterrence; *general* deterrence refers to preventing other potential offenders from engaging in crime by the example set in punishing specific offenders. With the deterrence rationale, no longer is punishment solely dependent on the nature of the offense. In addition, consideration is focused on offenders—actual and potential—and the deterrent effects to be derived from the severity of the punishment.

Rehabilitation involves the attempt to "correct" the personality and behavior of offenders through educational, vocational, and therapeutic intervention or treatment. The goal of rehabilitation is not based on the fear of punishment but on modifying the character of the offender so that he or she finds crime to be morally unacceptable or on giving the offender skills (education, job training, etc.) so that he or she can secure legitimate employment. "Treatment" may be carried out while an offender is incarcerated or while living in the community at large. Early US efforts were religious in nature, with the *penitentiary* built around the idea of penance, a process through which sins are forgiven after they are confessed with true sorrow and a promise to follow through on the priest's requirements. Penitentiaries gave way to *reformatories*, which offered a wider range of educational and vocational programs, although current "correctional institutions" tend to emphasize warehousing rather than actual correction (Irwin 2006).

Incapacitation usually refers to the removal (or restriction of the freedom) of those who have been convicted of a criminal violation. Typically, misdemeanants are incapacitated in jail with sentences of less than one year, while felons are incapacitated in prison with sentences of more than one year. This rationale emphasizes public safety in that incarcerated offenders, during their period of punishment, are virtually without access to committing further crimes in the free world. Two kinds of incapacitation are currently practiced in the United States: collective and selective. Collective incapacitation refers to sanctions applied to offenders without regard to their personal characteristics. Belonging to the offending crime categories such as violent offender, drug dealer, or child molester would qualify one for a lengthy prison sentence regardless of the circumstances involved in the offense. Selective incapacitation refers to efforts to identify high-risk offenders based on their criminal histories, drug use, schooling, employment records, and so on, and to set them apart from other offenders of the same group.

The newest rationale of punishment, restoration, refers both to restoring or making victims of crime whole through various forms of victim compensation programs and to successfully reintegrating offenders with their communities. Unlike the other forms of punishment, which focus almost exclusively on offenders and their punishments, *restorative justice* seeks to restore or repair the health of the community, meet the needs of victims, and involve the offender in the processes of restoration. Restitution and community service are two common forms of restorative practice by which convicted offenders, as part of their sentences, are required to pay money or provide services to their victims, their victims' survivors, or their community.

Currently, all of these punishment rationales are in use, although more than thirty years of "tough on crime" rhetoric and practice indicate retribution plays a primary role. During this period, legislation advanced as being tough on crime as well as "sentencing reform" that had the same aim, including: mandatory sentences; truth in sentencing (mandating federal offenders serve a minimum of 85 percent of their sentence); "habitual offender" laws (requiring enhanced prison terms for repeat felony offenders, in some cases regardless of the pettiness of the offense); "three strikes and you're out" (mandatory life sentences after repeat convictions); and moves to increase the number of offenses that count as strikes (see the opening narrative of chapter 8 about Leandro Andrade). Further, even while the rest of the world moved away from the death penalty, the United States has expanded the number of offenses that can potentially result in execution.

As a result of more people going to prison *and* those going to prison serving longer sentences, state and federal incarceration rates have increased dramatically, as shown in figure 10.1. As the financial crisis has hit various states, some have started to reduce their prison population. A substantial amount of the decrease is in California because of a 2011 Supreme Court order in *Brown v. Palta* to release 37,000 inmates in order to bring the system down to 137.5 percent of capacity (from 200 percent at the time of the original filing) and remedy conditions that the court found are causing "needless suffering and death" (09-1233, 3).

When looking at jail inmates as well as state and federal prisoners, the numbers have declined less than 100,000 since their peak in 2009 and were just over 2.2 million at the end of 2012 (Bureau of Justice Statistics 2013b, table 2). In addition, just under 4.8 million adults are under "community supervision," which means parole or probation. So about 6.9 million people—about one in every thirty-five adults—are under some form of supervision by the correctional system.

While incarceration rates from other countries are not always perfectly comparable, the picture still emerges that the United States leads the world with the highest incarceration rates, including rates of both developed and developing nations. This

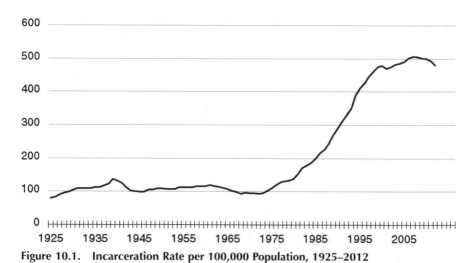

Figure 10.1. Incarceration Rate per 100,000 Population, 1925–2012

Source: Based on data from *Sourcebook of Criminal Justice Statistics*, table 6.28.2012.

is not a new phenomenon and dates back to at least the 1990s. Incarceration rates per 100,000, according to the International Centre for Prison Studies (2013), are as follows for the United States and selected developed nations:

- United States, 716 (2011)
- Russian Federation, 475 (2013)
- South Africa, 294 (2013)
- Brazil, 274 (2012)
- Mexico, 210 (2013)
- United Kingdom: England and Wales, 148 (2013)
- Australia, 130 (2012)
- China, 121 (2012)
- Canada, 118 (2011)
- Denmark, 73 (2013)
- Japan, 51 (2013)
- India, 30 (2012)

Importantly, criminologists have never been able to draw a connection between increases in incarceration and fluctuating crime rates (Currie 1998; Platt and Takagi 1980; Reiman and Leighton 2013). DiMascio (1998, 237) affirms: "Putting offenders behind bars may keep them from committing more crimes while they are there, but no significant overall deterrent effect has yet been proven." While many point to the decline in crime rates over the past ten years as "proof" that incarceration is effective at lowering the crime rate, this short term analysis overlooks how incarceration rates have been increasing for more than three decades, and during much of that time crime was also increasing (Selman and Leighton 2010). Figure 10.2 shows the lack of correlation between violent crime rates and state plus federal incarceration rates.

While most criminologists do not deny the increased incarceration rate has had some impact on crime, overall estimates tend to be low. Alfred Blumstein, based on his research for the book *The Crime Drop in America* (Blumstein and Wallman 2000), suggests that 25 percent of the reduction in crime is attributable to incarceration, although Harvard sociologist Bruce Western argues it is closer to 10 percent (see, generally, Reiman and Leighton 2013, 18–19). Although his estimate is in the upper range, John Conklin agrees in his 2003 book, *Why Crime Rates Fell*, but he also notes "the expansion of the inmate population certainly incurred exorbitant costs, both in terms of its disastrous impact on the lives of offenders and their families and in terms of the huge expenditure of tax revenue" (2003, 200).

While prison does prevent some crime by incarcerating offenders and perhaps offers some deterrence, it also has some negative side effects that counteract some of its public safety benefits. For example, prisons function as "schools for crime" by deepening an inmate's ties with other criminals, subjecting them to an environment that undermines personal responsibility and offers little rehabilitation. Ex-cons have

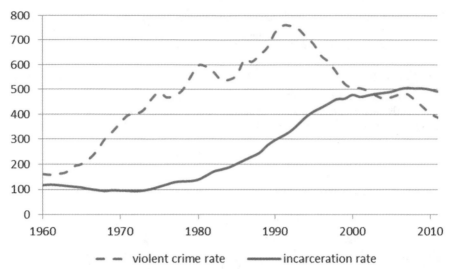

Figure 10.2.   Violent Crime and Incarceration Rates, 1960–2011

Source: Sourcebook of Criminal Justice Statistics, tables 6.28.2012 and 1.106.2009; UCR 2012, table 1.

reduced job possibilities because of their criminal records, and cynicism about the law and justice may reduce their commitment to obey the law. Prisons have crimino-genic (crime-producing) effects not only on individuals but also on family formation and on community well-being. For example, the children of inmates do less well in school and are more likely to become delinquent; under conditions of mass incarceration, the moving back and forth of offenders between prison and home leads to community disorganization (Reiman and Leighton 2013, 18–19).

In 2010, all governments spent over $80 billion on corrections (Bureau of Justice Statistics 2010, table 1). This number is based on current operations only and thus substantially underestimates corrections spending because it does not include new prison construction—a big expense that frequently comes out of capital budgets or is supported by issuing bonds. All this corrections spending comes with what economists call an opportunity cost: money spent here cannot fund other programs. Some trade-offs are inevitable, but increasingly, states are cutting budgets for schools, education, drug and alcohol treatment, and crime prevention programs that seek to create law-abiding citizens rather than simply punish them after a criminal act. One criminologist likens this tactic to "mopping the water off the floor while we let the tub overflow. Mopping harder may make some difference in the level of the flood. It does not, however, do anything about the open faucet" (Currie 1985, 85).

The US incarceration binge has been not only expensive and ineffective but also a source of injustice. Normally, sentencing and incarceration are the culmination of the criminal justice system, where criminals get what they deserve. But as the sections that follow explain, incarceration is almost exclusively for poor criminals. It is disproportionate for minorities—so much so that the movement of black men into prison and back into the community is creating disorganization and eroding informal social controls that help prevent crime. And though women represent a small portion of the incarcerated population, their sentences raise questions about gender and "equal justice."

CLASS AND THE PUNISHMENT OF OFFENDERS

Critics of the variability or disparity in sentencing have documented historical patterns of institutionalized discrimination against people of color and the poor (Lynch, Patterson, and Childs 2008; Mann and Zatz 1998; Platt and Takagi 1980; Reiman and Leighton 2013). Significant inequalities are also described in the two previous chapters—inequalities that favor the rich through legislation defining what a criminal violation is and secondarily through differential law enforcement, prosecutorial discretion, and superior legal resources. The legislative and court processes taken together have consistently failed to criminalize the *analogous social harms* of the rich and powerful or have "decriminalized" them through nonenforcement or with "slaps on the wrist." During the same period, these same legal institutions have consistently ratcheted upward the severity of pain and punishment for the poor and/or powerless.

In 2005, an oil refinery in Texas City belonging to BP exploded, killing 15 and injuring 170. Several investigations, including one by the US Chemical Safety and Hazard Board, traced maintenance problems to budget cuts (to increase profit) and noted that many ignored safety measures could have prevented the explosion. Carolyn Merritt, appointed by President Bush to chair the US Chemical Safety Hazard Board, noted, "The problems that existed at BP Texas City were neither momentary nor superficial. They ran deep through that operation of a risk denial and a risk blindness that was not being addressed anywhere in the organization" (quoted in Whiteside 2006). When asked on CBS's *60 Minutes* "if she thinks this accident could have been easily prevented, Merritt says, 'Absolutely'" (Whiteside 2006).

The plant had been built in the 1930s and was in "bad repair" when BP acquired it in 1999 (Knutson 2010). A 1992 OSHA citation specifically singled out a part called blowdown drums, which help release overpressure and failed in the 2005 explosion. After the acquisition, BP cut inspectors and maintenance workers and eliminated safety calendars. A 2002 outside audit found "serious concerns about the potential for a major site incident," and safety audits in the next two years noted similar problems (Knutson 2010). BP headquarters wanted more cuts to increase profits, even after an outside auditor surveyed one thousand employees and reported that they had an "exceptional degree of fear."

BP had to settle civil wrongful death suits and injury suits, and it had to pay a $21 million fine levied by the Occupational Safety and Health Administration. But as far as the criminal law went, BP pled guilty to one violation of the federal Clean Air Act; it agreed to a $50 million fine, made safety upgrades to the plant, and was on probation for three years (T. Fowler 2009). Many victims protested the fine in light of BP's profits, which were more than $22 billion in 2006—about $50 million a day. In a challenge to the plea bargain, BP stated that the penalty was sufficiently "harsh" and the felony criminal prosecution is an "extraordinary outcome to a workplace accident, even an accident that results in multiple fatalities" (quoted in Collette 2008). The company reviewed three thousand records involving three or more fatalities and found only four criminal prosecutions.

Obviously, the fine did not do much to deter BP, because in 2009, OSHA alleged that BP had failed in 270 cases to comply with the terms of agreements and found 439 new "egregious and willful" safety violations at the plant (Knutson 2010). The fine was $87 million—the largest in OSHA's history—for problems that included failure to review, upgrade, and inspect critical systems that resulted in the earlier refinery explosion. (Indeed, in the four years following the blast, four more workers died and two chemical releases sent 130 people to the hospital.)

Chapter 8 noted how "serious violations—those that pose a substantial probability of death or serious physical harm to workers—are subject to a maximum civil penalty of only $7,000" by OSHA. But that is a maximum, and in 2010 the average penalty for a serious violation was $1,000—and that was after some administrative adjustments to the schedule of fines to make it tougher. In 2007, the median initial penalty for cases involving the death of a worker was $5,900; the median final penalty after settlement was $3,675 (Reiman and Leighton 2013, 92).

Holding corporations and/or their executives accountable can be difficult because their financial resources or "deep pockets" give them numerous advantages, which can be seen in the outbreak of Enron-style corporate fraud that included Health South, Adelphia, WorldCom, Global Crossing, Xerox, Waste Management, and others. In commenting on these corporate frauds, William Greider (2005, 4) captures the spirit of this contradictory approach to "getting tough" on crime when he writes: "In the deregulated realm of U.S. banking and finance, crime does occasionally pay for its foul deeds, not in prison time but by making modest rebates to the victims." For example, the WorldCom and Enron swindles could not have been accomplished without the ingenious balance sheet deceptions that required the active participation of financiers at Citigroup, JPMorgan Chase, and other leading banks. A *Wall Street Journal* editorial called the banks "Enron Enablers" (in Leighton and Reiman 2002), and a cover of the mainstream business publication *Fortune* magazine included the title: "Partners in Crime: The Untold Story of How Citi, JPMorgan Chase and Merrill Lynch Helped Enron Pull Off One of the Greatest Scams Ever" (quoted in Leighton and Reiman 2004). An earlier *Fortune* story commented, "They appear to have behaved in a guileful way and helped their corporate clients undertake unsavory practices. And they appear to have had an entire division that, among other things, helped corporations avoid taxes and manipulate their balance sheets through something called structured finance, which is a huge profit center for each bank" (in Leighton and Reiman 2002).

For its role in the WorldCom fraud, Citigroup, the biggest and most blatant of Wall Street offenders at the turn of the twenty-first century, paid $2.65 billion in fines to cheated investors as a result of civil—not criminal—suits. Similarly, for their roles in the Enron conning of thousands of investors and pensioners, Citigroup and JPMorgan Chase settled their lawsuits with the Securities and Exchange Commission (SEC) in June 2005 by agreeing to provide $2 billion and $2.2 billion, respectively, to some of the injured parties. These fines sound like a lot of money; however, considering that shareholders and pension funds lost more than $60 billion on Enron alone, such punishments are actually petty.

As spelled out in the opening narrative of chapter 8, habitual offender laws apply to street crimes but not suite crimes. In the case of Citigroup, this global behemoth in international banking continued to engage in questionable banking practices and to grow despite its numerous fraudulent collaborations with other corporate giants such as Global Crossing, Dynegy, and Adelphia. Rather than face incarceration for executives or a breakup of the company, in 2008 the Federal Reserve declared that Citigroup was "too big to fail." As of the summer of 2009, Citigroup had already "received $45 billion in taxpayers' money, along with guarantees on $300 billion in toxic assets, to mitigate its reckless risk-taking during the reign of such obscenely rewarded (and now departed) executives as Charles Prince and Robert Rubin" (Rich 2009b, WK8). The bank that is too big to fail not only increased credit card interest rates (to nearly 30 percent in some cases) on the taxpayers whose money bailed them out but also raised its own base salaries by 50 percent.

This pattern continues with civil—not criminal—settlements for financial institutions and executives after the 2008 financial crisis. For example, Goldman Sachs settled in 2010 an SEC suit for $550 million for misleading investors about a subprime mortgage product called Abacus. Another firm, Countrywide, grew quickly to become one of the largest mortgage lenders by steering people into expensive subprime loans. Angelo Mozilo, its CEO, settled with the SEC for $67.5 million for assuring investors "that Countrywide was primarily a prime quality mortgage lender that had avoided the excesses of its competitors" just before the firm was spared bankruptcy by being sold to Bank of America.

These penalties might seem high. But consider that Goldman's penalty came after the government gave it $12.9 billion because it was a counterparty to AIG, which the government was rescuing with taxpayer money and paying AIG counterparties at very generous valuations (Walsh 2009). In the year of the SEC settlement, Goldman Sachs had revenue of $39 billion and posted profits of $8.35 billion, even after paying the half-billion-dollar SEC fine (Goldman Sachs 2011). Of Mozilo's $67.5 million settlement, Countrywide paid $20 million of it for him, leaving him personally on the hook for $47.5 million to pay from his total compensation of $521.5 million from 2000 to 2008. Indeed, Mozilo made $140 million on stocks he sold between November 2006 and October 2007, and the Department of Justice will not pursue criminal charges against him (Morgenson 2010).

Nobel Prize–winning economist Joseph Stiglitz puts these cases into the larger perspective: "Yeah, we fine them, and what is the big lesson? . . . You're still sitting home pretty with your several hundred million dollars that you have left over after paying fines that look very large by ordinary standards but look small compared to the amount that you've been able to cash in." Ultimately, "the fine is just a cost of doing business," and "we ought to go do what we did in the S&L [crisis] and actually put many of these guys in prison" (Stiglitz 2010). Barry Ritholtz, the author of *Bailout Nation*, agrees that fines have become a cost of doing business, with the government playing the role of a "meter maid" giving out parking tickets. But when we are "trying to reduce or eliminate a behavior with extremely negative repercussions for society, we bring out the big stick: Jail time" (Ritholtz 2013).

Sentences for some of those caught up in the corporate frauds have been long, certainly in comparison to previous sentences for white-collar crime (Leighton and Reiman 2004). For example, Bernard Ebbers received twenty-five years for his role as CEO of WorldCom, which filed for bankruptcy just after Enron and displaced it as the largest corporate bankruptcy in American history. The sentence is worth investigating, as it is one that has made people question whether we have gone "too far" in punishing corporate crime. In upholding the sentence, the U.S. Court of Appeals states, "The securities fraud here was not puffery or cheerleading or even a misguided effort to protect the company." Rather, "the methods used were specifically intended to create a false picture of profitability even for professional analysts that, in Ebbers' case, was motivated by his personal financial circumstances" (quoted in Reiman and Leighton, 2010, 96). While Ebbers had no criminal history, the sentence length was determined by the severity of the crime. The court described the calculation:

> The pre-sentence report ("PSR") recommended a base offense level of six, plus sentencing enhancements of 26 levels for a loss over $100 million, of four levels for involving more than 50 victims, of two levels for receiving more than $1 million from financial institutions as a result of the offense, of four levels for leading a criminal activity involving five or more participants, and of two levels for abusing a position of public trust. With Ebbers' criminal history category of I, the Guidelines range calculated in the PSR was life imprisonment. The Probation Department recommended a 30-year sentence. Judge Jones declined to apply the enhancements for deriving more than $1 million from financial institutions or for obstruction of justice. She also denied Ebbers' motions for downward departures based on the claims that the loss overstated the seriousness of the offense, his medical condition was poor, and he had performed many beneficial community services and good works. She determined that the advisory Guidelines range would be 30 years to life. She then sentenced Ebbers to 25 years' imprisonment and three years' supervised release, and imposed a $900 special assessment but no fines. (Quoted in Reiman and Leighton 2010, 96–97)

One question that comes up is whether Ebbers deserved a sentence longer than some people get for murder. But it is not inherently outrageous to say that causing $100 million in losses to more than fifty victims while leading a criminal activity involving others and a breach of public trust can be worse than taking one life. It is also true that his sentence was less than what Andrade received for two residential burglaries and two shoplifting charges over the course of decades (see chapter 8).

Perhaps such a sentence would not have been reasonable in the past, but the scale of financial crimes was also smaller then. The S&L losses were significantly smaller than the losses from WorldCom or Enron. Companies are now bigger, more powerful, and fraud—especially when it leads to a company's collapse—leaves a much larger financial crater. More people get hurt, and the losses are much more severe; there are more powerful ripple effects (including unemployment) through associated businesses and the economy in general (Reiman and Leighton 2010, 99). While the sentence is long, note that the judge declined to apply several other enhancements. The court's opinion also notes that the sentence is based on a $100 million loss estimate, when "a loss calculation of $1 billion is therefore almost certainly too low" (quoted in Reiman and Leighton 2010, 100).

Further, attention has focused disproportionately on a relatively small number of Enron-era sentences that are in the range of fifteen to thirty years. These were not run-of-the-mill white-collar crimes but systemic and widespread frauds that undermined the public's faith in the financial system and caused extensive harm to employees, communities, and shareholders. For example, the judge sentencing Enron's Jeffrey Skilling noted that he had "imposed on hundreds if not thousands of people a life sentence of poverty" (C. Johnson 2006). Focusing on the extreme cases gives a distorted sense of the overall picture of sentencing. An article in the *Federal Sentencing Reporter* (Barker et al. 2008) tracked 440 of the highest-profile cases of corporate fraud from the Enron era and found that by and large, the harsh sentences were reserved for those who went to trial and lost, although "the largest concentration of white-collar criminals convicted at trial received five-to-ten-year sentences."

Guilty pleas accounted for 57 percent of the cases, and only two of those defendants received sentences of more than fifteen years: "The vast majority of those who plead received sentences of fewer than five years—the beneficiaries of sentencing guidelines that reward cooperation" (Barker et al. 2008). So a substantial number of those involved in the biggest financial scandal up to that point in time ended up with fewer than five years in prison, which is equivalent to the mandatory sentence triggered by possession of five grams of crack cocaine. Those who were found guilty at trial did receive longer sentences, although a final assessment needs to wait until we see how much actual time they serve because of reductions for good time and participation in rehabilitation programs.

While people in the developed world seem not to understand what is going on, economist Stiglitz wrote: "In the developing world, people look at Washington and see a system of government that allowed Wall Street to write self-serving rules which put at risk the world economy—and then, when the day of reckoning came, turned to Wall Street to manage the recovery. They see continued re-distributions of wealth to the top of the pyramid, transparently at the expense of ordinary citizens" (quoted in Rich 2009b, WK8). Alyssa Katz argues in *Our Lot: How Real Estate Came to Own Us* (2009) that the real-estate bubble, like the Wall Street bubble, was a crime scene. But unlike other crimes, there are few chargeable criminal offenses and little punishment.

More generally, in the "old days" at least, Enron and WorldCom were allowed to fail and file for bankruptcy; under the current economic regime, some financial institutions are too big to fail. As for the future, without the proper regulatory rules in place, the financial executives and their government enablers will continue to loot the general taxpayer and consumer without any negative consequences for themselves. And although the criminal justice system has really come down hard on some recent cases here and there, the powers of crime control are still largely disengaged from addressing the structural problems of the economy and financial fraud. Similarly, whatever toughness may have prevailed on a relatively few corporate offenders, it has been limited to a narrow range of financial offenses and has not spread to other types of white-collar crimes such as willful violations of health and safety laws that result in death; these are still punishable by six months in prison—half the penalty for harassing a wild burro on federal land (see chapter 8).

While wealthy offenders for more serious offenses are often weeded out on the way to prison, poor offenders, often for less serious offenses, find themselves on the "fast track" to prison. In 2002—the last year these data were reported—29 percent of jail inmates were unemployed prior to arrest. Of those employed prior to arrest, 29.3 percent indicated that their position was part-time or "occasional," and 44.9 percent of jailed inmates made less than $7,200 per year (Bureau of Justice Statistics 2004c, 9).

These legal realities are even more pronounced when it comes to the administration of the death penalty in the United States. Sister Helen Préjean, author of *Dead Man Walking* (1993), has pointed out: "The death penalty is a poor person's issue. Always remember that after all the rhetoric that goes on in the legislative assemblies, in the end, when the deck is cast out, it is the poor who are selected to die in this country" (Préjean 1995). On this point, Robert Johnson (1998), death penalty researcher and author of *Death Work*, concurs: "In America, and indeed around the world, members of poor and other marginal groups have been selected for the gallows with disturbing regularity."

Although societies are "quick" to execute the poor, the ultimate punishment of death is not sought when the poor are killed. Préjean (1995) contends, "When the victim is poor, when the victim is a nobody, when the victim is homeless or a person of color— not only is the ultimate punishment not sought to avenge the death, but the case is not even seriously prosecuted." This pattern tells the poor and minorities that not only are they expendable, but their lives are not worth killing for. By contrast, wealthy individuals are more likely to "get away with murder" either literally or figuratively when they victimize the poor rather than someone closer to their own social class.

RACE AND THE PUNISHMENT OF OFFENDERS

The United States is the world leader for the rate at which it incarcerates its citizens, and minorities are overrepresented in the penal system, so they bear the brunt of this trend. Long before gaining this status as the leader in incarceration, the United States had significantly higher rates of punishment for minorities handed out by the criminal justice system. The disparities between whites and minorities, especially among blacks, Hispanics, and Native Americans, are glaring because they reflect the cumulative biases from all stages of criminal justice administration in addition to other contributing factors, as indicated in figure 10.3.

The cumulative effect of these biases is striking and growing more intense with time, even though the black imprisonment rates for both males and females have decreased recently. Most striking is the rate of incarceration in state and federal prisons compared with the respective populations, as shown in table 10.1. For example, the incarceration rate at year-end 2012 for white men is 483 per 100,000 population, compared with 2,841 for black men, and with Hispanic or Latino men in between. There is a similar pattern for women, with the rate for white women less than half of that for black women.

While the discussion of intersections later in this chapter further explores the race and gender breakdown, table 10.2 provides a breakdown of the incarceration rate by race and ethnicity for jails and prisons. The third column hints at the cumulative impact incarceration policies have had on the current population by indicating the percentage of the current population that has been to prison. The final column provides the likelihood of incarceration in prison based on the incarceration rate of

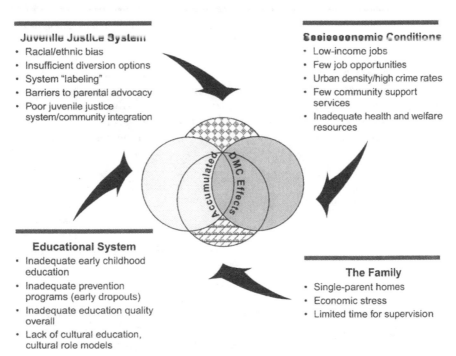

Juvenile Justice System
- Racial/ethnic bias
- Insufficient diversion options
- System "labeling"
- Barriers to parental advocacy
- Poor juvenile justice system/community integration

Socioeconomic Conditions
- Low-income jobs
- Few job opportunities
- Urban density/high crime rates
- Few community support services
- Inadequate health and welfare resources

Educational System
- Inadequate early childhood education
- Inadequate prevention programs (early dropouts)
- Inadequate education quality overall
- Lack of cultural education, cultural role models

The Family
- Single-parent homes
- Economic stress
- Limited time for supervision

Figure 10.3. Underlying Factors That Contribute to Minority Overrepresentation

Table 10.1.　Imprisonment Rates of Sentenced State and Federal Prisoners, Year-End 2012 (per 100,000 US Residents)

	All[a]	*White[b]*	*Black[b]*	*Hispanic*	*Other[a,b]*
Males	909	463	2,841	1,158	972
Females	63	49	115	64	90

Source: BJS. "Prisoners in 2012: Trends in Admissions and Releases, 1991–2012," table 18.

Note: Counts based on prisoners with sentences of more than one year under the jurisdiction of state or federal correctional officials. Imprisonment rate is the number of prisoners under state or federal jurisdiction with a sentence of more than one year per 100,000 US residents of corresponding sex, age, and race/ethnicity. Resident population estimates are from the US Census Bureau for January 1 of the following year. Illinois and Nevada did not submit 2012 data to the National Prisoner Statistics Program, so their jurisdiction counts are imputed.

[a] Includes American Indians, Alaska Natives, Asians, Native Hawaiians, other Pacific Islanders, and persons identifying two or more races.

[b] Excludes persons of Hispanic or Latino origin.

2001, which means that blacks are about five times more likely to go to prison in their lifetime and about one in five blacks will serve time in a state or federal prison. BJS does not publish racial breakdowns of parole and probation populations, so the racial breakdown of people under control of the criminal justice system is unknown.

The analysis of cumulative likelihoods of incarceration is important because this population still suffers from the stigma of arrest records, which makes employment more difficult, and it carries the burden of a number of "invisible punishments" that reinforce social exclusion and marginalization (Travis 2002). Arrest and incarceration take people away from jobs and connections to the labor market and establish a barrier to future employment because of the gap in employment history and the requirement of disclosing the conviction. Former National Institute of Justice director Jeremy Travis has also noted a number of punishments that continue after release, even though one has supposedly served the time for the crime. For example, those

Table 10.2.　Incarceration Rates by Race and Ethnicity

	No. of People in Prison and Jail (per 100,000), 2010	*% of Adult Population Ever Incarcerated in 2001*	*% Ever Going to Prison during Lifetime If Born in 2001*
White	380	1.4	3.4
Black	2,207	8.9	18.6
Hispanic	966	4.3	10.0

Source: BJS 2003, "Prevalence of Imprisonment in the U.S. Population, 1974–2001," tables 5 and 9; Prison Policy Initiative. "Incarceration Rates by Race and Ethnicity, 2010," http://www.prisonpolicy.org/graphs/raceinc.html.

convicted of certain types of crimes lose their right to vote, hold certain professional licenses, and receive benefits such as access to public housing, unemployment benefits, food stamps, and student loans (Travis 2002; see also Alexander 2012). These policies make it much more difficult for offenders to reenter society by denying access to affordable housing, denying them a source of legitimate income, and erecting barriers to the education and professional credentials necessary to enter the workforce.

Further, large numbers of formerly incarcerated people in a community can have negative effects on it as well. For example, incarceration "reduce[s] the marriageability of men and thereby reduces marriage formation. This, in turn, would increase the number of female-headed households in areas with high incarceration rates and, ultimately, increase crime rates due to an absence of supervision for young males in" areas of high incarceration (Lynch and Sabol 2000, 15). Criminologists also raise concerns about social disorganization from the removal ("coerced migration") of residents to prison and having them dumped back into the community with few resources—either not rehabilitated or ultimately worse off for their time in prison.

Todd Clear has summarized the point by stating that "very high concentrations of incarceration may well have a negative impact on public safety by leaving communities less capable of sustaining the informal social control that undergirds public safety" (2002, 181–82; see also Clear 2008). This is not a critique of prison in general but an analysis of how the effects of mass incarceration, when concentrated in areas with few resources such as inner cities, can erode informal social controls such as family, neighborhoods, and community groups. The results can mean the creation of criminogenic conditions, which are a potential exception to the general rule that incarceration adds to public safety by removing problem individuals from the community. If too many individuals are removed, especially for nonviolent offenses, the result could be different from the intended effect.

The increased rate of incarceration fueled a prison construction boom in rural, and thus white, areas, with important racial consequences. Because of globalization and other economic trends, manufacturing and related jobs have disappeared from the United States. To make up for lost jobs, many communities actively lobbied for a prison with unrealistic and exaggerated expectations about the economic development it would bring (Huling 2002). Having rural white guards oversee largely minority inner-city inmates creates problems with racial harassment. Also, for purposes of the census, inmates are counted as residents where they are incarcerated, not where their home is. As a result, the population of largely white rural areas gets a boost, while cities show lower numbers of residents (Huling 2002; see, generally, prisonersofthecensus.org). Using the census figures to allocate legislators to the state and the US Congress, as well as to distribute large amounts of government aid, therefore works against minority populations.

Collectively, higher rates of imprisonment for blacks and Hispanics also limit their abilities to participate in the political process and to effect changes in the system, criminal justice or otherwise. Several million Americans are currently or permanently disenfranchised from voting, including one in eight black males of voting age. According to the Sentencing Project in 2010, forty-eight states and the District of Columbia prohibit offenders from voting while on parole or probation, and fourteen states have reserved the right to permanently ban felons from voting (Porter 2010). When combined with population counts that affect legislators and financial aid, the sum total of these dynamics is to disadvantage racially diverse cities with large numbers of minority residents who have committed no crimes while economically and politically privileging white areas.

A final significant issue with race and punishment is the death penalty, which is exercised less frequently each year, although it is of great symbolic importance because it represents one of the ultimate exercises of state power. BJS claims that at year-end 2011, 55 percent of death row inmates are white and 42 percent are black (2013a, 1), but these figures are the result of classifying most Latinos as white. A table in the *Sourcebook* for April 2012 shows that whites make up 43 percent of death row, blacks are almost 42 percent, and Hispanics are about 12 percent (table 6.80.2012).

A forum sponsored by the American Bar Association on the death penalty reveals some of the deeper problems. For example, in capital cases, prosecutors routinely move to exclude all black jurors on the grounds that such jurors would not only be sympathetic to black defendants but also to white defendants, because they are generally less supportive of the death penalty than whites are. James Coleman argues:

> This can be traced to the legacy of our antebellum criminal justice system, in which slaves and free blacks were not considered equals and in which more severe punishment was accepted as normal. I think the country still believes that black defendants deserve more severe punishment . . . especially when the victim of the crime is white. The criminal justice system will never be fair or nondiscriminatory until it is administered by both black and white citizens, until prosecutors and jurors are forced routinely to deal with the experiences of black people and to factor those experiences into their decisions. There is no such thing as a race-neutral decision in the criminal justice system, when it affects black people and when their voice is not part of the discussion leading to the decision. (Quoted in Acker et al. 1998, 171)

While the overt discrimination has been reduced over time, disparity still remains. David Baldus, one of the foremost authorities on the subject, has explained, "The risk of race effects was very low in the most aggravated capital cases; however, in the *mid-range* cases, where the 'correct' sentence was less clear, and the room for exercise of discretion much broader, the race disparities are much stronger" (quoted in Acker et al. 1998, 172). But even where the "correct" sentence was clear, the actual guilt of the convicted person can still be an issue along racial lines. That is, while exonerations of death-row inmates make headlines, the racial pattern of wrongful convictions has received less attention. But a study published in the American Bar Association's *Criminal Justice* magazine examined 107 cases of people on death row who were wrongfully convicted. Of these exonerated inmates, 58 percent were minority defendants—45 percent were black, and another 13 percent were other minorities (Parker, DeWees, and Radelet 2003).

Finally, Leigh Bienen points out the plight of blacks in a system where whites hold the power, although her words are a reminder about the mix of class and racial discrimination in the use of the death penalty:

> The criminal justice system is controlled and dominated by whites, although the recipients of punishment, including the death penalty, are disproportionately black. The death penalty is a symbol of state control and white control over blacks. Black males who present a threatening and defiant persona are the favorites of those administering the punishment, including the overwhelming middle-aged white, male prosecutors who—in running for election or re-election—find nothing gets them more votes than demonizing young black men. The reasons for this have more to do with the larger politics of the country than with the death penalty. I would also argue that the class and economic discrimination affecting the death penalty are "worse," in the sense of being more unjust, than the racial elements. (Quoted in Acker et al. 1998, 171–72)

GENDER AND THE PUNISHMENT OF OFFENDERS

The environments of women's prisons are generally less oppressive than those of men's because there is less violence, conflict, interracial tension, and hostility toward staff. But women may experience imprisonment more negatively than men because of women inmates' separation from their family, especially children. Other contributing factors to this negativity are scarcity of resources, including a lack of work programs, vocational curriculum, and health services (compared with men's facilities); sexual harassment and abuse from prison staff; and fewer distinctions or classifications when it comes to custody and security levels (i.e., many states operate only one major prison for women).

As of year-end 2012, women made up about 7 percent of prison inmates. There were 108,772 female inmates in state and federal prisons compared with 1,461,625 males (Bureau of Justice Statistics 2013b, appendix table 6). However, for the past fifteen years, incarceration rates for females have grown faster than incarceration rates for men. Between 1995 and 2010, for example, the male prison population grew 41.6 percent while the female population grew 63.6 percent (*Stat Abs* 2013, table 357). Table 10.3 illustrates the recent rates as well as the faster projected growth in the number of women who will spend time in prison.

Because there are fewer women in prison does not mean the sentencing system is fair with respect to gender. Indeed, compared with men, women are differently situated with respect to crime, most notably in that they typically commit less serious crimes than men do, engage in less violent crime, and are less likely to have a prior record. With women, "the most common pathways to crime are based on survival (of abuse and poverty) and substance abuse" (Bloom, Owen, and Covington 2003, 52). Thus, women are typically arrested for "survival" crimes, mostly property and

Table 10.3.   Incarceration Rates by Gender

	No. of People in Prison and Jail (per 100,000), 2010	% of Adult Population Ever Incarcerated in 2001	% Ever Going to Prison during Lifetime If Born in 2001
Male	1,352	4.9	11.3
Female	126	0.5	1.8

Source: BJS 2003, "Prevalence of Imprisonment in the U.S. Population, 1974–2001," tables 5 and 9; BJS 2011, *Correctional Populations in the United States, 2010*, appendix table 3. BJS has not included the incarceration rate for prison and jail by gender for 2011 or 2012.

drug-related crimes, including but not limited to bad checks, welfare fraud, and credit card abuse. Such crimes can be related to the gender inequality in the labor market (see chapter 5) and fewer well-paying jobs open to women, although criminal opportunities have a similar gender inequality; even with economic crimes, women do not tend to be drug kingpins, ringleaders of retail theft organizations, or white-collar criminals to nearly the extent men are.

Further, women are disproportionately represented among those incarcerated for public order violations, such as prostitution, begging, and driving under the influence (Warren 2005). Examining more specific crimes within each of these general categories of offenses reveals that women are nearly twice as likely as men to be jailed for larceny/theft and fraud, which probably reflects the greater likelihood of women being arrested for shoplifting and writing bad checks (Harlow 1998). While there are some violent women, reading the statistics about the increasing number of women in jail for assault requires caution because of the effect of mandatory arrest laws discussed in the previous chapter. Indeed, an analysis by the Office of Juvenile Justice and Delinquency Prevention (OJJDP) Girls Study Group found that much of girls' assaultive behavior occurred at home among family members. At an earlier time, such behavior might have resulted in a referral to family services, but criminal justice practices have changed, and not for the better: "Charging girls for behavior arising from family chaos sweeps girls with trauma histories and chaotic families into secure juvenile justice confinement" (F. Sherman 2012, 1593).

Characterizations of the "typical" male and female prisoners are useful for the purpose of appreciating why men typically receive harsher punishments than women and how the diverse needs of men and women call for overlapping yet different kinds of punitive responses. The typical male prisoner at the turn of the twenty-first century was black, twenty-five to twenty-nine years of age, convicted of a violent offense (Gilliard and Beck 1998), and probably the victim of physical and/or sexual abuse or neglect as a child. One study of adult male felons in New York, for example, found that 68 percent reported some form of victimization before age twelve and that around one-third reported severe childhood physical abuse such as being kicked, bitten, burned or scalded, or threatened with a knife or gun (Weeks and Widom 1998). A typical woman prisoner was black, thirty to thirty-four years of age, convicted of a drug offense (Gilliard and Beck 1998), probably the victim of at least one sexual assault or rape (Warren 2005), and probably a mother of at least one child under the age of eighteen, with whom she lived before entering prison.

Unlike male prison inmates, who are usually incarcerated according to different levels of security (i.e., maximum, medium, minimum) and classification by type of offense, women prisoners are likely to be incarcerated at a facility with a diverse population of offenders. As measured on a per-inmate basis, expenditures for women for education, vocational, and other programs have been less than for men. The one notable exception has been for monies spent on health care, where women have received 60 percent more than men do. Reproductive issues are cited as one reason, but in a California investigation on the "state of female corrections," inmates told state legislators that they had not had a mammogram or Pap smear in years (Warren 2005). In fact, the greater expenditures are more likely related to the greater incidences of HIV and AIDS and with greater needs for mental health services.

In short, male facilities typically have more—and more diverse—programs than female facilities do, in part because of the occupational prevalence of stereotypical gender and sex roles and in part because of relatively more resources. Moreover, women's facilities tend to be smaller, fewer in number, and qualitatively different from men's prisons. For example, women's prisons are more likely than men's to have a cottage-style design and are less likely to have intimidating features such as gun towers, high concrete walls, and armed guards. This cottage form of imprisoning inmates dates back to the early twentieth century, when cottages were used to house small groups of women so that they could "live with a motherly matron in a family setting" (Rierden 1997, 7). The legacy of this era has meant that women's prisons are still tending to infantilize and domesticize women while reinforcing gender stereotypes (Belknap 2007). Over time, accommodation has moved toward the confinement model used in men's prisons, designed to hold hundreds of inmates. This development, however, is another example of seeming gender neutrality that is actually based on a male standard (see chapter 5) rather than a genuine effort to address the actual needs of women.

For example, Jill McCorkel's study of a New England women's prison found that "equal treatment" meant that women "received a much-needed law library" but also isolation cells, "boot camps, razor wire fences, and body cavity searches" (2013, 28). This did not make the prison system gender neutral or gender responsive; "it universally masculinized the physical structure of incarceration. In designing the new prison the way that they had, the Department of Corrections made men's prisons the model for *all* prisons" (2013, 28, emphasis in the original).

The problem of seeming gender neutrality can be compounded when classification and risk assessment surveys designed with men are used for women, drug or alcohol programs and staff are not given training about the different needs and expectations of women (Bloom, Owen, and Covington 2003). Further, "national studies, research and national focus group interviews have all identified negative attitudes and cultural stereotypes about the female as major obstacles to supervising women and providing services for them" (24). Women can be seen as "more trouble" than men because of their different style of communication that emphasizes connection and their "expectation that agents will provide help, in terms of concrete assistance in navigating the system and providing other aid" (15).

Another important difference with female inmates is their relationship with children. While a large number of incarcerated men are fathers, 70 percent of female offenders have a child under eighteen and are likely to be the primary caretaker. While "there is significant evidence that the mother-child relationship may hold significant potential for community reintegration," women in prison tend to be isolated because of geography, transportation, economic resources, and the termination of parental rights (Bloom, Owen, and Covington 2003, 56–57). However, after representatives from several states visited a mother-child prison unit in Germany, they became interested in adapting their women's prisons to allow newborns and infants to stay with mothers for up to several years. As the Vera Institute explains, "Research conducted on U.S. programs has found that these programs have a positive impact for both mothers and children. Evaluations of prison nursery programs have shown lower rates of recidivism, an increased likelihood of obtaining child custody post-release, higher rates of mother and child bonding, and self-reported increases in self-esteem and self-confidence" (Subramanian and Shames 2013, 16). However, programs do little to help women with job skills so that they are in a better economic position to support children or enhance their capacity in other ways to set up a life that would involve reunification with children.

Finally, although the Eighth Amendment does not mandate comfortable prisons, such sentences should not include *additional* punishments for women or men. Sexual and other abuses of inmates, particularly male inmates by other male inmates, female inmates by male staff, and juvenile inmates by both, continue to present serious problems in adult and juvenile institutions across the United States. Within women's prisons, inmates frequently form supportive "play family" or "prison family" arrangements, with substantially less inmate-on-inmate violence than in men's prisons. Victimization of female inmates has tended to come from male staff members who use the power differences between them and the inmates to coerce or exploit female inmates. An Amnesty International report noted that there is a "significant difference" between the law in the United States and international standards on the treatment of female inmates. The report, titled "Not Part of My Sentence," was based on a comment made by a female inmate that performing oral sex on male officers was not part of the judge's sentence. But deficits in cross-sex supervision coupled with inadequate procedures for reporting misconduct and fear of retaliation have led to numerous problems (Amnesty International 1999a).

International standards provide that female prisoners should be supervised only by female guards, but sex discrimination laws in the United States mean that men can work in women's prisons and women can work in men's prisons. Thus, "under the laws of the USA, a male guard may watch over a woman, even when she is dressing or showering or using the toilet. He may touch every part of her body when he searches for contraband" (Amnesty International 1999a, 2). In popular culture, sex in women's prison is eroticized, as evidenced by the "chicks in chains" film genre and the "jail babes" dating services that have sprung up to capitalize on the increasing number of women in prison. But the reality is very different, and "women prisoners with histories of abuse may be re-traumatized by sexual harassment and abuse in prison" (Bloom, Owen, and Covington 2003, 26). The result includes posttraumatic stress disorder, depression, "and decreased ability to participate in rehabilitative programs," which ultimately affect reintegration and recidivism (26).

In men's prisons, sexual violence tends to be inmate-on-inmate, and rape functions as a violent rite of passage to convert "men" into "punks" and create hierarchies of power and control, to meet part of the demand for sexual partners, and to establish claims to masculinity. Gresham Sykes (1958) noted that one of the pains of imprisonment was a deprivation of heterosexual contact. In this situation, men have to define "manhood" without women and do so by emphasizing the worst aspects of the male gender role—aggression, domination, and emotional coldness. The victims are symbolically transformed into women and even take on the "womanly" functions of the relationship. Punks will often do household chores that mimic those of the traditional female, such as doing the laundry, making the bunk, making coffee, or cleaning the cell. Prisoner subculture dictates that aggressive penetrative activity is not homosexual, while receptive penetrated activity is considered homosexual. While in prison, "the guys are not as concerned about whom you are in bed with so much as who is in charge, that is, who is doing the (expletive), the penetrating, who is the Man, who is 'normal'" (Tucker 1981). The phrase *homosexual rape* is thus misleading since the overwhelming majority of prisoner rape victims and perpetrators are heterosexual and resume heterosexual behavior when they are released from incarceration.

One strategy some men use to avoid sexual victimization is to "hook up" with another inmate. In exchange for sexual favors, men who fear victimization can pair off with a "Man" or predatory "Wolf" for protection from gang rapes or repeated threats of rape. The resulting relationships do not reflect consensual homosexuality as much as survival-driven behavior. Men who wish to avoid being turned out or who desire to undo its effect must often use violence. Sometimes they must even take on the characteristics of the perpetrator themselves. One Texas inmate explained: "It's fixed where if you're raped, the only way you [can stop the abuse is if] you rape someone else. Yes I know that's fully screwed, but that's how your head is twisted. After it's over you may be disgusted with yourself, but you realize you're not powerless and that you can deliver as well as receive pain. Then it's up to you to decide whether you enjoy it or not" (Human Rights Watch 2001).

INTERSECTIONS AND THE PUNISHMENT OF OFFENDERS

One classic illustration of corporate crime involved the manufacture and distribution of the Dalkon Shield, a birth control device, by the A. H. Robins Company. In 1971, the company started selling the intrauterine device (IUD) as a safe, modern, and effective product. Although A. H. Robins had performed few tests on the device, marketing and promotion went ahead quickly, and by 1975 some 4.5 million IUDs had been distributed. Early reports indicated many problems, including that the tail string from the device hung outside the vagina and wicked bacteria up into the woman's body, and the device was not especially effective at preventing pregnancy, either. Even worse, women suffered from a variety of crippling and life-threatening infections, some of which required emergency hysterectomies; others had unwanted pregnancies that resulted in miscarriages or spontaneous abortions; or, because of infections, they gave birth to children with severe birth defects. Conservative estimates indicated that some 200,000 women were injured (Clinard 1990).

Two court-appointed examiners in 1985 found that Robins had engaged "in ongoing fraud by knowingly misrepresenting the nature, quality, safety and efficacy" of its IUD. The fraud also "involved the destruction and withholding of relevant evidence" (quoted in Clinard 1990, 104). In spite of these facts, no prosecutor brought criminal charges against the company or its executives. Women were left on their own to file a variety of civil product liability suits. In response, Robins tried to file for bankruptcy in order to avoid liability. However, a judge required the company to establish a trust fund to compensate victims, and he had to reprimand Robins for giving substantial bonuses to its top executives in violation of the bankruptcy laws.

Judge Miles Lord, who heard some four hundred civil law cases, in a famous plea for corporate conscience, pointed out the class bias of the judicial process workings:

> If some poor young man was, by some act of his—without authority or consent—to inflict such damage on one woman, he would be jailed for a good portion of the rest of his life. And yet your company, without warning to women, invaded their bodies by the millions and caused them injury by the thousands. And when the time came for these women to make claims against your company, you attacked their characters. You inquired into sexual practices and into the identity of their sex partners. You exposed these women—and ruined families and reputation and careers—in order to intimidate those who would raise their voice against you. You introduced issues that had no relationship whatsoever to the fact that you planted in the bodies of these women instruments of death, of mutilation, of disease. (Quoted in Hills 1987, 42)

Judge Lord also noted that the underlying harm—inflicting harm without consent—is expressed in the street crime of assault and punishable with imprisonment, but there is no analogous crime for corporations. Indeed, A. H. Robins may have been more harshly punished if the victims of its birth control device had included more wealthy women. Or the consequences might have been harsher had the injured parties been men rather than women, who Judge Lord noted "seem through some strange quirk in our society's mores to be expected to suffer pain, shame and humiliation" (quoted in Hills 1987, 42). The executives from Robins ultimately had to listen to a lecture and return some bonus pay as punishment, whereas offenders who engage in other assaults face prison time.

In a different but powerful way, Jill McCorkel's *Breaking Women* illustrates the importance of examining intersections. The book uses the author's four years of observation of a drug program in a women's prison to analyze gender, race, and privatization. As noted earlier, "gender neutrality" means a male model of getting tough, which happens as increasing numbers of African American women arrive in prison. "The rehabilitative ideal died at the very same moment when the number of African Americans behind bars surpassed the number of incarcerated whites" (McCorkel 2013, 13). At this point in time, "staff began to distinguish between prisoners of old ('good girls') and the incoming tide of 'real criminals'" (2013, 16). McCorkel argues that "racial stereotypes of Black women, particularly as welfare dependent, crime prone, and drug addicted, became galvanizing symbols for abandoning the rehabilitative ideal and replacing it with control strategies that were both more coercive and more intrusive than earlier practices" (2013, 13).

One entity seizing on this new perspective was a for-profit company, which introduced a drug treatment plan that was accepted because it is also "tough": it "breaks down" women so they accept that addiction is caused by their diseased "self," which is a "permanent condition" that could be "treated but not cured" with a "lifetime of external management and control" (McCorkel 2013, 56). The program, billed as "habilation" (not "rehabilitation"), consists of verbal abuse of the inmates' mothering, sexuality, and (co)dependence on men and welfare. McCorkel notes that in the Canadian prison system, "prisoners are encouraged to deal with structural issues like poverty and violence by taking responsibility for their own choices and actions, and, ultimately, their own reform" (2013, 151). They seem to take more responsibility for their actions than the state does for the social problems, but the goal is "self-governing, rational and autonomous subjects." But with habilation, there is no building back up, because prisoners are seen as broken beyond repair, which McCorkel argues leads to disempowerment and confusion over their experiences with poverty, violence, and sexual abuse.

The realities of the disproportionate number of poor, blacks, and Hispanics in prison do not necessarily capture how the experience of being incarcerated breeds feelings of despair and hopelessness, and often anger and rage, for those individuals imprisoned, thus impacting their lives. For example, these feelings in combination with the stigma of having been incarcerated often make it difficult to find little else than minimum-wage employment, if that, on release. Moreover, businesses are less likely to locate in areas with large numbers of poor people, especially those with high concentrations of black men, because of concerns about the pool of labor, so these communities find it difficult, if not impossible, to build any type of economically viable base.

Higher rates of black incarceration for men and women weaken both the economic and familiar stability of black and other poor communities (Johnson, Farrell, and Stoloff 1998). Specifically, these correctional practices that disproportionately affect African Americans and other poor minorities have an impact on noncriminal impoverished women and their children (Danner 1998). In other words, as corrections budgets have increased nationwide, state funds to support poor and low-income families have been slashed along with other social services and social-service positions disproportionately staffed by women. These connections show problems with conventional discussions of punishment that tend to treat corrections as if it were a discrete and independent social institution. Far from being an entity separate unto itself, the entire criminal justice system, especially the correctional system, has become inextricably intertwined with the welfare system, the political system, and—with the increasing privatization of corrections—the economic system. For example, the impact of having one in three black men under the control of the criminal justice system cannot be separated from the welfare system's Temporary Assistance to Needy Families (TANF) program or the high percentage of single-female black households. Similarly, the secondary impact of incarceration of poor women on their children cannot be underestimated with respect to the increased likelihood of the children's delinquency.

Further, TANF, created by the Personal Responsibility and Work Opportunity Reconciliation Act of 1996, which replaced the Aid to Families with Dependent Children (AFDC), prohibits individuals who violate probation or parole orders and their families from receiving TANF or food stamps. The act does not distinguish between minor technical violations such as missing an appointment with a probation or parole officer and committing a new crime. Another provision bans persons convicted of drug felonies from receiving TANF or food stamps for the rest of their lives. Consequently, critics of the act were quick to express concern that children would feel the repercussions of provisions intended to punish their mothers and promote "personal responsibility." Hence, children of a poor woman suffer consequences for their mother's behavior in a way that middle-class children would not, should either of their parents be busted for using drugs.

Another important addition to the understanding of intersections comes from examining private prisons. While chapter 2 examined privatization in more detail, of interest here is that the dramatic growth in incarceration has attracted the interest of numerous business owners who see prison as a "growth industry" that they can cash in on. The most visible of these industries are for-profit companies, some of which have shares traded on the stock market, that build and run prisons (see box 10.1). A full review of the pros and cons is beyond the scope of this section; however, the important point is that those who are incarcerated are largely poor white, black, and Hispanic-Latino men, while those who benefit economically from private prisons are wealthy white men. The latter tend to own the most shares of publicly traded stock as well as businesses, and the economic links also tend to benefit other white men who are in financial services (which underwrite loans) or corporate law.

More generally, privatization of correctional services can end up harming many in prison while enriching business owners. Take, for example, the story of Prison Health

BOX 10.1. PUNISHMENT FOR SALE: PRIVATE PRISON, BIG BUSINESS, AND THE INCARCERATION BINGE

Chapter 1 identified privatization as one of the major trends that would continue to exert an influence on the criminal justice enterprise. Privatization refers to the practice of outsourcing government functions and services to private, for-profit businesses under a contract with the government. Punishment and incarceration may seem like odd functions to privatize, but private prisons are a multibillion-dollar-a-year business, and the two largest firms—Corrections Corporation of America (CCA) and GEO Group—are multinational businesses that are traded on Wall Street.

In a groundbreaking examination of prison privatization, criminologists Donna Selman and Paul Leighton argue in *Punishment for Sale* (2010) that understanding the nature of the contemporary criminal justice system requires understanding privatization, including the business model and financial dynamics of these firms. It's not just a multibillion-dollar business, but CCA has a billion-dollar credit line with various powerful Wall Street investment banks. They—and all the shareholders—ensure that the private prison firms are managing the business risk factors that they must disclose in filings with the SEC. Risk factors include not getting enough inmates from government to be profitable, sentencing reform (like the repeal of certain mandatory minimum sentences), steps toward the legalization of drugs, and immigration reform. While these are controversial topics, the debate over justice policy needs to be on the merits of reform—not based on the financial interests of wealthy shareholders and Wall Street. Indeed, research demonstrates that private prison firms have already influenced public policy to their own benefit through campaign donations, and they have rejected a shareholder proposal to fully disclose donations and lobbying money. (They have also rejected proposals to make the performance incentive portion of executives' pay include criteria related to the absence of human rights or labor violations.)

Selman and Leighton (2010) argue that privatization was born from two trends. First, the relentless war on crime and war on drugs caused massive prison overcrowding. Extremely costly prison expansion and renovation were the inevitable results of "getting tough," but ran into conflict with politicians' other favorite lines about lower taxes and less government. Second, President Ronald Reagan declared in his first inaugural address that "government is the problem," and he set the stage for antigovernment politicians to privatize a range of services. The historical moment was ripe for several politically well-connected individuals, backed by the same venture capital that facilitated the expansion of Kentucky Fried Chicken, to use private funds to build their own prison and collect money from government to house inmates from over-crowded facilities.

As briefly noted in this chapter, the incarceration binge has been costly and ineffective—and has contributed to social injustice (especially racial). Selman and Leighton (2010), after developing these points more fully, argue that the for-profit nature of the prison business depends on the continuation of those dynamics. Companies traded on the stock exchange owe a basic duty to shareholders to grow and become more profitable, regardless of the impact on others or on justice.

Privatization has several important implications for understanding the intersections of class, race, gender, and crime. First, in a variation of *The Rich Get Richer and the Poor Get Prison* (Reiman and Leighton 2013), with prison privatization, the rich whites get richer because the poor minorities go to prison. As noted in chapter 3, stock ownership is concentrated in the hand of relatively few wealthy families who are mostly white. As noted in this chapter, those going to prison are disproportionately minority—and private prisons have a substantial number of contracts to house immigrants (including detained families). Racial fear means business and profits for private prison companies.

Second, chapter 1 noted that private prison firms pay substantially less than their government counterparts for prison staff, a point that generates opposition to privatization from unions. But private prison firms also pay their executives substantially more than the head of a department of corrections who manages substantially more inmates. Paying those at the top substantially more while paying those at the bottom substantially less directly contributes to income and class inequality. Overhead costs for the directors, SEC lawyers, consultants, mergers and acquisitions, "customer acquisition" (advertising and lobbying), shareholder lawsuits, and shareholder relations mean a wide variety of criminal justice workers will have lower wages and less economic security than if they had a government job.

Services, Inc. The cover story of the *New York Times* for February 27, 2005, read: "As Health Care in Jails Goes Private, 10 Days Can Be a Death Sentence." The exposé of Prison Health revealed that as governments try to reduce the burden of soaring medical costs—due to the expanding and aging prison populations, exacerbated by the exploding problems of AIDS and mental illness among inmates—this new for-profit field has become a multibillion-dollar-a-year industry.

The yearlong examination of Prison Health Services (the leader in the field) by the *New York Times* revealed repeated instances of medical care that was flawed and sometimes lethal. "The company's performance around the nation has provoked criticism from judges and sheriffs, lawsuits from inmates' families and whistle-blowers, and condemnations by federal, state, and local authorities. The company has paid millions of dollars in fines and settlements" (von Zielbauer 2005, A1). Despite the similar patterns of abuse found across the nation, like the ones in New York, described below, Prison Health has been an ongoing concern:

> In the two deaths, and eight others across upstate New York, state investigators say they kept discovering the same failings: medical staffs trimmed to the bone, doctors under-qualified or out of reach, nurses doing tasks beyond their training, prescription drugs withheld, patient records unread and employee misconduct unpunished. Not surprisingly, Prison Health, which is based outside of Nashville, is no longer working in most of those upstate jails. But it is hardly out of work. Despite a tarnished record [from coast to coast], Prison Health has sold its promise of lower costs and better care, and become the biggest for-profit company providing medical care in jails and prisons. It has amassed 86 contracts in 28 states, and now cares for 237,000 inmates, or about 1 in every 10 people behind bars. (von Zielbauer 2005, A26)

IMPLICATIONS

Crime control policies constantly reward financial white-collar criminals, especially those corporate giants found on Main Street, Wall Street, and global streets alike, that line their pockets millions of times over at the expense of the general public and well-being of the world. At the same time, crime control policies overwhelmingly penalize the poor and people of color, especially black and Hispanic or Latino persons, for relatively harmless acts and numerous "crimes without victims." For the latter groups of people, who become inhabitants of US penal institutions, the behind-bars abuse, violence, and victimization come in a variety of forms, shapes, and practices. Penal violence, however, is pretty much hidden or invisible from public scrutiny, much like the disproportionate numbers of minority citizens contained in prisons. For example, Sykes and Piquero (2009, 214) have found with respect to contracting HIV inside and outside of prison as well as with other health testing in general that "the penal institution is an active agent in structuring and re-creating health inequalities within prisons, thereby exacerbating existing community health inequities when inmates are released."

Recent changes in state laws have been in the process of overturning a century-old juvenile justice system whose very reason for existence was to protect children from contact with adult prisoners. Despite the fact that whites commit most juvenile crimes, three out of four youths admitted to adult courts, jails, and prisons are children of color. In spite of the fact that penologists and criminologists almost all agree that these children are more likely to be physically and sexually abused in these institutions than in juvenile institutions and that they are more likely to continue committing crimes after their release, more and more prosecutors are moving young offenders into the adult system with little, if any, regard for the children's age or circumstances.

Ultimately, the institutionalization of penal violence cannot be divorced or separated from the structural conditions residing inside and outside the confining walls. Angela Davis (1998, 2) has reflected, the "prison industrial system materially and morally impoverishes its inhabitants and devours the social wealth needed to address the very problems that have led to spiraling numbers of prisons." The focus should thus not be only on a criminal justice system in need of reform but also on the "Perpetual Prisoner Machine" (Dyer 2000) that has been increasing its size and proportion of state and federal fiscal budgets relative to the declining dollars spent on education and social services since the late 1990s. In turn, these relationships cannot be separated from the structural changes of a postindustrial service economy caught within the contemporary epoch of globalization.

REVIEW AND DISCUSSION QUESTIONS

1. When it comes to disparities in punishment, sentencing, and imprisonment in the United States, which is more important—class, race, or gender—and why?
2. Historically, there have been five major rationales or justifications for punishment. Identify and briefly discuss each of these, and then make a case for the support or rejection of each.
3. Given that the United States is more punitive than any of the other developed nations and has the highest incarceration rates in the world, how can anybody make a case for mandatory sentencing laws?
4. What are some of the differences between men and women with respect to the crimes they commit, the punishments they receive, and the conditions of their imprisonment?
5. Though most critics of disparity in sentencing point to the more obvious patterns in discrimination against certain minorities and the poor, what are some of the less obvious or more subtle forms of inequity or disadvantageousness experienced by the lower and middle classes in relation to the analogous harms and crimes committed by both the powerful and the megacorporations of the United States?

Conclusion

Crime, Justice, and Policy

This book has considered a variety of ways in which the independent and interdependent experiences of class, race, and gender help to shape both crime and crime control in the United States. In multiple chapters, we have described and examined male and female patterns of crime, victimization, and interactions with systems of criminal justice. In the late 1980s and early 1990s, these unequal patterns of law enforcement and punishment were viewed in many jurisdictions as accounting for disproportionate minority confinement. Today, these institutionalized relations of inequality in the management of young persons caught up in the criminal justice apparatus are labeled by the Office of Juvenile Justice and Delinquency Prevention as "disproportionate minority contact" (OJJDP 2006).

Recent ethnographic studies of the experiences of marginalized blacks and Latinos in the "criminal justice pipeline" provide analyses of how the direct consequences of the enhanced policing, surveillance, and punitive treatment of these youths have been the development of a specific set of gendered (masculine) practices that obstruct both criminal desistance and social mobility (Rios 2009). Moreover, this "cumulative disadvantage" has unintended negative effects not only for those individuals caught up in the system but also for those families and communities that they have left behind and will most likely return to. Similarly, other ethnographic studies employing critical race theory and incorporating a "colonization" framework have revealed how structural and social conditions have created physically and psychologically threatening and insecure environments for racial and ethnic minorities. Gangs form in response to these harmful spaces, often enhanced by racially oppressed environments, limiting opportunities for more legitimate alternatives to self-protection and activism (Duran 2013). Reciprocally, these social relations of gang marginality increase both the illegitimate opportunities and the risks for arrest and incarceration.

More generally, our review and analysis of the latest crime control data demonstrate that four sets of relations continue to exist in the social realities of the administration of criminal law in the United States:

- Inequalities in class, race, and gender relations produce different lived experiences in society and in crime and crime control;
- Criminal law emphasizes the harms commonly perpetrated among the marginal members of society while it leaves the socially analogous harms committed by the more powerful well beyond incrimination;
- Discriminations based on class, race, and gender produce more prosecutions and harsher punishments for the "petty" offenses of the powerless and fewer prosecutions and softer punishments for the major offenses of the powerful; and
- Mass-mediated representations of class, race, and gender help to reproduce both the structural relations of oppression associated with crime and the repression associated with crime control.

In short, harms that are defined as crimes and the differential applications of criminal law enforcement, adjudication, and punishment are selective reflections and products of the social, political, and economic relations of class, race, and gender. We do not argue that the social realities of criminal justice in the United States are merely an expression of the inequalities and privileges of the larger society. On the contrary, the administration of justice is subject to many other factors and complex relationships, including bureaucratic needs of efficiency, economy, and effectiveness, and contradictory tensions between the rule of law (due process) and the rule of order (crime control). In addition, not only local politics are at work but also the politics of crime control in the context of a globalizing process that surrounds the criminal justice enterprise as a whole.

Finally, by incorporating legalistic analyses of crime and crime control with sociological analyses of inequality and privilege, we have conceptually broadened the traditional ("equal protection") framework for evaluating justice in the United States. In this regard, we have revealed those relationships not only between crime control and class, race, and gender but also, as explicitly recapitulated below, between the criminal justice system and the systems of political, economic, and ethical justice. By doing so, we have tried to demonstrate the need for the United States both to diversify its responses to crime and to expand its practices of justice.

MEDIA, CRIME, AND JUSTICE

What constitutes crime and crime control is not constant. The National Institute of Justice (NIJ) (2005, 1) declared of "crime" in its 2004 annual report: "The primary challenge for criminal justice professionals today is not from the number of crimes . . . but from the changing nature of the crime landscape. Although traditional criminal activities such as juvenile delinquency, gangs, burglary, and violent crimes remain problems for many communities, law enforcement agencies now face such new threats as the evolving globalization of crime, possible terrorism, and cybercrime." Omitted from the NIJ report, of course, was any mention of the traditional or new threats posed by corporate or governmental criminality. At the same time, in reference to changes in "crime control," the Justice Department underscored advances in technology "such as lower costs for the analysis of DNA samples" that "are changing how evidence is collected and crimes are investigated, as well as how judges and attorneys handle court cases" (NIJ 2005, 1).

Similarly, subtle transformations are occurring in who constitutes the criminal classes. The traditional stereotypes of dangerous criminals as poor, marginal, and nonwhite and as emanating from the streets remain, a subtext of much of the high-profile George Zimmerman trial as well as some pre- and postmedia coverage. However, the images of threatening persons now include young people with backpacks, especially if they are (or look as if they are) of Middle Eastern origins. Of course, the Boston Marathon bombings in the spring of 2013 reinforced this kind of "ethnic profiling." At the same time, six years after the Wall Street meltdown caused by an epidemic of securities frauds, the threatening or dangerous persons do not include images (or texts) about greedy executives perpetrating corporate or financial fraud or government bureaucrats deregulating business and financial services industries and committing "nonfeasance" (willful failure to perform a required duty) or colluding with the perpetrators (Barak 2012; Will, Handelman, and Brotherton 2013).

Take the "crime" of hiring undocumented workers. Every day, "illegal aliens" or undocumented workers are arrested, charged, and deported for breaking the law. However, those who employed them and broke the law have been given a virtual "free pass" to engage in this crime. In 2000, when the Bush administration took over, there had been little law enforcement or prosecution by the Clinton administration. This policy of nonenforcement escalated during the Bush presidency, and employers were rarely, if ever, charged with a criminal offense; if they were charged with "knowingly" hiring workers without papers, the first offense was a fine of $225. And despite thousands of arrests of Mexican nationals, for example, from 2000 to 2008, not one employer went to jail. It remains to be seen whether or not enforcement policies under the Obama administration will change. Throughout the first term of the Obama administration, record numbers of deportations occurred. In fact, near the end of 2013, deportations under Obama were "on track to reach two million, or nearly the same number of deportations in the United States from 1892 to 1997" (Shear 2013).

In the above cases, and more generally, the three *C*s of mass society—culture, consumption, and communication—mediate the social realities of crime and justice. Together, these help to shape the fundamental attitudes, values, and behaviors of not only Americans but non-Americans, too, through empire and globalization. In the processes of making and consuming ideas and things, our consciousness about life in general—and about crime and justice, perpetrators and victims, and cops and robbers in particular—are constantly forming and being reshaped. This constructing consciousness about "crime" expresses itself in our fears, discussions, and understandings about "crime control" and, more importantly, about what or who needs to be controlled. Ultimately, over and over vis-à-vis mass-mediated reconstructions, this consciousness (or sensitivity or perspective) on crime and justice spreads through our families, communities, nation-states, and beyond; in the process, our public and private policies on crime and crime control are developed both domestically and internationally.

The Internet, blogs, cell phones, and Twitter represent democratization in media as anyone can set up a web page or blog and "broadcast" their thoughts. But entertainment and news are still largely a mass-produced corporate phenomenon, relying for their very sustenance on advertisement as well as on the mass consumption of goods and services, ideas, and images. Even aspects of so-called independent media and alternative venues often consist of corporations playing on the rebellion against mass media and big corporations to appeal to consumers. Mass communication is quite expensive—bought and paid for by commercial advertising as well as by the owners and investors of private capital. For these reasons, what is aired, piped, or videoed into our consciousness are images and messages that are not value-free, objective, or neutral; rather, they reflect specific interests, and they are about selling, motivating, and reinforcing particular lifestyles and ideological points of view, not the least of which are about "crime and justice" in local, national, and international arenas.

Remember that corporations monopolize the ownership and distribution of newspapers, books, magazines, films, radio, video, television, and software. For example, General Electric (see chapter 8) has business interests in motors, transportation, turbines, electric equipment, communications, plastics, lighting, appliances, retail, medical services, music, financing, insurance, and software. Moreover, GE owns cable and network television stations, including NBC, MSNBC, CNBC, and USA. USA's series *White Collar* is an apolitical drama about white-collar crime; GE owns USA and does not want to bring attention to corporate crime, environmental pollution, or many other acts it—and the corporate advertisers who pay the bills—have done (Leighton 2010). Similarly, Westinghouse, in addition to its interests in communications and information, insurance, financing, banking, managing, electricity, nuclear power, and refrigeration, owns radio, cable, and television stations, including CBS.

The absorption of major media outlets by megacapital has merged, if not subverted, the interests of the "free press" with those of big business. So virtually all news and most entertainment, whether politically "left" (GE-owned MSNBC) or "right" (Fox) oriented, have fallen captive to the dominant ideologies of corporate-style free and unregulated enterprise. While there are more websites and blogs, corporate sites and news outlets still get the vast majority of the audience. As a result, there has arisen a greater uniformity in narrative discourses about most subjects, including crime and justice, especially considering media conglomerates can own radio, television, and newspapers in the same city.

Our argument is not a media conspiracy theory. Ultimately, the consumer is part of the equation. That is to say, our approach to mediated crime and justice recognizes superficially that "being profit-driven, the media respond to the actual demands of their audience rather than to the idealized 'thirst for knowledge' demand posited by public intellectuals and deans of journalism schools. They serve up what the consumer wants, and the more intense the competitive pressure, the better they do it" (Posner 2005, 9). But what does the average consumer of news and opinion want? What are audiences looking for? At the most general level, audiences want reinforcement of what they already believe. That is to say, "people don't like being in a state of doubt, so they look for information that will support rather than undermine their existing beliefs. They're also uncomfortable seeing their beliefs challenged on issues that are bound up with their economic welfare, physical safety or religious and moral views" (Posner 2005, 9). Accordingly, the news media, liberal or conservative, are careful not to step on the toes of their respective viewers, in the process further polarizing their respective deliveries (or "spins") on topical subjects. Each, in effect, defers to their loyal followings or audiences, selecting, slanting, and presenting their news accordingly. Further, the local presentations cannot be separated from the national or global portrayals that are constitutive of the "collective imaginations" pertaining to crime, law, and justice.

We suggest there is an interactive relationship between the so-called passive audience and the so-called active distributor of news, entertainment, and advertising. Generally, audiences consume crime news, for example, to learn of facts or trends that bear directly and immediately on their lives—hence the greater attention paid to local rather than to national or international crime news. They also listen and watch mass media to be entertained. In this context, distributors do not, for example, see the complexities of price-fixing or corporate fraud with limited exceptions—as "newsworthy" beyond their entertainment value because of an agreed-upon national narrative that precludes delving into the workings of the "higher-order" criminality found on Wall Street or in Washington, D.C. In effect, journalistic opinion or commentary of print, radio, and television supply pretty much what their respective audiences think they want or demand, but they do so within the groupthink of a mainstream media and mass culture that, for the most part, shapes a "local" demand that is invulnerable to the realities of crime and justice in the United States.

The relationship between the producers and the receivers of mediated crime and justice, or anything else for that matter, is symbiotic and serves more often than not to reinforce rather than to challenge the status quo. In terms of the "who," "what," "where," and "when" (if not "why") of the stories they report, news media typically strive for all the accuracy they can muster so long as they do not "step on the toes" of their advertisers and bosses or the relevant politicians or pundits. Investigative reporting does not have a high profit margin, and reporters represent high overhead costs that interfere with profit, so mainstream media reporters have become overly dependent on a short supply of news sources (including corporate press releases). Hence, when it comes to stories of crime and justice, the perspectives, biases, and distorted or slanted views of those in official positions of authority typically dominate the media. In short, the media whose beat is "law and order" rely almost exclusively on criminal justice professionals and their official statements or press releases about crime and crime control. As a result, there is a tendency to reproduce hegemonic or top-down views of crime and justice (Barak 1996; Ericson, Baranek, and Chan 1987; Kasinsky 1994). In this regard, Mark Fishman (1978) has referred to the news gathering and reporting on crime and violence as involving "procedures not to know."

As a market-driven enterprise, mainstream media do not want to bite the financial hands that feed them, nor do they want to bite the informational sources that provide the news and authority for their stories any more than they want to disappoint their audiences. Thus, it is in their journalistic interests not to ordinarily challenge areas of social and political consensus, no matter how fictional, stupid, vicious, or harmful that consensus may be. Consequently, both before and after the George W. Bush administration left office, the administration's lies to the American people and its acts of state-organized torture in violation of national and international law, for example, were primarily downplayed when not ignored altogether because confronting the normative beliefs and values that the United States does not engage in these types of crimes wins no friends and often alienates or turns off traditional audiences and mainstream sources. In the end, the narrative themes of crime and justice that are regularly reproduced by the mass media are highly reflective of selected and framed versions of social reality.

Take, for example, Sister Préjean's death-penalty book, *Dead Man Walking* (1993), and the Hollywood movie of the same title based on the book. In the book, Préjean notes that she became involved with prisons because she works with the poor, and part of her anti-death-penalty stance is out of concern about the effect of race and class inequalities. She is explicitly committed to a social justice perspective and notes that her mission is unsettling "because taking on the struggles of the poor invariably means challenging the wealthy and those who serve their interests. 'Comfort the afflicted and afflict the comfortable'—that's what Dorothy Day, a Catholic social activist said is the heart of the Christian gospel" (Préjean 1993, 5). Further, being kind to the oppressed in an unjust system is not enough, she says, and "to claim to be apolitical or neutral in the face of such injustices would be, in actuality, to uphold the status quo—a very political position to take, and on the side of the oppressors" (Préjean 1993, 5–6).

She notes explicitly that she "cannot believe in a God who metes out hurt for hurt, pain for pain, torture for torture." And she's skeptical about executions by the government, "which can't be trusted to control its own bureaucrats or collect taxes equitably or fill a pothole, much less decide which of its citizens to kill" (Préjean 1993, 21). The book approvingly quotes Camus, who thinks the followers of Christ "who have set at the center of their faith the staggering victim of a judicial error ought at least to hesitate before committing legal murder" (Préjean 1993, 89). And she asks the warden overseeing executions, "If Christ lived on Earth today, would he supervise this process?" (Préjean 1993, 103).

Interestingly, none of this critical content is included in the movie, which won praise for showing "both sides"—yet ultimately it presented no information or larger context on which to base further consideration about the death penalty. Given that most people in the United States are Christian, generally supportive of the death penalty, and do not want to be challenged about class or race inequality, the movie strips out anything that might offend them and combines the worst of both condemned men Préjean works with in the book into one character for the movie. The movie is about an individual bad guy who may or may not deserve to be executed; the book is an articulate critique using two men as examples of systemic inequalities that Christian gospel should challenge.

In addition, because issues of crime and crime control are too numerous, uncertain, and intricate, and because the benefits of being a well-informed audience member regarding crime and punishment are too small, viewers (and to a lesser extent listeners and readers) do not constitute audiences who are thriving for disinterested and sustained analyses of deviance. Instead, the average consumer wants to be entertained; she or he finds scandals, violence, crime, the foibles of celebrities, and some moral failings of the powerful too pleasurable to tune out.

Contemporary coverage of wrongful convictions in the United States is another example. Are we talking an occasional aberration or a statewide epidemic in the administration of criminal justice? While there is no definitive research revealing the magnitude of the problem, it is beyond question that we are not simply talking about a few, but rather many, innocent people who have been sent to prison, sometimes for decades. Freelance magazine writer, book author, and part-time journalism instructor at the University of Missouri Steve Weinberg (2008, 59) points out: "In each of those cases, the justice system failed. But so did journalism." More generally, the lack of serious journalistic reporting of crime and justice has serious consequences rarely discussed by the media, criminologists, or the general public. Weinberg (2008, 56) argues, "Unless journalists get better at covering the justice system, many criminals will continue to go unpunished, free to murder or rape or rob again. So investigating wrongful convictions is not—as perceived by too many police, prosecutors and judges—an assault by soft-on-crime bleeding hearts." The lack of investigative journalism of white-collar crime, its deficient control, and questionable justice also has deleterious effects across society.

Turning briefly to entertainment, the dramatic crime narratives found in books, on television, or at the movies are often more accurate and less distorted than are either the news stories of prime time or the so-called reality shows such as *COPS* (Barak 1994, 1996). The pictures of criminals are reflective of the multiracial and ethnic distributions of index and occupational crime (although equal time, once again, is not given to the crimes of the powerful and to corporate misbehavior). Conversely, when it comes to crime control, the greater distortion is with the entertainment media because of their tendency, for example, to overrepresent women and persons of color in positions of criminal justice leadership compared to their actual distributions. In either venue, however, underrepresentation of corporate deviance or of the crimes of the powerful is the norm. Unless the violations involve powerful celebrities or blatantly outrageous behavior (as exemplified by Enron or Bernard Madoff), they are typically glossed over. Even when there is coverage, corporate abuse, harm, and criminality is left unexamined in terms of the institutional or structural relations of crime control and its functionality to the upper echelons of power and influence in the United States. The reports leave the impression that the problem is a "few bad apples" rather than systemic.

Finally, what the mass media as a whole accomplish, consciously and unconsciously, is to separate the "criminals" from the "noncriminals," serving to reinforce the belief that "real" criminals are different from the rest of us. This has particularly been the case with respect to the sanctioning of torture distributed by the "good guys" to alleged terrorists in post-9/11 fictional entertainments. That is, on both small television and large movie screens, torture has been reconstituted as justifiable treatment for these monstrous others (Flynn and Salek 2012). Terrorists and other dangerous criminals alike may be subject to severe and draconian forms of crime control and criminal justice administration for both their good and ours. If persons can be portrayed as belonging to a strange and dangerous breed driven to crime not because of inequality or injustice but rather because they suffer from some kind of biological or psychological flaws, it becomes easier to sell "the idea of an increasingly punitive criminal justice system with fewer constitutional restraints to keep neighborhoods safe from the demonic 'Other'" that society has constructed as criminal (Kooistra, Mahoney, and Westervelt 1998, 147). And if inequality, poverty, or injustice cannot be the culprits in the scenarios of crime and crime control, then neither can privilege, wealth, or deregulation. Hence, for all practical purposes, mediated crime and crime control have been stripped of their social context while criminals and criminality are reduced to the idiosyncratic behavior of isolated and free-willed, if not rational, individuals.

In sum, even though our criminal justice system revolves around the rule of law, rational intent, and retributive justice, the cultural productions of crime and justice nevertheless convey the message that street criminals are fundamentally irrational or disturbed. As such, not only are they not entitled to be treated rationally, but we are not obligated to treat them rationally. Conveniently, however, when it comes to "suite" crimes, the message is quite different: these offenders are fundamentally decent and rational people whose potentially bad acts are not evidence of bad character. Complex circumstances beyond their individual control created some kind of aberration or deviation, but not a serious breach worth fixing, even when such behavior is habitually practiced and may have brought the economy to its knees, as with the recession of 2008–2010. On the other hand, on the rare occasions when stories about upper-class and/or corporate criminality are broached by mass media, these narratives and representations fail to challenge the larger economic system and do not communicate the real danger or threat of these crimes because their perpetrators are not only paragons of our socioeconomically stratified communities but also leaders of some of the most profitable corporations and financial institutions in the world. These paragons of market society, in the final analysis, must appear above all else to be rational and normative and therefore beyond serious incrimination. In the case of those Wall Street securities frauds or those "crimes of capitalist control" that caused the victimization of millions of people between 2008 and 2012, the US Department of Justice simply decided that it would be too costly to prosecute these high-profile fraudsters. Attorney General Eric Holder testified before the Senate Judiciary Committee on March 6, 2013: "I am concerned that the size of some of these institutions becomes so large that it does become difficult for us to prosecute them when we are hit with indications that if you do prosecute, if you do bring a criminal charge, it will have a negative impact on the national economy, perhaps even the world economy" (quoted in Gongloff, 2013).

THE ENDURING STRUGGLE FOR JUSTICE: EQUAL, RESTORATIVE, AND SOCIAL

Three systems of justice—equal, restorative, and social—cannot be separated from the modern evolution in the conceptualization of justice. Each of these justice systems or models represents a generation in the three-tier revolution of the rights of human beings to ultimately share in common the exact same formal rights as everybody else regardless of their class, race/ethnic, gender, religious, national, or sexual affiliation (Ishay 2004). The first generation of rights represented the struggle for *equal justice*, or the struggle for "negative rights," in that they called for restraint from the state and/or monarchy. These rights were derived from the American and French Revolutions and the struggle to gain freedom from arbitrary rule; they are also articulated in the Civil and Political Rights of the International Bill of Rights. Collectively, these rights have helped shape what we usually refer to as governmental control by "rule of law" rather than by "rule of man." A product of this struggle has been an emphasis on the impartial and fair enforcement of the procedural and substantive criminal law.

The second generation of rights represented the struggle for *restorative justice*, or the struggle for "positive rights," in that they called for "affirmative actions" on the part of the state. These rights are articulated in the Economic, Social, and Cultural Rights of the International Bill of Rights. Collectively, these rights have helped shape what we refer to as the minimal duties or social obligations of the state to facilitate the "self-realization" of the individual. A product of this struggle has been an emphasis on community social welfare, penitence/redemption, and victim-offender reconciliation.

The third generation of rights represents the contemporary struggle for *social justice* worldwide, also identified as the struggle for universal "human rights." Evolving out of the emerging conditions of global interdependence, these rights call for international cooperation between all nation-states, such as the establishment in 1999, in

The Hague, of the International Criminal Court. Collectively, these rights recognize that the delivery of human rights for all cannot be satisfied within the body of individual states acting alone. Products of this international struggle for human rights or social justice include the global emphasis on ending world hunger, forgiving the debt of underdeveloped "third-world" nations, and treating all the victims of AIDS/HIV and other life-threatening diseases, famines, and tsunamis worldwide.

Historically, the evolution of justice and the struggle for universal human rights has not followed a linear path forward. On the contrary, not only has every generation of rights met with resistance, but also each major stride on the pathway to human rights has been trailed by severe setbacks:

> The universalism of human rights brandished during the French Revolution was slowly superseded by a nationalist reaction incubated during Napoleon's conquests, just as the internationalist hopes of socialist human rights advocates were drowned in a tidal wave of nationalism at the approach of World War I. The human rights aspirations of the Bolshevik Revolution and of two liberal sister institutions, the League of Nations and the International Labor Organization (ILO), were crushed by the rise of Stalinism and fascism during the interwar period; the establishment of the United Nations (UN) and adoption of the Universal Declaration of Human Rights were eclipsed by intensifying nationalism in the emerging Third World and global competition between two nuclear-armed superpowers. Finally, the triumphant claims made after 1989 that human rights would blossom in an unfettered global market economy were soon drowned out by rising nationalism in the former Soviet Union, Africa, the Balkans, and beyond. (Ishay 2004, 4)

To be sure, reactionary forces have not totally nullified each chapter of progress in human rights. In fact, the record informs us otherwise: "History preserves the human rights record as each generation builds on the hopes and achievements of its predecessors while struggling to free itself from authoritarianism and improve its social conditions" (Ishay 2004, 4). Over time, the evolution of "human rights" has reflected the historical continuity and change that helped form the Universal Declaration of Human Rights (UDHR) adopted by the General Assembly of the United Nations in 1948. Drawing on the battle cry of the French Revolution, "liberty, equality, and brotherhood," on the demands of the Industrial Revolution for political, social, and economic equity, and on the communal and national solidarity movements associated with the postcolonial era of dignity for all, the articles of the UDHR brought together in one document the universal meanings of human rights. However, issues of how to obtain human rights for all and of what constitutes equal human rights still remain as, legally and socially, people disagree; for example, disagreements arise in the case of Darfur as whether or not to have persons prosecuted for genocide or for gross human rights violations. Even though Sudan has established special courts twice since 2003 and a new special prosecutor as recently as 2012 for the purposes of pursuing those guilty of war crimes, perpetrators of crimes allegedly committed in the course of Khartoum's war against armed rebels in Darfur had not yet been prosecuted in summer 2013.

In the everyday practices of crime and social control, these three models or approaches to justice are central—equal, restorative, and social. Inside and outside the United States, the ideals and realities of equal justice are older than the ideals and realities of restorative or social justice. The ideas and practices of equal justice compared with those of restorative and social justice are more individually and less collectively oriented approaches to justice.

In the modern evolution of justice, history has moved from individual to collective notions of justice, and there has been a widening of fundamental rights (Crawford 1988). These expanding ideas initially found expression in small philosophical or political circles, gradually finding acceptance, if not consensus, in a significant portion of the body politic and, ultimately, finding incorporation in the procedural as well as the substantive sides of the law. In terms of the contemporary period dating back to the end of World War II, the United States has more slowly than other developed nations experienced a transition away from the relative limits or constraints of legal rights and toward the blossoming or escalating possibilities of human rights such as civil unions and same-sex marriages. Politically, the USA is a signatory to or has ratified a number of United Nations conventions, and while the Supreme Court's decision striking down the death penalty for juveniles acknowledged "the overwhelming weight of international opinion against the juvenile death penalty," it pointed out that such opinion "is not controlling here, but provides respected and significant confirmation for the Court's determination that the penalty is a disproportionate punishment for offenders under 18" (*Roper v. Simmons*, 543 U.S. 551 [2005]).

Equal Justice

In the United States, equal justice assumes the rationality of the prevailing political, economic, and social arrangements in general and of the administration of criminal justice in particular. Within this system of justice, whether criminals are viewed as "bad" or "mad," they are disconnected from their socioeconomic conditions as well as from their class, racial, and gendered backgrounds, and they are held equally accountable for the harm they inflict regardless of context or situation. Whether defendants come from profoundly vulnerable or at-risk social environments or from privileged and advantaged elite milieus is not relevant to blind or equal justice.

The current model of equal justice practiced in the United States has its root in the mid-eighteenth century, when the European age of reason or Enlightenment was busy reforming the more arbitrary and barbaric justice practices from the medieval period. Although not driven by revenge or vengeance, these present-day models of equal justice are repressive in that they downplay flexible sentencing, community alternatives, and restitution. They also ignore the social structures, environmental milieus, and ecologies of crime. In addition, these models of justice have traditionally not considered the interests of either the injured parties or their communities or of the perpetrators themselves. In short, the adjudicative practices of equal justice serve to reinforce a repressive system of individualized justice that helps to sustain as well as institutionalize a permanent underclass of marginally threatening offenders.

In the final analysis, policies of equal justice do not take into account the concept of equal treatment of nonequal offenders or victims by class, race, gender, sexual orientation, and so on. Or, put differently, the unequal treatment of analogous social injuries or harms by the powerful and the powerless, respectively, serve to reproduce the status quo of crime, victimization, and discriminatory justice.

Restorative Justice

Whereas equal justice systems are more legalistically oriented and punitive-repressive and social justice systems are more structural and transformative in orientation, restorative justice systems may be thought of as located somewhere on a continuum between the other two systems. Globally speaking, restorative justice has been used more typically at the micro level, when the approach is used to bring individuals and offenders together. But it has also been used at the macro level as a means of dealing with collective injury and guilt involving, for example, "the crimes of genocide in Rwanda, war crimes in Bosnia Herzegovina, and even war zones in Israel" (Hanser 2009, 193). Fundamentally, restorative justice is about "de-centering punishment in regulatory institutions while acknowledging the significant place that punishment will always have within them" as a source of communicating the actual "shamefulness" of the act in question (Braithwaite, Braithwaite, and Ahmed 2005, 287).

Unlike equal justice policies that strive to isolate and exclude offenders from the rest of society based on the alleged differences between "criminals" and "noncriminals," restorative justice policies assume that most offenders and nonoffenders, whether perpetrators, victims, or both, share an intrinsic humanity in common. Howard Zehr and Harry Mika (1998, 54–55) have maintained that restorative justice is being pursued when citizens

- focus on the harms of wrongdoing more than on the rules that have been broken;
- show equal concern and commitment to victims and offenders, involving both in the process of justice;
- work toward the restoration of victims, empowering them and responding to their needs as they see them;
- support offenders while encouraging them to understand, accept, and carry out their obligations;
- recognize that while obligations may be difficult for offenders, they should not be intended as harms and they must be achievable;
- provide opportunities for dialogue, direct or indirect, between victims and offenders as appropriate;
- involve and empower the affected community through the justice process and increase its capacity to recognize and respond to community bases of crime;

- encourage collaboration and reintegration rather than coercion and isolation;
- give attention to the unintended consequences of [their] actions and programs [on particular communities]; and
- show respect to all parties, including victims, offenders, and justice colleagues.

Modern practices of restorative justice have their legal roots in the ancient patterns of such diverse cultures as the Sumerian Code of Ur-Nammu (2050 BC), the Hebrew scriptures and the Code of Hammurabi (1700 BC), the Roman Law of the Twelve Tables (449 BC), and the earliest collection of the Germanic tribal laws, the lex Salica (AD 496). Each of the legal systems of justice required that offenders and their families settle accounts with victims and their families, not simply to ensure that injured persons received restitution or compensation but also to restore or reestablish community peace. In many precolonial African and Native American societies, punitive sanctions were compensatory rather than retributive, intended primarily to make victims whole or to restore them to their previous position.

Today, the contemporary system of Japanese justice, emphasizing as it does "confession, repentance and absolution," is also about compensating the victim and restoring community peace (Haley 1989). Similarly, "indigenous populations in North America, New Zealand, Australia and elsewhere are experimenting with ways in which their traditional approaches to crime, which [were] restorative in intent, may exist in the context of the dominant Western legal systems" of colonization (Van Ness and Heetderks Strong 1997, 9). Moreover, since the 1980s, restorative justice has been represented both outside and inside the United States by a wide diversity of programs that may or may not contain the same "essential" elements or practices as ideally conceptualized.

In other words, the idea of restorative justice has come to have many different meanings and practices. It has come to be associated with innovations in community mediation, problem-solving justice, victim-offender reconciliation, alternative sentencing, and community service. Kathleen Daly and Russ Immarigeon (1998, 21–22) point out:

> The concept may refer to an alternative process for resolving disputes, to alternative sanctioning options, or to a distinctively different, "new" mode of criminal justice organized around principles of restoration to victims, offenders, and the communities in which they live. It may refer to diversion from formal court process, to actions taken in parallel with court decisions, and to meetings between offenders and victims at any stage of the criminal process (from arrest, presentencing, and prison release). It is a process used in juvenile justice, criminal justice, and family welfare/child protection cases.

Regardless of the myriad of practices that seem to be part of a larger movement to incorporate restorative justice programs throughout the criminal justice system and local communities, what they all share in common is a view of crime and criminals that moves beyond defining some behavior as illegal to include at least some of the basic needs of human respect and dignity and the relevant sources of conflict and dispute resolution. Unlike equal justice systems that revolve around how much pain and suffering has been inflicted by the actions of the wrongdoer, restorative justice systems revolve around how much harm has been repaired or prevented. Hence, restorative justice not only sees criminality as involving the needs of offenders and victims as well as the mutual obligations and liabilities between offenders and victims but also recognizes the different and often related harms that perpetrators and victims of street crimes experience in common.

In this way, restorative justice significantly views both the offenders and the victims as responding more or less rationally to their perceived needs, interests, and options. Unlike equal justice systems that view crime control as primarily a matter of individual perpetrators versus the state, restorative justice systems are preoccupied with the interpersonal (and larger mutualistic) relationships involving offenders, victims, family members, and the communities from which they are spawned. In short, restorative justice emphasizes the recovery of the victim through redress, vindication, and healing on the one hand and of the offender through fair treatment, recompense of the victim, and rehabilitation (or primary habilitation) on the other hand.

For example, reparation, restitution, and compensation programs are more concerned with healing injuries than they are with inflicting harm and pain. They are not about payback per se or about inflicting additional suffering, but they are about "getting even." While one concern is obviously public safety, their primary concerns are about seeing that victims are made whole and that offenders are involved in the process of mutual healing. The objectives of restorative justice are less about the narrow goal of diverting inmates from prison than they are about advancing the recovery of both the victims and the perpetrators, enabling or empowering both to "self-actualize" and to establish themselves as participating rather than marginal members of society.

In the final analysis, restorative justice relies on both the formal and informal mechanisms of social control in that it supports the role of government as responsible for preserving law and order and the community as responsible for establishing peace and justice. For example, victim-offender reconciliation programs offer a context in which the two parties to the crime have an opportunity to face each other in a nonadversarial setting. This encounter affords victims and offenders rather than the state prosecutors the chance to decide what they consider relevant to the crime. The encounter also tends "to humanize each of them to one another and permits them substantial creativity in constructing a response that deals not only with the injustice that occurred but with the futures of both parties as well" (Van Ness and Heetderks Strong 1987, 89).

Social Justice

Whereas equal justice models reduce "conflicts" between offenders and victims to legally relevant material evidence, restorative justice models try to converge some of the formal and informal aspects of social control and conflict resolution through victim-offender conciliation and community peacemaking (Hanser 2009). While equal justice systems revolve primarily around retribution between the offender and the state and restorative justice systems revolve primarily around reparation and healing between the offender and the victim, social justice systems venture beyond the immediate conflicts between particular offenders and their victims. Neither the retributive equal justice models nor the reparative restorative justice models have paid attention to the "big picture" or to the "patterns of social inequality or disadvantage, which make both victims and offenders, and indeed their communities, more prone to the experiences of criminal harm and to the processes of criminalization" in the first place (R. White 1998, 17).

The visions of social justice are broader and the policies more ambitious than the visions and policies of equal and restorative justice. Social justice models expand the notions of conflict and injury beyond what the law recognizes to include those harms identified as part of an evolving set of human rights, some established in treaties and covenants, some in international resolutions or tribunals. The violations of any of these fundamental rights constitute what are known in the world community as "crimes against humanity." These crimes generally, but not always, are committed by the authorities or agents of the state, such as the violation of a person and/or a group's inalienable rights to be free, for example, from exploitation, sexual slavery, hatred, impoverishment, discrimination, or genocide.

Social justice models also view "crime" as something more than an interpersonal violation between people and a particular nation-state's legal order. Moreover, these models see crime control as something more than the reparation, reconciliation, and reassurance of victims and offenders alike. Crimes are not merely personal expressions, but they are also institutional and structural expressions of fundamental political and economic arrangements. For example, rich folks, regardless of race and gender, do not ordinarily hold up fast-food markets, gas stations, or banking establishments. Likewise, poor folks, regardless of race and gender, do not violate insider trading rules, falsify corporate accounting statements, price-fix, or monopolize the sale, distribution, and production of goods and services. In other words, these are all crimes of structural opportunity, and it is no accidental convenience that the legal orders and their administration disadvantage the perpetrators of the street crimes while they advantage the perpetrators of the suite crimes.

More generally, social justice models recognize the indivisible relations between, for example, the "crime" of homelessness in an affluent society and the crimes by and against the homeless as rooted in the violence of poverty and inequality and in the creation of dependent classes of marginalized people. To address these structural inequities or injustices, social justice stresses the importance of public policies of crime control that go beyond the confines of the criminal justice system and the crimes of the poor and powerless. Attention and care are also given, for example, not only to the crimes of the rich and powerful but also more generally to the economic and social harms of corporate deregulation, to the formation of social and human capital, and to the oppression and exploitation of a multiethnic underclass. Thus, domestic policies of crime control in the United States also focus affordable and accessible programs on family development, health care, subsidized housing, public education, community efficacy, and political empowerment. To the extent that social factors create crime and make crime control repressive for the purposes of securing a legal order that supports or reinforces inequality and privilege, the social justice model advocates intervening to prevent those social factors.

Historically, advocates of social justice in the United States in the nineteenth century included members of various religious groups and others from organized labor. Its roots go as far back as the Quakers and their involvement with the development of the first penitentiary, the Walnut Street Jail, in Philadelphia in the early 1800s. More recently, the prisoner's movement of the 1960s, the second wave of feminism in the 1970s, the environmental movement of the 1980s, and the movement for universal human rights in the 1990s have nurtured and propelled forward models of social justice to this day.

Proponents of social justice, such as the late Michael Harrington (1989), talk in terms of the merits of "visionary gradualism" and "free-market socialism." Grounded in the global principles of feminist, antiracist, and ecologist communitarianism, this view of social justice ascribes to the capitalistic structure, but it also believes in the eradication of social subjugation, oppression, and exploitation of people and the establishment of fundamental human rights for all. Often referred to as "democratic socialism," this vision of social justice does not seek to do away with all forms of privilege and inequality, but it does rest on the capacity of people to choose and implement democratic forms of socialization and public policymaking in "the face of 'irresponsible,' 'unthinking' and 'unsocial' versions of corporate socialization" and private policymaking (West 1990, 59).

BEYOND "EQUAL JUSTICE" FOR ALL: A CRITIQUE

Persons who come before the various tribunals of justice have never been, nor are they now, equal before the law. Legalistic fairness, due process, and equal protection in actual practice are not synonymous with equal justice or the rule of law, in a court of law or in the larger court of public opinion. Anatole France (1844–1924), the French poet, journalist, and best-selling novelist, wrote in *The Red Lily* (1894): "The law, in its majestic equality, forbids the rich as well as the poor to sleep under bridges, to beg in the streets, and to steal bread" (chapter 7). Of course, such laws then and now are only relevant to the marginal, to the destitute, to the homeless, to the mentally ill, and so on. As in this illustration class matters, race and gender also matter, both at law and in society, as this book has depicted throughout.

When evaluators of justice—criminal, civil, or corporate—falsely treat persons of different or unequal socioeconomic status, race, ethnicity, gender, or sexual orientation as though they were the same or legally equal based on some kind of formal or abstract notion of the equality of all people, these evaluators ignore the very concrete inequalities that cut across the dynamic relations of class, race, gender, crime, justice, and society. Similarly, because of the common or ideological overemphasis on notions of individual or equal justice, most critiques of the administration of criminal justice focus on the procedural irregularities in the application of due process or the rule of law. Although recognition is often given to the selective enforcement and differential applications of the law in the facts of individual cases, less likely is much discussion of the systemic-discriminatory outcomes, let alone any mention or critique of the substantive "irregularities" in the labeling of "crime" or in the unequal definitions of harm or analogous injuries in the first place.

The point is that there is a long list of harms and injuries that could be legally prohibited but have not been. They have not been labeled or criminalized as constituting "crimes worth pursuing" because of the advantages they accrue for powerful interests in society. In other words, the pursuit of equal justice within a legally biased system against the marginally impoverished is not only a narrow or limited goal but also, more importantly, is one that obscures a multitude of oppressive dynamics that are of concern to social justice models because these would alleviate many of the roots of antisocial behavior in society.

The consequences, for example, of being free from racism, sexism, and other forms of discrimination or from these "omissions of equal justice" are that crime control is stacked against the powerless rather than the powerful, as we have underscored with respect to the unequal war on drugs and its adverse effects on minority communities of African and Latin backgrounds. For example, the large-scale removal of young black males from their communities contributes to the depletion of the supply of potential marriage partners for young black females and to the accumulation of generational impoverishment. Some commentators have argued that these social relations of crime, victimization, and punishment have encouraged young female-headed households, creating precisely the types of family formations that have been linked with higher rates of street crime and domestic abuse when not given adequate social support (Currie 1985; Foster and Hagan 2009; Messner and Rosenfeld 1994). In short, these trends in racial and gender punishment are countereffective as they exacerbate the problems of absentee parents, convict reentry, and the lack of community efficacy.

Similarly, the increased processing of less serious marginal offenders throughout the criminal justice system has not only created a state of megawarehouses of nonviolent offenders but has also undermined the capacity of formal systems of crime control to deliver on their promises of due process and equal protection during a period when the rates of crimes against the person, such as murders, and crimes against property, such as burglary, remain at multidecade lows in the United States. Nevertheless, assembly-line, plea-bargained "equal justice" pertains not only to defendants but to the convicted as well, as each of these groups become subject to the practices of actuarial justice or to the forecasting of the costs and risks associated with managing populations considered dangerous (Barak 2009; Feeley and Simon 1992, 1994). In the end, this type of bureaucratized equal justice for all helps to secure and reinforce stereotypic images of both crime and criminals through sophisticated systems of profiling and classification.

Working hand-in-hand with mediated images of crime and justice, bureaucratized justice helps to reinforce images of the "typical" criminal that do not include high-powered corporate executives, emphasizing the low-life predators who murder, rob, assault, kidnap, and do drugs rather than acts of inside trades, no-bid contractors, financial fraudsters, and so forth. Crimes are acts identified with poor and racial minorities, not with rich and powerful white folks. Crime control is represented by what the police, courts, and prisons do with the "dangerous classes," rarely providing background or context for the behavior in question. The images associated with these culprits and with the responses to their crimes only serve to inflame public fears and anxieties associated with crime and its control while reproducing scenarios of retributive and repressive justice that reifies class, racial, and gendered patterns of disparity, exclusion, and isolation.

The implication of this critique is not to argue for an end to equal justice for all. On the contrary, equal justice is certainly a good place to begin, but it is only a beginning. Indeed, all agents or workers of the criminal justice system should aspire to act impartially or neutrally, according to both the letter and the spirit of due process and equal protection under the law. In addition, however, equal justice must be assisted by the goals and objectives of both restorative justice and social justice. These alternative approaches to equal justice offer substantial ways to improve the quality of justice inside and outside the criminal justice system, serving better to curb and reduce all forms of criminality—personal, institutional, and structural. These models of justice engage in more humanistic and inclusive approaches to crime control and in more holistic or integrated approaches to crime and justice than does the model of equal justice by itself. Both restorative and social justice models actively encourage and support the participation of offenders, victims, and communities of interest in the processes of local democratic crime prevention. Social justice models also promote and advocate the institutionalization of human rights across society. From the vantage point of policy development, restorative and social justice aspires toward an evolution in justice based on healing, recovery, reconciliation, and the ongoing struggle for diversity, equity, and inclusiveness. Once again, these approaches do not abandon the legalistic models of the rule of law; rather, they play down the wars on crime as they struggle for peace and justice.

RECOMMENDED POLICIES AND REFORMS FOR ALLEVIATING HARM AND REDUCING CRIME

Based on a consensus of knowledge that a great deal of interpersonal crime and violence comes from the fault lines around economic and racial inequality and the absence of hope and opportunity in rural towns and inner cities alike, social control and crime control must be responsive to the life histories of offenders, victims, and communities. Furthermore, policy recommendations for reducing criminal behavior and improving the quality of crime control and justice not only call for a readdressing of our structural ills but also call for a healthy recognition of another criminological consensus; namely, that we cannot punish our way out of these structural conditions of crime and injustice.

Currie (2005, 303) has written: "If crime is heavily rooted in social structures and social policies that are created by human agency, then on its present level it is not an inevitable fact of modern life but is alterable through social action." In other words, if a market society establishes a nation with high rates of crime and violence because its competitive and consumptive lifestyles create a "toxic brew" of predatory social behavior, then domestic (and international) policies are required to ameliorate structural poverty and widening inequality in general and to avoid destroyed livelihoods, stressed-out families, dilapidated neighborhoods, and fragmented communities in particular. However, focusing on the production of crime has to be balanced by focusing on the infrastructure and groupthink that has dominated crime control in the United States. We are referring specifically to the war-on-crime mentality that for the past three decades has distorted our nation's approach to alleviating harm and reducing crime. The editors of *After the War on Crime* (2008) maintain:

> It emerged as a slogan more than thirty-five years ago, but, from the first, the "war on crime" was much more than rhetoric. As in the case of the "cold war" and, more recently, the "war on terror," the war on crime produced significant and enduring effects on the entire American population in social, political, economic, constitutional, and, far from least, racial terms. . . . This campaign mobilized tens of thousands in law enforcement agencies and prison systems and tens of thousands more in the related war industries stimulated by our society's commitment of billions of dollars to this effort. In a nod toward total war, every member of the population has contributed, federal and state taxes, general revenues, and bond issues, to the most rapid, most thoroughgoing, most extensive buildup in carceral and police systems this country has ever undertaken. More than merely paying taxes . . . millions of Americans have adopted war thinking in how they perceive and respond to crime risk as citizens, parents, and economic actors. (Simon, López, and Frampton 2008, 2–3)

Simon, López, and Frampton (2008, 3) argue further that the war on crime remade our society: "It reshaped our cities; transformed our social imagination about the nature of ourselves, our neighbors, and strangers; shifted the distribution of population between urban and rural areas; and ultimately changed the way motor vehicles, housing developments, shopping and office complexes look and operate." Optimistically, however, they argue more generally that the war on crime, if it is not over, has at least peaked. They also point out that "the issues that increasingly come to the fore are those emerging from the consequences of the war on crime itself; its effects are suddenly visible across almost every institution of importance to civic life, including family, schools, the labor market, the political field, and race relations" (Simon, López, and Frampton 2008, 3).

That is to say, now it is time to deal with the damage inflicted by the war on crime—to rescue those communities caught up in the grip of zero tolerance and aggressive policing as well as those young persons who have been extracted from them, for example. Now is the time to develop plans and policies to reintegrate into society more than 650,000 persons a year expected to return to the free world. Now is the time, as Obama's new drug czar, Gil Kerlikowske, has done, to call off the "war on drugs" (Fields 2009). Now is the time to reframe the problem of drug use and abuse as a public health issue, not a criminal one, as has been done in Vancouver, British Columbia, with positive results (Beiser 2008). Similarly, it is now time that the United States adopt those strategies of "harm reduction" that are more realistically geared to minimizing the damage inflicted on or by those folks, for example, who are abusing licit and illicit drugs or who are engaging in other destructive behaviors associated with the industries of vice.

Simon, López, and Frampton also argue that if we are to imagine a postwar on crime in the United States, moving in a different direction, it is important that people are made to reject the prohibitively expensive war on crime and to understand the viability of rehabilitative and reentry programs. They recognize, however, that these programs alone are not likely to fundamentally shake things up enough to end the war on crime. Nevertheless, they contend that

> There is some rhetorical value in simply declaring the war over. Maybe saying so will not, by itself, make it so. But saying so, loudly and often and in the context of an extended conversation regarding where we should go from here, can only help. (Simon, López, and Frampton 2008, 10)

We concur with Simon, López, and Frampton about the importance of reframing the discourse on harm and crime reduction in a context of how the war on crime has actually been self-defeating and counterproductive in at least three ways. First, the war on crime "represented a nationalizing project that promoted a highly artificial image of a crime problem that was more or less the same everywhere. Not only was this image highly misleading about the actual incidence and prevalence of different kinds of crime problems in different communities, but also it almost certainly created more fear and more readiness to respond harshly" (Simon, López, and Frampton 2008, 11). Second, the war on crime was a double-edged sword that "simultaneously made race less visible as a set of public problems while having an enormous impact on the construction of race in the United States" (2008, 12). In the same vein, having Obama as a multiracial president (or not—he's still regarded as black even though his mother was white) at a point in history when the fastest-growing census category is biracial still does not mean that our country is moving beyond racial hierarchies any more than it is moving beyond class or gender hierarchies. Third, in replacing the repressive older discourse of the war on crime, the new discourse needs to be more democratic or conversational in its orientation and more willing to apply principles of crime and social control that look well beyond systems of criminal justice to those other societal systems that address the whole range of human needs and services, both at home and abroad.

Finally, in recognition of the structural conditions of capitalist accumulation and labor exploitation that underlie both the crimes of the powerful and the powerless, the reciprocal relations between those violations in the suite and those violations in the street, which revolve around the social inequality in the distribution of goods, services, and resources, need to be redressed from the perspective of democratizing the ownership of wealth and serving the common welfare of communities (Barak 2012).

Lawmaking

In the area of lawmaking, at least two types of basic policy developments are called for as a means of curbing the emphasis on punitive retribution and of de-escalating the wars on crime in general and on drugs in particular. These policy alternatives include social capital investments and harm reduction strategies on intervention. Both of these types of legislation are aimed at structurally preventing crime and violence before they occur. Armed with the knowledge that many predatory criminals, adolescent or adult, have been victims of abuse and/or neglect before they become perpetrators, social capital anticrime bills are needed to tackle these early risks or symptoms of delinquency and criminality through community advocacy, efficacy, and development. In addition, socially realistic or responsible harm reduction bills are needed not only to decriminalize those personal-choice activities of individual morality that are better left as private rather than public matters but also to criminalize those structural or deregulated activities of corporate malfeasance and misbehavior that adversely affect the well-being of millions of people.

At the same time, regarding the few monopolistic financial institutions whose fraudulent behavior in the previous decade caused the housing and Wall Street meltdowns of 2007–2008 as well as the domestic and global recessions of 2008–2012 that cost some twenty million people to lose their jobs as well as the losses of some $20 trillion in savings and equities, we learned that these banking cartels and related firms were too big to fail or jail because of the havoc this would bring to the society as a whole if they were to be criminally prosecuted. Accordingly, we need to eliminate the risks of this type of mass victimization by breaking up "too big to fail" banks that place the United States at risk for systemic crises. We need to update "Glass-Steagall" to exempt securities trading, insurance operations, and real-estate transactions from the Federal Deposit Insurance Corporation rather than necessarily separating commercial and investment banks. We need to establish state-owned banks, create benefit or "B" corporations, and support environmental defense organizations such as the Business Alliance for Local Living Economies (BALLE) and the American Sustainable Business Council (ASBC). Similarly, we need to expand the number of some 10 million Americans who are involved in worker-owned companies and the 130 million Americans who belong to co-ops and credit unions. We need to pass both a comprehensive infrastructure-human development fund and jobs act and an act to forgive student loan debt. We also need to pass laws that tax earned, unearned, and "carried interest" income at the same rates as well as institute a financial transaction tax to discourage excessive trading and risk. While we are at it, we need to pass laws that integrate climate-change adjustments and financial market incentives (Barak 2013). All of these suggested legal-structural reforms would advance the cause of socializing the wealth for the benefit of the greatest number of people.

Furthermore, those interested in justice for injured crime victims should join forces with the emerging movement for socially responsible corporations that have been struggling to rescind corporate "personhood" through model local ordinances that eliminate those constitutional privileges benefiting corporations doing business within a township, city, or county at the expense of ordinary citizens. By resisting the corporate hegemony within the United States and abroad, these relatively recent laws are attempts by average people to remove themselves from the strangleholds of big corporations and to democratize their local governments (Hartmann 2002). These efforts, more specifically, are helping to rein in corporations that are doing away with worker rights and/or are contributing to the deterioration of the general welfare of society (Derber 1998). Of course, the key to the security and well-being of all rather than just the relatively affluent involves the balanced growth of dynamic and sustainable economies in tandem with domestic and international policies that promote more equitable and just social orders worldwide. A tall order, we know!

Investing in Harm Reduction

Policies of harm reduction are typically associated first and foremost with substance abuse, but the philosophy or strategy of "first, reduce harm" also applies to other demographic hot spots that cause avoidable pain and suffering, not to mention unnecessary financial costs to the victims, to law enforcement, and to the taxpayers. In terms of drug abuse and dependency and/or mental illness, policies of harm reduction make available on request drug, alcohol, and mental health treatment for all. These policies also provide syringes for shooting heroin, mouthpieces for crack pipes, and prescriptions of methadone for addicts at taxpayers' expense.

In the area of illicit drugs and/or substance abuse and in the spirit of de-escalating the war on drugs, there are those who philosophically call for decriminalization and others who call for legalization, regulation, and/or taxation. For examples of related legal changes, more than a dozen states have already decriminalized or legalized medical marijuana and the states of Colorado and Washington have legalized recreational use. Our position regardless of the preferred alternative is to recommend the wholesale shifting of the "drug problem" away from law enforcement and into the medical arena. The use and abuse of drugs becomes a matter of law enforcement and police concern when other violations of the criminal law are also involved, but otherwise the use and abuse of drugs should be treated as a public health concern. Age requirements, restrictions on driving while impaired, and similar necessary regulations remain in place. This kind of wholesale scaling back on the war on drugs would not only significantly reduce the number of persons jailed or imprisoned and lower the costs of incarceration but also free up hundreds of millions of dollars or more annually for community-based treatment programs. With this type of decriminalization policy in place, many fewer families, especially poor and minority, would find themselves needlessly ripped apart by the war on drugs.

De-escalating other public-order violations or crimes of morality such as prostitution or gambling by decriminalizing, deregulating, and so on respects freedom, privacy, and individual autonomy. It also seems to be a fairer policy in light of the highly unequal enforcement and application of current law.

Finally, there is the need to roll back a host of what have been collectively referred to as the new urban social-control techniques. These recently established measures of urban social regulation "have dispersed the logic and operations of spatial control beyond prison walls" and have broadened the range of behaviors and statuses subject to criminal justice intervention while they have diminished the rights of those people who have been targeted for exclusion (Beckett and Herbert 2008, 107). Such acts include the establishment from coast to coast of off-limits orders, trespass laws, and park exclusion laws. These ordinances all combine elements of criminal, civil, and administrative law to define the mere presence in urban space as a crime and promise to "cleanse" those areas of disorder caused by the mere presence of the socially marginal, increasing the state's abilities to search, detain, regulate, and monitor those subject to these new misdemeanor offenses without having to necessarily make an arrest or place someone in jail. In effect, these rules criminalize such statuses as homeless or mentally ill in a public space and, at least initially, require only a person's disappearance from the area (Barak 1991a). Attached to the discredited "broken windows" theory and "zero tolerance" policies of the 1990s, these new techniques of surveillance and social control are leading to skyrocketing violations and eventually to the arresting and jailing of mostly poor people for the crime of poverty. This type of criminalization, of course, expands the net of formal social control, becomes criminogenic, and needs to be stopped before it spreads as a law enforcement rather than a social problem.

Other demographic "hot spots" that cause more pain and injury than the mere presence of debilitated and unsightly people are often under the radar, invisible, and/or ignored by public and private policy alike. Harm reduction, for example, of high-powered, white-collar offenders and corporate abusers moves in the other direction. Since they are undercriminalized or lack the responsible enforcement and/or regulation needed, these behaviors call for the expansion of the law to regulate and/or criminalize. To put it simply, the United Stated needs more laws and socially appropriate penalties for harms perpetrated by the powerful players and institutions that damage the public, workers, and consumers. When acts such as toxic pollution, waste elimination, or environmental destruction adversely affect communities—that is, inflict disproportionate pain and suffering, especially on marginal communities— then some type of compensation and social restitution should be in order for those victims. Further, funds should be allocated to set up investigating and prosecuting teams against those perpetrators for their "impersonal" crimes and public disregard.

When it comes to penalizing corporate lawbreakers, sanctions should do away with the slap-on-the-wrist fines, all too often passed on to the consumers and taxpayers. For example, the use of debarment sanctions would prohibit habitually lawbreaking corporations from receiving any fraction of the $300 billion worth of government contracts given out annually. In addition, creative sanctions should be pursued that involve equity fines, behavioral restrictions, dechartering of corporations, and probationary treatment of corporations. For instance, the criminal justice apparatus now charges probationers and parolees for monitoring these persons where it can and often requires from them some form of restitution. There is no reason that corporations, which have far greater abilities to pay than most offenders, should not contribute to the costs of ensuring their compliance with the law. In other words, as irresponsible members of the community, these offenders should also have to pay back their debts to society with sizable social investments as their penalties.

By instituting polices that regulate in the public interest rather than in the corporate interest, two things become crucial: the ability, first, to ensure enough oversight and regulation of the major industries such as energy, banking, and accounting, and second, to scale back the corporate harms that have been taking a toll on the health, lives, and pocketbooks of average citizens for decades. It is well past time for government to put hundreds of federal cops on the corporate beats of Wall Street and Main Street. Much more in the way of resources for corporate law enforcement is required. The Justice Department, the Internal Revenue Service, the Securities and Exchange Commission, the Food and Drug Administration, and the Consumer Products Safety Commission, to name the most prominent, remain seriously underfunded, understaffed, and undermotivated. Beyond funding and morale, there should be established across these departments an interagency corporate crime division or the development of something like a tactical corporate crime team (TCCT).

More specifically, the US Department of Justice should provide for the collection and dissemination of comprehensive information about the nature and extent of corporate abuse and damage. The Justice Department should also help law enforcement officials identify emerging trends or patterns of corporate harm and direct resources appropriately. In terms of the creation of a permanent, well-funded corporate crime division with specially trained technical personnel, including those from the fields of law, accounting, and information sciences, the TCCT needs to develop strategies to handle such problems as major fraud, corruption, and safety violations as well as the legal-technical means to pursue and prosecute the complexities of corporate-state crime.

Investing in Social Capital

Since domestic and cross-cultural studies alike reveal strong associations between the production of marginal criminality and relative deprivation, economic frustration, social aggression, and family violence, policies of social maintenance are needed to reduce these sources of behavioral conflict. Policies designed to reduce poverty and inequality should be at the front of the agenda. One place to begin is to follow the lead of those communities, usually midsize cities with relatively secure economies, in the United States that have passed ordinances to establish a system of living wages rather than minimum wages. More broadly, legislation is called for that increases economic support and social services, inclusive of jobs programs, education and technical training, and the deployment of universal health care. Such policies, if they materialize, should not be limited to when the economy has tanked and is in need of a stimulus package to save it from another Great Depression; these policies should be deployed as a basic domestic strategy to prevent marginal criminality in good times and bad times alike.

For example, the reduced relative spending on children, families, and education in the United States that has occurred over the past several decades needs to be reversed and even expanded if the nation is to remain globally competitive over the next fifty years. Just as fundamentally, if not more so, monies need to be "earmarked" or redeployed from private-public sources and invested in those urban communities, such as Detroit, for the twin purposes of economic and human development. Holistically designed domestic policies of inclusion should be aimed at providing prenatal care and early childhood development for all. Likewise, to prevent childhood abuse and neglect and to enhance children's intellectual and social growth, social skills and counseling programs are needed in all impoverished communities. Policies are also needed that make programs available to vulnerable or at-risk youth in general as well as more intensive programs of intervention to serve habitual juvenile offenders in particular and to make available on request drug, alcohol, and mental health treatment for all.

Law Enforcement

In the areas of police behavior, at least five policy-related concerns need attention. These include continuing to upgrade the profession of law enforcement, reaffirming due process and equal protection, de-escalating the wars on crime and terrorism, controlling the abuse of power and corruption, and enriching community-based input, control, and participation.

Collectively, these policy recommendations are aimed at curbing aggressive policing, enhancing respect for the rule of law, intensifying police-community empathy, and amending the police mission.

Professionalizing the Police

Many would argue that the police have already obtained professional status, given their hundreds of hours of instruction at statewide academy programs, degrees in law enforcement, and police agency accreditation requirements. Nevertheless, continued education and training should become the norm wherever possible. Academy training devotes little time to domestic violence issues, and a number of other important topics could be the subject of required ongoing training. Continuing education improves one's law enforcement skills and technical knowledge, and it also helps to discourage police abuse of force and the condoning of racist and brutal tactics against marginal others.

Removing from the profession those officers who would, for example, participate in or overlook such beatings as those inflicted on Rodney King by the LAPD or on Abner Louima by the NYPD is absolutely essential if any significant progress is to be made in lessening racial antagonism and raising the perception of law enforcement as a profession worthy of trust and admiration. Many urban cops, in other words, bring to their jobs a negative attitude toward certain community members, undoubtedly a product of the stresses and frustrations of their job. Nevertheless, through educational awareness of human behavior and cultural differences, police officers can be taught to view their on-duty time as a "professional performance" geared toward providing the best service possible to all citizens regardless of class, race, and gender. Most police go into the profession to help make a difference in people's lives, and the training we have in mind will reconnect them with that spirit and provide tools to help them achieve that goal.

Curbing and/or eliminating overtime and moonlighting would probably go a long way toward improving the quality of police performance. For example, the National Institute of Justice (NIJ) (2005) pointed out that about one-third of police officers work twenty or more hours of overtime per month and more than half moonlight at other jobs. Although research has yet to determine how, exactly, fatigue affects police work, there is no doubt that "law enforcement suffers when officers are fatigued due to overtime, shift work, court appearances, and the emotional and physical demands of the job" (NIJ 2005, 13). While police salaries may need to be raised to compensate for the lost salary, such a move would make police work more consistent with many other occupations affecting or involving public safety, such as airline pilots, truck drivers, and nurses—all of whom must abide by working-hours standards and restrictions designed to prevent excess fatigue. Such standards should certainly apply to law enforcement officials, who have been delegated the only legitimate monopoly over the deadly use of force.

Reaffirming Due Process and Equal Protection

The erosion of due process and equal protection rights over the past decades in the United States gained momentum with the hurried passage of an antiterrorism law—the USA Patriot Act—in the weeks after 9/11. The original act had sixteen provisions that were scheduled to expire at the end of 2005 unless renewed by Congress. In the fall of that year, the 109th Congress made fourteen of those provisions permanent as part of the USA Patriot Improvement and Reauthorization Act that became law in 2006. The other two were passed with sunset clauses subjecting them to future congressional renewal. One of these provisions was on "roving wiretaps" and the other on "searches" of library records, business records, medical files, and other documents.

These administrative (rather than judicially approved) subpoenas are not totally new to federal investigators, for the FBI had already been employing these surveillance and investigative procedures in drug and health-care fraud cases. The second revision of the Patriot Act occurred in July 2008. It included the controversial immunity for the phone companies that cooperated in the National Security Agency (NSA) wiretapping program authorized by the Bush administration. Compared to the laws before and after 9/11, the most recent measure "gives the executive branch broader latitude in eavesdropping on people abroad and at home who it believes are tied to terrorism, and it reduced the role of a secret intelligence court in overseeing some operations" (Lichtblau 2008, 1), in spite of the very low rate of successfully prosecuting these cases, as shown in chapter 9.

Reinforcing the rule of law becomes all the more important not only in the context of homeland security, the increasing militarization of the police, and the revelations of NSA surveillance but also in light of the United States' denial of these rights to those suspected terrorists or "enemy combatants" incarcerated in places such as Guantanamo Bay Detention Camp in Cuba. For example, at a minimum, we must reinstate various legal safeguards that had previously been watered down, such as the so-called good faith exemptions in having probable cause when obtaining reasonable search warrants, or respecting the fundamental principle that no person should be deprived of his liberty without the right to habeas corpus, or most notably being charged and tried for a crime in a court of law or set free. We also recommend the suppression of supersurveillance activities that indiscriminately invade every person's rights to privacy by way of the "interception of wire, telephone, and computer communications, the searching of businesses and residences, the seizing of business and library records, or other similar items of evidence" (Logan 2007, 287).

Finally, we recommend the creation of independent oversight boards of law enforcement practices in general as well as the mandatory videotaping of interrogations and use-of-force incidents in particular.

De-escalating the Wars on Crime and Terrorism

Once again, in the context of the recent conflation of the "war on crime" and the "war on terrorism," we need to de-escalate our language and our practices, keeping the actions and the roles of the police and the military as separate and as unique as "real politics" will allow. For example, even the Bush administration in the summer of 2005 toned down its metaphor from a "war on terror" to the "global struggle against violent extremism." The Obama administration has also pledged wherever it can to use criminal courts rather than military tribunals to combat terrorists. Similarly, rather than a war metaphor for combating illicit drugs and drug abusers, policy should be guided by a medical metaphor that seeks not to punish but to assist those who have become drug-dependent victims to heal and recover. More generally, as law enforcement knows that most of the answers to crime lie elsewhere than within the administration of criminal justice, efforts of social control should involve institutions other than law enforcement whenever possible.

Two policy changes that would help to facilitate a de-escalation of the wars on crime, even during an era of heightened sensitivity to violent extremism, would include scaling back some paramilitary trends in law enforcement and curbing the use of zero-tolerance policies as discussed above and below. In the case of paramilitary approaches to a war on crime, for example, the use of SWAT teams has been extended from its original purposes of dealing with hostage negotiation situations to raiding public housing projects and college dormitories seeking out marijuana dealers. Such practices, especially in those marginal communities already disenchanted with the police, only serve to further alienate these groups of citizens. More selective and narrower uses of these tactics in law enforcement are called for.

Law enforcement must distinguish between battling murderers or terrorists on the one hand and confronting petty criminals or social nonconformists on the other hand. Zero-tolerance policies that disable police or judicial discretion are seldom good ideas, but where enacted they should distinguish between behaviors that pose serious risks of injury and harm and those nonviolent and unthreatening behaviors that pose no security risks or tangible harm. In other words, homeless addicts or veterans and the mentally ill should be referred by law enforcement to human services and/or voluntary agencies, thus "filtering" out from the criminal justice system all but hardcore or serious offenders.

Controlling Police Abuse of Power and Corruption

Since the creation of formal policing in the nineteenth century, police abuse of power and/or corruption has always been to varying degrees a fact of local law enforcement. From the very beginning, police officers were known for selling protection and administering "curbside justice," buying their positions and promotions, and ignoring violations of the law in exchange for money or other favors. Historically, the use and abuse of the police force has always been a controversial issue, especially in those communities of color where a disproportionate use of this behavior, including deadly force, has occurred. Over the years, several policies have been used to reduce both necessary and unnecessary use of force by police officers. We support the use of all of these policies and encourage their more extensive use. These include instituting tougher and clearer departmental guidelines, monitoring the levels of aggression and the use-of-force incidents with dashboard-mounted cameras and investigation, employing anger- and stress-management techniques, psychological counseling for officers who request such services, and administering psychological tests as a prescreening effort to identify individuals prone to abuse of power or who are vulnerable to handling stress badly.

Ellwyn Stoddard (1968, 204), in a classic article on police corruption, identified ten types of corruption that he described as constituting the "blue-coat code":

1. Bribery—accepting cash or gifts in exchange for nonenforcement of the law.
2. Chiseling—demanding discounts, free admission, and free food.

3. Extortion—the threat of enforcement and arrest if a bribe is not given.
4. Favoritism—giving breaks on law enforcement, such as for traffic violations committed by families and friends of the police.
5. Mooching—accepting food, drinks, and admission to entertainment.
6. Perjury—lying for other officers apprehended in illegal activity.
7. Prejudice—unequal enforcement of the law with respect to racial and ethnic minorities.
8. Premeditated theft—planned burglaries and thefts.
9. Shakedown—taking items from the scene of a theft or a burglary [or a drug deal] the officer is investigating.
10. Shopping—taking small, inexpensive items from a crime scene or an unsecured business or home.

Policy recommendations here simply encourage all police departments to incorporate into their organizational frameworks some of the more successful efforts to control and reduce corrupt activities, which naturally contribute to the erosion of public confidence and trust in law enforcement. Beyond setting high moral standards, training in ethical issues, and selecting the most qualified officers, departments should establish rigid policies of discipline and prosecution in response to violating customary policies, procedures, and laws. Departments should, of course, also strive for the uniform enforcement of the law, neither favoring the affiliations of some groups nor penalizing the affiliations of other groups. Where possible, internal affairs units of law enforcement departments should become proactive in ferreting out illegal and unethical activity, and supervisors, as a rule, should be held responsible or answerable for the actions of their subordinates. When and where corruption becomes too widespread and "out of control," then these departments should become subject to outside commissions, task forces, special prosecutors, and court oversight if necessary.

Enriching Community Control of the Police

In those marginal communities like the ghetto and the barrio, where both overzealous policing and underenforcement occur simultaneously, disadvantaged blacks and Latinos believe that "they are always under terror without protection from the authorities" (Wilkinson, Beaty, and Lurry 2009, 36). Without dependable legal protection, self- or crew protection exemplifies Black's theory of self-help, where crime by these youths becomes a means of social control (Black 1983, 1993). Accordingly, it is little wonder that in these marginal communities, the history of police-community relations and efforts aimed at improving them have received mixed reviews at best, including a variety of activities that have fallen under the rubric of "community policing." Moreover, the widespread skepticism and mistrust from many inner-city urban residents leads them to often view these efforts as little more than public relations gimmicks. To go beyond those social interactions that are seen primarily as image boosters for the police or as citizens becoming extensions of local law enforcement as police "informants," reforms and programs are called for that empower the police.

This means above all else that the police need to take the frameworks, norms, and grievances of these marginalized groups seriously or risk the consequences of more crime as self-help and self-protection. In other words, the state is subject to losing its moral authority when it fails to recognize the moral imperatives of self-defense, for example, when people are defending themselves or their families from violence. Also, the racial and ethnic profiling that often occurs in Latino or Afro-Caribbean communities, for example, buttressed by the uncertainty of immigrant status, aggravates the disrespectful treatment that residents experience (Lopez 2008; Solis, Portillos, and Brunson 2009). In response, what are called for are not only police strategies with youth in mind but also the involvement of those groups, young and old, in discussions of proposed police strategies, such outcomes allowing for the coproduction of local strategies of harm reduction.

Other related strategies of police-community reform include the implementation of a community ombudsman or the creation of marginally represented citizen review boards with reasonable authority and power to serve or guard against overzealous and/or abusive police practices in "high-crime" areas. When police must answer for their behavior and are accountable to the citizens from those communities that they serve, much can be done to improve police-community interaction and to build the public trust in local law enforcement. The police may also identify and train their officers to lead workshops on conflict and dispute resolution and on human dignity and multiculturalism. In a different but related vein of raising the public's confidence in these communities, the inclusion of all representative groups (e.g., minorities, women, gays) in neighborhood patrols, for example, should be highly visible as a means of sensitizing the police and the community to each other's needs.

Adjudication

The middle stage of the administration of criminal justice involving prosecutors, defense attorneys, and judges who are acting as legal agents of adjudication for the state and the accused, engaged in the processes of negotiated plea bargains or adversarial trials, is often thought of as the fulcrum of the system since who is and who is not guilty of a crime is ultimately determined here. Historically, until the decline of the indeterminate and the rise of the determinate sentencing systems that started in the late 1970s, judges used to wield a great deal of influence vis-à-vis their discretion during the sentencing phase to decide on the type and length of punishment. A consequence of these changes in the sentencing law was to transfer this power of sentencing discretion to prosecutors. Recently, there has been a resurrection in the discretionary authority as well as in the social activism of the judiciary. One product of this activism has been the development of problem-solving courts.

As part of the movement in restorative justice, problem-solving courts have blossomed throughout the United States. Today, every state has at least one problem-
solving court, and all told, there are more than two thousand of these courts. Of the
eleven different kinds of problem-solving courts, the three most common are drug
courts, domestic violence courts, and community courts. Originally designed for
low-level criminal cases, mostly misdemeanors (involving such crimes as drug possession, prostitution, and vandalism), now there is an array of other courts addressing
both the less serious and more serious felony offenses. These include mental health
courts, reentry courts, DWI courts, gun courts, family treatment courts, juvenile
drug courts, homeless courts, and youth courts (Berman and Feinblatt 2005).

These courts are the products of judges and attorneys who have turned the
traditional adversary system of case processing and adjudication into a caring and
problem-solving community tribunal. The goal here is to move away from treating
criminal cases as part of an undifferentiated mass of assembly-line equal justice and
toward a restorative model of case-by-case, individualized justice. Using a tailored
approach to justice, these problem-solving courts invite the community, victims, offenders, social service providers, and so on to participate in the adjudicative process
and to come up with some kind of community-based alternative to jail or prison,
usually involving social services and/or community restitution projects. The product
of this nonadversarial and nonbureaucratic approach to personalized justice has been
to change the behavioral patterns of habitual offenders, enhance the safety of victims,
and improve the quality of community life. These problem-solving courts operate in
the spirit of harm reduction.

Some prosecutors in this country have modified their roles and their use of prosecutorial discretion to become advocates for those who are vulnerable and/or cannot
defend themselves. For example, the prosecutors in Alameda and San Francisco,
California, instituted changes in the labeling and treatment of sexual molesters as
well as adolescent sex workers. In the case of teenage prostitutes, these adolescent
girls were legally transformed from delinquent criminals into victims of exploitation
and molestation. In these and other progressive offices of prosecution, the officers
of the court are redefining crime and public safety, moving away from incarceration
and throwing-away-the-key approaches to ones that also involve the prevention of
crime and violence. These prosecutors, like many of the problem-solving judges, are
adopting a public-health approach to crime and violence, where policies and strategies are employed to treat the victims and to assault the problems with heavy dosages
of early childhood intervention and preventions for those at high risk.

Curbing Prosecutorial Discretion and Misconduct

Despite the recent activism of judges and prosecutors involved in problem solving
courts, well over 95 percent of cases are resolved without a trial, and that unchecked
prosecutorial discretion and decision-making remains the most important factor in
adjudication outcomes. This unconstrained discretion often results in prosecutors

ignoring or not conforming to the Supreme Court's 1963 holding in *Brady v. Maryland* that required prosecutors to provide the defense with any exculpatory evidence that could materially affect a verdict or a sentence. Alex Kozinski, the chief judge of the United States Court of Appeals for the Ninth Circuit, wrote in a 2013 dissenting opinion in a case involving the conviction of Kenneth Olsen for producing ricin, a toxic poison, for use as a weapon: "There is an epidemic of Brady violations abroad in the land" (quoted in *New York Times* 2014, SR10). The problem stems from the fact that prosecutors have the discretion to decide when a piece of evidence would be helpful to the defense. Furthermore, prosecutors have little incentive to turn over a single piece of exculpatory evidence when they are in possession of a mountain of evidence proving guilt, especially since appellate courts do not commonly sanction these violations. The Center for Prosecutor Integrity has reported that over the past fifty years, the courts have punished prosecutorial misconduct in less than 2 percent of the cases in which it has occurred. Similarly, the National Registry of Exonerations has reported that 43 percent of wrongful convictions are the result of official misconduct (*New York Times* 2014).

These forms of prosecutorial discretion and/or misconduct could be curbed, in the case of *Brady* violations in particular, by adopting a standard "open file" policy of transparency, which would involve turning over all exculpatory evidence as a rule not subject to the discretion of prosecutors. Not only would this reduce the potential for errors, but it would also help to sensitize the criminal justice system to the unchecked powers of prosecutors more generally.

Improving Representation and Technology for Indigent Defendants

With respect to equal protection and other rights of due process for the indigent accused and convicted, there is a need to improve the criminal law competency and remuneration of legal counsel, especially those defense attorneys affiliated with court-appointed systems or in cases involving capital crimes and the death penalty. Wherever appropriate, defendants and their attorneys should also have access to the latest technological developments. For example, all persons accused or convicted of a crime where DNA tests would be relevant to proving or disproving guilt or innocence should have access to that technology. We agree with those forty-seven states that have passed laws providing convicted felons access to DNA evidence and not with the Supreme Court's 5–4 ruling in 2009 that convicted criminals do not have a constitutional right to obtain access to a state's biological evidence in order to conduct DNA testing pursuant to their claims of innocence.

Finally, in light of some three decades of contracting legal rights, it makes sense to reexamine, expand, or reinstate the rights of those convicted to appeal their verdicts, sentences, and living and working conditions. Such policies both resist the human rights violations of correctional workers and locked-up inmates alike, and they improve the morale and human dignity of all concerned and responsible parties.

Corrections

Prison growth has (1) had only a limited impact on the amount of crime, (2) been the product of intentional policy, not natural forces, (3) decreased social justice, and (4) damaged the well-being of poor communities (Clear 2008). Changes are called for that curb excessively long sentences (i.e., more than one hundred years), reverse the trends of increasing lengths of imprisonment for minor and nonviolent crimes, and create alternatives to incarceration for as many convicted offenders as possible. The types of policies we recommend include the abandonment of mandatory sentencing, increased judicial discretion in sentencing, the expansion of intermediate or community sanctions that go beyond slapping a tracking device on an offender, and the delivery of related human and social services. We also recommend abolishing the practices of treating adolescents as adult defendants and of housing juvenile or youthful offenders with adult offenders under any circumstances.

Most importantly, we recommend the repeal of the 1996 Prison Litigation Reform Act. This act has effectively barred inmate complaints from federal court and, in effect, has hidden prison operations from public view. Without the repeal of this act, subjecting correctional authorities once again to the rule of law, inmates are left unfree from the arbitrary and cruel practices associated with the incarceration binge in the United States.

In terms of professionalizing the field of corrections, educational and training requirements should be upgraded across the board, with a bachelor's degree in some behavioral or social science required as a minimum for gaining entrance into the field. Corrections is an occupation that can certainly benefit from workshops, experimentation, and research into institutionalized behavior and control. Finally, programs that promote the development of self-actualization and social integration for inmates or parolees are also advocated as essential for reintegrating offenders back into the community as fully participating citizens. Former NIJ director Jeremy Travis noted some five years ago that 630,000 people leave prison each year and reenter society, so "reentry is not an option. Reentry reflects the iron law of imprisonment: they all come back" (Travis 2005, xxi). In short, prison must do a better job in preparing inmates for their inevitable releases, and local communities should do a better job of assisting those returning to society.

Abandoning Mandatory Sentences, Reducing Minimum Sentencing, and Abolishing Capital Punishment

Current mandatory sentencing laws such as three strikes, even if uniformly applied, still have adverse, accumulatively negative effects on African and Latin male Americans in particular, as these groups of the marginal classes are disproportionately overrepresented in prison. Accordingly, we recommend a sentencing system that does away with the minimum aspect of the sentencing guidelines but keeps a "maximum time served" and allows for a fuller reinstitutionalization of "good time" reductions in sentences as an incentive for early release. In particular, we applaud the twenty-nine states that have moved to cut back on mandatory sentences since 2000, particularly for low-level and nonviolent drug offenders. Similarly, as this book goes to press, we are supportive of two bills pending before the US Congress: the Smarter Sentencing Act and the Recidivism Reduction and Public Safety Act. Together, these laws if passed would halve mandatory minimum sentences for certain nonviolent drug crimes, provide judges more discretion to sentence below the minimum in some cases, offer early release of thousands of inmates disproportionately punished for crack cocaine usage, and allow prisoners to earn credit toward earlier release by participating in education, job training, and drug treatment programs.

We also recommend abolishing the death penalty in the United States. First, its past and present use does not reflect equal justice for all. It is too selective and arbitrary in all but the most heinous crimes. More particularly, the death penalty is applied disproportionately to poor people and minorities with white victims. Second, the time is well past due for this nation, as one of only a few in the democratic nation-states worldwide to continue to violate the most basic of human rights—the right to life—to desist from this practice as it briefly did for a few years in the 1970s and, more recently, as several states instituted temporary (if unfortunately not permanent) moratoriums on state executions.

A Moratorium on Prison Construction and the Privatization of Prisons

The United States has the largest per capita prison population in the world at a time when rates of street criminality are generally as low as or lower than they have been in some forty years. Put simply, we do not need additional prisons that will be filled with minor offenders at high costs to taxpayers and communities. Politicians are not as eager to talk tough on crime as they once were and are more likely now than perhaps ever before to talk about runaway prison expenses because prisons are raiding state budgets everywhere, draining money from already tight and contracting budgets in education, social services, and other basic areas of crime prevention. Ultimately, this nation does not need more than 2.2 million cells, and a moratorium on building any new facilities still leaves plenty of room for those who need to be there.

Private prisons, more so than public prisons, create vested interests in increasing the amount of punishment by involving big business and Wall Street in crime control for profits (Selman and Leighton 2010). Whether we are talking about the privatization of prisons or the privatization of prison services such as the delivery of health care, wherever possible, corners are cut to the bare minimums to support high salaries for executives and a return on shareholders' investments. As corporate and not state bodies, privately owned prisons are exempt from many disclosure requirements because the Freedom of Information Act does not apply, so transparency and accountability are much more difficult to secure.

In a similar vein, private prisons do not, for example, provide lists of racial breakdowns of prisoners or other information considered vital in the public sector. They may also conceal some of their practices as these may be protected by "corporate policy" or "trade secrets." Finally, the movement for privatization inside and outside of the correctional apparatus provides one of the more obvious or conspicuous parts of what has become over the past couple of decades a growing criminal justice–industrial complex where interests other than those of the public in general and of crime control in particular are subject to the vagaries of the marketplace.

Intermediate Sanctions and Community-Based Alternatives

We strongly recommend the development, elaboration, and diversification of intermediate sanctions, including but not limited to: intensive-supervision probation and parole, day reporting centers, halfway houses, fines, and home confinement and electronic monitoring. These community-based alternatives to prison have mostly abandoned the "rehabilitative ideal," emphasizing instead the retributive, deterrence, and punitive objectives of corrections. We recommend that policies reaffirm rehabilitation and prisoner reentry programs. These forms of reintegration, as the primary goal of corrections, working in tandem with the developing practices of restorative justice, are not only more economical, but they are also preferred scientifically speaking as alternatives to jail and prison. Furthermore, expanding the use of intermediate sanctions in lieu of the more expensive and harsh methods of incarceration is more humane and constructive for offenders, victims, and communities alike.

Prisoner Reentry and Human Services Delivery

With the billions of dollars saved from expensive new prison construction and potentially from the lowered operating costs of serving hundreds of thousands of fewer inmates each year by way of intermediate sanctions and reduced sentencing structures, criminal justice could develop a whole range of human services inside and outside of prisons. In the spirit of both restorative and social justice and in the context of reintegration and community efficacy, victims and offenders both need access to programs in transition, employment, counseling, education, job training, and other types of reentry programs. Toward these ends, we strongly recommend a significant expansion of the $150 million allocated per year for the Second Chance Act signed into law by President Bush in April 2008.

Considering that there are at least 650,000 prisoners currently returning to the "free world" annually and that the United States currently spends more than $68 billion yearly on corrections, we think a more viable figure for reentry programs would be at least $2 billion dollars per annum. This figure would represent only one thirty-fourth of the current total correctional budget, amounting to $300 per returning parolee/prisoner rather than the current $25 per year (less the expenses for operating transition programs). As a preventive measure against the existing high rates of recidivism in this country as well as the prohibitive costs of incarcerating inmates averaging about $30,000 per annum, these additional dollars for prisoner reentry programs represent common sense, not rocket science.

With respect to the more than 650,000 released inmates each year for the foreseeable future, local communities may take various steps to facilitate reentry. These
include banning the boxes on application forms that ask whether or not one has
ever been convicted of a felony, city ordinances and laws prohibiting discrimination
against former prisoners, and resolutions and other incentives for employers who are
willing to assist ex-offenders. In addition, support should be available for families of
inmates and for "criminals anonymous" groups.

Finally, related policy measures such as the denial or restriction of welfare benefits,
public assistance, educational grants, and the loss of the right to vote for persons
convicted of crimes need to be seriously reconsidered and overhauled. For the most
part, these types of justice policies and practices of felon disenfranchisement tend to
worsen situations of deprivation and to stoke the flames of more, not less, criminality. These punitive approaches also serve to reinforce the social exclusion rather than
the social inclusion of ex-offenders.

References

Several common sources of data are referenced rather than through multiple similar entries for different years of the same publication:

BJS (Bureau of Justice Statistics) publishes annual data on prisoners, jail inmates, capital punishment, and victimization, to name a few. The Bureau of Justice Statistics is an agency of the US Department of Justice. Most of the publications are listed below, although some text references to BJS that include the name of the publication are not. The Bureau of Justice Statistics can be accessed online at http://www.ojp.usdoj.gov/bjs.

FBI or UCR (followed by year): US Department of Justice, Federal Bureau of Investigation, *Crime in America* (Washington, DC: US Government Printing Office). The Federal Bureau of Investigation can be accessed online at http://www.fbi.gov.

Sourcebook or *Sourcebook of Criminal Justice Statistics* (followed by year): Kathleen Maguire and Ann L. Pastore, eds. 2003. *Sourcebook of Criminal Justice Statistics*. Washington, DC: US Department of Justice, Bureau of Justice Statistics. The *Sourcebook* can be accessed online at http://www.albany.edu/sourcebook/.

Statistical Abstract of the United States (*Stat Abs* [followed by year]): The US Census Bureau annually publishes this reference volume. Current and historical volumes are available through http://www.census.gov/prod/www/abs/statab.html.

Acker, James, et al. 1998. "The Death Penalty: A Scholarly Forum." In *Selected Readings in Criminal Justice*, edited by Philip L. Reichel, 166–78. San Diego, CA: Greenhaven.

Agozino, Biko. 1997. *Black Women and the Criminal Justice System*. Aldershot, Eng.: Ashgate.

Alexander, Michelle. 2012. *The New Jim Crow: Mass Incarceration in the Age of Colorblindness*. New York: The New Press.

American Civil Liberties Union of Michigan. 2005. "Court Rules Every Michigan Citizen Is Entitled to Legal Representation." *Civil Liberties Newsletter* 4 (10): 1.

American Community Survey Reports. 2011. *Education and Synthetic Work-Life Earnings Estimates*. September. Washington, DC: US Census Bureau. http://www.census.gov/prod/2011pubs/acs-14.pdf.

American Society for Aesthetic Plastic Surgery. 2004. "Cosmetic Surgery Quick Facts." http://www.surgery.org/press/procedurefacts-asqf.php.

———. 2013. "Cosmetic Procedures Increase in 2012." News release, March 12. http://www.surgery.org/media/news-releases/cosmetic-procedures-increase-in-2012.

Amnesty International. 1999a. "'Not Part of My Sentence': Violations of the Human Rights of Women in Custody." Report, AI index AMR 51/019/1999, Amnesty International, New York, March 1. http://www.amnesty.org/en/library/asset/AMR51/019/1999/en/7588269a-e33d-11dd-808b-bfd8d459a3de/amr510191999en.pdf.

———. 1999b. "United States of America: Race, Rights, and Police Brutality." Report, AI index AMR 51/147/1999, Amnesty International, New York, January 9. http://www.amnesty.org/en/library/asset/AMR51/147/1999/en/735f2b8c-e038-11dd-865a-d728958ca30a/amr511471999en.pdf.

———. 2000. *Amnesty International: Annual Report 2000*. http://www.amnesty.org/en/library/info/POL10/001/2000/en.

Andersen, Margaret. 1988. "Moving Our Minds: Studying Women and Reconstructing Sociology." *Teaching Sociology* 16:123–32.

Andersen, Margaret L., and Patricia Hill Collins. 1998. *Race, Class and Gender: An Anthology*. 3rd ed. Belmont, CA: Wadsworth.

Anderson, Charles H. 1974. *The Political Economy of Social Class*. Englewood Cliffs, NJ: Prentice-Hall.

Anderson, S. E. 1995. *The Black Holocaust: For Beginners*. New York: Writers and Readers.

Anita Borg Institute. 2005. "Letter in Response to Summers." January 14. http://anitaborginstitute.org/news/archive/chronicle-of-a-controversy/.

Armstrong, David, and Peter Newcomb. 2004. "The Forbes 400." *Forbes*, October 11, 103.

Armstrong, Karen. 2005. "Ghosts of Our Past." In *Violence and Terrorism*, edited by Thomas Badey, 14–17. Dubuque, IA: McGraw-Hill/Dushkin.

Aronowitz, Stanley, and William DiFazio. 1994. *The Jobless Future: Sci-Tech and the Dogma of Work*. Minneapolis: University of Minnesota Press.

Arthur, Charles. 2013. "Symantec Discovers 2005 US Computer Virus Attack on Iran Nuclear Plants." *Guardian*, February 26. http://www.guardian.co.uk/technology/2013/feb/26/symantec-us-computer-virus-iran-nuclear.

Auerbach, Jerold S. 1976. *Unequal Justice: Lawyers and Social Change in Modern America*. New York: Oxford University Press.

Austin, Regina, and Michael Schill. 1991. "Black, Brown, Poor and Poisoned: Minority Grassroots Environmentalism and the Quest for Eco-Justice." *Kansas Journal of Law and Public Policy* (Summer): 69–82.

Baca Zinn, Maxine, Pierrette Hondagneu-Sotelo, and Michael Messner, eds. 2005. *Gender through the Prism of Difference.* 3rd ed. New York: Oxford University Press.

Bakan, Joel. 2004. *The Corporation: The Pathological Pursuit of Profit and Power.* New York: Free Press.

Balko, Radley. 2013. "Rise of the Warrior Cop." *Wall Street Journal,* August 7. http://online.wsj.com/news/articles/SB10001424127887323848804578608040780519904.

Barak, Gregg. 1980. *In Defense of Whom? A Critique of Criminal Justice Reform.* Cincinnati, OH: Anderson.

———, ed. 1991a. *Crimes by the Capitalist State: An Introduction to State Criminality.* Albany: State University of New York Press.

———. 1991b. *Gimme Shelter: A Social History of Homelessness in Contemporary America.* New York: Praeger.

———, ed. 1994. *Media, Process, and the Social Construction of Crime: Studies in Newsmaking Criminology.* New York: Routledge.

———, ed. 1996. *Representing O. J.: Murder, Criminal Justice and Mass Culture.* Albany, NY: Harrow and Heston.

———. 1998. *Integrating Criminologies.* Boston: Allyn & Bacon.

———. 2000. "Repressive versus Restorative and Social Justice: A Case for Integrative Praxis." *Contemporary Justice Review* 3 (1): 39–44.

———. 2001. "Crime and Crime Control in an Age of Globalization. A Theoretical Dissection." *Critical Criminology: An International Journal* 10 (1): 57–72.

———. 2003. *Violence and Nonviolence: Pathways to Understanding.* Thousand Oaks, CA: Sage.

———. 2004a. "Class, Race, and Gender in Criminology and Criminal Justice: Ways of Seeing Difference." *Race, Gender, and Class: An Interdisciplinary and Multicultural Journal* 11 (4): 80–97.

———. 2004b. "A Reciprocal Approach to Terrorism and Terrorist-Like Behavior." In *Terrorism and Counter-Terrorism: Criminological Perspectives,* edited by Mathieu Deflem, 33–49. Amsterdam: Elsevier.

———. 2005. "A Reciprocal Approach to Peacemaking Criminology: Between Adversarialism and Mutualism." *Theoretical Criminology* 9 (2): 131–52.

———, ed. 2007. *Violence, Conflict, and World Order: Critical Conversations on State Sanctioned Justice.* Lanham, MD: Rowman & Littlefield.

———. 2008. "Homeland Security Failed to Protect U.S. from Financial Harm." *Ann Arbor News,* December 12, A10.

———. 2009. *Criminology: An Integrated Approach.* Lanham, MD: Rowman & Littlefield.

———. 2012. *Theft of a Nation: Wall Street Looting and Federal Regulatory Colluding.* Lanham, MD: Rowman & Littlefield.

———. 2013. "The Flickering Desires for White-Collar Crime Studies in the Post-Financial Crisis: Will They Ever Shine Brightly?" *Western Criminology Review* 14 (2): 61–71.

Barak, Gregg, and Stuart Henry. 1999. "An Integrative-Constitutive Theory of Crime, Law, and Social Justice." In *Social Justice/Criminal Justice: The Maturation of Critical Theory in Law, Crime, and Deviance*, edited by Bruce A. Arrigo, 136–51. Belmont, CA: West/Wadsworth, 1999.

Barker, Emily, Brian Baxter, Alison Frankel, and Nate Raymond. 2008. "Progress Report." *Federal Sentencing Reporter* 20 (3) (February): 206–10.

Barlow, Melissa. 1998. "Race and the Problem of Crime in *Time* and *Newsweek* Cover Stories, 1946–1995." *Social Justice* 25 (2): 149–83.

Barstow, David. 2003. "When Workers Die: U.S. Rarely Seeks Charges for Deaths in Workplace." *New York Times*, December 22. http://www.nytimes.com/2003/12/22/national/22OSHA.html.

Beckett, Katherine, and Steve Herbert. 2008. "The Punitive City Revisited: The Transformation of Urban Social Control." In *After the War on Crime: Race, Democracy, and a New Reconstruction*, edited by M. L. Frampton, I. H. López, and J. Simon, 106–22. New York: New York University Press.

Beckett, Katherine, and Theodore Sasson. 2000. *The Politics of Injustice: Crime and Punishment in America*. Thousand Oaks, CA: Pine Forge.

Beirne, Piers, and James Messerschmidt. 1991. *Criminology*. San Diego, CA: Harcourt Brace Jovanovich.

———. 2000. *Criminology*. 3rd ed. Boulder, CO: Westview.

Beiser, Vince. 2008. "First, Reduce Harm." *Miller-McCune*, November–December, 60–71.

Belknap, Joanne. 2007. *The Invisible Woman: Gender, Crime, and Justice*. 3rd ed. Belmont, CA: Wadsworth.

Bell, Derrick. 1989. "Racism: A Prophecy for the Year 2000." *Rutgers Law Review* 42:93–108; revised and expanded version in "After We're Gone: Prudent Speculations on America in a Post-Racial Epoch." *St. Louis Law Review* 34 (1990): 1–8.

———. 1998. "Foreword." In *Images of Color, Images of Crime: Readings*, edited by Coramae Richey Mann and Marjorie S. Zatz, vii–viii. Los Angeles: Roxbury.

Benjamin, Daniel, and Steven Simon. 2002. *The Age of Sacred Terror*. New York: Random House.

Benjamin, Rich. 2012. "The Gated Community Mentality." *New York Times*, March 29. http://www.nytimes.com/2012/03/30/opinion/the-gated-community-mentality.html?_r=0.

Benson, Christopher. 2007. "A Renewed Call for Diversity among Supreme Court Clerks: How a Diverse Body of Clerks Can Aid the High Court as an Institution." *Harvard Black Letter Law Journal* 23:23–54.

Berman, Greg, and John Feinblatt. 2005. *Good Courts: The Case for Problem-Solving Justice*. New York: The New Press.

Bernard, April. 2013. "The Intersectional Alternative: Explaining Female Criminality." *Feminist Criminology* 8 (1): 3–19. doi:10.1177/1557085112445304.

Best, Joel. 1990. *Threatened Children: Rhetoric and Concern about Child-Victims*. Chicago: University of Chicago Press.

Binstein, Michael, and Charles Bowden. 1993. *Trust Me: Charles Keating and the Missing Billions*. New York: Random House.

Black, Donald. 1976. *The Behavior of Law*. New York: Academic.

———. 1983. "Crime as Social Control." *American Sociological Review* 48:34–45.

———. 1993. *The Social Structure of Right and Wrong*. New York: Cambridge University Press.

Blast, Carol. 1997. "Driving While Black: Stopping Motorists on a Subterfuge." *Criminal Law Bulletin* 33:457.

Blau, Judith, and Peter Blau. 1982. "The Cost of Inequality: Metropolitan Structure and Violent Crime." *American Sociological Review* 47 (1): 114–29.

Blitstein, Ryan. 2009. "Racism's Hidden Toll." *Miller-McCune*, July–August, 48–57.

Bloom, Barbara, Barbara Owen, and Stephanie Covington. 2003. "Gender-Responsive Strategies: Research, Practice, and Guiding Principles for Women Offenders." Report, National Institute of Corrections/US Department of Justice, Washington, DC. http://www.nicic.org/pubs/2003/018017.pdf.

BloombergView. 2013. "The NSA's Alarming Misbehavior." August 16. http://www.bloomberg.com/news/2013-08-16/the-nsa-s-alarming-misbehavior.html.

Blum, Deborah. 2005. "Solving for XX: What Science Can (and Can't) Tell Larry Summers about the Difference between Men and Women." *Boston Globe* online edition, January 23. http://www.boston.com/news/globe/ideas/articles/2005/01/23/solving_for_xx/.

Blumstein, Alfred. 1993. "Interview with Professor Alfred Blumstein of Carnegie Mellon University." *Law Enforcement News* 422:10.

———. 2002. "Why Is Crime Falling—Or Is It?" *Perspectives on Crime and Justice: 2000–2001 Lecture Series*. Washington, DC: National Institute of Justice. http://www.ncjrs.gov/pdffiles1/nij/187100.pdf.

Blumstein, Alfred, and J. Wallman. 2000. *The Crime Drop in America*. New York: Cambridge University Press.

Body-Gendrot, Sophie. 2000. *The Social Control of Cities? A Comparative Perspective*. Oxford: Blackwell.

Bohm, Robert. 1998. "Understanding Crime and Social Control in Market Economies: Looking Back and Moving Forward." In *Cutting the Edge: Current Perspectives in Radical/Critical Criminology and Criminal Justice*, edited by Jeffrey Ross, 18–33. Westport, CT: Praeger.

Bohm, Robert M., and Keith N. Haley. 2004. *Introduction to Criminal Justice*. 3rd ed. Boston: McGraw-Hill.

———. 2005. *Introduction to Criminal Justice*. 4th ed. Boston: McGraw-Hill.

Bombardieri, Marcella. 2005. "Harvard Women's Group Rips Summers." *Boston Globe* online edition, January 19. http://www.boston.com/news/education/higher/articles/2005/01/19/harvard_womens_group_rips_summers/.

Bonilla-Silva, Eduardo. 1997. "Rethinking Racism: Toward a Structural Interpretation." *American Sociological Review* 62:465–80.

Braithwaite, John. 1989. *Crime, Shame, and Reintegration.* Cambridge: Cambridge University Press.

———. 1992. "Poverty, Power and White-Collar Crime: Sutherland and the Paradoxes of Criminological Theory." In *White Collar Crime Reconsidered,* edited by Kip Schlegel and David Weisburd, 78–107. Boston: Northeastern University Press.

Braithwaite, John, Valerie Braithwaite, and Eliza Ahmed. 2005. "Reintegrative Shaming." In *The Essential Criminology Reader,* edited by Stuart Henry and Mark Lanier, 286–96. Boulder, CO: Westview.

Brewer, Rose M., Cecilia A. Conrad, and Mary C. King. 2002. "The Complexities and Potential of Theorizing Gender, Caste, Race, and Class." *Feminist Economics* 8 (2): 3–17. doi:10.1080/1354570022000019038.

Bricker, Jessie, Arthur B. Kennickell, Kevin B. Moore, and John Sabelhaus. 2012. "Changes in U.S. Family Finances from 2007 to 2010: Evidence from the Survey of Consumer Finances." *Federal Reserve Bulletin* 98 (2). http://www.federalreserve .gov/pubs/bulletin/2012/pdf/scf12.pdf.

Britton, Dana M. 1997. "Gendered Organizational Logic: Policy and Practice in Men's and Women's Prisons." *Gender and Society* 11 (6): 796–818.

Brouwer, Steve. 1998. *Sharing the Pie: A Citizen's Guide to Wealth and Power in America.* New York: Henry Holt.

Brown, Robert McAfee. 1987. *Religion and Violence.* 2nd ed. Philadelphia: Westminster.

Brune, Tom. 1999. "Census Will for First Time Count Those of Mixed Race." *Seattle Times* online edition, August 17. http://community.seattletimes.nwsource.com/ar chive/?date=19990817&slug=2977786.

Buhrke, Robin A. 1996. *A Matter of Justice: Lesbians and Gay Men in Law Enforcement.* New York: Routledge.

Bullard, Robert. 1990. *Dumping in Dixie: Race, Class and Environmental Quality.* Boulder, CO: Westview.

———. 1994. *Unequal Protection: Environmental Justice and Communities of Color.* San Francisco: Sierra Club.

Bureau of Justice Statistics. 1992. "Drugs, Crime and the Justice System." NCJ 133652.

———. 1993. "Survey of State Prison Inmates, 1991." NCJ 136949.

———. 1997a. "HIV in Prisons and Jails, 1995." NCJ 164260.

———. 1997b. "Lifetime Likelihood of Going to State or Federal Prison." NCJ 160092.

———. 1998a. "Changes in Criminal Victimization, 1994–1995." NCJ 162032.

———. 1998b. "Profile of Jail Inmates, 1996." NCJ 164620.

———. 1998c. "Stalking in America." NCJ 169592.

———. 1998d. "Violence by Intimates." NCJ 167237.

———. 1999. "American Indians and Crime." NCJ 173386.

———. 2000. "The Sexual Victimization of College Women." NCJ 182369.

———. 2001. "Federal Drug Offenders, 1999, with Trends 1984–1999." NCJ 187285.

———. 2004a. "American Indians and Crime, 1992–2002." NCJ 203097.

———. 2004b. "Criminal Victimization, 2003." NCJ 205455.

———. 2004c. "Profile of Jail Inmates, 2002." NCJ 201932.

———. 2005a. "Contacts between Police and the Public: Findings from the 2002 National Survey." NCJ 207845.

———. 2005b. "Family Violence Statistics." NCJ 207846.

———. 2005c. "Probation and Parole in the United States, 2004." NCJ 210676.

———. 2006a. "Federal Law Enforcement Officers, 2004." NCJ 212750.

———. 2006b. "Local Police Departments, 2003." NCJ 210118.

———. 2006c. "Mental Health Problems of Prison and Jail Inmates." NCJ 213600.

———. 2006d. "National Survey of Prosecutors: Prosecutors in State Courts, 2005." NCJ 213799.

———. 2009a. "Asian, Native Hawaiian, and Pacific Islander Victims of Crime." NCJ 225037.

———. 2009b. "Capital Punishment, 2008—Statistical Tables." NCJ 228662.

———. 2009c. "Jail Incarceration Rates by Race and Ethnicity, 1990–2008."

———. 2009d. "Key Facts at a Glance." http://bjs.ojp.usdoj.gov/content/glance/tables/corr2tab.cfm.

———. 2009e. "Prisoners in 2008." NCJ 228417.

———. 2009f. "Stalking Victimization in the United States." NCJ 224527.

———. 2013a. "Capital Punishment, 2011—Statistical Tables." NCJ 242185.

———. 2013b. "Correctional Populations in the United States, 2012." NCJ 243936.

———. 2013c. "Criminal Victimization, 2012." NCJ 243389.

———. 2013d. "Intimate Partner Violence: Attributes of Victimization, 1993–2011." NCJ 243300.

Bureau of Labor Statistics. 1999a. *Employment and Earnings* (monthly), January. Table 10. ftp://ftp.bls.gov/pub/special.requests/lf/aat10.txt.

———. 1999b. "Highlights of Women's Earnings in 1998." Report 928. Washington, DC: US Department of Labor.

———. 1999c. "National Employment and Wage Data from the Occupational Employment Statistics Survey by Occupation, 1998." *Occupational Employment Statistics*, December. Table 1, table A-1.

———. 2004. "November 2004 National Occupational Employment and Wage Estimates: Legal Occupations." Washington, DC: US Department of Labor.

———. 2004–2005. *Occupational Outlook Handbook*, 9–10 of 12. Washington, DC: US Department of Labor.

———. 2008–2009. *Occupational Outlook Handbook*. Washington, DC: US Department of Labor. http://www.bls.gov/oco/.

———. 2012. "Occupational Employment Statistics." Washington, DC: US Department of Labor. http://www.bls.gov/oes/current/oes_stru.htm.

————. 2012–2013. *Occupational Outlook Handbook.* Washington, DC: US Department of Labor. http://www.bls.gov/ooh/protective-service/police-and-detectives.htm; http://www.bls.gov/ooh/legal/lawyers.htm; http://www.bls.gov/ooh/legal/judges-and-hearing-officers.htm; http://www.bls.gov/ooh/legal/arbitrators-mediators-and-conciliators.htm; http://www.bls.gov/ooh/protective-service/correctional-officers.htm.

Burnley, Jane, Christine Edmunds, Mario T. Gaboury, and Anne Seymour. 1998. *1998 National Victim Assistance Academy.* Washington, DC: Office of Justice Programs, US Department of Justice.

Business Week. 2005. "Death, Taxes, and Sarbanes-Oxley?" January 17. http://www.businessweek.com/magazine/content/05_03/b3916031_mz011.htm.

Butler, Anne. 1997. *Gendered Justice in the American West: Women Prisoners in Men's Penitentiaries.* Urbana: University of Illinois Press.

Calavita, Kitty, Henry Pontell, and Robert Tillman. 1997. *Big Money Crime.* Berkeley: University of California Press.

Callanan, Valerie J. 2012. "Media Consumption, Perceptions of Crime Risk and Fear of Crime: Examining Race/Ethnic Differences." *Sociological Perspectives* 55 (1): 93–115.

Camp, Camille Graham, and George M. Camp. 2002. *The Corrections Yearbook 2001: Adult Systems.* Middletown, CT: Criminal Justice Institute.

Campbell, J. C., D. Webster, J. Koziol-McLain, C. R. Block, D. Campbell, M. A. Curry, F. Gary, J. McFarlane, C. Sachs, P. Sharps, Y. Ulrich, and S. A. Wilt. 2003. "Assessing Risk Factors for Intimate Partner Homicide." In "Intimate Partner Homicide," *NIJ Journal* (250): 14–19. http://www.nij.gov/topics/crime/violence-against-women/selected-results.htm.

Cannon, Louis. 2000. "One Bad Cop." *New York Times,* October 1, 32. http://www.nytimes.com/2000/10/01/magazine/one-bad-cop.html.

Cantor, Nathaniel E. 1932. *Crime: Criminals and Criminal Justice.* New York: Henry Holt.

Carceral, K. C. 2005. *Prison, Inc.* New York: New York University Press.

Carmichael, Stokely, and Charles Hamilton. 1967. *Black Power: The Politics of Liberation in America.* New York: Vintage.

Catalyst. 2004. *Women in Business: A Snapshot.* New York: Catalyst.

CCA (Corrections Corporation of America). 2009. Form DEF 14A, filed with the Securities and Exchange Commission April 7. http://www.sec.gov/Archives/edgar/data/1070985/000095014409002981/g18453def14a.htm.

————. 2013. Form DEF 14A, filed with the Securities and Exchange Commission April 4. http://www.sec.gov/Archives/edgar/data/1070985/000119312513143512/d475112ddef14a.htm.

Census Bureau. 2005a. *Income, Poverty and Health Insurance Coverage in the United States: 2004.* Washington, DC: US Department of Commerce. http://www.census.gov/hhes/www/income/income.html.

———. 2005b. *Voting and Registration in the Election of November 2004.* Washington, DC: US Department of Commerce. http://www.census.gov/population/www/socdemo/voting/cps2004.html.

———. 2008. "Current Population Reports," table 1. "Income and Earnings Summary. Measures by Selected Characteristics: 2006 and 2007," table 3. "People and Families in Poverty by Selected Characteristics: 2006 and 2007," table B-1. "Poverty Status of People by Family Relationship, Race, and Hispanic Origin: 1959 to 2007," in *Income, Poverty, and Health Insurance Coverage in the United States: 2007.* Washington, DC: US Government Printing Office.

———. 2009. *Income, Poverty, and Health Insurance Coverage in the United States: 2008.* Washington, DC: US Government Printing Office.

———. 2012. "Full-Time Wage and Salary Workers—Number and Earnings: 2000 to 2010," table 648; "Nonfinancial Assets Held by Families by Type of Asset: 2007," table 720; "Family Net Worth—Mean and Median Net Worth in Constant (2007) Dollars by Selected Family Characteristics: 1998 to 2007," table 721. In *2012 Statistical Abstract: Income, Expenditures, Poverty, and Wealth.* Washington, DC: US Census Bureau.

———. 2013. "People in Families by Relationship to Householder, Age of Householder, Number of Related Children Present, and Family Structure: 2012." http://www.census.gov/hhes/www/cpstables/032013/pov/pov05_100.htm.

Center for the American Woman and Politics (CAWP). 2005. "Women in Elected Office 2005." http://www.cawp.rutgers.edu/fast_facts/levels_of_office/documents/elective05.pdf.

Center for Public Integrity. 2007. "EPA Document Lists Firms Tied to Superfund Sites." https://web.archive.org/web/20111203054327/http://projects.publicintegrity.org/superfund/report.aspx?aid=849.

Center for Research on Criminal Justice. 1975. *The Iron Fist and Velvet Glove.* Berkeley, CA: CRCJ.

Center for Responsive Politics. 2009a. "Lobbying: Top Spenders." *OpenSecrets.org.* http://www.opensecrets.org/lobby/top.php?indexType=s.

———. 2009b. "Top All-Time Donors, 1989–2010." *OpenSecrets.org.* http://www.opensecrets.org/orgs/list.php?order=A.

Chalk, Frank, and Kurt Jonassohn. 1990. *The History and Sociology of Genocide.* New Haven, CT: Yale University Press.

Chambliss, William. 1988. *Exploring Criminology.* New York: Macmillan.

Chambliss, William, and Milton Mankoff. 1976. *Whose Law? What Order?* New York: John Wiley.

Chambliss, William, and R. B. Seidman. 1982. *Law, Order and Power.* 2nd ed. Reading, MA: Addison-Wesley.

Chang, Mariko Lin. 2010. *Shortchanged: Why Women Have Less Wealth and What Can Be Done about It.* New York: Oxford University Press.

ChattahBox. 2009. "Pentagon to Create New Cyber-Command: Turf War with NSA Looming." May 29. http://chattahbox.com/us/2009/05/29/pentagon-to-create-new-cyber-command-turf-war-with-nsa-looming/.

Chesney-Lind, Meda. 1996. "Sentencing Women to Prison: Equality without Justice." In *Race, Gender, and Class in Criminology: The Intersections*, edited by Martin D. Schwartz and Dragan Milovanovic, 127–40. New York: Garland.

———. 1998. Foreword to *Crime Control and Women*, edited by Susan L. Miller, ix–x. Thousand Oaks, CA: Sage.

———. 2006. "Patriarchy, Crime, and Justice: Feminist Criminology in an Era of Backlash." *Feminist Criminology* 1 (1): 6–26.

Chesney-Lind, Meda, and Joycelyn M. Pollock. 1995. "Women's Prisons: Equality with a Vengeance." In *Women, Law, and Social Control*, edited by Alida V. Merlo and Joycelyn M. Pollock, 155–75. Boston: Allyn & Bacon.

Christianson, Scott. 1998. *With Liberty for Some*. Boston: Northeastern University Press.

Christie, Nils. 2000. *Crime Control as Industry: Towards Gulags, Western Style?* 3rd ed. London: Routledge.

Churchill, Ward, and Jim Vander Wall. 1990a. *Agents of Repression: The FBI's Secret Wars against the Black Panther Party and the American Indian Movement*. Boston: South End Press.

———. 1990b. *The COINTELPRO Papers: Documents from the FBI's Secret Wars against Dissent in the United States*. Boston: South End Press.

Clark, R., and B. M. Peck. 2012. "Examining the Gender Gap in Life Expectancy: A Cross-National Analysis, 1980–2005." *Social Science Quarterly* 93:820–37. doi:10.1111/j.1540-6237.2012.00881.x.

Clarke, D. A. 1981. *Banshee*. Portland, ME: Peregrine.

Clear, Todd. 2002. "The Problem with 'Addition by Subtraction.'" In *Invisible Punishment: The Collateral Consequences of Mass Imprisonment*, edited by Meda Chesney-Lind and Marc Mauer, 181–93. New York: The New Press.

———. 2008. "The Great Penal Experiment: Lesson for Social Justice." In *After the War on Crime: Race, Democracy, and a New Reconstruction*, edited by M. L. Frampton, I. H. López, and J. Simon, 61–72. New York: New York University Press.

Clinard, Marshall. 1990. *Corporate Corruption: The Abuse of Power*. New York: Praeger.

Cockburn, Alexander. 2009a. "Derail the 'Hate Crimes' Bandwagon!" *Nation*, June 15, 9.

———. 2009b. "Twittergasms." *Nation*, July 13, 9.

Coger, Robin N. 2012. "Why STEM Fields Still Don't Draw More Women." Dave Cutter was the illustrator for the article. https://chronicle.com/article/Why-STEM-Fields-Still-Dont/135302/.

Cole, David. 1999. *No Equal Justice: Race and Class in the American Criminal Justice System*. New York: The New Press.

Coleman, James. 1985. "Law and Power: The Sherman Antitrust Act and Its Enforcement in the Petroleum Industry." *Social Problems* 32 (3): 264–74.

Collette, Mark. 2008. "BP: Fine Is Sufficiently 'Harsh.'" *Galveston Daily News*, January 23. http://galvestondailynews.com/story.lasso?ewcd=411b93ca9e93157f.

Collins, Patricia Hill. 1990. *Black Feminist Thought: Knowledge, Consciousness, and the Politics of Empowerment.* New York: Routledge.

———. 1998. *Fighting Words: Black Women and the Search for Justice.* Minneapolis: University of Minnesota Press.

———. 2004. *Black Sexual Politics: African Americans, Gender and the New Racism.* New York: Routledge.

Collins, William C., and Andrew W. Collins. 1996. *Women in Jail: Legal Issues.* Washington, DC: National Institute of Corrections.

Conklin, John. 2003. *Why Crime Rates Fell.* Boston: Allyn & Bacon.

Conley, John, ed. 1994. *The 1967 President's Crime Commission Report: Its Impact 25 Years Later.* Cincinnati: Anderson.

Connell, R. W. 1987. *Gender and Power: Society, The Person, and Sexual Politics.* Stanford, CA: Stanford University Press.

———. 1995. *Masculinities.* Los Angeles: University of California Press.

Conover, Ted. 2000. "Guarding Sing Sing." *New Yorker*, April 3. http://www .tedconover.com/2010/01/guarding-sing-sing/.

Coontz, Stephanie. 2012. "The Myth of Male Decline." *New York Times*, September 29. http://www.nytimes.com/2012/09/30/opinion/sunday/the-myth-of-male-decline.html?pagewanted=all&_r=0.

Corak, Miles. 2013. "Income Inequality, Equality of Opportunity, and Intergenerational Mobility." *Journal of Economic Perspectives* 27 (3): 79–102.

Costello, Cynthia, and Barbara Kivimae Krimgold, eds. 1996. *The American Woman, 1996–1997: Where We Stand.* New York: Norton.

Cotton, Allison. 2008. *Effigy: Images of Capital Defendants.* Lanham, MD: Lexington Books.

Crawford, James. 1988. *The Rights of Peoples.* Oxford: Oxford University Press.

Crenshaw, Kimberlé. 1991. "Mapping the Margins: Intersectionality, Identity Politics, and Violence against Women of Color." *Stanford Law Review* 43:1258–99.

Creswell, Julie. 2011. "Even Funds That Lagged Paid Richly." *New York Times,* March 31. http://www.nytimes.com/2011/04/01/business/01hedge.html.

———. 2013. "Hedge Fund Titans' Pay Stretching to 10 Figures." *New York Times*, April 15. http://dealbook.nytimes.com/2013/04/15/pay-stretching-to-10-figures/?_r=0.

Cronin, Brenda. 2013. "Some 95% of 2009–2012 Income Gains Went to Wealthiest 1%." *Wall Street Journal*, September 10. http://blogs.wsj.com/economics/2013/09/10/some-95-of-2009-2012-income-gains-went-to-wealthiest-1/.

Cullen, Francis T., and Robert Agnew, eds. 1999. *Criminological Theory: Past to Present—Essential Readings.* Los Angeles: Roxbury.

Cuomo, Andrew. 2009. "No Rhyme or Reason: The 'Heads I Win, Tails You Lose' Bank Bonus Culture." New York Attorney General's Office. http://www .oag.state .ny.us/media_center/2009/july/pdfs/Bonus%20Report%20Final%207 .30.09.pdf.

Currie, Elliott. 1985. *Confronting Crime: An American Challenge.* New York: Pantheon.

———. 1998. *Crime and Punishment in America*. New York: Henry Holt.

———. 2005. "Inequality, Community, and Crime." In *The Essential Criminology Reader*, edited by Stuart Henry and Mark Lanier, 299–306. Boulder, CO: Westview.

Dahrendorf, Ralf. 1959. *Class and Class Conflict in Industrial Society*. Stanford, CA: Stanford University Press.

Dai, Dajun. 2010. "Black Residential Segregation, Disparities in Spatial Access to Health Care Facilities, and Late-Stage Breast Cancer Diagnosis in Metropolitan Detroit." *Health and Place* 6 (5): 1038–52.

Daly, Kathleen. 1994. *Gender, Crime, and Punishment*. New Haven, CT: Yale University Press.

———. 1995. "Looking Back, Looking Forward: The Promise of Feminist Transformation." In *The Criminal Justice System and Women*, 2nd ed., edited by Barbara Raffel Price and Natalie J. Sokoloff, 443–57. New York: McGraw-Hill.

———. 2006. "Feminist Thinking about Crime." In *The Essential Criminology Reader*, edited by S. Henry and M. Lanier, 205–13. Boulder, CO: Westview.

Daly, Kathleen, and Meda Chesney-Lind. 1988. "Feminism and Criminology." *Justice Quarterly* 5:497–538.

Daly, Kathleen, and Russ Immarigeon. 1998. "The Past, Present, and Future of Restorative Justice: Some Critical Reflections." *Contemporary Justice Review* 1 (1): 21–45.

Danner, Mona J. E. 1998. "Three Strikes and It's Women Who Are Out: The Hidden Consequences for Women of Criminal Justice Police Reforms." In *Crime Control and Women*, edited by Susan L. Miller, 1–14. Thousand Oaks, CA: Sage.

Davis, Angela. 1998. "What Is the Prison Industrial Complex? Why Does It Matter?" *Colorlines Magazine*, September 10, 1–8.

Day, Kathleen. 1993. *S&L Hell: The People and the Politics behind the $1 Trillion Savings and Loan Scandal*. New York: Norton.

DeCarlo, Scott. 2009. "What the Boss Makes." *Forbes*, April 22. http://www.forbes.com/2009/04/22/compensation-chief-executive-salary-leadership-best-boss-09-ceo-intro.html.

———. 2012. "America's Highest Paid CEOs". *Forbes*, April 4. http://www.forbes.com/sites/scottdecarlo/2012/04/04/americas-highest-paid-ceos/.

DeFrances, Carol. 2002. "Prosecutors in State Courts, 2001." *Bureau of Justice Statistics Bulletin*, May.

DeKeseredy, W. S., M. Rogness, and M. D. Schwartz. 2004. "Separation/Divorce and Sexual Assault: The Current State of Social Scientific Knowledge." *Aggression and Violent Behavior* 9:675–91.

DeKeseredy, Walter S., and Martin D. Schwartz. 1996. *Contemporary Criminology*. Belmont, CA: Wadsworth.

Delaney, Kevin. 1999. *Strategic Bankruptcy*. Berkeley: University of California Press.

Delgado, Richard, ed. 1995a. *Critical Race Theory: The Cutting Edge*. Philadelphia: Temple University Press.

———. 1995b. "Rodrigo's Sixth Chronicle: Intersections, Essences, and the Dilemma of Social Reform." In *Critical Race Theory*, edited by Richard Delgado, 242–52. Philadelphia: Temple University Press.

Delgado, Richard, and Jean Stefancic. 1991. "Derrick Bell's Chronicle of the Space Traders: Would the U.S. Sacrifice People of Color If the Price Were Right?" *University of Colorado Law Review* 62:321–29.

———. 1997. *Critical White Studies: Looking behind the Mirror*. Philadelphia: Temple University Press.

Demos, Telis, Richard Morgan, and Christopher Tkaczyk. 2004. "America's 40 Richest under 40." *Fortune*, September 20.

DeNavas-Walt, Carmen, Bernadette D. Proctor, and Jessica C. Smith. 2013. *Income, Poverty, and Health Insurance Coverage in the United States: 2012*. Washington, DC: United States Census Bureau. https://www.census.gov/prod/2013pubs/p60-245.pdf.

Denver Business Journal. 2009. "Obama's Cyber Czar an 'Important 1st Step' to Security, Says Qwest CEO." May 29. http://www.bizjournals.com/denver/stories/2009/05/25/daily77.html.

Department of Health and Human Services. 2011. "Vulnerabilities in FDA's Oversight of State Food Facility Inspections." Report from the Office of the Inspector General. https://oig.hhs.gov/oei/reports/oei-02-09-00430.pdf.

Department of Justice. 1998. *The Challenge of Crime in a Free Society: Looking Back, Looking Forward*. Washington, DC: US Department of Justice.

Department of Labor. 2006. *All about OSHA*. Washington, DC: Department of Labor. http://www.osha.gov/Publications/all_about_OSHA.pdf.

Derber, Charles. 1998. *Corporation Nation: How Corporations Are Taking Over Our Lives and What We Can Do about It*. New York: St. Martin's.

DiMascio, William M. 1998. "Why Inmate Populations Are Up." In *Selected Readings in Criminal Justice*, edited by Philip L. Reichel, 237–45. San Diego, CA: Greenhaven.

Dinan, Stephen. 2013. "Report: Deportations Plummet in 2013, Lowest since 2007." *Washington Times*, October 30, http://www.washingtontimes.com/news/2013/oct/30/deportations-plummet-2013-lowest-2007/?page=all.

Dinkes, R., J. Kemp, and K. Baum. 2009. "Indicators of School Crime and Safety: 2008 (NCES 2009–022/NCJ 226343)." Washington, DC: National Center for Education Statistics, Institute of Education Sciences, US Department of Education, Bureau of Justice Statistics, Office of Justice Programs, US Department of Justice.

Domhoff, G. William. 1998. *Who Rules America?* 3rd ed. Mountain View, CA: Mayfield.

Douglas, Danielle. 2013. "Attorney General Says Big Banks' Size May Inhibit Prosecution." *Washington Post*, March 6. http://www.washingtonpost.com/business/economy/holder-concerned-megabanks-too-big-to-jail/2013/03/06/6fa2b07a-869e-11e2-999e-5f8e0410cb9d_story.html.

Douglas, William O. 1954. *An Almanac of Liberty*. Garden City, NY: Doubleday.

Doyle, James. 1992. "'It's the Third World Down There!': The Colonialist Vocation and American Criminal Justice." *Harvard Civil Rights—Civil Liberties Law Review* 27:71.

DuBois, Ellen Carol, and Lynn Dumenil. 2005. *Through Women's Eyes: An American History*. Boston: Bedford/St. Martin's.

Duffee, David. 1980. *Explaining Criminal Justice: Community Theory and Criminal Justice Reform*. Prospects Heights, IL: Waveland.

Duran, Robert. 2013. *Gang Life in Two Cities: An Insider's Journey*. New York: Columbia University Press.

Durkheim, Emile. (1893) 1964. *The Division of Labor in Society*. Reprint, New York: Free Press.

Dyer, Joel. 2000. *The Perpetual Prisoner Machine: How America Profits from Crime*. Boulder, CO: Westview.

Dyer, Richard. 2005. "The Matter of Whiteness." In *White Privilege: Essential Readings on the Other Side of Racism*, edited by Paula Rothenberg, 9–14. New York: Worth.

Dyson, Michael Eric. 2005. *Is Bill Cosby Right? (or Has the Black Middle Class Lost Its Mind?)*. New York: Basic Civitas/Perseus.

Edelstein, Charles D., and Robert J. Wicks. 1977. *An Introduction to Criminal Justice*. New York: McGraw-Hill.

Edwards, Adam, and Peter Gill, eds. 2003. *Transnational Organized Crime: Perspectives on Global Security*. New York: Routledge.

Eichstaedt, Peter. 1994. *If You Poison Us: Uranium and Native Americans*. Santa Fe, NM: Red Crane Books.

Eisenhower, Dwight. 1961. Farewell address. Transcript, http://en.wikisource.org/wiki/Eisenhower%27s_farewell_address.

Elias, Robert. 1986. *The Politics of Victimization: Victims, Victimology and Human Rights*. New York: Oxford University Press.

Emmelman, Debra S. 2004. "Defending the Poor: Commonsense Class-ism in the Adjudication of Criminal Cases." In *For the Common Good: A Critical Examination of Law and Social Control*, edited by Robin Miller and Sandra Lee Browning, 49–67. Durham, NC: Carolina Academic.

Engel, Robin Shepard, and Jennifer M. Calnon. 2004. "Examining the Influence of Drivers' Characteristics during Traffic Stops with Police: Results from a National Survey." *Justice Quarterly* 21 (1): 49–90.

Engen, Rodney. 2009. "Assessing Determinate and Presumptive Sentencing—Making Research Relevant." *Criminology and Public Policy* 8 (2) (May): 323–36.

Ericson, R., P. Baranek, and J. Chan. 1987. *Visualizing Deviance: A Study of News Organizations*. Toronto: University of Toronto Press.

Essed, P. 1990. *Everyday Racism: Reports from Women in Two Cultures*. Claremont, CA: Hunter House.

————. 1991. *Understanding Everyday Racism: An Interdisciplinary Theory.* Newbury, CA: Sage.

Etzioni, Amitai. 1990. "Going Soft on Corporate Crime." *Washington Post*, April 1.

Ezekiel, Raphael. 1995. *The Racist Mind: Portraits of American Neo-Nazis and Klansmen.* New York: Penguin.

Fairfield, Hannah. 2013. "Girls Lead in Science Exam, but Not in the United States." *New York Times*, February 4. http://www.nytimes.com/interactive/2013/02/04/science/girls-lead-in-science-exam-but-not-in-the-united-states.html.

Faith, Karlene. 1993. "Gendered Imaginations: Female Crime and Prison Movies." *Justice Professional* 8 (1): 53–70.

Fanon, Frantz. 1963. *The Wretched of the Earth.* New York: Prentice-Hall.

————. 1967. *A Dying Colonialism.* New York: Grove.

Farrell, Amy, Geoff Ward, and Danielle Rousseau. 2009. "Race Effects of Representation among Federal Court Workers: Does Black Workforce Representation Reduce Sentencing Disparities?" *Annals of the American Academy of Political and Social Science* 623 (May): 121–33.

Fausto-Sterling, Anne. 2000. *Sexing the Body: Gender Politics and the Construction of Sexuality.* New York: Basic.

Faux, Jeff. 2006. *The Global Class War: How America's Bipartisan Elite Lost Our Future and What It Will Take to Win It Back.* Hoboken, NJ: Wiley.

Feagin, Joe, and Clairece Booher Feagin. 1996. *Racial and Ethnic Relations.* Upper Saddle River, NJ: Prentice-Hall.

Feagin, Joe, and Hernan Vera. 1995. *White Racism: The Basics.* New York: Routledge.

Feeley, Malcolm, and Jonathan Simon. 1992. "The New Penology. Notes on the Emerging Strategy of Corrections and Its Implications." *Criminology* 30 (3): 449–74.

————. 1994. "Actuarial Justice: The Emerging New Criminal Law." In *The Futures of Criminology*, edited by David Nelken, chap. 8. London: Sage.

FHFA (Federal Housing Finance Agency). 2011. "FHFA Sues 17 Firms to Recover Losses to Fannie Mae and Freddie Mac." News release, September 2. http://www.fhfa.gov/webfiles/22599/PLSLitigation_final_090211.pdf.

Fields, Gary. 2009. "White House Czar Calls for End to 'War on Drugs.'" *Wall Street Journal Online*, May 14. http://online.wsj.com/article/SB124225891527617397.html.

File, Thom. 2013. "The Diversifying Electorate—Voting Rate by Race and Hispanic Origin in 2012 (and Other Recent Elections)." Report, US Census Bureau, Washington, DC, May. http://www.census.gov/prod/2013pubs/p20-568.pdf.

Fishman, Laura T. 1998. "The Black Bogeyman and White Self-Righteousness." In *Images of Color, Images of Crime: Readings*, edited by Coramae Richey Mann and Marjorie Zatz, 109–26. Los Angeles: Roxbury.

Fishman, Mark. 1978. "Crime Waves as Ideology." *Social Problems* 25 (5): 531–43.

Flavin, Jeanne. 2001. "Feminism for the Mainstream Criminologist: An Invitation." *Journal of Criminal Justice Education* 29 (4): 271–85.

———. 2009. *Our Bodies, Our Crimes: The Policing of Women's Reproduction in America*. New York: New York University Press.

Fletcher, Connie. 1995. *Breaking and Entering*. New York: HarperCollins.

Florian, Ellen. 2002. "Executive Pay: Don't Go Buying That Third House Just Yet." *Fortune*, November 18, 30.

Flynn, Michael, and Fabiola Salek, eds. 2012. *Screening Torture: Media Representations of State Terror and Political Domination*. New York: Columbia University Press.

Foley, Neil. 2005. "Becoming Hispanic: Mexican Americans and Whiteness." In *White Privilege: Essential Readings on the Other Side of Racism*, edited by Paula Rothenberg, 55–66. New York: Worth.

Fontanarosa, Phil, Drummond Rennie, and Catherine DeAngelis. 2004. "Postmarketing Surveillance—Lack of Vigilance, Lack of Trust." *Journal of the American Medical Association* 292 (21) (December 1): 2647–50.

Forbes. 2008. "The 400 Richest Americans." September 17. http://www.forbes.com/lists/2008/54/400list08_The-400-Richest-Americans_FinalWorth.html.

———. 2009. "The Celebrity 100." (June 3). http://www.forbes.com/lists/2009/53/celebrity-09_The-Celebrity-100_EarningsPrevYear.html.

———. 2013a. "The Forbes 400: The Richest People in America". *Forbes*. http://www.forbes.com/forbes-400/list/#page:1_sort:0_direction:asc_search:_filter:All%20industries_filter:All%20states_filter:All%20categories.

———. 2013b. "The World's Most Powerful Celebrities." *Forbes*. http://www.forbes.com/celebrities/#page:1_sort:3_direction:asc_search:_filter:All%20categories.

Forell, Caroline, and Donna Matthews. 2000. *A Law of Her Own*. New York: New York University Press.

Fortune. 2005. "The Largest U.S. Corporations." April 18.

Foster, Holly, and John Hagan. 2009. "The Mass Incarceration of Parents in America: Issues of Race/Ethnicity, Collateral Damage to Children, and Prisoner Reentry." *Annals of the American Academy of Political and Social Science* 623 (May): 179–94.

Foucault, Michel. 1980. *The History of Sexuality*. Vol. 1, *An Introduction*. New York: Vintage.

Fowler, Bree. 2013. "Combined Net Worth of America's Richest Rises." Salon.com, September 16. http://www.salon.com/2013/09/16/combined_net_worth_of_americas_richest_rises/.

Fowler, Tom. 2009. "OSHA Punishes BP over Safety." *Houston Chronicle*, October 31. http://www.chron.com/disp/story.mpl/business/energy/6695722.html.

Francis, David. 2005. "The American Dream Gains a Harder Edge." *Christian Science Monitor*, May 23. http://www.csmonitor.com/2005/0523/p17s01-cogn.html.

Frank, Jerome. 1963. *Courts on Trial: Myth and Reality in American Justice*. New York: Atheneum.

Frank, Nancy. 1988. "Unintended Murder and Corporate Risk-Taking: Defining the Concept of Justifiability." *Journal of Criminal Justice* 16:17–24.

Frank, Robert, and Amir Efrati. 2009a. "'Evil' Madoff Gets 150 Years in Epic Fraud." *Wall Street Journal,* June 30, A1, A12.

———. 2009b. "Madoff Plays Fate Like His Fraud." *Wall Street Journal,* June 27–28, B1, B3.

Frankenberg, Ruth. 1993. *White Women, Race Matters: The Social Construction of Whiteness.* Minneapolis: University of Minnesota Press.

Franklin, H. B. 1989. *Prison Literature in America.* New York: Oxford University Press.

Free, Marvin D., Jr., and Mitch Ruesink. 2012. *Race and Justice: Wrongful Convictions of African American Men.* Boulder, CO: Lynne Rienner.

Friedman, Lee, and Linda Forst. 2007. "The Impact of OSHA Recordkeeping Regulation Changes on Occupational Injury and Illness Trends in the US." *Occupational and Environmental Medicine* 64:454–60.

Friedrichs, David. 1996. *Trusted Criminals.* Belmont, CA: Wadsworth.

Funnell, Ben. 2009. "Debt Is Capitalism's Dirty Little Secret." *Financial Times,* June 30. http://www.ft.com/cms/s/0/e23c6d04-659d-11de-8e34-00144feabdc0.html.

Fussell, Paul. 1983. *Class: A Guide through the American Status System.* New York: Summit.

Fyfe, James J. 1990. "Blind Justice: Police Shootings in Memphis." In *Violence: Patterns, Causes, and Public Policy,* edited by S. A. Weiner, M. A. Zahn, and R. J. Sagi, 232–40. New York: Harcourt Brace College.

Gabbidon, Shaun, and Helen Taylor Greene. 2005. *Race and Crime.* Thousand Oaks, CA: Sage.

Gabe, Thomas. 2013. "Poverty In the United States. 2012." Report, Congressional Research Service, Washington, DC, November 13. http://www.fas.org/sgp/crs/misc/RL33069.pdf.

Gamble, Sarah, ed. 1999. *The Routledge Critical Dictionary of Feminism and Postfeminism.* New York: Routledge.

Gandy, Oscar. 1993. *The Panoptic Sort: A Political Economy of Personal Information.* Boulder, CO: Westview.

Garland, David. 1990. *Punishment and Society: A Study in Social Theory.* Chicago: University of Chicago Press.

———. 1999. "The Commonplace and the Catastrophic: Interpretations of Crime in Late Modernity." *Theoretical Criminology* 3 (3): 353–64.

———. 2001. *The Culture of Control.* Oxford: Oxford University Press.

GEO Group. 2009. Form DEF 14A, filed with the Securities and Exchange Commission March 30. http://www.sec.gov/Archives/edgar/data/923796/000095014409002717/g18277def14a.htm.

———. 2013. Form DEF 14A, filed with the Securities and Exchange Commission March 28. http://www.sec.gov/Archives/edgar/data/923796/000119312513132372d507253ddef14a.htm.

Geronimus, Arline, Cynthia Colen, Tara Shochet, Lori Barer Ingber, and Sherman James. 2006a. "Urban-Rural Differences in Excess Mortality among High-Poverty

Populations: Evidence from the Harlem Household Survey and the Pitt County, North Carolina, Study of African American Health." *Journal of Health Care for the Poor and Underserved* 17 (3): 532–58.

Geronimus, Arline, Margaret Hicken, Danya Keene, and John Bound. 2006b. "Weathering and Age-Patterns of Allostatic Load Scores among Blacks and Whites in the United States." *American Journal of Public Health* 96:826–33.

Gerth, Jeff, and Brady Dennis. 2009. "How a Loophole Benefits GE in Bank Rescue." *Washington Post*, June 29. http://www.washingtonpost.com/wp-dyn/content/article/2009/06/28/AR2009062802955.html.

Gilbert, Dennis. 1998. *The American Class Structure*. 5th ed. Belmont, CA: Wadsworth.

Gilliard, Darrell K., and Allen J. Beck. 1998. "Prisoners in 1997." Washington, DC: US Department of Justice.

Gladwell, Malcolm. 2005. "The Moral Hazard Myth." *New Yorker*, August 29. http://www.newyorker.com/archive/2005/08/29/050829fa_fact?currentPage=all.

Glazer, Myron, and Penina Glazer. 1989. *The Whistle-Blowers*. New York: Basic.

Gonzales, Alberto. 2005. "Prepared Remarks of Attorney General Alberto Gonzales: Sentencing Guidelines Speech." June 21. http://www.justice.gov/archive/ag/speeches/2005/06212005victimsofcrime.htm.

Goldman Sachs. 2011. Form 10-K (annual report) filed with the Securities and Exchange Commission. http://www.goldmansachs.com/investor-relations/financials/archived/10k/docs/2010-10-k.pdf.

Goldstein, Joseph. 2013. "Judge Rejects New York's Stop-and-Frisk Policy." *New York Times*, August 12. http://www.nytimes.com/2013/08/13/nyregion/stop-and-frisk-practice-violated-rights-judge-rules.html?pagewanted=all&_r=0/.

Gongloff, Mark. 2013. "Eric Holder Admits Some Banks Are Just Too Big to Prosecute." *Huffington Post*, March 6. http://www.huffingtonpost.com/2013/03/06/eric-holder-banks-too-big_n_2821741.html.

Goodstein, Lynne. 1992. "Feminist Perspectives and the Criminal Justice Curriculum." *Journal of Criminal Justice Education* 3 (2): 165–81.

Gordon, Diana. 1990. *The Justice Juggernaut: Fighting Street Crime, Controlling Citizens*. New Brunswick, NJ: Rutgers University Press.

Gordon, Kathryn H., Castro, Y., Sitnikob, L., and Holm-Denoma, J. 2010. "Cultural Body Shape Ideals and Eating Disorder Symptoms among White, Latina, and Black College Women." *Cultural Diversity and Ethnic Minority Psychology* 16 (2): 135–43. doi:10.1037/a0018671.

Gorman, Tessa. 1997. "Back on the Chain Gang: Why the 8th Amendment and the History of Slavery Proscribe the Resurgence of Chain Gangs." *California Law Review* 85 (2): 441–78.

Grabosky, P., J. Braithwaite, and P. Wilson. 1987. "The Myth of Community Tolerance toward White-Collar Crime." *Australia and New Zealand Journal of Criminology* 20:33–44.

Greene, Judith. 2002. "Entrepreneurial Corrections: Incarceration as a Business Opportunity." In *Invisible Punishment*, edited by Meda Chesney-Lind and Marc Mauer, 95–113. New York: The New Press.

Greenfeld, Lawrence A. 1997. *Sex Offenses and Offenders*. Washington, DC: US Department of Justice.

Greenwood, Peter. 1995. "Juvenile Crime and Juvenile Justice." In *Crime*, edited by James Q. Wilson and Joan Petersilia, 91–117. San Francisco: Institute for Contemporary Studies.

Greider, William. 1994. "Why the Mighty GE Can't Strike Out." *Rolling Stone*, April 21, 36.

———. 1996. *Who Will Tell the People? The Betrayal of American Democracy*. New York: Simon & Schuster.

———. 2005. "Sins & the Citi." *Nation*, July 4, 4–6.

———. 2009. "Obama's False Reform." *Nation*, July 13, 8–9.

Grossman, Lev, and Jay Newton-Small. 2013. "The Secret Web: Where Drugs, Porn and Murder Live Online." *Time*, November 11, 26–33.

Guardian. 2008. "Countrywide Financial Faces Unethical Business Practices Prosecution." Bay Ledger News Zone, January 28. http://www.blnz.com/news/2008/06/25/Countrywide_Financial_faces_unethical_business_9812.html.

Hacker, Andrew. 1995. *Two Nations: Black and White, Separate, Hostile, Unequal*. New York: Ballantine.

Hagan, F. E. 2013. *Introduction to Criminology*. Los Angeles, CA: Sage.

Hagan, John. 1994. *Crime and Disrepute*. Thousand Oaks, CA: Pine Forge.

Hale, Donna C. 1998. "Keeping Women in Their Place: An Analysis of Police women in Videos, 1972 to 1996." In *Popular Culture, Crime and Justice*, edited by Frankie Bailey and Donna Hale, 159–79. Belmont, CA: West/Wadsworth.

Haley, John. 1989. "Confession, Repentance and Absolution." In *Mediation and Criminal Justice*, edited by Martin Wright and Burt Galaway, 195–211. Newbury Park, CA: Sage.

Hammond, R. W. 1999. "School-Associated Violent Deaths: United States, 1994–1998." Paper presented at the annual meeting of the American Society of Criminology, Toronto, Canada, November.

Hanser, Richard. 2009. "Conflicts and Geographical Flashpoints around the World: The Effective Application of Restorative Justice and Peacemaking Perspectives." *Contemporary Justice Review* 12 (2): 191–206.

Haraway, Donna. 1991. "Situated Knowledges: The Science Question in Feminism and the Privilege of Partial Perspective." In *Simians, Cyborgs, and Women: The Reinvention of Nature*, 183–201. New York: Routledge.

Hare, R. M. 1990. "Public Policy in a Pluralist Society." In *Embryo Experimentation*, edited by Peter Singer, Helga Kuhse, Stephen Buckle, Karen Dawson, and Pascal Kasimba, 183–94. Cambridge: Cambridge University Press.

Harlow, Carolina Wolf. 1998. "Profile of Jail Inmates 1996." Special report NCJ 164620. US Department of Justice, Washington, DC.

Harring, Sidney L. 1983. *Policing a Class Society: The Experience of American Cities, 1865–1915*. New Brunswick, NJ: Rutgers University Press.

Harrington, Michael. 1989. *Socialism: Past and Future*. Berkeley, CA: Arcade.

Harris, Angela P. 1990. "Race and Essentialism in Feminist Legal Theory." In *Critical Race Theory: The Cutting Edge*, edited by Richard Delgado, 253–66. Philadelphia: Temple University Press.

———. 1997. "Race and Essentialism in Feminist Legal Theory." In *Critical Race Feminism: A Reader*, edited by Adrien K. Wing, 11–18. New York: New York University Press.

Harris, David. 1999. "The Stories, the Statistics, and the Law: Why 'Driving While Black' Matters." *Minnesota Law Review* 84 (2): 265–326. http://academic.uday ton.edu/race/03justice/dwb01.htm.

Harris, Kamala. 2008. "Smart on Crime." In *After the War on Crime: Race, Democracy, and a New Reconstruction*, edited by M. L. Frampton, I. H. López, and J. Simon, 145–52. New York: New York University Press.

Hart, Lynda. 1994. *Fatal Women: Lesbian Sexuality and the Mark of Aggression*. Princeton, NJ: Princeton University Press.

Hartmann, Thom. 2002. *Unequal Protection: The Rise of Corporate Dominance and the Theft of Human Rights*. New York: Rodale.

Harvard Law Review. 1988. "Developments in the Law: Race and the Criminal Process." *Harvard Law Review* 101:1472.

Hatty, Suzanne. 2000. *Masculinities, Violence, and Culture*. Thousand Oaks, CA: Sage.

Hawkins, Darnell. 1995. *Ethnicity, Race and Crime*. Albany: State University of New York Press.

Hawkins, Richard, and Geoffrey Alpert. 1989. *American Prison Systems: Punishment and Justice*. Englewood Cliffs, NJ: Prentice-Hall.

Hayes, Christopher. 2009. "Bucking the Banks." *Nation*, July 13, 7.

Headlee, Sue, and Margery Elfin. 1996. *The Cost of Being Female*. Westport, CT: Praeger.

Heidensohn, Frances. 1995. *Women and Crime*. 2nd ed. New York: New York University Press.

Henry, Stuart, and William Hinkle. 2001. *Careers in Criminal Justice*. 2nd ed. Salem, WI: Sheffield.

Henry, Stuart, and Dragan Milovanovic. 1996. *Constitutive Criminology: Beyond Postmodernism*. London: Sage.

———. 1999. *Constitutive Criminology at Work*. Albany: State University of New York Press.

Hightower, Jim. 1998a. "All the Free Speech Money Can Buy." *Detroit Metrotimes*, August 19–25.

———. 1998b. *There's Nothing in the Middle of the Road but Yellow Stripes and Dead Armadillos*. New York: HarperPerennial.

Hills, Stuart, ed. 1987. *Corporate Violence: Injury and Death for Profit*. Savage, MD: Rowman & Littlefield.

Hinkle, William G., and Stuart Henry, eds. 2000. *School Violence*. Annals of the American Academy of Political and Social Science. Thousand Oaks, CA: Sage.

Hinojosa, Ricardo. 2008. Statement of Ricardo Hinojosa, Chair, United States Sentencing Commission, before the Senate Judiciary Committee, February 12. http://www.ussc.gov/testimony/Hinososa_Testimony_021208.pdf.

Hitt, Jack. 2005. "The Newest Indians." *New York Times Magazine*, August 21. http://www.nytimes.com/2005/08/21/magazine/21NATIVE.html.

Holmes, Malcolm D. "Minority Threat and Police Brutality: Determinants of Civil Rights Criminal Complaints in the U.S. Municipalities." *Criminology* 38 (2): 343–68.

Horton, Paul B., and Chester L. Hunt. 1976. *Sociology*. 4th ed. New York: McGraw-Hill.

Huisman, Kimberly, Jeri Martinez, and Cathleen Wilson. 2005. "Training Police Officers on Domestic Violence and Racism." *Violence against Women* 11 (6): 792–821.

Huling, Tracy. 2002. "Building a Prison Economy in Rural America." In *Invisible Punishment: The Collateral Consequences of Mass Imprisonment*, edited by Meda Chesney-Lind and Marc Mauer, 197–213. New York: The New Press.

Hull, Gloria T., Patricia Bell Scott, and Barbara Smith, eds. 1982. *All the Women Are White, All the Blacks Are Men, but Some of Us Are Brave: Black Women's Studies*. New York: Feminist Press.

Human Rights Watch. 1996. *All Too Familiar Sexual Abuse of Women in U.S. State Prisons*. New York: Women's Rights Project.

———. 1999. *Human Rights Watch World Report 1999: United States*. New York: Human Rights Watch.

———. 2001. "No Escape: Male Rape in U.S. Prisons." Report, Human Rights Watch, April 1. http://www.hrw.org/reports/2001/prison/.

Humm, Maggie. 1990. *The Dictionary of Feminist Theory*. Columbus: Ohio State University Press.

Humphries, Drew. 1999. *Crack Mothers: Pregnancy, Drugs, and the Media*. Columbus: Ohio University Press.

Hurtado, Aida. 1989. "Relating to Privilege: Seduction and Rejection in the Subordination of White Women and Women of Color." *Signs* 14 (4): 833–55.

Indian Law and Order Commission. 2013. *A Roadmap for Making Native America Safer: Report to the President and Congress of the United States*. http://www.aisc.ucla.edu/iloc/report/index.html.

International Centre for Prison Studies. 2013. "World Prison Brief." King's College, London. (http://www.prisonstudies.org/info/worldbrief/wpb_stats.php?area=all&category=wb_poprate).

Irwin, John. 2005. *The Warehouse Prison*. Los Angeles: Roxbury.

Irwin, John, and James Austin. 1997. *It's about Time: America's Imprisonment Binge.* Belmont, CA: Wadsworth.

Irwin, Neil. 2006. "Our Financial Failings: Family Savings Look Scary across the Board." *Washington Post*, March 5, F01.

Ishay, Micheline. 2004. *The History of Human Rights: From Ancient Times to the Globalization Era.* Berkeley: University of California Press.

Isikoff, Michael. 1990. "Justice Dept. Shifts on Corporate Sentencing." *Washington Post*, April 28.

Jacob, Herbert. (1973) 1980. *Urban Justice: Law and Order in American Cities.* Reprint, Englewood Cliffs, NJ: Prentice-Hall.

Jenkins, Philip. 1994. *Using Murder: The Social Construction of Serial Homicide.* New York: Aldine de Gruyter.

Johnson, Carrie. 2006. "Skilling Gets 24 Years for Fraud at Enron." *Washington Post*, October 24, A1.

Johnson, Gene. 2005. "Utilities Win Forum against Enron." *Washington Post*, March 13, A14.

Johnson, James H., Jr., Walter C. Farrell Jr., and Jennifer A. Stoloff. 1998. "The Declining Social and Economic Fortunes of African American Males: A Critical Assessment of Four Perspectives." *Review of Black Political Economy* 25 (4): 17–40.

Johnson, Robert. 1998. *Death Work: A Study of the Modern Execution Process.* 2nd ed. Belmont, CA: Wadsworth.

———. 2000. "American Prisons and the African-American Experience: A History of Social Control and Racial Oppression." *Corrections Compendium* 25 (9): 6–30.

———. 2001. "Village Life." *American Weekly*, November. http://stopviolence.com/9-11/arts/villagelife.htm.

———. 2002. *Hard Time.* Belmont, CA: Wadsworth.

Johnson, Robert, and Paul Leighton. 1999. "American Genocide: The Destruction of the Black Underclass." In *Collective Violence: Harmful Behavior in Groups and Governments*, edited by Craig Summers and Eric Markusen, 95–140. Lanham: Rowman & Littlefield. http://paulsjusticepage.com.

Johnston, David. 2005. "Richest Are Leaving Even the Rich Far Behind." *New York Times*, June 5. http://www.nytimes.com/class.

Jones, N. A., and J. J. Bullock. 2013. "Understanding Who Reported Multiple Races in the U.S. Decennial Census: Results from Census 2000 and the 2010 Census." *Family Relations* 62 (1): 5–16.

Jones, Nikki. 2011. "Something Smells Like a Pig, You Say?" *Public Intellectual*, May 2. http://thepublicintellectual.org/2011/05/02/if-it-smells-like-a-pig/.

Jordan, Carol. 2004. "Intimate Partner Violence and the Justice System." *Journal of Interpersonal Violence* 19 (12): 1412–34.

Jordan, Emma. 2009. "A Fair Deal for Taxpayer Investments." *Harvard Law School Forum on Corporate Governance and Financial Regulation* (blog). http://blogs.law.harvard.edu/corpgov/2009/09/24/a-fair-deal-for-taxpayer-investments/.

Kandal, Terry. 1988. *The Woman Question in Classical Sociological Theory.* Miami: Florida International University Press.

Kangas, Steve. 1996. "Myths about Affirmative Action." *Liberalism Resurgent.* http://www.aliveness.com/kangaroo/LiberalFAQ.htm.

Karlgaard, Rich. 2011. "What Is Wealth in America?" *Forbes*, September 21. http://www.forbes.com/forbes/2011/1010/opinions-innovation-rules-wealth-america-rich-karlgaard.html.

Kasinsky, Renee. 1994. "Patrolling the Facts: Cops, Media, and Crime." In *Media, Process, and the Social Construction of Crime: Studies in Newsmaking Criminology*, edited by Gregg Barak, 203–34. New York: Routledge.

Katz, Alyssa. 2009. *Our Lot: How Real Estate Came to Own Us.* New York: Bloomsbury.

Katz, Jackson. 1999. *Tough Guise.* DVD, 88 min. Northampton, MA: Media Education Foundation.

Kaufman, J. S., Arline Geronimus, and Sherman James. 2007. "Faulty Interpretation of Observed Racial Disparity in Recurrent Preterm Birth." *American Journal of Obstetrics and Gynecology* 197 (3): 327–37.

Kennedy, Marc C. 1970. "Beyond Incrimination: Some Neglected Facets of the Theory of Punishment." *Catalyst* 5 (Summer): 1–30.

Kennedy, Randall. 1997. *Race, Crime, and the Law.* New York: Random House.

Kennickell, Arthur. 2003. "A Rolling Tide: Changes in the Distribution of Wealth in the U.S., 1989–2001." Working paper, Federal Reserve Board, Washington, DC, March 3. http://www.federalreserve.gov/pubs/feds/2003/200324/200324pap.pdf.

———. 2006. "Currents and Undercurrents: Changes in the Distribution of Wealth, 1989–2004." Working paper, Federal Reserve Board, Washington, DC, January 30. http://www.federalreserve.gov/pubs/feds/2006/200613/200613pap.pdf.

———. 2009. "Ponds and Streams: Wealth and Income in the U.S., 1989 to 2007." Working paper, Federal Reserve Board, Washington, DC, March 7. http://www.federalreserve.gov/pubs/feds/2009/200913/200913abs.html.

———. 2012. "Tossed and Turned: Wealth Dynamics of U.S. Households 2007–2009." Working paper 2011-51, Federal Reserve Board, Washington, DC, May 29. http://www.federalreserve.gov/pubs/feds/2011/201151/revision/201151pap.pdf.

Kent, Mary Mederios. 2010. "Large Wealth Gap Among U.S. Racial and Ethnic Groups." Population Reference Bureau. http://www.prb.org/Publications/Articles/2010/usnetworth.aspx.

Kilbourne, Jean. 2000. *Can't Buy My Love: How Advertising Changes the Way We Think and Feel.* New York: Free Press.

Killingbeck, Donna. 2005. "A Sociological History of Prison Privatization in the Contemporary United States." PhD diss., Western Michigan University, Kalamazoo.

Kim, Jane. 2009. "Hunt Goes on for Missing Madoff Money." *Wall Street Journal*, June 29, CI.

King, Jeanne. 1998. "Two NYPD Officers Charge Discrimination against Gays." Reuters, October 28.

Kipnis, Kenneth. 2001. "Criminal Justice and the Negotiated Plea." In *Criminal Justice Ethics*, edited by Paul Leighton and Jeffrey Reiman, 362–371. Upper Saddle River, NJ: Prentice-Hall.

Klein, Dorie. (1973) 1995. "The Etiology of Female Crime: A Review of the Literature." In *The Criminal Justice System and Women*, 2nd ed., edited by Barbara Raffel Price and Natalie J. Sokoloff, 30–53. New York: McGraw-Hill.

———. 1998. "An Agenda for Reading and Writing about Women, Crime, and Justice." *Social Pathology* 3 (2) (Summer): 81–91.

Klein, Naomi. 2007. *The Shock Doctrine: The Rise of Disaster Capitalism*. New York: Picador.

Knutson, Ryan. 2010. "Blast at BP Texas Refinery in '05 Foreshadowed Gulf Disaster." *ProPublica*, July 2. http://www.propublica.org/article/blast-at-bp-texas-refinery-in-05-foreshadowed-gulf-disaster.

Kochhar, Rakesh. 2004. "The Wealth of Hispanic Households: 1996 to 2002." Pew Research Hispanic Trends Project, Washington, DC. http://www.pewhispanic.org/2004/10/18/the-wealth-of-hispanic-households/.

Kocieniewski, David. 2011. "G.E.'s Strategies Let It Avoid Taxes Altogether." *New York Times*, March 24. http://www.nytimes.com/2011/03/25/business/economy/25tax.html?pagewanted=all&_r=0.

Kooistra, Paul. 1989. *Criminals as Heroes: Structure, Power and Identity*. Bowling Green, OH: Bowling Green State University Popular Press.

Kooistra, Paul G., John S. Mahoney, and Saundra D. Westervelt. 1998. "The World of Crime According to COPS." In *Entertaining Crime*, edited by M. Fishman and G. Cavender, 141–58. New York: Aldine de Gruyter.

Korton, David. 1995. *When Corporations Rule the World*. Bloomfield, CT: Kumarian Press.

Kozol, Jonathan. 1991. *Savage Inequalities: Children in America's Schools*. New York: HarperCollins.

Kraska, Peter. 1999. "Militarizing Criminal Justice: Exploring Possibilities." *Journal of Political and Military Sociology* 27 (2): 205–16.

———. 2004. *Theorizing Criminal Justice: Eight Essential Orientations*. Long Grove, IL: Waveland.

———. 2007. "The Blurring of War and Law Enforcement." In *Violence, Conflict, and World Order: Critical Conversations on State-Sanctioned Justice*, edited by G. Barak, 161–87. Lanham, MD: Rowman & Littlefield.

Krieger, Nancy, and Elizabeth Fee. 1994. "Man-Made Medicine and Women's Health: The Biopolitics of Sex/Gender and Race/Ethnicity." In *Women's Health, Politics, and Power: Essays on Sex/Gender, Medicine, and Public Health*, edited by Elizabeth Fee and Nancy Krieger, 11–29. Amityville, NY: Baywood.

Krisberg, Barry. 1975. *Crime and Privilege: Towards a New Criminology*. Englewood Cliffs, NJ: Prentice-Hall.

Krivo, Lauren, and Ruth Peterson. 2009. Introduction to the special issue, "Race, Crime, and Justice: Contexts and Complexities." *Annals of the American Academy of Political and Social Science* 623 (May): 7–10.

Kroll, Luisa. 2013. "Inside the 2013 Forbes 400." *Forbes,* September 16. http://www.forbes.com/sites/luisakroll/2013/09/16/inside-the-2013-forbes-400-facts-and-figures-on-americas-richest/.

Kuper, Leo. 1985. *The Prevention of Genocide.* New Haven, CT: Yale University Press.

Kurtz, Karl, and Brian Weberg. 2009. "The State of Staff: July/August 2009." National Conference of State Legislatures. http://www.ncsl.org/default.aspx?tabid=17904.

Labaton, Stephen. 2002. "Now Who, Exactly Got Us into This? Enron? Arthur Andersen? Shocking Say Those Who Helped It Along." *New York Times,* February 3, C01.

Lamy, Philip. 1996. *Millennium Rage.* New York: Plenum.

Lanier, Mark M., and Stuart Henry. 2004. *Essential Criminology.* Boulder, CO: Westview.

Lasswell, Thomas E. 1965. *Class and Stratum.* Boston: Houghton Mifflin.

Lattman, Peter, and Annelena Lobb. 2009. "Victims' Speeches in Court Influenced Judge's Ruling." *Wall Street Journal,* June 30, A12.

Lauritsen, Janet. 2004. "Searching for a Better Understanding of Race and Ethnic Differences in Violent Crime." *Criminal Justice Ethics* (Winter/Spring): 68–73.

Layton, Lyndsey. 2009. "Peanut Processor Knowingly Sold Tainted Products." *Washington Post,* January 28. http://www.washingtonpost.com/wp-dyn/content/article/2009/01/27/AR2009012702992.html.

Lazarus, Edward. 1991. *Black Hills, White Justice: The Sioux Nation versus the United States, 1775 to the Present.* New York: HarperCollins.

Le, Cuong Nguyen. 2005. "Socioeconomic Statistics and Demographics." *Asian Nation.* http://www.asian-nation.org/demographics.shtml.

Leaf, Clifton. 2005. "Enough Is Enough: White-Collar Criminals; They Lie They Cheat They Steal and They've Been Getting Away with It for Too Long." In *Annual Editions: Criminal Justice,* 29th ed., edited by Joseph L. Victor and Joanne Naughton, 35–42. Dubuque, IA: McGraw-Hill/Dushkin. (Reprinted from *Fortune,* March 18, 2002, 62–65.)

Lederman, Josh. 2013. "Obama Signs Violence against Women Act." *Huffington Post,* March 7. http://www.huffingtonpost.com/2013/03/07/obama-violence-against-women-act_n_2830158.html.

Lee, Charles. 1992. "Toxic Waste and Race in the United States." In *Race and the Incidence of Environmental Hazards: A Time for Discourse,* edited by Bunyan Bryant and Paul Mohai, 10–27. Boulder, CO: Westview.

Lee, Jennifer. 2000. "The Salience of Race in Everyday Life: Black Customers' Shopping Experiences in Black and White Neighborhoods." *Work and Occupations* 27:353–76.

Lees, Loretta. 2003. "Super-gentrification: The Case of Brooklyn Heights, New York City." *Urban Studies* 40 (12): 2487–2509.

Leighton, Paul. 1999. *Mopping the Floor While the Tub Overflows.* Monograph written for the Citizen's Alliance on Prisons and Public Safety. http://www.paulsjusticepage.com.

———. 2002. "Should Sept. 11 Victims Be Counted in the Crime Reports?" StopViolence.com, http://stopviolence.com/9-11/law/crimerates.htm. Originally published as "Decision on 9/11 Victims Is a Crime." *Newsday,* August 29.

———. 2005. "The Challenge of Terrorism to Free Societies in the Global Village." In *Terrorism and Counter-Terrorism: Criminological Perspectives,* edited by Mathieu Deflem, 199–218. Amsterdam: Elsevier Science.

———. 2006. "Demystifying Terrorism: Crazy Islamic Terrorists Who Hate Us Because We're Free?" In *Demystifying Crime and Criminal Justice,* edited by Robert M. Bohm and Jeffery T. Walker, 63–70. Los Angeles: Roxbury.

———. 2007. "Judge Removed from Indian Trust Case for Saying Interior Dept. Is Racist." *Critical Criminologist* 17 (2). http://paulsjusticepage.com.

———. 2010. "A Professor of White Collar Crime Reviews USA's "White Collar" Series." *Paul's Justice Blog.* http://www.paulsjusticeblog.com/2010/02/a_professor _of_white_collar_cr.php.

———. 2013. "Corporate Crime and the Corporate Agenda for Crime Control: Disappearing Awareness of Corporate Crime and Increasing Abuses of Power." *Western Criminology Review* 14 (2): 38–51. http://wcr.sonoma.edu/v14n2/Leighton.pdf.

Leighton, Paul, and Donna Killingbeck. 2001. "Professional Codes of Ethics." In *Criminal Justice Ethics,* edited by Paul Leighton and Jeffrey Reiman, 527–32. Upper Saddle River, NJ: Prentice-Hall.

Leighton, Paul, and Jeffrey Reiman, eds. 2001. *Criminal Justice Ethics.* Upper Saddle River, NJ: Prentice-Hall.

———. 2002. "Getting Tough on Corporate Crime? Enron and a Year of Corporate Financial Scandals." Boston: Allyn & Bacon. http://www.paulsjusticepage.com/ RichGetRicher/fraud.htm.

———. 2004. "A Tale of Two Criminals: We're Tougher on Corporate Criminals, but They Still Don't Get What They Deserve." Boston: Allyn & Bacon. http:// paulsjusticepage.com/RichGetRicher/fraud2004.htm.

———. 2014. "A Suitable Amount of Street Crime and a Suitable Amount of White Collar Crime: Inconvenient Truths about Inequality, Crime and Criminal Justice." In *Routledge Handbook of International Crime and Justice Studies,* edited by B. Arrigo and H. Berscot. New York: Routledge.

Leighton, Paul, and Donna Selman. 2012. "Private Prisons, the Criminal Justice-Industrial Complex and Bodies Destined for Profitable Punishment." In *Routledge Handbook of Critical Criminology,* edited by W. DeKeseredy and M. Dragiewicz, 266–79. New York: Routledge.

Leinen, Stephen. 1993. *Gay Cops.* New Brunswick, NJ: Rutgers University Press.

Lenzner, Robert. 2013. "The Top 25 Hedge Fund Managers Earn More Than All the 500 Top CEOs Together." *Forbes*, August 6. http://www.forbes.com/sites/robertlenzner/2013/08/06/the-top-25-hedge-fund-managers-earn-more-than-all-the-500-top-ceos-together/.

Leonard, Eileen B. 1982. *Women, Crime, and Society: A Critique of Criminology Theory*. New York: Longman.

———. 1995. "Theoretical Criminology and Gender." In *The Criminal Justice System and Women*, 2nd ed., edited by Barbara Raffel Price and Natalie J. Sokoloff, 54–70. New York: McGraw-Hill.

Levine, James. 1997. "The Impact of Racial Demography on Jury Verdicts in Routine Adjudication." *Criminal Law Bulletin* 33:523.

Levy, Barrie, ed. 1998. *Dating Violence: Young Women in Danger*. Seattle, WA: Seal.

Lichtblau, Eric. 2005. "Profiling Report Leads to a Demotion." *New York Times*, August 24. http://www.nytimes.com/2005/08/24/politics/24profiling.html.

———. 2008. "Senate Approves Bill to Broaden Wiretap Powers." *New York Times*, July 10. http://www.nytimes.com/2008/07/10/washington/10fisa.html.

Lichtblau, Eric, David Johnston, and Ron Nixon. 2008. "FBI Struggles to Handle Financial Fraud Cases." *New York Times*, October 18. http://www.nytimes.com/2008/10/19/washington/19fbi.html.

Lichter, Robert, and Daniel R. Amundson. 1997. "Distorted Reality: Hispanic Characters in TV Entertainment." In *Latin Looks*, edited by Clara E. Rodriguez, 57–72. Boulder, CO: Westview.

Light, John. 2013. "Rethinking Our Minimum Wage." *Moyers & Company*, February 22. http://billmoyers.com/2013/02/22/rethinking-our-minimum-wage/.

Lipsitz, George. 2005. "The Possessive Investment in Whiteness." In *White Privilege: Essential Readings on the Other Side of Racism*, 2nd ed., edited by Paula S. Rothenberg, 67–90. New York: Worth.

Little Rock. 1989. "The American Indian in the White Man's Prisons: A Story of Genocide." *Journal of Prisoners on Prisons* 1 (1): 41–56.

Loftus, Elizabeth, and K. Ketcham. 1991. *Witness for the Defense*. New York: St. Martin's.

Logan, Keith. 2007. "Foreign Intelligence Surveillance Act." In *Battleground: Criminal Justice*, edited by G. Barak, 1:287–98. Westport, CT: Greenwood.

Lopez, Gerald. 2008. "Rebelling against the War on Low-Income, of Color, and Immigrant Communities." In *After the War on Crime: Race, Democracy, and a New Reconstruction*, edited by M. L. Frampton, I. H. López, and J. Simon, 151–65. New York: New York University Press.

Lopez, Mark, and Paul Taylor. 2009. "Dissecting the 2008 Electorate: Most Diverse in U.S. History." Pew Research Hispanic Trends Project, Washington, DC. http://www.pewhispanic.org/2009/04/30/dissecting-the-2008-electorate-most-diverse-in-us-history/#end1.

Lusane, Clarence. 1991. *Pipe Dream Blues: Racism and the War on Drugs*. Boston: South End.

Lynch, James, and William Sabol. 2000. "Prison Use and Social Control: Policies, Processes, and Decisions of the Criminal Justice System; Criminal Justice 2000." NCJ 182410. Washington, DC: US Department of Justice.

Lynch, Michael J. 1996. "Class, Race, Gender and Criminology: Structured Choices and the Life Course." In *Race, Gender, and Class in Criminology: The Intersection*, edited by Martin D. Schwartz and Dragan Milovanovic, 3–28. New York: Garland.

Lynch, Michael J., and Nancy K. Frank. 1992. *Corporate Crime, Corporate Violence*. Albany, NY: Harrow and Heston.

Lynch, Michael, and W. Byron Groves. 1989. *A Primer in Radical Criminology*. 2nd ed. Albany, NY: Harrow and Heston.

Lynch, Michael, Ray Michalowski, and W. Byron Groves. 2000. *The New Primer in Radical Criminology*. 3rd ed. Monsey, NY: Willow Tree.

Lynch, Michael, and E. Britt Patterson, eds. 1991. *Race and Criminal Justice*. Albany, NY: Harrow and Heston.

Lynch, Michael, E. Britt Patterson, and Kristina K. Childs. 2008. "Racial Divide: The Context of Racial and Ethnic Bias in Criminal Justice Processes." In *Racial Divide: Racial and Ethnic Bias in the Criminal Justice System*, edited by M. Lynch, E. Patterson, and K. Childs, 1–14. Monsey, NY: Criminal Justice.

Lynch, Michael, and Paul Stretesky. 1998. "Uniting Class, Race and Criticism through the Study of Environmental Justice." *Critical Criminologist* 9 (1): 1, 4–6.

Ma, Yue. 2008. "Prosecutorial Discretion and Plea Bargaining in the United States, France, Germany, and Italy: A Comparative Perspective." In *Global Criminology and Criminal Justice: Current Issues and Perspectives*, edited by Nick Larsen and Russell Smandych, 281–310. Buffalo, NY: Broadview.

Macartney, Suzanne. 2011. *Child Poverty in the United States 2009 and 2010: Selected Race Groups and Hispanic Origin*. Washington, DC: United States Census Bureau. http://www.census.gov/prod/2011pubs/acsbr10-05.pdf.

Macartney, Suzanne, Alemayehu Bishaw, and Kayla Fontenot. 2013. "Poverty Rates for Selected Detailed Race and Hispanic Groups by State and Place: 2007–2011." American Community Survey Briefs, United States Census Bureau. http://www.census.gov/prod/2013pubs/acsbr11-17.pdf.

MacKinnon, Catharine A. (1984) 1991. "Difference and Dominance: On Sex Discrimination." In *Feminist Legal Theory*, edited by Katharine T. Bartlett and Rosanne Kennedy, 81–94. Boulder, CO: Westview.

Madriz, Esther. 1997. *Nothing Bad Happens to Good Girls: Fear of Crime in Women's Lives*. Berkeley: University of California Press.

Mallicoat, Stacy L., and Gregory C. Brown. 2008. "The Impact of Race and Ethnicity on Student Opinions of Capital Punishment." *Journal of Ethnicity in Criminal Justice* 6 (4): 255–80. doi:10.1080/15377930802530296.

Mandle, J. R. 1978. *The Roots of Black Poverty: The Southern Plantation Economy after the Civil War*. Durham, NC: Duke University Press.

———. 1992. *Not Slave, Not Free: The African American Economic Experience since the Civil War.* Durham, NC: Duke University Press.

Mann, Coramae Richey, and Marjorie S. Zatz, eds. 1998. *Images of Color, Images of Crime: Readings.* Los Angeles: Roxbury.

Manning, Jennifer E. 2012. "Membership of the 112th Congress: A Profile." Report, Congressional Research Service, Washington, DC, November 26. http://www.fas.org/sgp/crs/misc/R41647.pdf.

Marable, Manning. 1983. *How Capitalism Underdeveloped Black America: Problems in Race, Political Economy, and Society.* Boston: South End.

Marshall, Eliot. 1998. "DNA Studies Challenge the Meaning of Race." *Science* 282:654.

Martin, Susan E. 1990. *On the Move: The Status of Women in Policing.* Washington, DC: Police Foundation.

———. 1992. "The Interactive Effects of Race and Sex on Women Police Officers." *Justice Professional* 6 (1): 155–72.

Martin, Susan E., and Nancy C. Jurik. 1996. *Doing Justice, Doing Gender.* Thousand Oaks, CA: Sage.

Maruschak, Laura M., and Erika Parks. 2012. "Probation and Parole in the United States, 2011." Bureau of Justice Statistics. http://www.bjs.gov/content/pub/pdf/ppus11.pdf.

Massey, Douglas, and Nancy Denton. 1993. *American Apartheid: Segregation and the Making of the Underclass.* Cambridge, MA: Harvard University Press.

Mauer, Marc. 1997. *Intended and Unintended Consequences: State Racial Disparities in Imprisonment.* Washington, DC: Sentencing Project.

Mauer, Marc, and Meda Chesney-Lind, eds. 2002. *Invisible Punishment: The Collateral Consequences of Mass Imprisonment.* New York: The New Press.

Mazzetti, Mark, and Scott Shane. 2009. "Interrogation Memos Detail Harsh Tactics by the C.I.A." *New York Times,* April 16. http://www.nytimes.com/2009/04/17/us/politics/17detain.html?pagewanted=all.

McCorkel, Jill A. 2013. *Breaking Women: Gender, Race, and the New Politics of Imprisonment.* New York: New York University Press.

McDonald, J. 2001. "Some Question Police Tactics at Biotech Protest." *San Diego Union-Tribune,* August 18, A1. http://www.signonsandiego.com.

McGee, Susan. 2004. "Why Battered Women Stay." *StopViolence.com* (blog). http://stopviolence.com/domviol/whytheystay.htm.

McGrath, Charles. 2005. "In Fiction, a Long History of Fixation on the Social Gap." *New York Times,* June 8. http://www.nytimes.com/2005/06/08/national/class/08fict-FINAL.html?pagewanted=all.

McGurrin, Danielle, Melissa Jarrell, Amber Jahn, and Brandy Cochrane. 2013. "White Collar Crime Representation in the Criminological Literature Revisited, 2001–2010." *Western Criminology Review* 14 (2): 3–19. http://wcr.sonoma.edu/v14n2/McGurrin.pdf.

McIntosh, Peggy. 1984. "Interactive Phases of Curricular Revision." In *Toward a Balanced Curriculum*, edited by Bonnie Spanier, Alexander Bloom, and Darlene Boroviak, 25–34. Cambridge, MA: Schenkman.

———. (1988) 1997. "White Privilege and Male Privilege: A Personal Account of Coming to See Correspondences through Work in Women's Studies." In *Critical White Studies*, edited by Richard Delgado and Jean Stefancic, 291–99. Philadelphia: Temple University Press.

McNeely, Robert. 2011. "Census: Education Level Main Factor in Determining Income." *NEA Today*, September 20. http://neatoday.org/2011/09/20/census-education-level-main-factor-in-determining-income/.

Meeks, Gregory W. 1999. "Q: Does the Supreme Court Need Affirmative Action for Its Own Staff?" *Insight on the News* 15 (3): 24–27.

Messerschmidt, James W. 1993. *Masculinities and Crime: Critique and Reconceptualization of Theory*. Lanham, MD: Rowman & Littlefield.

———. 1995. "From Patriarchy to Gender: Feminist Theory, Criminology, and the Challenge of Diversity." In *International Feminist Perspectives in Criminology*, edited by N. H. Rafter and F. Heidensohn, 167–88. Philadelphia: Open University Press.

———. 1997. *Crime as Structured Action: Gender, Race, Class, and Crime in the Making*. Thousand Oaks, CA: Sage.

———. 2004. *Flesh and Blood: Adolescent Gender Diversity and Violence*. Lanham, MD: Rowman & Littlefield.

Messner, Steven F., and Richard Rosenfeld. 1994. *Crime and the American Dream*. Belmont, CA: Wadsworth.

Meyer, Josh. 2009. "FBI Planning a Bigger Role in Terrorism Fight." *Los Angeles Times*, May 28. http://www.latimes.com/news/nationworld/washingtondc/la-na-fbi28-2009may28,0,329005,print.story.

Meyers, Jim. 2009. "DHS Chief Napolitano: Illegal Immigration Is Not a Crime." Newsmax, April 22. http://newsmax.com/InsideCover/napolitano-illegals-crime/2009/04/22/id/329647.

Michalowski, Raymond. 1985. *Order, Law and Crime*. New York: Random House.

Michalowski, Raymond, and Susan Carlson. 1999. "Unemployment, Imprisonment, and Social Structures of Accumulation: Historical Contingency in the Rusche-Kirchheimer Hypothesis." *Criminology* 37 (2): 217–50.

Michalowski, Raymond, and Ronald Kramer, eds. 2006. *State-Corporate Crime: Wrongdoing at the Intersection of Business and Government*. New Brunswick, NJ: Rutgers University Press.

Miller, Jerome G. 1996. *Search and Destroy: African-American Males in the Criminal Justice System*. Cambridge: Cambridge University Press.

Miller, Jody. 1998. "Up It Up: Gender and the Accomplishment of Street Robbery." *Criminology* 36 (1): 37–65.

———. 2001. *One of the Guys: Girls, Gangs, and Gender*. New York: Oxford University Press.

———. 2002. "The Strengths and Limits of 'Doing Gender' for Understanding Street Crime." *Theoretical Criminology* 6 (4): 433–60.

———. 2008. *Getting Played: African American Girls, Urban Inequality, and Gendered Violence*. New York: New York University Press.

Miller, Robin, and Sandra Lee Browning. 2004. "A Critical Examination of Law and Social Control: Introductory Remarks." In *For the Common Good: A Critical Examination of Law and Social Control*, edited by Robin Miller and Sandra Lee Browning, 3–8. Durham, NC: Carolina Academic Press.

Miller, Susan L. 1998. "Introduction." In *Crime Control and Women*, edited by Susan L. Miller, xv–xxiv. Thousand Oaks, CA: Sage.

———. 1999. *Gender and Community Policing: Walking the Talk*. Boston: Northeastern University Press.

Miller, Susan, and Michelle Meloy. 2006. "Women's Use of Force." *Violence against Women* 12 (1): 89–115.

Millett, Kate. 1970. *Sexual Politics*. New York: Doubleday.

Mills, C. Wright. 1956. *The Power Elite*. New York: Oxford University Press.

Mills, Mark. 2004. "The Security-Industrial Complex." *Forbes*, November 29. http://www.forbes.com/forbes/2004/1129/044.html.

Mohamed, A. Rafik, and Erik Fritsvold. 2011. *Dorm Room Dealers: Drugs and the Privileges of Race and Class*. Boulder, CO: Lynne Rienner.

Mohn, Tanya. 2012. "America's Most Exclusive Gated Communities." *Forbes*, July 3. http://www.forbes.com/sites/tanyamohn/2012/07/03/americas-most-exclusive-gated-communities/.

Money.cnn.com. 2013. "Fortune 500." http://money.cnn.com/magazines/fortune/fortune500/2013/full_list/.

Mooney, G. 2008. "Explaining Poverty, Social Exclusion and Inequality." In *Understanding Inequality, Poverty and Wealth*, edited by T. Ridge and S. Wright, 61–78. Bristol, UK: Policy.

Morgenson, Gretchen. 2010. "Lending Magnate Settles Fraud Case." *New York Times*, October 15. http://www.nytimes.com/2010/10/16/business/16countrywide.html.

Morrison, Toni, ed. 1992. *Race-ing Justice, En-gendering Power: Essays on Anita Hill, Clarence Thomas, and the Construction of Social Reality*. New York: Pantheon.

Moss, Jeremiah. 2014. "On Spike Lee and Hyper-Gentrification, the Monster That Ate New York." *Jeremiah's Vanishing New York* (blog), March 3. http://vanishing-newyork.blogspot.com/2014/03/on-spike-lee-hyper-gentrification.html.

Moulds, Elizabeth F. 1980. "Chivalry and Paternalism: Disparities of Treatment in the Criminal Justice System." In *Women, Crime, and Justice*, edited by Susan Datesman and Frank Scarpitti, 277–99. New York: Oxford University Press.

Mullings, Leith. 1994. "Images, Ideology, and Women of Color." In *Women of Color in U.S. Society*, edited by Maxine Baca Zinn and Bonnie Thornton Dill, 265–89. Philadelphia: Temple University Press.

Murphy, Sheigla B., and Marsha Rosenbaum. 1997. "Two Women Who Used Cocaine Too Much: Class, Race, Gender, Crack, and Coke." In *Crack in America:*

Demon Drugs and Social Justice, edited by Craig Reinarman and Harry G. Levine, 98–112. Berkeley: University of California Press.

Myrdal, Gunnar. 1944. *An American Dilemma: The Negro Problem and Modern Democracy*. New York: Pantheon.

NAACP (National Association for the Advancement of Colored People). 2009–2013. "Criminal Justice Fact Sheet." http://www.naacp.org/pages/criminal-justice-fact-sheet.

Nagel, Ilene H., and Barry L. Johnson. 1994. "The Role of Gender in a Structured Sentencing System." *Journal of Criminal Law and Criminology* 85 (1): 181–221.

Nation. 2009. "Noted." *Nation*, July 13, 5.

National Association of Criminal Defense Attorneys. 2004. "Getting What They Pay For: The Fallacy of Quality Indigent Defense." *Indigent Defense* (May/June). http://www.nacdl.org/public.nsf/DefenseUpdates/Louisiana029.

National Center for Health Statistics. 2004. "Americans Slightly Taller, Much Heavier Than Four Decades Ago." http://www.cdc.gov/nchs/pressroom/04news/americans.htm.

National Center for Women in Policing. 2002. *Equality Denied: The Status of Women in Policing, 2001*. Washington, DC: National Center for Women in Policing.

National Council on Crime and Delinquency. 1995 (January). "National Assessment of Structured Sentencing Final Report."

National Institute of Justice. 2005. *2004 Annual Report*. Washington, DC: US Government Printing Office, 1–24.

National Narcotics Intelligence Consumers Committee. 1995. *The NNICC Report 1994: The Supply of Illegal Drugs to the United States*. Washington, DC: DEA.

Nelson, J., ed. 2000. *Police Brutality: An Anthology*. New York: Norton.

Newman, Katherine S., Cybelle Fox, David J. Harding, Jal Mehta, and Wendy Roth. 2004. *Rampage: The Social Roots of School Shootings*. New York: Basic.

New Webster's Dictionary of the English Language. 1984. New York: Delair.

New York Times. 2005. "Text: Victim Impact Statement." August 11.

———. 2009a. "A Shift on Immigration." May 3.

———. 2009b. "The Torturers' Manifesto." April 18, WK9. http://www.nytimes.com/2009/04/19/opinion/19sun1.html?_r=1.

———. 2014. "Rampant Prosecutorial Misconduct." January 5, SR10.

Nordstrom, Carolyn. 2007. *Global Outlaws: Crime, Money, and Power in the Contemporary World*. Berkeley: University of California Press.

Norris, Floyd. 2008a. "Can Mary Schapiro Save the SEC?" *New York Times*, December 17. http://norris.blogs.nytimes.com/2008/12/17/can-she-save-the-sec/.

———. 2008b. "Misleading Numbers at the SEC." *New York Times*, September 11. http://norris.blogs.nytimes.com/2008/09/11/misleading-numbers-at-the-sec/.

Norton, M., and D. Ariely. 2011. "Building a Better America—One Wealth Quintile at a Time." *Perspectives on Psychological Science* 6 (1): 9–12.

NYSOAG (New York State Office of the Attorney General). 1999. "Results of Investigation into NYPD 'Stop and Frisk' Practice." Albany, NY: Office of the Attorney General.

Obama, Barack. 2007. "Remarks at Howard University Convocation." Howard University, Washington, DC, September 28. http://www.barackobama .com/2007/09/28/remarks_of_senator_barack_obam_26.php.

———. 2009. "Remarks at NAACP Centennial." *Politico*, July 16. http://www.po litico.com/news/stories/0709/25053.html.

———. 2013. Transcript of President Obama's speech on US drone and counterterror policy, as provided by the White House. May 23.

O'Connell, John P. 1995. "Throwing Away the Key (and State Money)." *Spectrum: Journal of State Government* 68 (1) (Winter): 28–31.

Ogawa, Brian, and Aurelia Sands Belle. 1999. "Respecting Diversity: Responding to Underserved Victims of Crime." In *1999 National Victim Assistance Academy*, edited by Grace Coleman, Mario Gaboury, Morna Murray, and Anne Seymour, chap. 7. Washington, DC: Office for Justice Programs. https://www.ncjrs.gov/ ovc_archives/nvaa99/chap7.htm.

O'Hehir, Andrew. 2013. "The NSA-DEA Police State Tango: This Week's DEA Bombshell Shows Us How the Drug War and the Terror War Have Poisoned Our Justice System." *Salon*, August 10. http://www.salon.com/2013/08/10/the_nsa_ dea_police_state_tango/.

OJJDP (Office of Juvenile Justice and Delinquency Prevention). 1998. *Disproportionate Minority Confinement*. Washington, DC: U.S. Department of Justice. NCJ 173420.

———. 2006. *Disproportionate Minority Contact Technical Assistance Manual*. 3rd ed. Washington, DC: US Department of Justice.

Omi, Michael, and Howard Winant. 1994. *Racial Formation in the United States*. 2nd ed. New York: Routledge.

Ontiveros, Maria L. (1995) 1997a. "Rosa Lopez, Christopher Darden, and Me: Issues of Gender, Ethnicity, and Class in Evaluating Witness Credibility." In *Critical Race Feminism: A Reader*, edited by Adrien Katherine Wing, 269–77. New York: New York University Press.

———. (1993) 1997b. "Three Perspectives on Workplace Harassment of Women of Color." In *Critical Race Feminism*, edited by Adrien Katherine Wing, 188–91. New York: New York University Press.

OpenSecrets.org. n.d. "Donor Demographics." http://www.opensecrets.org/bigpic ture/DonorDemographics.php.

Oshinsky, David. 1996. *Worse Than Slavery: Parchman Farm and the Ordeal of Jim Crow Justice*. New York: Free Press.

Packer, Herbert. 1964. "Two Models of the Criminal Process." *University of Pennsylvania Law Review* 113:1–23.

Padilla, Laura M. 1997. "Intersectionality and Positionality: Situating Women of Color in the Affirmative Action Dialogue." *Fordham Law Review* 66:843–929.

Painter, Matthew, and Jonathan Vespa. 2008. "Race/Ethnicity, Cohabitation, and Marital Wealth Accumulation." Paper prepared for the annual meeting of the Population Association of America, Detroit, MI, April 30–May 2. http://paa2009 .princeton.edu/download.aspx?submissionId=91404.

Paley, Amit, and David Hilzenrath. 2008. "SEC Chief Defends His Restraint." *Washington Post*, December 24, A1.

Paltrow, Lynn, and Jeanne Flavin. 2013. "Arrests of and Forced Interventions on Pregnant Women in the United States, 1973–2005: Implications for Women's Legal Status and Public Health." *Journal of Health Politics, Policy and Law* 38 (2): 299–343.

Parenti, Christian. 1999. *Lockdown America: Police and Prisons in the Age of Crisis*. New York: Verso.

Parker, Karen, Mari DeWees, and Michael Radelet. 2003. "Race, the Death Penalty and Wrongful Convictions." *Criminal Justice Magazine* (Spring): 48–54. http://www.abanet.org/crimjust/spring2003/death_penalty.html.

Pasztor, Andy. 1995. *When the Pentagon Was for Sale*. New York: Scribner.

Patterson, William, ed. (1951) 1970. *We Charge Genocide: The Crime of Government against the Negro People*. Reprint, New York: International.

———. 1971. *The Man Who Charged Genocide: An Autobiography*. New York: International.

Pease, Bob. 2010. *Undoing Privilege*. London: Zed.

Pepinsky, Harold E., and Richard Quinney, eds. 1991. *Criminology as Peacemaking*. Bloomington: Indiana University Press.

Perkins, John. 2007. *The Secret History of the American Empire: The Truth about Economic Hit Men, Jackals, and How to Change the World*. New York: Plume.

Pew Hispanic Center. 2005. "Hispanics: A People in Motion." Pew Research Hispanic Trends Project, Washington, DC. http://www.pewhispanic.org/2005/01/24/hispanic-trends/.

Pfohl, Stephen J. 1985. *Images of Deviance and Social Control*. New York: McGraw-Hill.

Pinkney, Alphonso. 1984. *The Myth of Black Progress*. Cambridge: Cambridge University Press.

Pizzo, Stephen, Mark Fricker, and Paul Muolo. 1991. *Inside Job: The Looting of America's Savings & Loans*. New York: HarperPerennial.

Pizzo, Stephen, and Paul Muolo. 1993. "Take the Money and Run: A Rogues Gallery of Some Lucky S & L Thieves." *New York Times Magazine*, May 9.

Platt, Anthony. 1969. *The Child Savers: The Invention of Delinquency*. Chicago: University of Chicago Press.

———. 1974. "Prospects for a Radical Criminology." *Crime and Social Justice* 1 (Fall): 1–14.

Platt, Anthony, and Randi Pollock. 1974. "Channeling Lawyers: The Careers of Public Defenders." *Issues in Criminology* 9 (1): 1–31.

Platt, Anthony, and Paul Takagi, eds. 1980. *Punishment and Penal Discipline*. San Francisco: Crime and Social Justice Associates.

Pollak, Otto. 1950. *The Criminality of Women*. Philadelphia: University of Pennsylvania Press.

Pollock-Byrne, Joycelyn. 1990. *Women, Prison, and Crime*. Pacific Grove, CA: Brooks/Cole.

Pomykala, Joseph. 2000. "Bankruptcy's Origins in Debtor-Perpetrated Crime." Working paper, Department of Economics, Towson University, Towson, MD. Available at Social Science Research Network, http://ssrn.com/abstract=222377.

Population Reference Bureau (PRB). 2009. "2009 World Population Data Sheet." http://www.prb.org/Publications/Datasheets/2009/2009wpds.aspx.

Porter, Eduardo. 2005. "How Long Can Workers Tread Water?" *New York Times*, July 14. http://www.nytimes.com/2005/07/14/business/14income html?pagewanted=all.

Porter, Nicole. 2010. "Expanding the Vote: State Felony Disenfranchisement Reform, 1997–2010." Report, Sentencing Project. http://www.sentencingproject .org/doc/publications/publications/vr_ExpandingtheVoteFinalAddendum.pdf.

Posner, Richard. 1992. *Sex and Reason*. Cambridge, MA: Harvard University Press.

———. 2005. "Bad News." *New York Times Book Review*, July 21, 1, 8–11.

Potter, Gary W., and Victor E. Kappeler, eds. 1998. *Constructing Crime: Perspectives on Making News and Social Problems*. Prospect Heights, IL: Waveland.

Potter, Hillary. 2008. *Battle Cries: Black Women and Intimate Partner Violence*. New York: New York University Press.

Préjean, Helen. 1993. *Dead Man Walking*. New York: Vintage.

———. 1995. "Dead Man Walking." Speech in Albany, NY. January 24. Transcript available from archive of *Radical Catholic Page*. http://web.archive.org/ web/20020209203423/http://www.bway.net/~halsall/radcath/prejean1.html.

Quinney, Richard. 1975. *Criminology: An Analysis and Critique of Crime in America*. Boston: Little, Brown.

———. 1977. *Class, State and Crime*. New York: Longman.

Radcliffe-Brown, A. R. (1933) 1965. *Structure and Function in Primitive Society: Essays and Addresses*. New York: Free Press.

Radelet, Michael. 1989. "Executions of Whites for Crimes against Blacks." *Sociological Quarterly* 30 (4): 529–44.

Raeder, Myrna S. 1993. "Gender and Sentencing: Single Moms, Battered Women, and Other Sex-Based Anomalies in the Gender-Free World of the Federal Sentencing Guidelines." *Pepperdine Law Review* 20:905–90.

Rafter, Nicole Hahn. 1990. *Partial Justice: Women, Prisons and Social Control*. New Brunswick, NJ: Transaction.

———. 1994. "Eugenics, Class, and the Professionalization of Social Control." In *Inequality, Crime, and Social Control*, edited by George Bridges and Martha Myers, 215–26. Boulder, CO: Westview.

———. 1997. *Creating Born Criminals*. Urbana: University of Illinois Press.

Rand, Michael. 2008. "Criminal Victimization." *Bureau of Justice Statistics Bulletin*. Washington, DC: US Department of Justice (December): 1–11.

Rasche, Christine E. (1988) 1995. "Minority Women and Domestic Violence: The Unique Dilemmas of Battered Women of Color." In *The Criminal Justice System and Women*, edited by Barbara Raffel Price and Natalie J. Sokoloff, 246–61. New York: McGraw-Hill.

Reaves, Brian A. 2011. "Census of State and Local Law Enforcement Agencies, 2008." Bureau of Justice Statistics. http://www.bjs.gov/content/pub/pdf/csllea08 .pdf.

———. 2012. "Federal Law Enforcement Officers, 2008." Bureau of Justice Statistics. http://www.bjs.gov/content/pub/pdf/fleo08.pdf.

Redstockings, Inc. 1978. *Feminist Revolution*. New York: Random House.

Reed, Diane F., and Edward L. Reed. 1997. "Children of Incarcerated Parents." *Social Justice* 24:152–69.

Reeve, Simon. 1999. *The New Jackals: Ramzi Yousef, Osama bin Laden, and the Future of Terrorism*. Boston: Northeastern University Press.

Reiman, Jeffrey. 1990. *Justice and Modern Moral Philosophy*. New Haven, CT: Yale University Press.

———. 1998. "Against Police Discretion: Reply to John Kleinig." *Journal of Social Philosophy* 29 (1): 132–42.

Reiman, Jeffrey, and Paul Leighton. 2010. *The Rich Get Richer: A Reader*. Boston: Allyn & Bacon.

———. 2013. *The Rich Get Richer and the Poor Get Prison*. 10th ed. Boston: Allyn & Bacon.

Renzetti, Claire M. 1998. "Connecting the Dots: Women, Public Policy, and Social Control." In *Crime Control and Women*, edited by Susan L. Miller, 181–89. Thousand Oaks, CA: Sage.

Revell, Janice. 2003. "Mo' Money, Fewer Problems." *Fortune*, March 31.

Rice, Marcia. 1990. "Challenging Orthodoxies in Feminist Theory: A Black Feminist Critique." In *Feminist Perspectives in Criminology*, edited by Loraine Gelsthorpe and Allison Morris, 57–69. Milton Keynes: Open University Press.

Rich, Frank. 2009a. "The Banality of Bush White House Evil." *New York Times*, April 26, WK14.

———. 2009b. "Bernie Madoff Is No John Dillinger." *New York Times*, July 8, WK8.

Richie, Beth E. 1996. *Compelled to Crime: The Gender Entrapment of Battered Black Women*. New York: Routledge.

———. 2012. *Arrested Justice: Black Women, Violence, and America's Prison Nation*. New York: New York University Press.

Ridgeway, James. 1995. *Blood in the Face*. New York: Thunder's Mouth.

Rierden, Andi. 1997. *The Farm: Life inside a Women's Prison*. Amherst: University of Massachusetts Press.

Rifkin, Jeremy. 1995. *The End of Work*. New York: Putnam.

Rios, Victor. 2009. "The Consequences of the Criminal Justice Pipeline on Black and Latino Masculinity." *Annals of the American Academy of Political and Social Science* 623 (May): 150–62.

———. 2011. *Punished: Policing the Lives of Black and Latino Boys*. New York: New York University Press.

———. 2013. "We Are All George Zimmerman: Trayvon Martin and the Youth Control Complex." *From the Square* (blog), July 22. http://www.fromthesquare .org/?p=5256.

Ripley, Amanda. 2000. "Unnecessary Force?" *Time*, July 24, 34–37.

Ritholtz, Barry. 2008a. "CEO Clawback Provisions in the Bailout?" *The Big Picture* (blog). http://bigpicture.typepad.com/comments/2008/09/ceo-clawback-pr.html.

———. 2008b. "A Memo Found in the Street: Uncle Sam the Enabler." In *The Rich Get Richer and the Poor Get Prison: A Reader*, edited by Jeffrey Reiman and Paul Leighton, 100–102. Boston: Allyn & Bacon/Pearson.

———. 2008c. "What Is 'Nonfeasance'?" *Seeking Alpha*, August 18. http://seekingalpha.com/article/91465-what-is-nonfeasance.

———. 2008d. "Where's the Ref?" *Forbes*, September 12. http://www.forbes.com/home/2008/09/12/lehman-greenspan-regulation-opinions-cx_br_0912ritholtz.html.

———. 2009a. *Bailout Nation*. Hoboken, NJ: Wiley.

———. 2009b. "Is Consumer Protection 'Too Big to Fail'?" *The Big Picture* (blog), November 4. http://www.ritholtz.com/blog/2009/11/is-consumer-protection-regulation-too-big-to-fail/.

———. 2009c. "Tactical Error: Health Care vs. Finance Regulatory Reform." *The Big Picture* (blog). http://www.ritholtz.com/blog/2009/09/finance-reform-vs-health-care-reform/.

———. 2011. "Word of the Day: Precariat." *The Big Picture* (blog). http://www.ritholtz.com/blog/2011/03/word-of-the-day-precariat/.

———. 2013. "Meet Uncle Sam, Your Partner in Crime." *Bloomberg*, November 5. http://www.bloomberg.com/news/2013-11-05/meet-uncle-sam-your-partner-in-crime.html.

Ritzer, George. 2004. *The McDonaldization of Society*. Thousand Oaks, CA. Pine Forge.

Rivera, Jenny. 1994. "Domestic Violence against Latinas by Latino Males: An Analysis of Race, National Origin, and Gender Differentials." *Third World Law Journal* 14 (2): 231.

Rivlin, Gary. 2011. "The Billion-Dollar Bank Heist: How the Financial Industry Is Buying Off Washington—and Killing Reform." *Newsweek*, July 11. http://www.thedailybeast.com/newsweek/2011/07/10/the-billion-dollar-bank-heist.html.

Roach, Stephen. 2006. "Globalization's New Underclass." Morgan Stanley Global Economic Forum. March 3.

Robers, Simone, Jana Kemp, Jennifer Truman, and Thomas Snyder. 2013. "Indicators of School Crime and Safety: 2012." Report, US Department of Education (NCES 2013-036) and US Department of Justice (NCJ 241446), Washington, DC, June. http://nces.ed.gov/pubs2013/2013036.pdf.

Roberts, Dorothy E. 1993. "Crime, Race, and Reproduction." *Tulane Law Review* 67 (6): 1945–77.

Robinson, Matt. 1998. "Tobacco: The Greatest Crime in World History?" *Critical Criminologist* 8 (3): 20–22.

Rodriguez, Clara E. 1997. "The Silver Screen: Stories and Stereotypes." In *Latin Looks: Images of Latinas and Latinos in the U.S. Media*, 73–79. Boulder, CO: Westview.

Roman, John. 2013. "Stand Your Ground Laws and Racial Bias." *MetroTrends Blog*, June 5. http://blog.metrotrends.org/2013/06/stand-ground-laws-racial-bias/.

Rosenbaum, Marsha, and Katherine Irwin. 1998. "Pregnancy, Drugs, and Harm Reduction." In *Drug Addiction Research and the Health of Women*, edited by Cora Lee Wetherington and Adele B. Roman, 309–18. Rockville, MD: National Institute on Drug Abuse.

Rosenfeld, Richard. 2002. "Why Criminologists Should Study Terrorism." *Criminologist: The Official Newsletter of the American Society of Criminology* 27 (6) (November/December): 3–4.

Rosenwald, Michael S. 2013. "A Drone of Your Very Own: These Aren't Your Average Remote-Controlled Aircraft." *Washington Post*, August 17. http://www.washingtonpost.com/local/personal-drones-delivering-wedding-rings-instead-of-missiles/2013/08/17/75ed2092-ff7e-11e2-9711-3708310f6f4d_story.html.

Ross, Sherwood. 2009. "Solitary Confinement in U.S. Prisons Making Thousands Psychotic." *Opednews.com*, March 24, 1–2. http://www.opednews.com/articles/Solitary-Confinement-In-U-by-Sherwood-Ross-090324-708.html.

Rubenstein, R. L. 1987. "Afterword: Genocide and Civilization." In *Genocide and the Modern Age: Etiology and Case Studies of Mass Death*, edited by Isidor Wallimann and Michael Dobkowski, 283–297. New York: Greenwood.

Rusche, Georg, and Otto Kirchheimer. (1939) 1968. *Punishment and Social Structure*. Reprint, New York: Russell and Russell.

Russell, Katheryn K. 1998. *The Color of Crime: Racial Hoaxes, White Fear, Black Protectionism, Police Harrassment, and Other Macroaggressions*. New York: New York University Press.

Samborn, Hope Viner. 1999. "Profiled and Pulled Over." *ABA Journal* 85:18.

Sample, Albert. 1984. *Racehoss: Big Emma's Boy*. New York: Ballantine.

SAMHSA (Substance Abuse and Mental Health Administration). 2012. Results from the 2012 National Survey on Drug Use and Health: Detailed Tables. http://www.oas.samhsa.gov.

Sampson, Robert, and W. J. Wilson. 1995. "Toward a Theory of Race, Crime, and Urban Inequality." In *Crime and Inequality*, edited by J. Hagan and R. Peterson, 37–54. Stanford, CA: Stanford University Press.

Satter, Robert. 1990. *Doing Justice: A Trial Judge at Work*. New York: Simon & Schuster.

Schell, Jonathan. 2009. "Torture and Truth." *Nation*, June 15, 15–18.

Schemo, Diana Jean. 2000. "Despite Options on Census, Many to Check 'Black' Only." *New York Times*, February 12, A1.

Schlabach, Mark. 2005. "From a Stool, Tyson Ends It." *Washington Post*, June 12.

Schlosser, Eric. 1998. "The Prison-Industrial Complex." *Atlantic*, December 1. http://www.theatlantic.com/doc/199812/prisons.

Schmitt, Richard. 2008. "FBI Saw Threat of Loan Crisis." *Los Angeles Times*, August 25, 2008, A1.

Schwartz, Martin D., and Dragan Milovanovic, eds. 1996. *Race, Gender, and Class in Criminology: The Intersections.* New York: Garland.

Schwartz, Nelson, and Michael Cooper. 2013. "Racial Diversity Efforts Ebb for Elite Careers, Analysis Finds." *New York Times,* May 27. http://www.nytimes.com/2013/05/28/us/texas-firm-highlights-struggle-for-black-professionals.html?nl=todaysheadlines&emc=edit_th_20130528&_r=0.

Schwendinger, Herman, and Julia Schwendinger. 1970. "Defenders of Order or Guardians of Human Rights?" *Issues in Criminology* 5:123–57.

Scott, Janny, and David Leonhardt. 2005. "Class in America: Shadowy Lines That Still Divide." *New York Times,* May 15.

Scully, Diana. 1990. *Understanding Sexual Violence: A Study of Convicted Rapists.* London: HarperCollins Academic.

Seagal, Debra. 2001. "Tales from the Cutting Room Floor." In *Criminal Justice Ethics,* edited by Paul Leighton and Jeffrey Reiman, 503–11. Upper Saddle River, NJ: Prentice-Hall.

Securities and Exchange Commission. 2010. "Former Countrywide CEO Angelo Mozilo to Pay SEC's Largest-Ever Financial Penalty Against a Public Company's Senior Executive." http://www.sec.gov/news/press/2010/2010-197.htm.

Sekhon, Nirej. 2011. "Redistributive Policing." *Journal of Criminal Law and Criminology* 101 (4): 1171–1226.

Sellers, Patricia. 2003. "Power: Do Women Really Want It?" *Fortune,* October 13.

Sellin, Thorsten. 1928. "The Negro Criminal: A Statistical Note." *Annals of the American Academy of Political and Social Science* 140:52–64.

———. 1976. *Slavery and the Penal System.* New York: Elsevier.

Selman, Donna, and Paul Leighton. 2010. *Punishment for Sale.* Lanham, MD: Rowman & Littlefield.

Selman-Killingbeck, Donna. 2005. "A Sociological History of Prison Privatization in the Contemporary United States." PhD diss., Western Michigan University, Kalamazoo, MI.

Sentencing Project. 1994. "Why '3 Strikes and You're Out' Won't Reduce Crime." Washington, DC: Sentencing Project.

Shaw, Clifford R., and Henry D. McKay. 1942. *Juvenile Delinquency and Urban Areas: A Study of Rates of Delinquents in Relation to Differential Characteristics of Local Communities in American Cities.* Chicago: University of Chicago Press.

Shear, Michael. 2013. "Seeing Citizenship Path Near, Activists Push Obama to Slow Deportations." *New York Times,* February 22. http://www.nytimes.com/2013/02/23/us/advocates-push-obama-to-halt-aggressive-deportation-efforts.html?pagewanted=all&_r=0.

Sheets, Virgil L., and Sanford L. Braver. 1999. "Organization Status and Perceived Sexual Harassment: Detecting the Mediators of a Null Effect." *Personality and Social Psychology Bulletin* 25 (9): 1159–71.

Shelden, Randall. 1999. "The Prison Industrial Complex and the New American Apartheid." *Critical Criminologist* 10 (1): 1, 3–5.

————. 2000. *Controlling the Dangerous Classes: A Critical Introduction to the History of Criminal Justice*. Boston: Allyn & Bacon.

Sheptycki, James, and Ali Wardak, eds. 2005. *Transnational and Comparative Criminology*. Oxford: GlassHouse.

Sherman, Francine. 2012. "Justice for Girls: Are We Making Progress?" *UCLA Law Review* 59:1584–1627.

Sherman, Mark. 2013. "DOJ Secretly Obtains Months of AP Phone Records; AP Condemns 'Unprecedented Intrusion.'" *Huffington Post*, May 13. http://www.huffingtonpost.com/2013/05/13/ap-phone-records-government-intrusion-unprecedented_n_3268569.html.

Shine, Cathy, and Marc Mauer. 1993. "Does the Punishment Fit the Crime? Drug Users and Drunk Drivers, Questions of Race and Class." Report, Sentencing Project, Washington, DC.

Siegel, Steven. 2009. "The Public Interest and Private Gated Communities." *Loyola Law Review* 55 (4): 805–38.

Simon, David. 1999. *Elite Deviance*. 6th ed. Boston: Allyn & Bacon.

Simon, Jonathan, Ian Haney López, and Mary Louise Frampton. 2008. Introduction to *After the War on Crime: Race, Democracy, and a New Reconstruction*, edited by M. L. Frampton, I. H. López, and J. Simon, 1–20. New York: New York University Press.

Skolnick, Jerome. (1967) 1996. *Justice without Trial: Law Enforcement in a Democratic Society*. Reprint, New York: Wiley.

Smith, Chris. 2013. "The Highest-Paid Coaches In U.S. Sports". *Forbes*. http://www.forbes.com/sites/chrissmith/2013/05/22/the-highest-paid-coaches-in-us-sports.

Smith, Dorothy. 1990. *The Conceptual Practices of Power*. Boston: Northeastern University Press.

Smith, E. B., and P. Kuntz. 2013. "CEO Pay 1,795-to-1 Multiple of Wages Skirts U.S. Law." *Bloomberg*, April 29. http://www.bloomberg.com/news/2013-04-30/ceo-pay-1-795-to-1-multiple-of-workers-skirts-law-as-sec-delays.html.

Smothers, Ronald. 1995. "Wave of Prison Uprisings Provokes Debate on Crack." *New York Times*, October 24, A12.

Solis, Carmen, Edwardo Portillos, and Rod Brunson. 2009. "Youth Violence—Crime or Self-Help? Marginalized Urban Males' Perspectives on the Limited Efficacy of the Criminal Justice System to Stop Youth Violence." In *After the War on Crime: Race, Democracy, and a New Reconstruction*, edited by M. L. Frampton, I. H. López, and J. Simon, 39–51. New York: New York University Press.

Spohn, Cassia. 1990. "Decision Making in Sexual Assault Cases: Do Black and Female Judges Make a Difference?" *Women and Criminal Justice* 2 (1): 83–105.

Spohn, Cassia, and David Holleran. 2000. "The Imprisonment Penalty Paid by Young Unemployed Black and Hispanic Male Offenders." *Criminology* 38 (1): 281–306.

Spohn, Cassia, and Katharine Tellis. 2011. "Justice Denied: The Exceptional Clearance of Rape Cases in Los Angeles." *Albany Law Review* 74 (3): 1379–1420.

Stark, Rodney. 1987. "Deviant Places: A Theory of the Ecology of Crime." *Criminology* 25:893–411.

Starkman, Dean. 2009. "The Most Important Financial Journalist of Her Generation: Gretchen Morgenson of the *New York Times*." *Nation*, July 6, 11–18.

Starr, Douglas. 1998. *Blood: An Epic History of Medicine and Commerce*. New York: Quill.

Staub, Ervin. 1989. *The Roots of Evil: The Origins of Genocide and Other Group Violence*. New York: Cambridge University Press.

Steffensmeier, Darrell. 1995. "Trends in Female Crime: It's Still a Man's World." In *The Criminal Justice System and Women*, 2nd ed., edited by Barbara Raffel Price and Natalie J. Sokoloff, 89–104. New York: McGraw-Hill.

Steffensmeier, Darrell, Jennifer Schwartz, and Michael Roche. 2013. "Gender and Twenty-First-Century Corporate Crime: Female Involvement and the Gender Gap in Enron-Era Corporate Frauds." *American Sociological Review* 78 (3): 448–76.

Stephenson, Neal. 1992. *Snow Crash*. New York: Bantam.

Stiglitz, Joseph E. 2009. "A Real Cure for the Global Economic Crackup." *Nation*, July 13, 11–14.

———. 2010. Interview with Sam Gustin and Michael Rainey. *Daily Finance*, October 20. http://www.dailyfinance.com/2010/10/22/joseph-stiglitz-interview-transcript/.

Stoddard, Ellwyn. 1968. "The Informal 'Code' of Police Deviancy: A Group Approach to Blue-Coat Crime." *Journal of Criminal Law, Criminology, and Police Science* 59:191–212.

Stolzenberg, Lisa, David Eitle, and Steward D'Alessio. 2006. "Race, Economic Inequality, and Violent Crime." *Journal of Criminal Justice* 34 (3): 303–16.

Strasser, Annie-Rose. 2012. "Romney's Advice to Students: Borrow Money from Your Parents." ThinkProgress, April 27. http://thinkprogress.org/election/2012/04/27/473096/romney-borrow-money-parents/.

Strauss, David. 2007. "Militarization of Policing." In *Battleground: Criminal Justice*, edited by G. Barak, 454–59. Westport, CT: Greenwood.

Subramanian, Ram, and Alsion Shames. 2013. "Sentencing and Prison Practices in Germany and the Netherlands: Implications for the United States." Report for Vera Institute of Justice, New York, October. http://www.vera.org/sites/default/files/resources/downloads/european-american-prison-report-v3.pdf.

Sum, Andrew, and Tess Forsell. 2009. "Wealth in America." Report, Center for Labor Studies, Northeastern University, January 1. http://www.clms.neu.edu/publication/documents/Wealth_in_America.pdf.

Summers, Lawrence. 2005a. "Letter from President Summers on Women and Science." http://wiseli.engr.wisc.edu/archives/summers.php.

———. 2005b. "Remarks at NBER Conference on Diversifying the Science and Engineering Workforce." Cambridge, MA, January 14. http://www.president.harvard.edu/speeches/summers_2005/nber.php.

Sumter, Melvina. 2008. "The Correctional Work Force Faces Challenges in the 21st Century." Research Notes. *Corrections Today* 70 (4): 100–102.

Swift, Pat. 1997. "At the Intersection of Racial Politics and Domestic Abuse." *Buffalo News*, December 27, B7.

Sykes, Bryan, and Alex Piquero. 2009. "Structuring and Re-creating Inequality: Health Testing Policies, Race, and the Criminal Justice System." *Annals of the American Academy of Political and Social Science* 623 (May): 214–29.

Sykes, Gresham. 1958. *The Society of Captives: A Study of a Maximum Security Prison.* Princeton, NJ: Princeton University Press.

Tafoya, Sonya. 2004. "Shades of Belonging." Report, Pew Hispanic Center, December 6. http://pewhispanic.org/files/reports/35.pdf.

Taibbi, Matt. 2009. "Inside the Great American Bubble Machine." *Rolling Stone*, July 2, 2009. http://www.rollingstone.com/politics/story/28816321/the_great_american_bubble_machine.

———. 2011. "Why Isn't Wall Street in Jail?" *Rolling Stone*, March 3. http://www.rollingstone.com/politics/news/why-isnt-wall-street-in-jail-20110216.

Talvi, Silja. 2004. "Could You Repeat the Question, Please?" AlterNet, October 6. http://www.alternet.org/story/20101.

Tatum, B. 1996. "The Colonial Model as a Theoretical Explanation of Crime and Delinquency." In *African-American Perspectives on Crime Causation, Criminal Justice Administration, and Crime Prevention*, edited by A. Sutton, 33–52. Boston: Butterworth-Heinemann.

This American Life. 2008. "Giant Pool of Money." April 9, program 355. Transcript available at http://www.thisamericanlife.org/radio-archives/episode/355/The-Giant-Pool-of-Money.

Taylor, Mac. 2013. "The 2013–14 Budget: Governor's Criminal Justice Proposals." Report, Legislative Analyst's Office. http://www.lao.ca.gov/analysis/2013/crim_justice/criminal-justice-proposals/criminal-justice-proposals-021513.pdf.

Tjaden, Patricia, and Nancy Thoennes. 1998. *Stalking in America: Findings from the National Violence against Women Survey.* Washington, DC: US Department of Justice.

Tobias, Carl. 2009. "Diversifying California's Federal District Courts." *Findlaw.com.* http://writ.news.findlaw.com/commentary/20090903_tobias.html.

Toch, Hans. 1990. "The Shape of Police Violence." In *Violence: Patterns, Causes, and Public Policy*, edited by N. A. Weiner, M. A. Zahn, and R. J. Sagi, 223–32. New York: Harcourt Brace College.

Tolnay, S. E., and E. M. Beck. 1995. *A Festival of Violence: An Analysis of Southern Lynchings, 1882–1930.* Urbana: University of Illinois Press.

Tong, Rosemarie. 1989. *Feminist Thought: A More Comprehensive Introduction.* Boulder, CO: Westview.

Tonry, Michael. 1995. *Malign Neglect: Race, Crime, and Punishment in America.* New York: Oxford University Press.

Toth, Jennifer. 1995. *The Mole People: Life in the Tunnels beneath New York City.* Chicago: Chicago Review.

Totten, Mark D. 2000. *Guys, Gangs, and Girlfriend Abuse.* Petersborough, ON: Broadview.

Travis, Jeremy. 1999. *NIJ Request for Proposals for Comparative, Cross-National Crime Research Challenge Grants.* US Department of Justice, National Institute of Justice, April.

———. 2002. "Invisible Punishment: An Instrument of Social Exclusion." In *Invisible Punishment: The Collateral Consequences of Mass Imprisonment,* edited by Meda Chesney-Lind and Marc Mauer, 15–36. New York: The New Press.

———. 2005. *But They All Come Back.* Washington, DC: Urban Institute Press.

Trawalter, Sophie, Andrew R. Todd, Abigail A. Baird, and Jennifer A. Richeson. 2008. "Attending to Threat: Race-Based Patterns of Selective Attention." *Journal of Experimental Social Psychology* 44:1322–27.

Tucker, Donald. 1981. "A Punk's Song: View from the Inside." In *Male Rape: A Casebook of Sexual Aggressions,* edited by Anthony M. Scacco Jr., 58–79. New York: AMS.

Unnever, James, and Shaun Gabbidon. 2011. *A Theory of African American Offending: Race, Racism and Crime.* London: Routledge.

US Congress, House of Representatives, Subcommittee on Financial Institutions Supervision, Regulation and Insurance of the Committee on Banking, Finance, and Urban Affairs. 1990. *When Are the Savings and Loan Crooks Going to Jail?* Hearing Before the Subcommittee. June 28. 101st Cong., 2nd Session. Washington, DC: US Government Printing Office.

Uscourts.gov. 2009. "Summary of Judicial Vacancies." http://www.uscourts.gov/judicialvac.cfm.

US Department of Health and Human Services. 2004. "Women's Health USA 2004." http://mchb.hrsa.gov/whusa04/index.htm.

US Department of Justice. 1994. "An Analysis of Non-Violent Drug Offenders with Minimal Criminal Histories." February 4.

———. 2009. *United States Attorneys' Annual Statistical Report: Fiscal Year 2008,* 7, 42. Washington, DC: Executive Office for the United States Attorneys.

US Sentencing Commission. 1991. *Mandatory Minimum Penalties in the Federal Criminal Justice System* (August). Washington, DC: US Sentencing Commission.

———. 1992. *Sentencing Commission Guidelines Manual.* Washington, DC: US Sentencing Commission.

———. 1999. *Sourcebook of Federal Sentencing Statistics.* Washington, DC: US Sentencing Commission.

———. 2012. *Annual Report and Sourcebook of Federal Sentencing Statistics.* Washington, DC: US Sentencing Commission. http://www.ussc.gov/Data_and_Statistics/index.cfm.

Van Ness, Daniel, and Karen Heetderks Strong. 1997. *Restoring Justice.* Cincinnati, OH: Anderson.

Van Riper, Tom. 2009. "The Highest-Paid Coaches." *Forbes*, May 14. http://www.forbes.com/2009/05/13/highest-paid-coaches-business-sports-nba.html?partner=contextstory.

Veblen, Thorstein. (1919) 1969. *The Vested Interests and the Common Man*. New York: Capricorn.

Vespa, Jonathan. 2009. "Gender Ideology Construction: A Life Course and Intersectional Approach." *Gender and Society* 23 (3): 363–87.

Visano, Livy A. 1998. *Crime and Culture: Refining the Traditions*. Toronto: Canadian Scholars' Press.

Vold, George, and Thomas Bernard. 1986. *Theoretical Criminology*. 3rd ed. New York: Oxford University Press.

Von Zielbauer, Paul. 2005. "As Health Care in Jails Goes Private, 10 Days Can Be a Death Sentence." *New York Times*, February 27, A1, A26.

Walker, Samuel. 1980. *Popular Justice: A History of American Criminal Justice*. New York: Oxford University Press.

———. 1992. "Origins of the Contemporary Criminal Justice Paradigm: The American Bar Foundation Survey, 1953–1969." *Justice Quarterly* (9) 1: 47–76.

Walker, Samuel, Cassia Spohn, and Miriam DeLone. 1995. *The Color of Justice*. Belmont, CA: Wadsworth.

Walsh, Mary Williams. 2009. "A.I.G. Lists Banks It Paid with U.S. Bailout Funds." *New York Times*, March 15. http://www.nytimes.com/2009/03/16/business/16rescue.html.

Warren, Jennifer. 2005. "Rethinking Treatment of Female Prisoners." *Los Angeles Times*, June 19, A1.

Warren, Patricia, and Amy Farrell. 2009. "The Environmental Context of Racial Profiling." *Annals of the American Academy of Political and Social Science* 623 (May): 7–10.

Warrick, Joby. 2006. "Safety Violations Have Piled Up at Coal Mine." *Washington Post*, January 6, A04.

Washington Post. 2002. "Are CEOs Worth Their Salaries?" October 2.

Weeks, Robin, and Cathy Spatz Widom. 1998. *Early Childhood Victimization among Incarcerated Adult Male Felons*. Washington, DC: US Department of Justice.

Weinberg, Steve. 2008. "Innocent until Reported Guilty." *Miller-McCune*, October, 54–63.

Weinstein, Henry, and David Rosenzweig. 2005. "Sentence Ruling Not Clear." *Ann Arbor News*, January 13, 1, 12.

Weiss, Eric. 2006. "At U.S. Urging, Court Throws Lamberth off Indian Case." *Washington Post*, July 12, A13.

Weitzman, Susan. 2000. *Not to People Like Us: Hidden Abuse in Upscale Marriages*. New York: Basic.

Welch, Michael. 1996a. *Corrections: A Critical Approach*. New York: McGraw-Hill.

———. 1996b. "The Immigration Crisis: Detention as an Emerging Mechanism of Social Control." *Social Justice* 23 (3): 169–84.

———. 1999. *Punishment in America: Social Control and the Ironies of Imprisonment.* Thousand Oaks, CA: Sage.

———. 2000. *Punishment in America.* Thousand Oaks, CA: Sage.

West, Candace, and Don H. Zimmerman. 1987. "Doing Gender." *Gender and Society* 1:125–51.

West, Cornel. 1990. "Michael Harrington, Socialist." *Nation*, January 8, 59–60.

Weyler, Rex. 1992. *Blood of the Land: The Government and Corporate War against First Nations.* Philadelphia: New Society.

White, Jack. 1990. "Genocide Mumbo Jumbo." *Time*, January 22, 20.

White, Nicole. 1999. "NYPD White." *Village Voice* 44 (10), 23.

White, Rob. 1998. "Social Justice, Community Building and Restorative Strategies." Paper presented at the International Conference on Restorative Justice for Juveniles, Fort Lauderdale, Florida, November 7–9.

Whiteside, John. 2006. "BP, Texas City, and the Nature of the Corporation." *Houston Chronicle Blog*, October 31. http://blogs.chron.com/bluebayou/2006/10/bp_texas_city_and_the_nature_o_1.html.

Whitty, Stephen. 2005. "Racism, Raw, and Modern: Film Review of *Crash*." *Ann Arbor News*, May 6, E1–2.

Wightman, Linda F. 1997. "The Threat to Diversity in Legal Education: An Empirical Analysis of the Consequences of Abandoning Race as a Factor in Law School Admission Decisions." *New York University Law Review* 72:50–51.

Wildman, Stephanie M. (1996) 1997. "Reflections on Whiteness: The Case of Latinos(as)." In *Critical White Studies: Looking behind the Mirror*, edited by Richard Delgado and Jean Stefancic, 323–26. Philadelphia: Temple University Press.

Wildman, Stephanie M., and Adrienne D. Davis. 1997. "Making Systems of Privilege Visible." In *Critical White Studies: Looking behind the Mirror*, edited by Richard Delgado and Jean Stefancic, 314–19. Philadelphia: Temple University Press.

Wilkinson, Deanna, Chauncey Beaty, and Regina Lurry. 2009. "Latino Youths' Experiences with Perceptions of Involuntary Police Encounters." In *After the War on Crime: Race, Democracy, and a New Reconstruction*, edited by M. L. Frampton, I. H. López, and J. Simon, 25–38. New York: New York University Press.

Will, Susan, Stephen Handelman, and David Brotherton, eds. 2013. *How They Got Away with It: White Collar Criminals and the Financial Meltdown.* New York: Columbia University Press.

Willhelm, Sidney. 1970. *Who Needs the Negro?* Cambridge: Schenkman.

Williams, Chancellor. 1987. *The Destruction of Black Civilization.* Chicago: Third World Press.

Williams, Wendy W. (1982) 1991. "The Equality Crisis: Some Reflections on Culture, Courts, and Feminism." In *Feminist Legal Theory*, edited by Katharine T. Bartlett and Rosanne Kennedy, 15–34. Boulder, CO: Westview.

Wilson, James Q. 1972. *Varieties of Police Behavior: The Management of Law and Order in Eight Communities.* New York: Atheneum.

Wilson, William J. 1987. *The Truly Disadvantaged: The Inner City, the Underclass, and Public Policy*. Chicago: Chicago University Press.

———. 1996. *When Work Disappears: The World of the New Urban Poor*. New York: Knopf.

Winerip, Michael. 2000. "Why Harlem Drug Cops Don't Discuss Race." *New York Times*, July 9, A1.

Wing, Adrien Katherine, ed. 1997. *Critical Race Feminism: A Reader*. New York: New York University Press.

Winslow, George. 1999. *Capital Crimes*. New York: Monthly Review.

Wise, Tim. 2012. *Dear White America: Letter to a New Minority*. San Francisco: City Lights.

Withrow, Brian. 2006. *Racial Profiling: From Rhetoric to Reason*. Upper Saddle River, NJ: Prentice-Hall.

Wolfgang, Marvin, and Bernard Cohen. 1970. *Crime and Race: Conceptions and Misconceptions*. New York: Institute of Human Relations Press.

Wonders, Nancy. 1999. "Postmodern Feminist Criminology and Social Justice." In *Social Justice/Criminal Justice: The Maturation of Critical Theory in Law, Crime, and Deviance*, edited by Bruce A. Arrigo, 109–28. Belmont, CA: West/Wadsworth.

Woods, Jewel. 2008. "The Black Male Privileges Checklist." http://radicalprofemi nist.blogspot.com/2008/10/introducing-jewel-woods-and-black-male.html.

Wooldredge, John. 2009. "Short- versus Long-Term Effects of Ohio's Switch to More Structured Sentencing on Extralegal Disparities in Prison Sentences in an Urban Court." *Criminology and Public Policy* 8 (2) (May): 285–313.

World Health Organization. 2005. "Gender and Reproductive Rights." http://www .who.int/reproductive-health/gender/.

Wray, Matt, and Annalee Newitz, eds. 1996. *White Trash Studies: Race and Class in America*. New York: Routledge.

Wright, Kai. 2013. "Boxed In." *Nation*, November 25, 20–24, 26.

Wyatt, Edward. 2011. "Promises Made, and Remade, by Firms in S.E.C. Fraud Cases." *New York Times*. November 7. http://www.nytimes.com/2011/11/08/ business/in-sec-fraud-cases-banks-make-and-break-promises.html?partner=rss&e mc=rss&src=ig.

Yoshihama, Mieko, Asha L. Parekh, and Doris Boyington. 1998. "Dating Violence in Asian/Pacific Communities." In *Dating Violence: Young Women in Danger*, edited by Barrie Levy, 184–95. Seattle, WA: Seal.

Young, Jock. 2011. *The Criminological Imagination*. Malden, MA: Polity.

Young, Vernetta D. 1986. "Gender Expectations and Their Impact on Black Female Offenders and Their Victims." *Justice Quarterly* 3:305–27.

Zehr, Howard, and Harry Mika. 1998. "Fundamental Concepts of Restorative Justice." *Contemporary Justice Review* 1 (1): 47–55.

CASES

Brown v. Topeka, Kansas, Board of Education, 347 U.S. 483. 1954.

Floyd v. City of New York, 08 Civ. 1034. 2013.

Lockyer v. Andrade, 538 U.S. 63. 2003.

Loving v. Virginia, 388 U.S. 1. 1967.

Plessy v. Ferguson, 163 U.S. 537. 1896.

R.A.V. v. St. Paul, 507 U.S. 377. 1992.

Roe v. Wade, 410 U.S. 113. 1973.

Roper v. Simmons, 543 U.S. 551. 2005

Rummel v. Estelle, 445 U.S. 263. 1980.

State v. Mitchell, 485 NW2d 807. 1992.

Terry v. Ohio, 392 U.S. 1. 1968.

United States v. Booker, 125 S. Ct. 738. 2005.

United States v. Brandt, 907 F2d 31. 1990.

United States v. Fanfan, 125 S. Ct. 738. 2005.

United States v. City of Chicago, 549 F2d 415. 1977.

United States Securities and Exchange Commission v. Citigroup Global Markets, 11 Civ. 7387. 2011.

University of California v. Bakke, 438 U.S. 265. 1978.

Virginia v. Black, 538 U.S. 343. 2003.

Whitney v. California, 274 U.S. 357. 1927.

Whren v. U.S., 517 U.S. 806. 1996.

Wisconsin v. Mitchell, 508 U.S. 476. 1993.

Yick Wo v. Hopkins, 118 U.S. 356. 1886.

Name Index

Subject Index

Abu Ghraib, 173
actuarial justice, 307
affirmative action (diversity), 38–39, 40, 51, 116, 118, 159, 299; college admissions, 157–58; executive order, 38; gender, 129, 223; Supreme Court clerks, 42–43
Affordable Care Act (Obamacare), 188, 203
agency capture, 239–40
AIDS, 162, 228, 254, 281, 288, 289, 300
Aid to Families with Dependent Children (AFDC), 286
American Bar Association, 229, 278–79
American dream, 54, 66, 83, 88, 96, 102
American Indian Movement, 169
American Society of Aesthetic Plastic Surgery, 145
American Sociological Association, 63
Amnesty International, 176, 282, 283
analogous social injury, 61, 209, 269
anomie, 58, 69, 170, 186
antimiscegenation laws, 111
arrests: class, 7, 82, 274, 293; gender, 12, 228–29, 251–53, 279–80; law enforcement, 32, 34, 236; race, 9, 218, 219, 277–78, 234, 247–50; stigma, 276; UCR, 227

bankruptcy, 3, 91, 92, 183, 207, 271–72, 274, 284
battered women. *See* domestic violence
biological determinism, 58, 66–67
Bitcoin, 31–32
black codes, 2, 8, 9, 218
black-on-black violence, 170, 188, 251, 255. *See also* intraracial crime
Bosnia, 302
bourgeoisie, 85
BP oil spill, 269–70
Bureau of Indian Affairs, 169
Bureau of Justice Statistics, 178, 202, 248

capital punishment, 42, 57, 152, 213, 236, 266; abolishment, 324; deterrence, 62; executions, 255; incarceration vs., 57, 62; juveniles, 301; race, 219, 255, 274, 278, 279, 296–97; social class, 83, 274, 279, 296–97, 322
census, 119, 277; racial categories, 109–10, 111, 113, 118, 159–60, 310
Center for Prosecutor Integrity, 322
Central Intelligence Agency (CIA), 238
chain gangs, 11, 252
Chinese Exclusion Act, 108, 218
chivalry, 11, 136, 252

381

About the Authors

Gregg Barak is professor of criminology and criminal justice at Eastern Michigan University. He received his Ph.D. in criminology from UC Berkeley in 1974. In 2003 he became the 27th Fellow of the Academy of Criminal Justice Sciences and in 2007 he received the Lifetime Achievement Award from the Critical Division of the American Society of Criminology. Barak is a two-time award-winning author and/or editor of numerous books on crime, justice, media, violence, criminal law, homelessness, human rights, and related topics. His *Theft of a Nation: Wall Street Looting and Federal Regulatory Colluding* received the 2012 Outstanding Publication Award given by the White Collar Crime Research Consortium of the National White Collar Crime Center. Barak is also a general editor for the International Routledge Series, Crimes of the Powerful.

Paul Leighton is a professor in the Department of Sociology, Anthropology and Criminology at Eastern Michigan University. He received his Ph.D. from American University in sociology/justice. He is a coauthor with Jeffrey Reiman of *The Rich Get Richer and the Poor Get Prison*; they also coedited *The Rich Get Richer: A Reader* and *Criminal Justice Ethics*. He is coauthor, with Donna Selman, of *Punishment for Sale: Private Prisons, Big Business and the Incarceration Binge*. He was North American editor of *Critical Criminology: An International Journal* and was named Critical Criminologist of the Year by the American Society of Criminology's Division on Critical Criminology. He is a past president of the board of SafeHouse, the local shelter and advocacy center for victims of domestic violence and sexual assault.

Allison M. Cotton is associate professor of criminology at the Metropolitan State University of Denver. A Colorado native, Dr. Cotton received a bachelor's degree in sociology from the University of Colorado at Boulder in 1991, a master's degree in sociology from Howard University in Washington, D.C., in 1995, and a Ph.D. in sociology from the University of Colorado at Boulder in 2002. Dr. Cotton's publications range in subject from the death penalty, eyewitness identifications, lethal behavior, and expert witnesses to issues around race, class, gender, and crime. Lexington Books released her first book, *Effigy: Images of Capital Defendants*, in the summer of 2008. Dr. Cotton is a member of the Academy of Criminal Justice Sciences and the American Society of Criminology. A two-time Fulbright scholar, Dr. Cotton now serves as a board member of the Colorado Fulbright Foundation. She is also a member of Delta Sigma Theta Sorority, Inc.